# THIS
# THOUSAND
# YEARS

# THIS THOUSAND YEARS

## L. B. BROOKS

BRIDGE PUBLISHING
South Plainfield, NJ

This Thousand
ISBN 0-88270-711-6
Library of Congress Catalog Card #94-071926
Copyright © 1994 by L.B. Brooks

Published by:
Bridge Publishing Inc.
2500 Hamilton Blvd.
South Plainfield, NJ 07080

# Contents

Foreword ................................................................................ ix

Acknowledgments .................................................................. xv

Introduction ........................................................................ xix

1. 1001-1100 .......................................................................... 1
2. 1101-1200 ....................................................................... 43
3. 1201-1300 ....................................................................... 61
4. 1301-1400 ....................................................................... 83
5. 1401-1500 ..................................................................... 115
6. 1501-1600 ..................................................................... 135
7. 1601-1700 ..................................................................... 163
8. 1701-1800 ..................................................................... 187
9. 1801-1900 ..................................................................... 211
10. 1901-2000 .................................................................... 263
11. The Next Thousand Years ............................................ 345

Bibliography ...................................................................... 359

Picture Credits .................................................................. 363

Index by Person ................................................................ 365

Index by Subject ............................................................... 383

# Foreword

## To the Moon

When I flew to the moon on Apollo 12 in 1969, I looked back at the earth and the thing that amazed me the most was the fact that everybody I knew, had seen on TV or in the movies, or had read about in magazines and newspapers, had lived or was living on that beautiful blue-and-white ball. The love, the sacrifices, the dedication and the struggles that humans had experienced to make the world what it is today could not be seen. My awareness centered on the fact that there was this beautiful blue-and-white ball in the distance; it was home, and it was special.

I still feel that way today. Our planet earth is special. But can we keep it in the form of a beautiful blue-and-white world? It seems especially appropriate that, as the year 2001 approaches, we should try to prepare ourselves for the important decisions that future events will demand of us and our children. These challenges will require our very best choices if the human race is to survive.

I believe that one helpful way to prepare for the future is to study the past. Future events will not be exactly the same as past ones but some of them will be somewhat similar to past events. Niccolo Machiavelli (1469-1527), a brilliant observer who was much maligned, remarked:

Prudent men are wont to say--and this not rashly or without good ground--that he who would foresee what has to be, should reflect on what has been, for everything that happens in the world at any time has a genuine resemblance to what happened in ancient times. This is due to the fact that the agents who bring such things about are men, and that men have, and always have had, the same passions, whence it necessarily comes about that the same effects are produced.

## Man's Future

Will human beings be around for the next millennium? I believe the answer to this question depends on several things. The unchanging fact is that human beings have difficulty living together on our planet because of personal feelings of love, hate, fear, revenge, greed, self-aggrandizement, and their own egos--to name some of the most important motives. I believe that most of the problems in history have been caused by some of these very basic individual characteristics. When a person has these feelings, there is little he can do about it other than what he can accomplish on the level of one person to another. However, if he were a king, president, or emperor and he had these same feelings, he could cause a whole country to go to war if he felt strongly enough about something or were just a little crazy or uncooperative.

Can leaders of the future, who will have these same motivations, understand the situation well enough not to take whole countries to war? Can individuals and institutions become more effective in dealing with these matters than they have in the past? These questions are important because how we answer them will influence the outcome for the two major problems that humanity faces now: the threat of nuclear annihilation, and the possibility of some sort of global ecological disaster that seems to be beginning at the present time.

## Nuclear Annihilation

I believe that the atomic bomb is the best weapon that has been created in all history to prevent major, premeditated war because it is the first weapon to insure that the person or persons who start the war will die in it. Not only will they die, but their parents and their children will die as well. Would Adolf Hitler (1889-1945) have started World War II if he had known with certainty that, win or lose, he and the people he knew and loved would be dead within a few weeks after the war started? How about Napoleon (1769-1821) or Genghis Khan (circa 1162-1227) ?

But even with the threat of major premeditated wars almost eliminated, there will be mistakes. I think that it is highly likely that at some time in the future someone will launch a nuclear missile--a renegade military unit or some individual will accidentally or purposely do so. As nuclear weapons proliferate into the hands of more and more countries, the same motivation that made pharaohs kill their wives and slaves and bury them with them in their tombs, is likely to make some individual want to take other people and other countries with him or her into death.

Therefore, we need to provide some well-thought-out, pre-planned restraints so that when such tragic events threaten, we do not respond with a knee-jerk reaction by blowing up the whole planet. I think it is only a matter of time until such an event occurs— maybe we will have to destroy the person or the nuclear potential of the country responsible, but we must be certain to avoid doing anything that will make the whole planet unfit for human habitation. This kind of plan should be in place right now in every country that has a nuclear arsenal.

## Earth's Ecology and Man's Future

We are also approaching several serious global ecological disasters. The depletion of the ozone layer, the Greenhouse Effect, and the spread of nuclear waste are the three most important threats to earth's environment.

There is an interesting relationship between our relatively new but growing ability to monitor these potentially devastating global events--mostly through the efforts of the space program--and their occurrences. In a time when certain emissions from our industrialized society have just begun to deplete the ozone layer, we have also just recently acquired the ability to monitor the amount of that depletion. If we had begun depleting the ozone layer at the present rate 500 years ago (when we had no ability to monitor it), the ozone layer would have been eliminated before we would have even known of its existence. Then too, we have begun to follow the types of emissions that contribute to the Greenhouse Effect which, if left unchecked, have the potential of ending all life on earth. Finally, the spread of nuclear waste from reactors in electrical generating plants, on ships and submarines, and the manufacturing and dismantling of nuclear weapons, must concern us all. Careful study of what happens to these wastes is essential for the safety of life on earth.

## Back to Space

In 1973 I flew in space again. I was on Skylab, which was America's first space station--270 miles above the earth which it orbited every ninety-three minutes. I could look down and see cities, wakes of ships in the ocean and the beauty of the vastness of the earth. Because I spent fifty-nine days in Skylab, I had a chance to think about and try to see places that interested me in history. I tried to see where Captain James Cook (1728-1779), the English explorer, had gone on his voyages of discovery. I scanned the area where Hannibal (247-circa 182 B.C.), the Carthaginian general, had crossed the Alps and I wondered how difficult it had been for him to do so. I traced some of the overland trade routes from the western world to the eastern world. I looked towards the source of the Nile. I was able to cover all the land that Alexander the Great (356-323 B.C.) spent his life conquering in a few brief minutes.

The world is different now than it was when these individuals made their conquests, and the world of our children, grandchildren, and great-grandchildren will be different from ours. I believe it is very important for us to try to understand the present condition of the planet and the human race so that we might be able to help facilitate and direct the changes that take place in the future for the benefit of succeeding generations.

Why should we be concerned for the welfare of tomorrow's world and our descendants? It is the right thing to do. After all, we benefited from the efforts of such men as Francis Bacon (1561-1626), Sir Isaac Newton (1642-1727), Leonardo da Vinci (1452-1519), Johann Sebastian Bach (1685-1750), William Shakespeare (1564-1616), Vincent van Gogh (1853-1890), and Louis Pasteur (1822-1895). Though they did not live to see our present world these men and others, through their hard work and dedication, caused the world to be more beautiful and enjoyable. Can we do less for our tomorrow?

To those among us who speak of our world with negative comments--to those who suggest that our world is not as good as it used to be, and to those who long for the "good ol' days" because they feel we are really living in a difficult time--I say to them, —read this book! The facts are here and they are accurate. I believe we are living in the best time that's ever been--but the reader can decide for himself or herself.

We must be ready to make the right choices. We have the duty to know the past for it can make us responsible citizens of the present and of the future.

What better time to prepare for the future by remembering the past than now?

*Captain Alan L. Bean, USN*
*Apollo and Skylab Astronaut*

# Acknowledgments

Special thanks to the following individuals for their help:

Nick Apple, Public Affiars Specialist, Dept. of the Air Force, United States Air Force Musuem, Wright-Patterson AF Base, Ohio.

Richard Boijen, Head of the Print Room, Ministere De La Defense Nationale, Musee Royal De L'armee, Et D'Historie Militaire, Bruselles.

Georgia Maddox Engle, Manager Public Relations, LTV Aircraft Products Group.

Ms. Julie Esser.

Carla M. Fischer, Public Relations Representative, Corporate Public Relations, General Electric Company.

Bert Cull.

Rev. James H. Groves.

R. Hardy, Curator: Photographs, DIRECTOR, South African National Museum of Military History, Johannesburg.

Bill Harris.

Charles M. Hebble.

Elizabeth Hey, Hughes Tool Company, Houston, Texas.

Werner Hey, United States Department of Internal Revenue.

Tom Haynes, Manager, Marketing Services, Hughes Tool Company.

Cathy Hurst.

Renee' Hurst.

Z. M. Hurwitz, Adviser to the Prime Minister of Israel.

Dr. J.A.M.M. Janssen, Royal Netherlands Air Force, Historical Branch.

Bruce Kates Sr., Martin Marietta.

Mr. Norm Kelly, Kelly Graphic Ad-Ventures Ltd.

Col. Floyd Kendrick, United States Army, Retired.

Victor Manuel Martinez, United States Army Reserve.

Norma H. McCormick, Historical Photograph Specialist, A.T.&T.

Fred Mittag.

Donald J. Montoya, Acting Public Affairs Officer, Dept. of the Army, U.S. Army White Sands Missile Range, New Mexico.

P. G. Murton, BA, ALA, Keeper of Aviation Records, Royal Air Force Museum, Hendon, London.

Monsignor C. Sepe, Assessor for His Holiness Pope John Paul II, the Vatican.

Kenton Pate.

Ms. Laura Robinson.

Ms. Louise Rountree.

Rabbi Jack Segal.

Tom Sharman.

Ruth Shoemaker, Archives, General Electric.

Bernice Singleton, Community Relations Representative, United Technologies, Otis Elevator Company.

Darrell Smith, Public Affairs, National Railroad Passenger Corporation.

Judith A. Stowell, Manager, Public Relations, Martin Marietta Astronautics Group.

Dr. John Sutterby.

(Mrs.) Elinore S. Thomas, Senior Advisor, Editorial Services, Public Affairs Department, Aluminum Company of America.

Dr. William R. Turner, pastor South Main Baptist Church, Houston, Texas.

H. A. Vadnais, Jr. Head, Curator Branch, Naval Historical Center, Washington, D.C.

Captain Mark M. Vaught, Secretary of the General Staff, Dept. of the Army, U.S. Army Missile Command, Redstone Arsenal, Alabama.

Marie Wuttke, Public Relations Coordinator, R.C.A., Thomson Consumer Electronics, Inc.

# Introduction

It may seem trivial to say, but it's over. In the decade of the 1990s, the users of the Gregorian calendar are watching the final curtain fall on this thousand years. This is a significant event because we will observe the passing of a year, a decade, a century, and a millennium on the same evening.

On a practical level, it is important to realize that decades, centuries, and millennia do not end with a nine but with a zero. It seems logical, though, that the official worldwide celebration of this great event should begin on New Year's Eve, 1999, and continue until the technical end of the millennium on December 31, 2000. We will be reminded of it in the media, and we will do a few spectacular things to celebrate. The setting off of fireworks in outer space would seem appropriate if it were possible.

How did the present become like it is? What forces compelled humanity to emerge from the relative "darkness" of the Middle Ages when ignorance and superstition ruled into an age of heart transplants, successful treatments of some forms of cancer, vaccinations against polio, splitting the atom, sending men to the moon, and flinging probes toward the very stars themselves?

The answers are found within these pages. With a solid foundation of organization and a design that highlights the important social, scientific, religious, and political events of the last ten centuries, this book examines the major events and developments of world history in the light of God's eternal plan and purpose for mankind. Each chapter covers one century and, except for necessary background information, all events have been kept within the context of their centuries.

The reader will find the comparison of this thousand years to a single day a useful device in following the chronology of events. The occasional clock notations give the reader an idea concerning the time of day when a particular event would have occurred if the thousand years had been compressed into a day.

The events portrayed, the wars and their resolutions, the triumphs and tragedies of individuals and nations, the continuing struggle between good and evil that started in the Garden of Eden, are but pieces in the yet-unfinished puzzle of life, the maker of which is God. After all, what is history but —*His story?* The last chapter speculates on the next thousand years.

*L. B. Brooks*
*Houston, Texas*

# 1

# 1001 - 1100

## {12:00 a.m. - 2:23 a.m.}

---

The times are waxing late;
Be sober and keep vigil,
The Judge is at the gate.
—*Bernard of Morlaix*

---

Our comparison of this thousand years to a day begins at midnight. Around us is the relative darkness of what came to be called the Age of Darkness. Ignorance and superstition have replaced objective inquiry in many places. Let us see what the next two hours and twenty-three minutes bring.

## Overview

### 1. 1001

The arrival of the year 1001 had little significance to most medieval men who were largely ignorant of the fact that there even was such a thing as the year 1001. In a world shrouded in social, spiritual, and intellectual darkness, there was no wide spread appreciation that the first Christian millennium was apparently ending (see chapter endnote 1-1) and a new one was beginning. Even among the clergy there were only a comparatively few zealots who took seriously the suggestion in Revelation 20:1-7 that a thousand years symbolized the ongoing spiritual hegemony of Christ and applied it to their present. These dedicated monks trimmed their lamps and watched, as they anticipated the imminent return of Jesus and the final judgment. The end of the millennium seemed to them to be a logical time for this to take place.

## 2. The Dominance and Burden of Feudalism

Yet even if the medieval masses had been in a position to contemplate the fearful meaning of the apocalyptic symbolism that surrounded the period of a thousand years and the final judgment of Christ, it would have competed with the burdensome quality of life in medieval times, especially among the poor who were subject to *feudalism*. This term has been used since the end of the eighteenth century to describe the major social and political system of much of the world at the beginning of this millennium. The major characteristic of this system was the association of landholding with a personal relationship of loyalty between lord and men.

Various forms of feudalism had, of course, been practiced throughout history as the need arose. Certain agricultural states of early Greece had made use of the practice. The Hans dynasty in China (reigned 206 B.C.-220 A.D.) introduced a modified form of feudalism when they created 103 feudal principalities. They were, though, centralized under the jurisdiction of appointed civil governors, whereas the European system consisted of random and isolated communities governed by the local lord. A form of feudalism was also found in cases where one barbarous community conquered another but did not have the manpower to make complete slaves of the conquered peoples.

Feudalism arose in medieval Europe because of many reasons, but an important factor was the invasions of Italy and Gaul by successive waves of barbarian tribes, beginning in the early 5th century. These invasions made these places unsafe. Prudent aristocrats moved to the country and engaged dependents who performed various services for them in return for protection. Such arrangements were unfairly balanced since the largest segment of the population, the poor, did most of the labor-intensive tasks, the results of which afforded them relatively little hope of improving their condition.

Even so, this model of feudalism found acceptance in Europe (more so in the north than in the south) and elsewhere, especially in places where there was an abundance of land and not much money, since feudalism was an economy based on the land. If a person owned land on which crops could be grown and a small dwelling could be built, and on which a tower or castle could be erected to protect people when they were threatened by enemies, the rest of the people in the area might look to the owner-lord as his or her overlord. Then too, the bond between vassal and overlord was stronger in places where it was commonly believed that the aristocrats or overlords received their authority from God, an early stage in the development of the doctrine of the Divine Right of Kings which received wide acceptance in later centuries (see section 117).

In Europe deteriorating roads contributed to the breakdown of communication and commerce which tended to accentuate the isolation of these and other similar communities and encouraged them towards self-sufficiency. Travel became difficult and sometimes dangerous. The old Roman roads (see chapter endnote 1-2) had not entirely disappeared, but they did not lead everywhere and roads damaged by battle might remain neglected for years. So there were few good roads and even fewer bridges in and about the forests that surrounded the monasteries, castles, and feudal estates. Then too it was very likely that highwaymen lurked in the woods and along the usable roads, so it was considered foolish for a peasant to set off on foot alone through such dangerous wildernesses. Even persons traveling in groups were not immune from attack by these bandits.

Therefore, except for the knights and other nobles, few medieval people had any real knowledge of the world beyond their own manors, and rarely did they see anybody from other areas. At most, one might travel no more than a few miles from one's place of birth during a lifetime. Travel for pleasure, especially as we know it today, was out of the question. Only something as important as a war, religious persecution, a crusade, a pilgrimage, or impending starvation provided enough reason for one to go on a major journey. Even when such a decision was reached it was not made lightly. An extensive journey was a serious matter, likely to take months or possibly years, depending on the destination.

3

Medieval feudalism eventually controlled all aspects of society where its influence was felt. It thus came to meet the needs of this rather unruly period, an era of comparative ignorance which has been called the Middle Ages. The adjective *medieval* (from the Latin word *medium,* meaning "middle," and *aevum* meaning "age") is also used to describe this period. Sometimes this period is erroneously labeled the "Dark Ages." The years between 476 (following the decline of Rome), and 1453 (the year in which Constantinople fell), have been characterized by these designations (see chapter endnote 1-3). Further, because feudalism was so prevalent by 1001, the second half of the Middle Ages is sometimes called the *Feudal Age.* It was found in western Europe through the thirteenth or fourteenth centuries, depending on location. In some oriental countries, various forms of feudalism survived until the nineteenth and twentieth centuries.

## 3. Vassalage

A *vassal* was a person who held land from a lord or superior. When one person became another's vassal, the relationship was recognized by a ceremony known as *homage* (from the Latin root— *homo*—meaning "man"). In this rite the vassal knelt before the lord and promised to be the lord's "man." The lord usually gave the vassal something to indicate the relationship between them—perhaps a piece of dirt or a stick if farming was to be his assignment. Yet to be a vassal did not always suggest a state of inferiority. Vassals themselves could actually hold a high rank.

Feudal landholders were also called *lords* or *suzerains,* and the land granted to them was called a *fief* or a *feud.* Usually a fief was so large one man could not manage it well as an estate and the nobles and other land-holders discovered it was to their benefit to subdivide their lands among men who became vassals to them. This produced some curious effects. Counts or knights could be vassals to the nobles. If a person was a vassal of two lords and the two of them fought, the vassal had to decide which one he would support. Even the church held property in feudal relationships. A bishop or other church official represented the church as the holder of a section of land. This practice produced a complex and sometimes confusing system of management.

## 4. Feudal Estates and Their Occupants

Feudal land was also divided among the *villeins,* a rather large segment of the population which ranked below the nobles. They were called *villeins* because they lived in villages or villas, but the term had an additional meaning as well. It was commonly used to denote certain people who held an intermediate position between freedom and slavery. Villeins were assumed to be free persons by birth, but the lands they held could not be disposed of freely due to their relationship to their lord. The term "villein" was used in the *Domesday Book* (sometimes called *Doomsday Book*) compiled by William (circa 1027-1087) the Conqueror (see section 28). Out of 240,000 households listed in it, 100,000 were marked as belonging to villeins. There were also the classifications of full villeins and half villeins. The former had reference to persons who held about thirty acres and the latter to those with fifteen acres . The *bordarii* held plots of five acres, more or less, and the *cottagers* were connected with mere cottages and *crofts.* A *croft* was a small, enclosed field. A tract of 120 acres was known as a *hide.*

In addition to the villeins, there were other classes of workers on feudal estates. These included *freemen, serfs,* and *slaves.* It would not be appropriate to call such workers vassals. The term vassal referred to a certain class of landholders, and it applied to a direct feudal relationship and not to manual labor (see section 3). Villeins were vassals in this respect. Freemen were those workers who were not bound by special obligations to anyone. At first there were relatively few freemen, but as time passed they became more numerous. They might rent land from a landowner and then work it for themselves or others would pay them to work it.

The notion of serfdom was distinct from concepts of freedom and slavery. The serfs were not their own masters; they were part of an estate in the same way that animals belonged to it. They received no pay. Instead, they performed specific services as directed by the lord of the castle or manor.

Slaves were not as common as serfs simply because the idea of individual freedom was very strong among the Germanic peoples, and they were not accustomed to the buying and selling of human beings in any form. As time passed, even slaves were able to become serfs or else they were able to gain their freedom.

Christianity discouraged the use of slaves and, therefore, indirectly

5

gave rise to the later technological developments that eventually reduced or replaced the need for forced human labor. Yet slavery persisted in Christian nations for many centuries.

## 5. Obligations and Rights Under Feudalism

Many services were due to the lord for the use of his land. For at least three days a week, the peasant farmers had to work the lord's land under the supervision of the overseer whose job it was to see that the work was done properly. The rest of the time the peasants were free to work their own land. But at harvest time the lord received a part of their grain. The peasants could grind their grain at the lord's mill or bake bread in his oven, but they had to leave a portion of grain or baked bread in payment for these services.

Not all the workers on a manor were farmers. Some took care of the herds, protecting them from wild animals. Since sheep were of great value, medieval man had more experience in herding them than he had with other animals. Sheep and goats were the source of important food products, such as milk and meat, and other necessities as well as skins.

The smith was available to repair wagons, doors, or other things and the carpenter was expected to maintain the premises and supervise new construction as the lord required. The shoemaker prepared the leathers for the nobles who spent their days training for battle. In the castle, cooks and other domestic servants did the household work. The miller ran the lord's mill, the vintner made the wine, and the brewer made the ale and beer.

There were also certain other obligations inherent in the relationship between the peasants and the lord. The peasants had to agree to fight for the lord whenever necessary and to give him certain feudal "aids." For example, he had to make a gift when the lord's eldest son became a knight or his eldest daughter was married. If the lord was taken captive and money was demanded as ransom for him the vassal was expected to come to his aid. If the lord held court the vassal had to help with the cases that came up. If a vassal failed to carry out his part of the agreement, he could lose the use of his land.

As has already been mentioned, this agreement was not completely one-sided. It was the lord's responsibility to protect the vassal and his family from harm and wrong and to see that a guilty party was punished.

> **Reflection:**
>
> *The Christian belief in the Fatherhood of God implied to many a corresponding belief in the brotherhood of man under God. Christianity sought to improve the condition of all men by encouraging respect for each other. Consider how this might have influenced the attitude of the lord of a manor toward his serfs or the serfs toward their lord. What positive influences could such attitudes have contributed to the welfare of the manor?*

## 6. Farming

The methods of farming employed on the medieval feudal estates had been used for centuries. In the spring, the peasants plowed the land with their big, clumsy plows, drawn by slow-moving oxen. The Japanese used something called a *mattock* (a tool like a pickax, but with a flat blade on one or both sides) to loosen the soil, and dig up and cut roots. The *harrow* (a device used to break up clods of soil into a fine tilth) was also popular. Most sowing was done by the *broadcast method* (the scattering of seed), as row cultivation had not yet been adopted.

In the fall, the grain was reaped with sickles, bound into sheaves, piled high on carts, and hauled to the lord's barn. Then the grain was spread on the floor and the heads were mashed with long, jointed clubs called *flails*, or they were trodden out by animals. The straw or rye was cut for thatching roofs. Hay was cut and stacked for the animals' winter food. The lack of cultivation to control weeds was dealt with by allowing the land to lie fallow every third year, then burning the wood crop that sprang up and plowing again for grain.

## 7. Characteristics of the Manor

It would be difficult to describe a "typical" manor, but it is possible to identify some common characteristics shared by manors. The peasants' houses were small and shabby with only one room. They were thatched with straw, had a floor of packed earth, and one little window. Chimneys were nonexistent, so when fires were built in the middle of the floor, the smoke escaped through a hole in the roof.

Often a shed was joined to the house and the cattle spent their days foraging, roaming the same paths or streets where the children played. Sometimes the cattle were placed on a "common" piece of land where everybody's cattle could be pastured. Occasionally the houses were built around a "green" or on the two sides of a narrow street, initially just outside the wall of the tower or castle. One might expect to find a church in the village as well as a mill if there was running water available. It was also possible for more than one village to be located on a manorial estate. Often a section of trees was set aside for the peasants to cut wood for their fires or for making what little furniture they needed. Most of the things used on a manor were made by its inhabitants, thus the manor was a little world in itself, both economically and socially. Most manors had to import salt, iron, and stone; sometimes the products of the manor—things its own people did not need—were used in trade.

## 8. Military Architecture

The heart of the manor was the *castle*, a large fortified building or set of buildings—the seat of the feudal lord. It was a combination of a residence and a fortification. Warfare was an inherent part of feudalism. The best home, therefore, had to be not only a man's castle but his fortress as well. The medieval castle developed out of the old fortresses known as *mottes* which were originally constructed of wood. These became the basis for the castle after they were introduced by the Norsemen.

A *tower* was commonly the first structure to be considered in the plans for a castle, or it might remain an independent structure. Eventually the early wood structures were replaced by stone buildings. One example is the massive masonry fortress, the Tower of London, started by William the Conqueror in 1078.

The security of towers and castles was enhanced by carefully planning their location. As often as possible, towers and castles were built in nearly inaccessible places. This was true of the Chateau de Chinon which was originally built in this century at the edge of a cliff.

Much attention was also given to the construction of these military bastions to enhance their security. Many castles had a *portcullis* (a strong gate of iron that slid up and down in groves in the main gateway). A *drawbridge* was sometimes included as well. For

8

additional safety, towers were built with a single window near the top but with no door at the bottom. The only access, therefore, was by a ladder which could be pulled into the window near the top. Some tower designers made the tops of towers different in order to meet various needs. Towers could be made high enough for long-range observations in order to provide early detection of an approaching enemy. A defensive tower built over a castle gate or bridge was called a *barbican*. The *keep* (*donjon* in Middle French) was a massive central tower that was the last place of refuge for the occupants of the manor. The keep also contained living quarters and defense structures. After the Norman conquest more reliance was placed on the prison of the fortress. The modern and restricted use of the word "dungeon" is derived from donjon. Enemies were kept in the basement "dungeon" which was typically dark, wet, and infested with rats. Some contained instruments of torture.

Before the introduction of *gunpowder* into Europe (the formula for its manufacture was first published there in the thirteenth century by Roger Bacon), a castle or tower could be attacked [see figure 1-1] effectively only by the use of innovative machines such as the ones ancient Romans used for throwing big stones or other missiles (*catapults*). The *movable tower* was also useful for attacking a castle. Less spectacularly, an enemy might simply surround a castle and eventually starve out its inhabitants. Castle defenders could hold off an attacking party by shooting arrows or throwing stones at them, or by pouring boiling oil on them. Sometimes they issued from the castle in a counter-attack.

Traditional illustrations of magnificent castles such as figure 1-1 may suggest that living in them was a pleasing experience. Of course, compared to the peasant dwellings of this time period, castle living was luxurious, but even castles were hot in the summer and in some locations they were humid as well. They were certainly cold and damp in winter. The few windows that were built into their thick stone walls allowed wind and dust in as well as light and fresh air. Castles of this century had no external chimney shafts and flues were carried through the wall at some height above the fireplace and then out the side of the wall. It was not until later in the 1400s that buildings were designed so that smoke could emerge from the tops of their roofs. These conditions often militated against good health.

## 9. Customs and Traditions in Castles

During the eleventh century, more emphasis was placed on domestic needs in the keep which eventually consisted of a great hall and principal rooms of state. The hall became an important part of medieval social life for informal and solemn occasions. Feudal lords accommodated many people there by serving them food and drink and by providing entertainment.

The use of eating utensils was not as it is today. There were spoons, but they were used only for soup and gravy. Since forks were not introduced until later (in the late thirteenth century), if diners wanted a piece of pie, they would take it with their hands in whatever amount they thought they could eat and then they would wipe sticky fingers on a piece of bread. These pieces of bread were then commonly thrown to the dogs that waited eagerly for such scraps.

For their amusement, kings and lords had a "fool," or court jester. These early entertainers were required to have a license and they spent their days telling jokes and humorous stories, or doing amusing stunts. Court jesters remained popular until the seventeenth century. Traveling minstrels sometimes went around from castle to castle, singing songs or spreading the latest gossip. Wandering actors sometimes came to castles and performed parts of plays at court.

About this time it also became the custom to build castles with an inner court with walls and towers, a bailey or courtyard, rooms for servants, knights and guests, gardens, gatehouses, stables, and all the requirements for a self-contained existence.

## 10. Warfare, Knighthood, and Chivalry

It was the Persians (now Iranians) who first realized the advantages of putting an armed soldier on a horse. A warrior thus equipped could be a significant threat to foot soldiers in much the same way a tank is a threat to foot soldiers today. In fact, one might make a legitimate argument that the mounted knight, though primitive by today's standards, was similar in function and purpose to a modern tank. The big and powerful mounts necessary to carry these heavy loads were imported from Europe and the Near East. The Byzantine Empire (the ancient name of Constantinople) had large numbers of these warriors. They were called cataphracti, and they wore heavy suits of chain mail. They traveled from the east into such western European countries as France. By the time William the Conqueror landed in England, most of his army consisted of knights in chain mail.

Under feudalism, military services were extremely important because they were needed for defense and the maintenance of law and order. This military class of landholders was known as the knights. The words knight and knighthood are merely the modern forms of the Anglo-Saxon or Old English cniht and cnihthad.

## 11. Becoming a Knight

There was a process by which young men of noble rank became knights. They were first assigned to the role of "page" in the family of a friend or relative where they often became a type of errand-boy and learned how to behave in noble society.

When they reached the age of fourteen, they were usually assigned to a nobleman as a "squire." Squires were instructed in how to ride a horse and how to use weapons of war.

After the trainee reached the age of twenty-one, he could be "knighted," but only after he had been through a period of fasting and prayer. After this, a ceremony of initiation into knighthood took place, during which someone of higher rank initiated the subject. This process usually included the saying of a few words and the "laying on" of the sword on the subject's shoulder.

Knights were trained in tournaments. These medieval war games were often staged in the same type of festive atmosphere that is found in football games and wrestling matches today. Practiced techniques, such as the *tilt*, where two mounted knights charged at each other with their lances [see figure 1-2] were included in tournaments.

## 12. Disadvantages of the System of Selecting Knights

The system of selecting knights as warriors had its problems. While all men of noble rank were taught the art of combat, they were not necessarily chosen because of their skills in the tactics of warfare. The choice was based on the assumption that a person was a good warrior if he was a good rider and could handle a lance and sword with skill. The thought that discipline or tactical skill were as

11

important as courage had little or no acceptance, and undisciplined mobs often resulted. To compound the problem, the hierarchy of command was based on social status rather than on professional experience. The noble who led the largest group or held the highest rank felt himself entitled to assume the leadership of battle.

## 13. The Joy of Fighting

The fighting was not especially confined to conflicts between groups. A significant number of nobles looked upon fighting as a joy and it became their occupation. They were soldiers of fortune who dedicated themselves to the practice of fighting without giving much, if any thought to the broader question as to why wars are fought. Private combat—fighting between one noble and another—was common even though it was outlawed in England and engaged in without regard to the Truce of God (see section 14). Sometimes property was damaged or destroyed during these fights or innocent people were hurt or killed.

## 14. Feudalism and Chivalry

To address this feudalistic attitude and the problems it caused, the church and the nobles themselves developed a code of conduct which became known as *chivalry*. Chivalry has been defined as the "flower of feudalism." The ethical ideas of chivalry were a combination of Christian and military ideals. The main chivalric virtues were piety, bravery, loyalty, and honor. Loyalty was due to the spiritual master (God); the temporal master (the suzerain); and to the mistress of the heart (the woman the knight loved).

In 1041 the Truce of God declared that there should be no private fighting from Wednesday evening of any week until the next Monday, and none on religious holidays. The church wanted the knight to be a true soldier of Christ, acting in the spirit of "Do unto others as you would have them do unto you" (the Golden Rule). The church also tried to prevent private combat which would harm children, women, or weak or defenseless persons who were connected with the church. In the spirit of Jesus' command for Christians to love their enemies (See Matt. 5:43-48 and Luke 6:27), the church preached that it was improper to take booty in war and that knights should do all they could to put an end to crime.

12

## 15. Women in Medieval Society

The women of the upper classes in feudal society spent their days spinning, sewing, and running their households. Women were commonly, but not always, in the custody of a man, either a husband or a guardian. The universal subjugation of women was widely accepted. Women had to defer their rights to their husbands, and husbands were permitted to deal with their wives as they saw fit, even to the point of abusing them. In Europe, the church tried to protect wives to some extent by laying down rules about the size of the stick with which their husbands could beat them, and about not doing too much damage to them in the process. The unfortunate argument of the times was that women were the chief source of the world's sins because Eve ate the fruit in the Garden of Eden and seduced her husband to join her. This was a classic case of the improper use of theology to subjugate women. It was used as an unreasonable excuse to enable men to exploit women. Women did have a place in the church itself (see section 66).

> **Reflection:**
>
> *Consider the effect Christianity had on the position of women in society. Marriage was seen as a religious sacrament instead of a mere civil contract. The church opposed divorce and insisted that both men and women live pure lives.*

# Other Medieval Disciplines and Institutions

## 16. Astronomy

The astronomy of this century was rooted in the Ptolemaic system. Although the exact date of his birth is unknown, Claudius Ptolemy was known to be living in the second century. His theories, which placed the earth at the center of the universe, were discussed in his *Almagest*, a series of thirteen books (circa 137). His works were so impressive that they dominated scientific research for 1400 years, but their effect on social, political, moral, and theological theories lasted

13

even longer, until the period of the Industrial Revolution (1700s). His assumptions of a man-centered earth in a geocentric universe were widely known and accepted as fact. The church interpreted his theories as suggesting a great hierarchy or chain of being, with God and the angels as the highest order; then man, woman, animals, plants, and stones formed the lower parts of the chain.

With such a strong religious association with the heavens, it is no wonder then, that "events" there (such as the appearance of a comet) were subject to a religious interpretation rather than a scientific one. In 1054, for example, there occurred what today we call a *supernova*. We now know that a supernova is a star that has exploded. This explosion causes the star's brightness to increase rapidly (over a few hours, days, or weeks) before it quickly fades. The expanding, glowing gases from the star form an interesting object called a *nebula* (not visible without a telescope). Supernovas become so bright that they can be seen in the daylight. Such was the case of the supernova that occurred in 1054. Today we call the nebula it left behind the *Crab Nebula* because its shape suggests that creature. Asian astronomers documented the nova and in America, a Native American rock carving is also believed to show that the exploding star was observed there. Europeans must have observed the explosion but there is little evidence that they did. Perhaps they saw it as an omen of the great schism between the Greek and Roman churches (see section 34).

## 17. Astrology and Astronomy

*Astrology* has long been regarded as the practice of studying the celestial bodies to predict future events on earth. Astrologers and their followers believed that the heavenly bodies controlled the affairs of men and that their movements and positions could be used to predict the future.

Astrology has long been seen as a *pseudo* (false) science but its association with astronomy in this millennium was common and logical in the minds of many. Some astronomers were also astrologers. Astrologers performed services such as predicting the best days for doing various things and the best locations for building temples and other structures. They sometimes practiced medicine and diagnosed diseases which they did by observing the positions of the planets, each of which was supposed to represent a particular organ of the human body. That astrology is still popular today (some people still take it

14

seriously; others use it for entertainment purposes only) may be verified by the fact that many newspapers still carry a daily column on astrology.

## 18. Introduction to Medieval Education

In any discussion of European education in this time period, it is necessary to distinguish between formal and informal education. It was reasoned that the peasants needed to know just enough to carry out their duties on the manor and it was not considered necessary or even desirable to provide something like what we now call public schools for them, even if they had been considered possible. Thus, peasant children entered into a type of informal, narrowly focused vocational education as might be found when growing up in a family of farmers. Eventually a type of apprenticeship developed which formalized vocational education and which foreshadowed the guilds and their formidable apprenticeship programs that came later. Becoming a knight was a highly formal process that was reserved for the nobility. The wealthy hired tutors for their children and the abbey schools, which had been created by Charlemagne's decree (787) that established a school at every abbey in his domain, were available for young and older adults who wanted to enter the service of the church, become teachers themselves, or study logic or one of the other disciplines.

The founding of the universities, developed largely from the demands made by the professions of law, medicine, and theology, and from the increasing knowledge that followed the rediscovery of Aristotle and the study of the liberal arts, represented outstanding educational achievements. At Bologna a university was established (1088) that specialized in law. In other centuries, similar institutions were founded (see section 47).

The medieval abbey schools and universities came to be dominated by something called *scholasticism*.

## 19. Scholasticism

Scholasticism was a type of medieval western European intellectualism. The thinking of the *schoolmen*, as they were called, was a sort of mixture of theology and philosophy. To them Aristotle and the early Christian writers were about the only sources worth

15

studying. Whatever they had said or thought must be so. There was no experimenting, no work in laboratories, no study to find new facts. Too much of the time their arguments were only arguments over the meaning of words.

The choice of language for instruction in these schools was Latin since the Greek language had been lost (it was rediscovered in the 13th century) as had the original philosophical writings of the ancients. The schoolmen did have Boetius's translations of Aristotle's *Categories* and *De interpretatione,* Plato's (circa 427-circa 347 B.C.) *Timaeus* in Chalcidius's version, and Boetius's translation of Porphyry's (233-circa 304) *Eisagoge* (an introduction to the logic of Aristotle). With these four manuscripts available, all but one of which was from the mind of Aristotle, it is no wonder then that scholasticism basically became an Aristotelian system.

The typical curriculum of these medieval schools followed the *Seven Liberal Arts.* These were *grammar* (the reading of Latin), *rhetoric* (the speaking and writing of Latin), *logic* (the methods of argument and proof), *arithmetic, geometry* (geometry included some geography), *astronomy,* and *music.* The first three of the Seven Liberal Arts dealt with language and logic and were called the *Trivium,* or "three ways to learning." The last four were known as the *Quadrivium.* The study of the Trivium led to the Bachelor of Arts degree, and the Quadrivium to the Master of Arts.

Scholasticism was eventually seen by certain thinkers, especially in the Renaissance, as being inadequate, but it served as a bridge between the ancient thinkers and more modern times.

## 20. Attitudes on Health and Medicine

In this medieval time there was an inadequate understanding of the relationship between cleanliness and good health, and illness and disease remained constant threats. Standards of hygiene and sanitation were at very low levels and preventive measures were mostly practiced by accident. During the Crusades European soldiers had observed that Moslems bathed regularly, so in the thinking of many Christians, bathing was erroneously considered pagan.

The human body was generally regarded with contempt because of the church's teachings and the writings of the ancients (see section 21). It was not until much later that it was suggested by Fracastoro (see Chapter 5 Overview) that invisible "seeds" might exist and that these unknown entities could cause diseases. A verification of this theory had to await the development of the microscope centuries later (see sections 128 and 133), and the further research of certain scientists who gave validity to the understanding of germs, microbes, and viruses (see section 170).

## 21. Christian Medicine

The primary places of medical learning in the medieval period were the *monasteries.* It was the *copyists,* those generations of dedicated monks who spent their years laboring in dim, damp rooms with quill and paper, that kept the medical knowledge of the ancients from passing into total obscurity.

Yet the growth of Christian medicine in the Middle Ages was often limited by prejudice, superstition, and dogmatism. Quintus Tertullian (circa 150-circa 230) felt that investigation of the body was made unnecessary by the gospel (what good was objective inquiry anyway in the face of miracles worked by faith?) and Saint Gregory of Tours (circa 538-circa 594) thought that it was blasphemy to seek secular medical aid. Also the medieval monks and *doctors* (a term that meant someone who taught logic) of the church preserved only some of the ancient medical writings. Works by non-Christians were often discarded in favor of those written by Christians, or by those whose theology was similar to Christianity. Some were either permitted to decay or were erased or burned.

As a result, by this century, much of European monastic medical knowledge was based on the philosophy of Hippocrates (circa 460-circa 370 B.C.) and the discoveries and theories of Claudius Galen who had been born in 131 in Pergamum. Galen's works especially had dominated the medicine of the Roman Empire and became the most sacred laws of medieval medicine—with all that was in them—truth, half-truth, and pure error. Galen never became a Christian but he appealed to Christians because he believed in one God and felt that the Creator had made everything for a reason. Hippocrates was not a Christian either but his famous oath was based on good moral ideals.

When the ancient knowledge was inadequate, the doctors of the church turned to prayer and faith. This philosophy gave comfort to

17

those who accepted the healing power of prayer and faith. The historical basis for this hope may be seen in the acts and teachings of Jesus, who healed many during His ministry, using prayer and faith (see Matt. 15:29-31). Also the writings of Saint James contributed to this idea:

> Is any sick among you: Let him call for the elders of the church; and let them pray over him, anointing him with oil in the name of the Lord.
> And the prayer of faith shall save the sick, and the Lord shall raise him up... (James 5:14, 15).

It is not surprising that the later doctors of the church thought they could heal the sick using prayer and faith. Evidence reveals, though, that they were not as successful at it as Jesus or His disciples were.

The improper use of prayer and a lack of faith persistently degenerated into unbiblical practices such as dabbling in the occult. Often, pain was attributed to demons and evil spirits. As in Babylon, astrology often ruled prognoses and diagnoses that were mainly limited to an inspection of the patient's urine. Therapy regressed into magic and often revolting medicines, charms, and amulets were employed. *Venesection* (blood-letting) served only to weaken patients in most instances.

Yet, because the Christians placed great value on life and the human spirit, their important contributions to medieval medicine, aside from preserving certain ancient medical writings, came in their methods of patient care since they paid considerable attention to the comfort of their patients.

## 22. Secular European Medicine

From about the sixth century until about the end of the first century in this millennium, the great secular center for European medical learning was in Salerno and its origin is shrouded in obscurity. It is known that Salerno was the home of a Benedictine monastery (see section 35) by the end of the seventh century and that the monks there were noted for their practice of medicine, but the institute in question here was purely a secular one. The physicians of this secular institution eventually attained such a reputation for restoring health that, by the beginning of this millennium, it was common for the nobility and other important persons to go there for treatment. One of these was William of Normandy, who later became known as William the Conqueror.

## 23. Introduction of Arabian Medicine to Europe

It was in this century that the Western world received its first important introduction to Arabian medicine in the form of Latin translations and to a discipline that eventually competed with the monastic and secular medicine of Europe. Constantine the African (circa 1020-circa 1087), a Benedictine monk, was the author of the earliest of such versions (1050). This was the beginning of what is sometimes called the scholastic period of European medieval medicine and is, of course, closely tied to the great scholastic movement that influenced all forms of medieval European education (see section 19).

## 24. Medieval Chinese Medicine

The practice of *acupuncture* by the Chinese offered many advantages to both surgeons and patients. In this century, acupuncture involved the insertion of needles to treat disease, but not to prevent pain. The knowledge of this discipline was generally not available to others because China was a relatively closed society at this time. Even when outsiders learned of the practice, they typically regarded it with skepticism.

## 25. Music

During the Middle Ages much of the music was played by the churches and synagogues which had developed long and varying traditions. The music of the early Christians was vocal because their meetings were prohibited by Roman law and thus it was necessary to keep their secret meetings as inconspicuous as possible. Then, too, musical instruments had been used by the Romans in the worship of their pagan gods and early Christians thought they should not copy such practices from paganism.

Eventually the *lyre* and *cithara* were cautiously allowed as was the *organ* even later, but music in the early church was mostly in the form of very simple chants (also broadly called "plainsongs" or "plain chants"), that were a type of *unison* music. These forms dominated church music for nearly a thousand years.

Saint Athanasius (circa 296-373), who was a proponent of the doctrine of the Trinity (325), believed that the Psalms should be sung with so little variety that they should sound more like speaking than singing. Even after Pope Gregory I (circa 540; served 590-604) helped to systematize church music with his *Gregorian chants* and other works, it remained illegal for Catholics to experiment with music. Friars and monks were thus restricted from being creative because of what the church fathers perceived to be a way of maintaining a strictly defined theological message. Music and all art forms were justifiable only as long as they could be made to serve God.

The Jews, however, used music freely in their worship services before and during this period of time. The Jews had no prejudice against music because of their rich heritage of scriptural references to the use of instruments in worship. (See Ps. 150).

The office of cantor originated in the Jewish synagogues. The *cantillation* (*canticle* means a short song, hymn, or chant used in church services) of prayers, and later of parts of the Scriptures, was transmitted by oral tradition. Originally the notation of the chants was forbidden but later the cantor's musical position became more important.

The early Christian church adopted the idea of the *cantor*. A *precentor* (from the Latin meaning "one who sings first"), was the director of the music of a cathedral or a monastic church and also a cantor and played a part in the medieval church services.

The oral tradition contributed to the form of music known as the *ballad* (from the Latin verb *ballare*, meaning "to dance"). The word acquired other connotations as well, since it eventually came to refer broadly to any short verse, piece, lyric, or narrative whether it was sung or not. During this century the ballad more narrowly referred to the music of the common people, and more emphasis was placed on the narrative than the tune.

The professional musicians of this century were known by various names. In the south of France the *troubadours* (from the Provencal verb *trobar*, meaning "to compose") wrote songs of love and chivalry and were largely responsible for the popularization of music. The Spanish had "The Song of the Cid" which was based on the life of Rodrigo Diaz (circa 1030-1099) whom the Arabs called "the Cid" (*Al Sayyid,* "the lord"). Often the songs of the minstrels were affectionate stories of courtly love and chivalry or tributes to the glories and beauty of women. The psychology advanced in the songs suggested that a lady improved the life of a man, and the knight who loved a lady should live to make her happy. In the north of France minstrels were called *trouveres.*

# Background of Countries and Nations

### 26. The Byzantine Empire

The Byzantine Empire was the successor state to the Roman Empire where in eastern Europe it preserved the Roman tradition of law and order for nearly a thousand years after the disposition of Romulus Augustulus (birth uncertain; reigned 475-476). It was named after Byzantium, which Emperor Constantine I (circa 288; reigned 306-337) rebuilt (330) as Constantinople and made the capital of the entire Roman Empire. A division into Eastern and Western empires became permanent after the death of Theodosius I (circa 346; reigned in the East 379-395; reigned in the West 392-395) who divided the Roman Empire between his elder and his younger son. Honorius (384; reigned 395-423) ruled in the West and Arcadius (circa 377; reigned 395-408) ruled in the East. After 476 the East was often called the "Greek Empire," since it became more and more Greek in character, because of the loss of the western provinces in the fifth century and then of Syria and Egypt in the seventh century. The core of the empire consisted of the Balkan Peninsula (Thrace, Macedonia, Epirus, Greece proper, the Greek isles, and Illyria), and of Asia Minor.

That the Byzantine Empire lasted as long as it did (Mohammed II conquered it in 1453) is remarkable when one considers the many factors that worked against its survival. It had no easily defensible frontiers, contained a vastly divergent population with little in common, and on all sides it faced hostile adversaries. But its great wealth and resources, its despotic centralized government with its strong military, and the nearly impregnable position of Constantinople, long balanced the scales in its favor. Greek was the dominant language, but Latin long continued in official use. With the

21

crowning of Charlemagne as Emperor of the West at Rome (800), the Byzantine Empire lost any claim to universality. The political division of East and West was paralleled by the religious division between the Roman and the Orthodox Eastern Church (see section 34).

At the beginning of this millennium, the Macedonian Dynasty was in power in the Byzantine Empire (867-1081). One of its greatest accomplishments was to consolidate the empire.

The difficult reign of Basil II (circa 957; reigned 976-1025) was characterized by nearly continuous warfare as he successfully brought Bulgaria into his realm (1018). He negotiated friendly relations with the Russian Prince Vladimir (died 1015) and trade was started between the two countries.

When the second of Basil II's daughters died unmarried, the Macedonian line ended as there was no heir to the throne. Additional problems followed since there was no orderly method of succession in place and incompetent rulers found license to engage in palace intrigue to seize power. Under them the last signs of imperial rule in Italy ended, an open breach developed between the papacy and the Church at Constantinople (1054), and a new attack from the Moslems endangered Byzantine possessions in Asia. In 1071 the Seljuk Turks defeated the army of Romanus IV at Manzikert.

The Comneni Dynasty (1081-1204) was founded by the Emperor Alexius Comnenus (1048; reigned 1081-1118). Alexius I took advantage of the First Crusade to recover some territory in Asia Minor and to restore Byzantine prestige (see section 42), but his successors were able at best to postpone the disintegration of the empire (1453).

## 27. England

The *Angles* gave their name to England—Angleland—"the land of the Angles." The Angles were probably the same people who came from what is now Schleswig in the later decades of the fifth century. The Saxons, a Germanic tribe that had lived near the Angles, also settled in England in the late fifth century, after earlier marauding forays there. The later kingdoms of Sussex, Wessex, and Essex were the outgrowths of their settlements. Some of the Saxons became kings. The Danes forced some of the Saxon kings to pay them tribute, called Danegeld. One Danish chief named Sweyn (sometimes Swain) actually conquered England (see chapter endnote 1-4). His son, Canute (reigned 1016-1035), ruled over not only England but Denmark and Norway as well. Harold I, also known as Harefoot (reigned 1037-1040), an illegitimate son of Canute, then came to power, after a lengthy struggle with his half-brother, Hardecanute (sometimes Harthacanute). Hardecanute (reigned 1040-1042) assumed the throne when Harold died.

Edward the Confessor (circa 1002; reigned 1042-1066) became king upon the death of Hardecanute, his half-brother. Earl Godwin (died 1053), Edward's father-in-law, sensing Edward's lack of interest in politics, became a strong influence in the government by managing to secure the support of influential men such as Stigand (died 1072), Archbishop of Canterbury. Edward acted more like a monk than a king. He believed in the king's touch and stood around in public so his subjects could touch him for healing.

It was during this time that the story of Lady Godiva (1040-circa 1080), a Saxon lady, took place. According to the legend, she rode naked through the streets of Coventry to gain from her husband, Earl Leofric of Mercia and Lord of Coventry, a remission of the oppressive toll imposed on his tenants. She must have been a very devout person because she assisted in the founding of a monastery at Stow, Lincolnshire, in 1040.

## 28. The Norman Conquest

In Saxon England the kings were elected by the popular leaders who were known as the Witan. When Edward died in 1066 without an heir, the Witan elected as his successor a brave Saxon named Harold Godwinson (circa 1022-1066) who became the Earl of Wessex and the wealthiest and most noted man in England after the death of his father, Earl Godwin. He thus easily assumed the throne as Harold II in 1066, but it was not an easy matter to keep it. He faced three problems with his claim. There was his own brother Edgar Atheling, who had a claim to the throne, as well as the invasion by both the Vikings from Scandinavia and the Normans from the French coast who were led by William, Duke of Normandy.

Harold successfully defended his claim against his brother and he soundly put down the invasion by the Vikings, but he was not so successful in dealing with the threat from William.

23

William (circa 1027-1087) was the illegitimate son of Robert the Devil, Duke of Normandy (also known as Robert I), by Arletta. Robert induced the Norman barons to acknowledge William as his successor in 1034, since he did not have a legitimate son. The barons kept their agreement when Robert died in 1034, though William was only seven or eight years old at the time. There followed a period of violence during which three of William's guardians were murdered.

William demonstrated an early aptitude for war and government. When he was twenty, he received aid from Henry I of France and established his power. In turn he aided Henry against Geoffrey Martel, Count of Anjou.

William did other things to strengthen his claim to the English throne. He visited England in 1051 and there probably received from Edward the Confessor a promise of the English succession. He also married Matilda in 1053, a daughter of Baldwin V of Flanders, who traced her descent in the female line from Alfred the Great. William also claimed that Harold had sworn to support him for the throne as a favor he once did for him. An unsubstantiated story suggests that Harold had been shipwrecked in 1064 and William had taken care of him. As part of the bargain for his care, William had made Harold swear to support him in his quest for the throne of England. Such promises were not worth much because, as already mentioned, it was the custom of the Saxon nobles to elect their own king.

Harold's election thus aroused William's ire as he began to plan the Norman invasion of England in 1066. William gained the support of his followers and made his peace with Philip I, the new king of France, by promising that he would hold England as Philip's representative. He also got the support of Pope Alexander II (served 1061-1073). With the pope's backing William assembled a mighty army which crossed the channel toward England to attack Harold's army. Harold was killed in the ensuing battle and William had himself elected and crowned as king in 1066.

One of his first acts as king was to found Battle Abbey in East Sussex, England. Soon afterwards, William began construction on the great tower (now called the Tower of London).

## 29. How France Began to Take Form

After the disintegration of Charlemagne's empire under the incompetent rule of Louis I (778-840), the Treaty of Verdun in 843 gave

24

to Charles the Bald (823; reigned 843-877), one of Charlemagne's grandsons, much of the territory we know today as France. This region, however, was not a united nation. Since the power of the king had been weakened under Louis I, dukes, lords, and other personages with feudal titles ruled over different parts of it in their own name. Sometimes these barons demanded and received certain rights from the king in return for their support. This strengthened the feudal system in France.

When Hugh Capet (circa 940; reigned 987-996) took the throne, he avoided issues with the powerful barons that could have given him problems. To prevent disputes of succession, he originated the practice of a king naming his son king during his own lifetime. No wonder, then, that the dynasty he established lasted until 1328.

Hugh's son, Robert II (circa 971; reigned 996-1031) continued his father's policy of appeasing the barons and acquired small territories in the southeast and northwest.

Robert's son, Henry I (circa 1011; reigned 1031-1060), faced a serious rebellion by Eudes, Count of Troyes and Chartress. To build internal strength, Henry I was forced to surrender certain territories to Emperor Conrad II of Germany and to acknowledge his (Henry's) brother's claim to Burgundy.

Henry's son Philip I (1052; reigned 1060-1108) became king at the age of eight upon the death of his father. During his minority he spent most of his time around Paris where he was sometimes subjected to injury by the powerful lawless barons that came to town. His minority came to an end in 1066 and in the long reign that followed, he demonstrated little administrative skill but he was able to increase the lands of his house around Paris and maintained order in them. He also was able to hold his own in the occasional conflicts that arose between himself and William the Conqueror.

## 30. Germany

The area that is today known as Germany is a region of Europe with a history dating from Roman times. This long history involved many changes in government and many shifts of boundaries so that it was not the home of a united nation for hundreds of years. Barbarian tribes invaded the area in the fifth and sixth centuries after the fall of Rome. Saxony was seized by the Franks in the sixth and seventh centuries and the Merovingian Dynasty (448-751) was replaced by the Carolingian Dynasty (reigned 751-987) under Pepin III (circa 714; reigned 751-768). The empire of his son Charlemagne was divided by the Treaty of Verdun in 843 (see section 29). The eastern portion, the Kingdom of the East Franks, composed the nucleus of a German state, and was expanded by the Treaty of Mersen (870). Powerful feudal duchies developed during this time.

At the beginning of this millennium Otto III was in power in Germany (980; reigned 983-1002). During his minority, authority was exercised by Otto III's mother, Theophano (regent 983-991), and by his grandmother Adelaide (regent 991-995) after Theophano's death. Upon the death of Pope John XV (served 985-996), Otto III placed his cousin Bruno in the vacant papacy as Gregory V (996) and restored him (998) after his expulsion by a Roman revolt. After Gregory's death (999) Otto made his tutor Gerbert of Aurillac the pope. He called himself Sylvester II (circa 940; served 999-1003) and he was, therefore, the pope of the Roman Catholic Church at the beginning of this millennium. Otto III was very talented, extremely well educated, and deeply religious. After 998 he lived mainly in Rome where he constructed a palace. He was not popular either in Germany nor Italy. In the first year of this millennium, Otto III was blockaded in his palace by a mob but eventually he was allowed to retire to Paterno where he died.

Imperial power over the church reached its peak under Henry III, also known as "the Black," German king (1017; reigned 1039-1056) and Holy Roman Emperor (1046-1056), but then declined during the rule of his son Henry IV as a result of the Investiture Controversy, civil disturbances, and rebelling dukes (see sections 39 & 40). Henry III thought of himself as a *priest-king*, and his primary concern was with religious matters. He supported the Cluniac Order (see section 37). In 1043 (two years after the Truce of God was first proclaimed— see section 14) he announced that he was forgiving his private enemies and giving up all thought of vengeance and urged the nobles to do the same, but he failed in his purpose of giving his empire permanent peace. He supported reform in the church by denouncing the marriage of priests and the buying of *offices* (positions of responsibility in the church). He was succeeded by his young son, Henry IV.

Henry IV became German king during his minority (1050-1106;

reigned 1056-1105) and Holy Roman Emperor during his majority (reigned 1084-1105). During his minority the nobles and high ecclesiastics greatly increased their power at the expense of the royal authority. In 1075 he became the central figure in the opening stages of the long struggle between the empire and the papacy, that great matter known as the Investiture Controversy (see sections 39-40).

## 31. The Jews

In this century the Jews continued to be a "scattered people" since their expulsion from Palestine after a revolt there in 135. During this dispersion, the Jews maintained their language and religion and even managed to compile the *Talmud* (the sixty-three volumes of the Jewish civil and canonical law) in the sixth century. The "ownership" of Jerusalem itself changed over the years. Until 614 it was a Christian city. Between 614 and 629 it was a Persian city. Until 637 it was once again Christian and until the end of the First Crusade in 1099 it was a Moslem provincial capital.

Living in many different countries, the Jews were not universally welcome and were often mistreated. In Germany the feudal system debarred the Jews from holding land and they were subject to moral injury by being driven exclusively into finance and trade since they could practice usury (the lending of money at an extremely high rate of interest), which was prohibited by Christians. Because they had assisted the Moslems in the defense of Jerusalem, the surviving Jews of the First Crusade were forced into a synagogue and were burned to death (1099).

It was mostly in Spain (circa ninth to eleventh centuries) that the Jews found opportunity to become doctors, lawyers, teachers, or other professionals in a type of golden age. But even their comparative good fortune in Spain came to an end in this century when, during the revolt (1066) of the Arabs and Berbers (see chapter endnote 1-5), 4000 Jews in Granada were murdered. Those who survived this tragedy were forced to sell their property and get out of the country.

## 32. Important Jewish Leaders

Gershom ben Jehuda (960-1028) known as the "light of the exile," settled in Mainz, Germany, where he founded a rabbinical academy

27

and wrote a Hebrew commentary on the Talmud. He also published his ordinance forbidding polygamy in Jewish law (circa 1000) as it had been long prohibited in Jewish practice. This was the beginning of the *synodal* government of Judaism (in which leaders gathered to decide policy). This became a marked feature of medieval life in the synagogues of northern and central Europe.

Soon after Gershom's death, Rabbi Rashi (1040-1105) founded a new school of learning at Troyes which taught Jewish traditions and the Law. Rashi is credited with writing two important commentaries on the Hebrew Bible.

## 33. The Vikings

The *Vikings*, also known as *Norsemen* or *Northmen*, were seafaring warriors who raided Scandinavia (during the ninth to eleventh centuries). They extended their raids outward from the British Isles, France, Spain, Italy, and North Africa. Sometimes they settled in the conquered territories. Norwegian Vikings settled in Scotland and Ireland. Normandy also came under their influence.

There is some evidence to support the belief that the Vikings discovered North America in circa 1000, and that they tried unsuccessfully to make a settlement there. It was a place they called *Vinland*, a name derived from the wild grapes they found there. Leif Ericson (found living 1000) is credited with this discovery. They stayed for several years before abandoning the place (circa 1006).

Another noted Viking was Leif Ericson's father, Eric the Red (circa 950-circa 1010), who explored the southwest coast of Greenland (982-985) and founded a colony there. He was motivated to look for a new place to live when he fled from Iceland to escape persecution on a charge of murder.

The Vikings discontinued their raiding parties in this century and they instituted the emerging feudal system that was spreading across the rest of Europe, which narrowed the scope of their raids. Others became better organized at opposing them. The Normans who invaded England in 1066 were Viking descendants.

# Matters of Religion

## 34. Christianity

In the second century after Christ, the unfortunate peoples of the Mediterranean area were wracked by a series of devastating plagues that moved across their land and which claimed the lives of many thousands. Torn also by famine, economic devastation, revolt, and the barbaric invasions, they gladly sought refuge in the great number of cults and faiths that flourished in that area then. Three of them especially were popular.

There was the worship of *Mithra* (the god of light), an ancient god of Iran and India (where he is called "Mitra"). His special day was Sun-day which was later adopted by the Christians as was the practice of burning candles in religious services.

Followers of the *Seraphic* faith believed that their god was a savior who could bring salvation to all who believed in him. They believed in the existence of a father, a son, and the mother, known as Isis.

*Christianity*, which taught that Jesus could heal all the ills of the spirit as well as the flesh, soon became the dominant religion. Its ideas appealed to all men regardless of their nationality, race, or class. Constantine I (see section 26) saw the wisdom of using this force to bring unity to a world in turmoil. He officially recognized Christianity in 313. In 325 he called the Council of Nicaea where the concepts of the Holy Trinity and the divinity of Christ were officially acknowledged.

Yet the Council of Nicaea was characterized by turmoil as well as by agreement. It was said that the Church fathers even exchanged blows there, an early indication that there was a diversity of ideas about how Christianity should be defined. As mentioned earlier these disagreements eventually brought about a division of Eastern and Western Christianity. By the ninth century, a central figure in this matter was the Greek churchman and theologian, Photius (circa 820-circa 892) who questioned certain Latin practices and challenged the pope's right to judge the validity of the election of the patriarch. Disagreements such as these persisted until the split between the East and West Church became permanent. In 1054 Michael Cerularius, Patriarch of Constantinople, attacked the papacy, an act which caused Pope Leo IX (served 1049-1054) to respond by excommunicating him.

29

This so enraged the leaders of the Eastern Church that they made permanent the rift between the two churches that had been widening for so many years.

The Eastern or Greek Church had for its spiritual head the Patriarch of Constantinople, just as the Western or Roman Church had a head in the Pope or Bishop of Rome. The missionary efforts of the Greek Church resulted in the conversion of the barbarians who entered southeastern Europe during the early Middle Ages. Its greatest victory was the conversion of the Russians to Christianity under the direction of Vladimir the Great (died 1015). He sent out envoys to investigate the various merits of Islam, the Jewish religion, and Latin and Greek Christianity. The commissioners reported in favor of the religion of Constantinople. The beginning of this millennium, then, saw Christianity accepted in Russia.

The medieval church in western Europe was a catholic church in the original sense of the word. The word *catholic* means "universal" or "all inclusive." One would not think in medieval terms of the German, Roman, or French church, but of the church. Everywhere in western Europe, Latin was the language used in church services. All Christians were expected to admire and respect the pope as the representative of God on earth.

## 35. The Benedictines

An important influence on religion in Europe in the medieval period was an organization known as the *Benedictines*, founded by Saint Benedict (died circa 547). Also known as "Black Monks," they were first established at Monte Cassino, Italy, and quickly became the symbolic center of western monasticism. The concept of the *monastery*, or *abbey*, was seen as a devout Christian family of men, directed by an abbot, who spent their lives in service to others. In this century, this group underwent a significant change which resulted in the formation of a new organization, known as the *Cistercians*.

## 36. The Cistercians

Saint Stephen Harding (died 1134) was the founder of the Cistercians (1098), whose monks were also called "White Monks."

They organized as a reaction to the *Cluniac Revival* (see section 37) in effect rejecting what they felt was an inappropriate and worldly direction for the Benedictines. They saw themselves as returning to what the Benedictines had been when they were first formed, and not what they had become by the end of this century. They restored farming as a chief occupation of monks and became leaders in the development of new agricultural techniques in Europe. Another influential monk, Saint Bernard, is usually considered to be the "second founder" of this organization because of his zealous efforts on behalf of it (see section 50).

## 37. The Cluniac Revival

At the beginning of this millennium, a movement known as the Cluniac Revival swept across Europe. It was an organization of Benedictine monks centered in the abbey (founded in 910) of Cluny, France. It rapidly became the center of a broad reform of religious life, directed by a series of zealous abbots. Many men came to Cluny and new priories (religious houses) were opened. Abbeys that had been established long before the revival became involved. Outside the monastery the Cluniac monks worked for reform of Christian life and ecclesiastic independence. From circa 950 to circa 1130 Cluny had the greatest following in the West after the pope.

## 38. Christian Church Architecture

In this century a new style of architecture appeared which was known as *Gothic*. The Goths did not originate this new style, and the name at first was applied rather negatively, as if it were a barbarian style as compared with the Romanesque (Roman style). In Gothic architecture, in place of the rounded arch, there was a high-pointed arch. Ribs in the roof of the structure transferred some of the weight of the roof to the pillars. A type of external support for the walls of Gothic cathedrals was called the "flying buttress." They made it possible for walls to be less massive than before, and allowed more windows to be set in place.

Later, many cathedral windows were made of stained glass, and were beautiful works of art (see sections 91 and 97). An early Gothic design was employed in the building of Winchester Cathedral.

31

(Winchester was the original capital city of England.) Begun under the Norman Period in 1079 {1:52 a.m.}, its tower, which was completed many years later, was low but massive. Later, when the tower fell (1107), it was commonly believed that it was because William Rufus, "the bad king" (circa 1056; reigned 1087-1100),was buried under it (see chapter endnote 1-6).

# Matters of Church and State

## 39. The Holy Roman Emperor

When the German Prince Otto I was elected king by the Germanic nobles in 936, they decided to give the name *Holy Roman Empire* to the territory over which he reigned. The logic behind this idea was that just as there was a "universal church," which should include all people, there should also be a universal authority in charge of secular affairs. Since the Roman Empire, at least under Constantine and for a time following, seemed to provide for such a universal rule of both church and empire, the name "Holy Roman Empire" was used to suggest the rather vague concept of a worldwide authority outside of the church.

Men sometimes said it was the pope's duty to rule men's souls and it was the emperor's responsibility to rule men's bodies. Popes and emperors could not always make clear distinctions between their activities, and this often caused harsh feelings to arise, not to mention serious conflicts. The matter itself was classified as the Investiture Controversy which was the name for the struggle between the papacy and secular rulers for the right to elect and install bishops. In England, the controversy took the form of a long quarrel between Henry I and Anselm, Archbishop of Canterbury (1033; served 1093-1109). In Germany these feelings were especially strong during Henry IV's reign (1056-1105). He took issue with Pope Gregory VII (circa 1021; served 1073-1085) who claimed the right to rule in purely political matters and who wanted his bishops to rule as princes. When Henry IV made appointments (known as "lay investitures"—a formal investing of a person with a religious office) to the sees of Milan, Fermo, and Spoleto (1075), Gregory VII excommunicated him. Henry IV summoned a council at *Worms* (a city in Germany) which declared Gregory VII deposed and absolved his subjects of their oaths of fealty to the pope. But a powerful coalition of German nobles agreed (1076) not to

32

recognize Henry IV as king unless he obtained absolution from the pope by February, 1077, and in any event to decide the question of his fitness to rule at a diet to be held at Augsburg under the chairmanship of the pope.

## 40. Henry IV Goes to Canossa

To forestall the action of this diet, Henry IV crossed the Alps in the dead of winter to seek absolution. By his humiliation and penitence he moved the pope to grant him absolution at Canossa in January, 1077, a month earlier than the appointed deadline. Disappointed, the German nobles elected Rudolf of Swabia king, plunging Germany into civil war. Gregory VII remained neutral until March, 1080, when he renewed Henry IV's excommunication and deposition and recognized Rudolf's title. But Henry IV was now supported by a large party; German and Italian bishops joined him in declaring Gregory VII deposed and in electing an antipope, Clement II (served 1046-1047). One of these supporters was Sigebert of Gembloux (circa 1030-1112), the Benedictine monk and teacher. His writings on this question favored Henry IV's cause over that of the pope's and these works encouraged others to support Henry IV. At the death of Rudolf (1080) the German revolt was practically broken, and in 1081 Henry IV carried the war into Italy. After several unsuccessful attempts he occupied Rome before the advance of the Normans under Robert Guiscard (circa 1015-1085), who liberated Gregory VII, but upon Henry's return Gregory VII went into final exile where he died.

The matter of investiture in Germany was finally settled in compromise by the Concordat of Worms in 1122 between German king Henry V (1081; reigned 1105-1125) and Calixtus II (Pope 1119-1124.) (see section 53). The matter in England was settled by compromise somewhat sooner (1107).

### Reflection:

*This contest between Henry IV and Gregory VII, over an issue known as investiture and its settlement, represented the climax between the temporal and spiritual powers in the Middle Ages. It originated in the growing confusion which prevailed in those days over the question of the division of powers between the church and the state. Did people of the Middle Ages understand the words of Jesus: "My kingdom is not of this world" (John 18:36)? Do people of our own time appreciate the meaning of this statement of our Lord?*

## 41. The Crusades

In their day, the *Crusades* (a series of military expeditions made by Christians of Western Europe to recover Jerusalem and the Holy Land from the Moslems) were generally seen as "holy wars." They were sparked partly by the surge of religious revival which had begun in western Europe in the tenth century and which reached a peak during this century. As holy wars, the Crusades must be seen from the perspective of an age in which the spirit of man was dominated by thoughts of heaven. The Crusades became the "foreign policy" of the papacy, directing its faithful subjects to the great war of Christianity against those they called the "infidels"—the Moslems. The church effectively used the instinct for private war to this end (see section 14).

Because the crusaders wore a cross (from the Latin word *crux*) made from blood-red cloth on their breasts as they went to war, and on their backs as they returned, they were called "crusaders."

## 42. The First Crusade (1096-1099) {2:17 a.m. - 2:21 a.m.}

When the Seljuk Turks captured Jerusalem from the *Saracens* (nomads of the Syro-Arabian desert) in 1071, they began a cruel persecution of the Christians who resided in the Holy City and the scared places of the church were profaned or destroyed. The tomb of Christ, the Mount of Olives, Golgotha, and all places and things associated with the life and death of Christ in the Holy Land were so sacred that Christians thought they had divine powers to heal and forgive sins. Pilgrims on their way to the Holy City were attacked, robbed, and beaten. There was great anger among the Europeans when they learned of these events. The eastern Emperor Alexius Comnenus, whose predecessor had been defeated and slain by the Turks, feared for the safety of Constantinople itself and sent a request for help to Pope Urban II (served 1088-1099) at Rome. The response by the Latin Crusaders that followed is interesting when one considers that it came only forty-one years after the break between the Eastern and the Western church had been declared official. Whether Urban II was more interested in retaking Jerusalem than preventing the potential threat to Constantinople is a matter of conjecture. What is obvious is that Christian brothers became united in a common cause against the Turks.

The sermon of Urban II at Clermont, France (1095), became the standard discourse used by wandering preachers, among whom Peter the Hermit (died circa 1151) distinguished himself by his fiery zeal. Riding on a donkey from place to place through France and along the Rhine, he "captured" the attention of thousands of the poor through his eloquence. This crusade, therefore, became known as the people's crusade. Some three or four months before the term fixed (August 15, 1096) by Urban II, the peasants began to gather. Not willing to wait until August, at least four separate bands of these unorganized peasants started for the East in the spring of 1096. A knight named Walter the Penniless (died 1096) successfully led a large number of peasants to Constantinople. Another group under the leadership of the Hermit was not so fortunate since they were completely unprepared for the long journey. Many of these peasants died of starvation or were captured by slave traders as they passed through Bulgaria on their way to Jerusalem. They crossed the *Bosporus* (a strait that joins the Black Sea to the Sea of Marmara and separates Europe from Asia Minor) and were defeated by the Turks in October, 1096.

Meanwhile, the knights began to assemble. In small bands, they came eastward in 1096. Urban II estimated their numbers at 300,000 by March, 1096. Their first operation was the siege of Nicaea, defended by a Turkish garrison which they eventually captured (1097). Antioch fell (1098) but only after a lance was discovered which was said to be the lance that had pierced Jesus' side on the cross. This "holy lance" excited the whole army and the nervous strength it gave them enabled them to meet and defeat the Moslems. Jerusalem itself was captured (1098).

---

**Reflection:**

*In an age when nobles loved to fight, consider both sides of the debate surrounding the Crusades. Was the church justified in channeling the love of fighting into their holy wars or could the church have approached the solution to the problem in another way?*

---

### 43. The Kingdom of Jerusalem

Four Crusader states were established including the Latin Kingdom of Jerusalem, the principality of Antioch, and the counties of Edessa (now Urfa) and Tripoli. Godfrey of Bouillon (circa 1060; reigned 1099-1100) became the first ruler of the Holy Land and was given the title of "Defender of the Holy Sepulchre." Upon his death, he was replaced by his brother Baldwin I (circa 1058; reigned 1100-1118) who assumed the title of the King of Jerusalem and was crowned on December 25, 1100 {2:23 a.m.}.

The Latin Kingdom became an outpost of Christendom which provided the Italian cities with opportunities for trade with the east. A continuous stream of pilgrims and adventurers arrived to visit the Holy Sepulchre, to seek their fortunes, or to find employment in the defense of the kingdom. The great military orders, particularly the *Hospitalers* and the *Templars*, which were organized to defend and provide for pilgrims, garrisoned the castles, and in general carried on the defense of the Latin Kingdom.

**Reflection:**

*Christianity placed much emphasis on benevolence as a duty and, therefore, supported all institutions to help the poor, the sick, and the downtrodden. Consider how the various organizations that were started by the knights (see sections 43 and 45) helped meet these needs and why they received the support of the church.*

# Chapter Endnotes

1-1. The establishment of the Christian Era came in 532 when the Roman biblical scholar Dionysius Exiguus (died circa 545) designated the beginning of the year A.D. 1 to have been March 25 (it was later changed by Gregory XIII to January 1), and therefore Dec. 25, A.D. 1, was called the birth date of Christ. The correctness of this determination has long been subject to debate, and contemporary research suggests that December 25, 4 B.C. is a more accurate date for the Incarnation. The use of the number 1, instead of zero, to designate the beginning of the Christian Era, is why years such as 1501 and 1901 are regarded as the first of a new century and years such as 1500 and 1900 are regarded as the last years of an old century.

1-2. The years 476 and 1453 are what might be termed dates of convenience. They represent important events that are convenient references to the approximate beginning and end of the medieval period. Medieval attitudes and practices were found prior to the decline of Rome and after the fall of Constantinople. Some sources use such vague references as the late fifteenth century, or approximately 1500 to identify the end of the Middle Ages.

1-3. The ancient Romans had a very good method of making roads. Two parallel trenches were cut to mark the breadth of the road and loose earth was removed until a solid foundation was reached. It was replaced with local materials. Streets were paved with large polygonal blocks and footways with rectangular slabs. There is no evidence that the Roman methods were used in road construction in Europe during the Middle Ages, which is curious because there were sufficient examples then for them to copy. Indeed, It was not until about the beginning of the eighteenth century that the building of roads by Europeans was taken seriously, starting at first in France, whose example was soon copied by other European nations.

1-4. Sweyn was the king of Denmark (circa 960; reigned 986-1014) and son of Harold Bluetooth. At the battle of Svolder (1000) the Swedes and Danes defeated and killed King Olaf I of Norway (circa 963; reigned 995-1000) and divided his kingdom. Sweyn, who had already previously invaded England, returned in 1003-1004 and again

37

in 1013, when the English submitted and accepted him as king. He died before his coronation and was succeeded in Denmark and England by his son Canute.

1-5. The Berbers were aboriginal peoples of North Africa. The native languages were of the Hamitic group, but Arabic was prevalent, being the language of their religion, Islam.

1-6. William II, also known as William Rufus, (d. 1100), was king of England (reigned 1087-1100). His reign was characterized by much conflict, especially with the Scottish king, Malcom III, and intermittently with his brother Henry I for the throne. He exacted enormous taxes from his subjects on the flimsiest of pretexts, and inspired terror among the clergy by his sale of various churches and church lands.

## Chapter Terms

| | | | |
|---|---|---|---|
| Angles | croft | king's touch | tilt |
| ballad | Danegeld | mattock | tournament |
| Benedictines | Dark Ages | Middle Ages | Trivium |
| Berbers | Feudal Age | plainsongs | troubadours |
| Black Monks | feud | portcullis | trouveres |
| bordarii | feudalism | Quadrivium | venesection |
| Byzantine Empire | flail | Romanesque | villein |
| catapult | Gothic | Saracens | Vinland |
| catholic | homage | scholasticism | White Monks |
| Cistercians | freemen | schoolmen | |
| Cluniac Revival | knighthood | serf | |
| cottager | harrow | suzerain | |

## Chapter Review Questions/Exercises

1. What religious significance did the coming of the year 1001 have to a few Christian monks? (1)
2. Why were the masses of medieval men not in a position to appreciate or even know abut the symbolism of a thousand years? Would they have cared much if they had known? Why or why not? (1-2)

3. What was the dominant social and political system in much of the world at the beginning of this millennium? (1-2)
4. Describe this system and list conditions that caused it to become popular. (1-2).
5. List places where modified forms of this system had been used elsewhere. (2)
6. Why was this system so hard on the poor? (2)
7. List reasons why a medieval person might decide to go on a major journey. (2)
8. What are some of the terms used to describe the medieval period? (2)
9. Describe vassalage and the ceremony associated with it. (3)
10. List the different classifications of people that were found on a feudal estate. (4)
11. List the different kinds of workers that were found on a manor. (5)
12. What were the responsibilities of the occupants of a manor to their lord? (5)
13. What were the obligations of the lord of the manor to the occupants of the manor? (5)
14. Describe some of the characteristics of medieval farming.(6)
15. List some characteristics that manors had in common. (7)
16. Explain how castles were protected (consider both location and construction). (8)
17. Before the use of gunpowder, what were some of the ways a castle could be attacked? (8)
18. How could the castle occupants protect themselves? (8)
19. Describe the conditions in a typical castle. Was living in them really pleasant, like pictures of them suggest? (8)
20. What was the hall of the castle used for? (9)
21. Without eating utensils, how did medieval man eat his food?(9)
22. Who originated the concept of the armed soldier on a horse? (10)
23. Describe the process of becoming a knight. (11)
24. Explain the disadvantages of the system in use in medieval times to select knights. (12)
25. Describe the attitude the medieval nobles had toward fighting. (13)

26. Who developed the code of conduct known as chivalry and what were some of its characteristics? (14)
27. What was the Truce of God and why was it used? (14)
28. Describe the position of women in medieval society. (15)
29. What was the Ptolemaic system of astronomy? (16)
30. How did the church interpret the Ptolemaic theory? (6)
31. How did medieval man interpret things in the heavens, such as comets? (16)
32. Name some of the characteristics of medieval astrology. (17)
33. Distinguish between formal and informal medieval education. (18)
34. What was scholasticism? (19)
35. What were the Seven Liberal Arts and the Trivium? (19)
36. What were some of the medieval attitudes on health? (20)
37. What were some of the limitations of medieval Christian medicine? (21)
38. Why was faith and prayer so important to the medieval medical practitioners? (21)
39. What was the main contribution the Christian medieval monks made to medicine? (21)
40. How did medieval Europe learn about Arabian medicine? (23)
41. How was acupuncture used by the medieval Chinese? (24)
42. Why was the music used by the early Christians vocal? (25)
44. How did the Jews feel about using music in their worship services? (25)
45. Explain the term ballad and the broader meaning that later came to be associated with it. (25)
46. What were the professional musicians of the eleventh century called? (25)
47. Describe the background of the Byzantine Empire. (26)
48. What factors helped the Byzantine Empire last as long as it did? (26)
49. List some of the rulers of the Byzantine Empire in the eleventh century. (26)
50. How did England originate? (27)
51. How was Edward the Confessor different from other rulers? (27)
52. Why did William invade England? (28)

53. Describe the background of France. (29)
54. List some of the French rulers of the eleventh century. (29)
55. How did Germany originate? (30)
56. List some of the German rulers in the eleventh century. (30)
57. Describe some of the problems experienced by the medieval Jews. (31)
58. Who were two important Jewish leaders in the eleventh century? (32)
59. Who were the Vikings and what did they do in the year 1000? (33)
60. Describe the status of Christianity after the decline of Rome. (34)
61. What was the Council of Nicaea and what did it accomplish? (34)
62. Describe the events leading to the permanent split between the East and West church. (34)
63. Explain how medieval Russia accepted Christianity. (34)
64. Who were the Benedictines and the Cistercians? (35-36)
65. What was the Cluniac Revival? (37)
66. What was Gothic architecture? (38)
67. How did the idea of the Holy Roman Emperor originate? (39)
68. What was the Investiture Controversy? (39-40)
69. What happened to Henry IV in Canossa? (40)
70. What were the Crusades? (41)
71. Describe the First Crusade (42)
72. Who was Peter the Hermit? (42)
73. What was the kingdom of Jerusalem? (43)

# 2

# 1101-1200

## {2:24 a.m.-4:47 a.m.}

Sometime during the next two hours and twenty-three minutes, the Persian poet Omar Khayyam (circa 1050-circa 1123) will pen his famous saying:

> The bird of time has but a little way
> To flutter—and the bird is on the wing.

The German chronicler Otto of Freising (died 1158) will write his important medieval world history book *The Two Cities* (1146). It will be important because of its extensive information and the philosophy of history it will present.

## Overview

The plight of the peasants did not change much in the first hundred years of this millennium. As the year 1101 emerged, the feudal system found itself more and more entrenched in people's lives. There were more estates, villages, castles, and towers in this century than there had been in the preceding 100 years. These new and enlarged communities needed new approaches to government that had not been necessary when they had been smaller. Some of them used forms of organization that had been developed in the days of the Roman Empire. Others worked out their own institutions to meet their own needs. A city or town usually had a mayor or burgomaster as a sort of chief executive and some kind of council to assist him.

## 44. The Formation of Medieval Towns

Some of the old Roman towns, despite the devastation wrought by the barbarian invasions, did not disappear and larger centers of population, such as London, York, Paris, Vienna, Venice, Marseilles, Florence, and Milan, were of some importance throughout the Middle Ages. Constantinople, the heart of Byzantine civilization, was the largest and most populous place in medieval Europe. Yet as long as most people depended upon farming for their living, there was no particular incentive for towns to form, but often a town grew out of the manor around a tower or castle, or a village on a feudal manor, and expanded into a sizable center of population. As a result, trade between villages and manors increased, in spite of the difficulties and dangers of travel, and trade needed towns with people. Villas and manors were located where busy roads crossed, or where a river crossed a road, or where there was a natural harbor. These places · were visited often by many people.

Some towns had to struggle against lords and kings for the privilege of self-government. When many of the lords went away on the Crusades, they frequently sold privileges to towns. If the power of the lords could be weakened by doing so, kings usually encouraged towns to seek their freedom. But sometimes kings themselves had to make concessions to towns and grant them charters that recognized new rights of self-government.

Some medieval towns held annual *fairs* (from the Latin word *feria*, "a festival") which promoted economic growth and trade. They were held under charters granted by the king or the lord of the district. Such was the case with the Bartholomew Fair (named after the saint whose name means "son of a drawer of water"). The Bartholomew Fair began in 1133 at Smithfield, London, on Saint Bartholomew's Day.

## 45. The Knights

The knights continued to organize themselves during this century. The *Knights Templars* was a military and religious order whose men had fought bravely in the Crusades. This order was founded in Jerusalem in 1119 when several French knights pledged themselves to defend the Holy Sepulchre (presumed to be the tomb in which Jesus was buried), and to protect Christian pilgrims in the Holy Land. Baldwin II (reigned 1118-1131), King of Jerusalem, accommodated them by allowing them to occupy a part of his palace, and the abbots and canons of the church and convent of the Temple gave them a building in which to keep their arms. Thus, they were called Templars. The order was confirmed in 1128 by Pope Honorius II (served 1124-1130), and in the tradition of the crusaders themselves, these knights wore a red cross on their left breasts and on their banners. The Templars exercised a wide influence in Palestine until Jerusalem was captured by the Saracens under Saladin (circa 1138-1193) in 1187, when they transferred to Cyprus. Pope Alexander III (served 1159-1181) conferred extensive privileges upon them in 1162 and they became numerous in all the countries of southern and western Europe, establishing themselves in England (circa 1185). They recruited warriors for the crusading armies and took care of travelers' funds. They were thus drawn into the banking business as well.

The powerful *Teutonic Knights* organization was also founded in this century (1190-1191) by citizens of Bremen and Lubeck for the purpose of aiding the soldiers who suffered during the Siege of Acre (a port of Israel) in the Third Crusade. German king Frederick I Barbarossa (see section 56), raised the organization to an order of knighthood (1198). The grand master first stayed at Jerusalem, but when Palestine fell into the hands of the Turks, he moved to Venice, and later the headquarters was established in Germany.

## 46. Superstitions

In this century some men continued to rely on superstitions to explain the unknown. Evil spirits were credited with major disasters. Smaller problems were credited to gnomes, goblins, elves, and sometimes even to comets.

One superstition that was widely held involved sneezing. Sneezing was thought to be a sign that the soul was in danger of leaving the body. The German word *Gesundheit* ("your health") was originated as a blessing to use when one sneezed in order to prevent that from happening.

The concept of *abracadabra*, which had been a magical formula used by the Gnostics of the secnd century to seek the aid of spirits to prevent disease had, by this century, been extended to include any hocus-pocus. It thus became a common saying in the use of magic.

Other superstitions abounded during the Middle Ages. Belief in werewolves was common and it was said that some men changed into wolves at night. The Moslems believed in *jinn*, evil spirits that lived in the ground and appeared to man in the form of small animals or occasionally in human form. It was believed that they were responsible for disease and even accidents. There were also good jinn who helped people. In the tales of the Arabian Nights, for example, Aladdin called a *jinni* (genie) from the magic lamp. It was believed that jinn liked to occupy the threshold of a door and that is how the custom of carrying a bride over the threshold originated.

Some Jews believed in *Lilith* (from Hebrew *lilatu*, "night;" hence "night-monster"), a female demon equivalent to the Transylvanian *vampire* (a night demon who supposedly sucked blood from people who were sleeping). The personality and Hebrew name are derived from a Babylonian-Assyrian demon named Lilu. It was thought that Lilith had a special power for evil over children. The superstition was extended to a cult surviving among the Jews in the Middle Ages. In the rabbinical literature, Lilith became the first wife of Adam but she flew away from him and became a demon.

# Other Medieval Disciplines and Institutions

## 47. Higher Education in Medieval Europe

The founding of a university at Bologna in the previous century represented a tremendous achievement and was an example that came to be repeated, not only in this century, but in others as well. In England, Oxford and Cambridge universities grew out of the informal groups of young scholars in this century who gathered around the learned monks and teachers of the towns to study.

At first, these universities were not much like our modern

universities since they were characterized largely by their informality. The teacher might have been the only one in the class who owned a book. Formal lesson plans rarely existed, if at all, and the focus of attention in these classes might just as easily be determined by the students as by the teacher. There were no transcripts to record a student's progress as are found at today's universities. A student might change schools without any records being transferred.

The rediscovery of the works of Aristotle continued in this century. The Arab philosopher and commentator on Aristotle, Rushd Averroes (1126-1198), greatly influenced this trend. But his doctrines had a strong materialistic tone and his *pantheism* (the belief that God and the universe are identical) was condemned by the pope.

One of the first to become famous by teaching people to think was Peter Abelard (1079-1142) of Paris, who had the reputation of being the "greatest teacher since Aristotle's day." He became famous for the method of instruction represented in his *Sic et non*, ("So and not so," or "Yes and No") in 1121. He listed under "sic" the points in favor of some debated question and under "non" those against it. After doing so, he let his students draw their own conclusions.

## 48. The Oral Tradition and Literature

The *oral tradition* continued throughout this period since writing was still not a common skill. In England the ballads and carols of the previous century and the present one reflected Norman-Britain thought. The lore of King Arthur, Charlemagne, and Alexander the Great were important themes. The French had *The Song of Roland*, an imaginative poem based on one line in a medieval biography of Charlemagne, in which Roland was referred to as "perfect of the *marches* (land along the border of a country) of Brittany." Roland was the ideal medieval knight. The Spanish had the legend of Bernardo del Carpio who fought Alfonso II for the release of his father from prison. The clergy continued to preach about the life of Jesus and the saints, and the *cabala*, the oral traditions of the Jews (see chapter endnote 2-1), found its place all through the medieval period. As medieval culture evolved, these forms and many others developed.

Manuscripts were sometimes originated by the *copyists* (scribes) who preserved the ancient works. Among these was the Benedictine historian and teacher, Sigebert of Gembloux (circa 1030-1112). His

47

most important work was *Chronographia* or *Universal* Chronicle which covered nearly 700 years (from 381 to 1154). His *Anglo-Saxon Chronicles* (circa 891-circa 1154) was a meaningful series of national histories, but it was compiled mainly from the works of the Venerable Bede (673-735). It ended with the ascension to the throne of English King Henry II in 1154.

---

**Reflection:**

*Consider the importance of the Byzantine copyists, monks who spent their lives copying and preserving the ancient texts. It is largely due to their efforts that we understand the past as well as we do. Though they have been criticized for sometimes preserving certain of the ancient works and not others, these dedicated clergymen helped to preserve knowledge which might otherwise have been lost.*

---

Another manuscript from this century is the earliest known copy of *Beowulf,* an epic poem which came from the oral tradition in the 700s and which told about the adventures of Beowulf, including his fight with the monster Grendel. Beowulf, the hero, killed a dragon, but died from the encounter. This poem demonstrated that the Anglo-Saxons admired courage and were interested in the unknown.

An important historian of this century from Iceland was Snorri Sturluson (1179-1241). He distinguished himself early in his life as a poet by glorifying the exploits of the contemporary Norse kings and earls. It was his legal training, though, that prepared him for his role as an historian of his times, and his works provide important insights into the influential people and significant events of his day.

A significant Jewish writer of this century was Abenezra (circa 1092-1167). His writings were so well received that he influenced many medieval thinkers. His works included poems and writings in the field of Hebrew *philology* (linguistics) and biblical *exegesis* (a scholarly explanation of the Bible). He thus made accessible to the Jews of primarily Christian Europe the treasures of knowledge contained in the works written in Arabic which he had brought with him from Spain. His grammatical writings, among which *Moznayim* ("The Scales"), written in 1140, and *Zaahot* ("Correctness"), written in 1141 are the most valuable, were the first expositions of Hebrew grammar in the Hebrew language.

# Matters of Religion

## 49. Anti-Semitism

Christians found many excuses for disliking the Jews but they all centered around a religion one. Because Jesus's own people did not accept His divinity, it seemed logical to the Christians to blame all of the Jews for what a few had done to Jesus when they crucified Him. During medieval celebrations of Easter, the Jews stayed home to avoid the anger of zealous Christians who were reminded of the bitter story through the annual obligatory sermon.

An important non-religious reason why the Christians disliked the Jews, it will be recalled, was an economic one (see section 31). The Jews were subject to criticism when they were allowed to practice usury. Jewish lenders became the object of hostility over interest rates that reflected the insecurity of loans. Some Christian bankers actively promoted anti-Semitism to entice lenders to them and Jews who collected taxes were easy targets of Christian hatred. Faced with these problems, the Jews found it easy to dislike Christian things.

The Moslems disliked the Jews partly because they rejected their prophet Mohammed (circa 570-632, Prophet of Islam). In Spain it was announced by the Moslems that the Jews had told Mohammed that they would accept Islam 500 years after the Hegira (the flight of the prophet Mohammed from Mecca in 622) if, by that time (1122), the Messiah had not come. In 1107 the emir (an Arabian chief, prince, or military leader) demanded that all Jews in Spain convert to Islam or pay an enormous sum. Many Jews elected to leave Spain rather than pay the tax.

## 50. Saint Bernard

An important monk who left his mark on the affairs of his time was Saint Bernard of Clairvaux (circa 1090-1153). He was born in Burgundy, France, and founded many reformed Cistercian monasteries, including the famous Cistercian monastery at Clairvaux. Some of his many writings included the treatises *On the Steps of Humility and Pride* (circa 1125) and *On the Love of God* (circa 1127). He established the rules which governed the new Order of Knights Templars in 1128 (see section 45). He sought and obtained the condemnation of Abelard for his stand on scholasticism and preached sermons that persuaded many Christians to join the Second Crusade.

## 51. The Antichrist

From antiquity, belief in the *antichrist*, expected by some to be an evil figure whose appearance will precede the Second Coming of Christ, moved in and out of popularity through the years. Information about the antichrist is found chiefly in certain places in the Bible (for example, 2 Thess. 2: 1-12 and Rev. 13). The original idea of a mighty ruler who would appear at the end of time and whose essence would be enmity to God is older than Christian literature and probably originated in Jewish *eschatology* (theology which deals with the final end of man and the end of the world) in the prophecy of Daniel. The term itself came from the early Christian usage of it (see 1 John 2:18, 22; 4:3), after which it passed into general use.

The first prototype for the antichrist was thought to be Antiochus IV Epiphanes (circa 215 B.C.; reigned 175-circa 163 B.C.), King of Syria and persecutor of the Jews. He attempted to *Hellenize* (to impose Greek culture on a non-Greek culture) the Jews which provoked the revolt of the Maccabees. This was the name of a distinguished Jewish family prominent in Jerusalem at this time. The revolt, which began circa 168 B.C., continued with interruptions for over thirty years. When Daniel's doomsday prophecy was not fulfilled in this era, the concept of the antichrist developed into merely a figure of prophecy which was applied to different historical figures and phenomena throughout history.

With the growing demands of Islam in this period, interest in the antichrist reached a high point, especially during the Crusades. It became popular once again in this century, prompted largely by the works of the Italian Cistercian monk and mystic, Joachim of Floris (circa 1130-1202). His work entitled, *Expositio in Apocalypism*, a mystical interpretation of history, revived the controversy, and name-calling became fashionable once more.

In Germany the controversy was revived by the *Guelphs* and the *Ghibellines*, the names of two opposing political factions that originated in the rivalry between two German families. The Guelphs supported the popes in their struggle with the emperors of the Holy Roman Empire in Italy and the Ghibellines opposed them. It is not surprising, therefore, that the popes bestowed the title of antichrist upon the emperors, or that the emperors responded by calling the popes the same. The Guelphs used the same appellation against the Ghibellines and the Ghibellines did likewise against the Guelphs.

## 52. The European Cathedrals in the Life of the People

Cathedrals continued to be built during this century partly from the enthusiasm generated by the crusades which popularized their existence. Yet it was not the architecture or even the size of the structure that earned it the name of "cathedral." A cathedral was the primary church of a diocese where the archbishop or bishop had his headquarters. Beverly Saint Mary [see figure 2-1] looks like what one might expect a cathedral to be, but without a bishop it was called a church, not a cathedral.

While the more important aspect of the cathedral was its connection with church administration, it was the architectural splendor of cathedrals that made them the object of popular interest. Commonly, a cathedral was the most obvious building in a city. Usually it was placed on a commanding site, rising from a cluster of lower, secular buildings. It became important not only for religious matters, but also for political activities of local scope and sometimes even national scope such as the crowning of a king. Reims Cathedral in France was often used for coronations. Westminster Cathedral served the same function in England. Other uses of cathedrals included weekly markets, happy patriotic celebrations, solemn religious pageants, annual fairs, political rallies, horse races, and noisy demonstrations.

# Matters of Church and State

## 53. The Concordat of Worms

The struggles between the civil and ecclesiastical authorities made up a large part of medieval history (see sections 39 and 40). The struggle over investiture that began in the last century was settled after a time by an agreement known as the Concordat of Worms in 1122 {2:54 a.m.}. A *concordat* is an agreement made between a secular ruler and the pope to regulate the affairs of the Roman Catholic Church within a particular country and Worms is the name of a city in West Germany on the Rhine. Through the Concordat of Worms, it was decided that the church should elect its own abbots and bishops and

51

that the ring and staff which symbolized their religious duties should be presented by the pope or his representatives. The emperor, however, was to supervise the elections of the church officials in Germany and present them with the authority which they should exercise outside of religious matters.

## 54. The Murder of Becket

Similar controversies caused a famous struggle in England. King Henry II (see section 58), who tried to be a good king, appointed Thomas a' Becket (circa 1117-1170) as the Archbishop of Canterbury in 1162, the highest position in England's Roman Catholic Church. Henry resolved that the clergy, like laymen, should be subject to the civil courts. To this end, he had drawn up the so-called Constitutions of Clarendon in 1164, a collection of "a certain part of the customs, liberties, and dignities of his ancestors," which among other things provided that persons working in the church accused of crime should be tried by the king's judges, if these judges deemed the cases to be such as should come before them. It was further established that no case should be appealed from the courts of the archbishops to the pope without the king's consent. Becket, though, refused to recognize Henry's authority and would not take orders from him. In a remark that was probably the result of careless anger, Henry asked in the hearing of his knights, "Have I not about me one man of enough spirit to rid me of a single insolent prelate?" Four knights assumed this was an invitation for them to do so, and murdered Becket while he was at evening service in the cathedral (December 29, 1170). Becket was made a saint in 1172 and a beautiful monument was erected at Canterbury where he was buried. It was long a goal of pilgrims until the shrine was destroyed during the reign of Henry VIII.

## 55. The Second Crusade (1147-1149) {3:30 a.m.-3:33 a.m.}

The Second Crusade was preached by Saint Bernard when it was learned that Edessa had fallen to the Turks (1144). Edessa, it will be recalled, had been captured by the Crusaders in 1098. When word that the Moslems had recaptured Edessa reached Louis VII (circa 1120; reigned 1137-1180), king of France, he took the crusading vow on Christmas Day, 1145. Bernard also gained the support the German King Conrad III (circa 1093; reigned 1138-1152) by his sermon in the cathedral of Spires, Germany. Thus began the Second Crusade.

Difficulties arose in 1147 over whether the Crusaders should follow the land route through Hungary or go by sea to the Holy Land. Conrad III decided in favor of the land route, but the others went by sea. This major disagreement contributed to the failure of the Crusade. Nor was there any real unity among the Crusaders themselves. The Crusaders of northern Germany never went to the Holy Land at all and the Crusaders of the low countries and of England took the sea route and attacked and captured Lisbon on their way.

Among the great army of Crusaders who actually marched to Jerusalem, there was little real unity. Conrad III and Louis VII started separately and at different times in order to avoid dissensions between their armies. When they reached Asia Minor they still acted independently. Eager to win the first victories, the German Crusaders, who were in advance of the French, attempted a raid into the Sultanate of Iconium; but after a tough fight in October, 1147, they were forced to retreat.

Louis VII, who then appeared, was persuaded by this failure to take the long route by the west coast of Asia Minor; but even so he had lost most of his troops by the time he reached the Holy Land (1148). There he joined Conrad III and Baldwin III, king of Jerusalem (1130; reigned 1143-1163) and after some deliberation, the three rulers decided to attack Damascus. The attack failed after only four days (July 28, 1148), and the Second Crusade thus ended. Conrad III returned to Constantinople in the autumn of 1148 and Louis VII returned by sea to France in the spring of 1149. The only effect of this great movement was to prejudice others against the ends towards which it was directed. The position of the Franks in the Holy Land was not improved by the attack on Damascus. The incredible failure of a Crusade led by two kings brought the whole crusading movement into discredit in western Europe, and it was utterly in vain that a third one was attempted forty years later.

## 56. The Third Crusade (1189-1192) {4:31 a.m.-4:35 a.m.}

The capture of Jerusalem in 1187 by Saladin, the Moslem warrior and sultan of Egypt, caused the Christians to mount the Third Crusade. The Third Crusade, unlike the first, did not originate from within the church. It arose from the people, and was represented by the three strong monarchies of Germany, England, and France. In France and England the agreement between Augustus (Philip II) (1165; reigned 1180-1223) and Henry II (see section 58) was for a joint crusade and this revealed its origin in the laity. The Saladin tithe, a scheme of taxation named after the Moslem conqueror, was imposed on those who did not join the Crusade. This taxation drove many to take up the Cross so they wouldn't have to pay it. There is a sense in which the lay basis of this Crusade made it the greatest one of all but the involvement of the kings of France and England, who brought their political rivalries to it, contributed to its failure. Therefore, spiritually, this Crusade was inferior to the first.

Several factors contributed to the failure of the Third Crusade. German Emperor Frederick Barbarossa (circa 1122; reigned 1152-1190) and Holy Roman Emperor (reigned 1155-1190), drowned in Asia Minor after his army had exhausted itself in fighting its way overland. There was also the untimely death of English King Henry II (1189) and the ascension to the throne of his son Richard I, also known as Richard the Lion-Hearted (see section 59). The great jealousy between Richard, and Philip Augustus prevented them from working together. Acre was recaptured, largely through the fighting ability of Richard and Augustus went home, leaving his rival to win some victories against the Moslems, but without enough strength to take Jerusalem. Richard concluded a three-year truce with Saladin in the fall 1192, securing only a guarantee of free access for Christian pilgrims to the Holy City.

## 57. Background for the Fourth Crusade

In Europe the wars between the great princes prevented the launching of the Fourth Crusade for a time. There was also the unexpected death of its main advocate, German king Henry VI (1165; reigned 1190-1197), which delayed the start of the new crusade. Henry had been eager to resume the efforts to take Constantinople which had ended when his father, Frederick Barbarossa, drowned in Asia Minor during the Third Crusade (see above). While working on the preparations for the Fourth Crusade, Henry VI also died and the Crusade collapsed. His death was the result of a cold he caught while hunting. But Innocent III became Pope (circa 1160; served 1198-1216) and used his power and outstanding ability to bring peace in Europe to revive the crusade as a papal undertaking, an event that finally saw reality in the next century (see section 74).

# Matters of State

## 58. England Under Henry II

Henry II (1133; reigned 1154-1189) was the first of a line of kings known as *Plantagenets,* so called because this branch of the royal family used the broom plant (plantagenesta) as their crest. This symbolism began when Geoffrey IV of Anjou, Henry's father, wore a sprig of the broom plant in his cap. By an invasion of England (1152-1153) Henry forced King Stephen (circa 1097; reigned 1135-1154), who had become the English king after breaking his promise to support Henry II's claim to the throne, to acknowledge him (Henry) as heir. Henry ascended to the English throne in 1154. Henry married Eleanor of Aquitaine (circa 1122-1204) after her marriage to Louis VII of France was annulled in 1152. This union brought Henry Aquitaine, Guienne, and much territory in South France. It also became the source of numerous conflicts between France and England since it transferred Eleanor's estates of Aquitaine to English power. Henry ruled over the western half of France and all of England. He also became master of Scotland, Wales, and Ireland. He held this domain until his death, and laid the foundation for what is now the United Kingdom.

Henry II's accomplishments included extending the rights granted under the Charter of Liberties issued by Henry I. He also extended his power when he appointed his own judges to travel around the country to hear cases which would have been tried in the courts of feudal lords or local justices. In so doing, he put the king's law and justice ahead of any other's justice in the whole country.

## 59. England Under Richard I

Henry II was followed by Richard I, his third son by Eleanor of Aquitaine, known also as Richard, the Lion-Hearted (1157; reigned 1189-1199). As a king of England he was frequently absent from his duties because he chose to tend to other interests. He spent several years in the Third Crusade, it will be recalled, and during only one of the ten years (of his indicated reign) was he the designated ruler; this was the year when he was actually in his own country. His absence made it easier to challenge his claim to the guardianship of Arthur I (1187-1203), of Brittany, posthumous son of Geoffrey (the

55

fourth son of Henry II of England). Arthur's mother, Constance, profited from Richard's absence by governing the Duchy of Brittany. She had Arthur proclaimed Duke of Brittany by an assembly of barons and bishops (1194). Richard invaded Brittany in 1196, but was defeated the next year and became reconciled to Constance. He was killed by an arrow during the siege of the castle of Chaluz. The nobles of Anjou, Maine, and Touraine refused to recognize John of England, and did homage to Arthur, who declared himself the vassal of Philip Augustus, king of France.

## 60. A Disunited "Germany"

The vagueness that characterized German territorial outlines in the last century continued to exist during this one. The only person who had any idea that he might make himself ruler of this loosely defined territory was the Holy Roman Emperor. The right to choose the emperor came to be held by seven "electors," three of whom were churchmen and four were rulers.

If these emperors had been content with being emperors in Germany, they might have gotten somewhere. But some of the best of them were carried away with the concept that Italy was also a part of the Holy Roman Empire and that it was their business to bring under their rule as much of that peninsula as possible. This ambition was not realized, and in attempting to accomplish it they lost some of their influence. An emperor was seldom much more than a chairman over German kings and princes.

# God in History

Q. In this chapter we identified some of the common superstitions that filled the lives of medieval man (see section 46). What place did these have in the religious lives of the people and how did these superstitions relate to their need for religion?

A. There is something in each of us that needs God. When man misses the truth, he is likely to fill the void reserved for God with fear and superstitions. Superstitions were not new when this millennium began. The Apostle Paul (died circa 67) spoke of the men of Athens, Greece, who had built an altar to the unknown god (Acts 17:22), just to be sure they had not left one out. There were also the mythologies of the ancient Egyptians, Greeks, Romans, Chinese, and others which were all rooted in ideas about gods and spirits, which played an important role in personal and national affairs. During this century and later, stories about alchemists, sorcerers, and witches were rampant throughout western Europe.

Q. Are we superstitions today?

A. Whether we are aware of it or not, many things that people do today are linked with superstitious practices or beliefs, some having to do with deities or spirits. Birthdays, for example, had their origin in astrology, which attached great importance to one's exact date of birth. The birthday cake itself was probably related to rituals honoring the Greek goddess Artemis, whose birthday was celebrated with moon-shaped honey cakes topped with candles. Wearing black at funerals was originally thought of as a way to escape the attention of evil spirits that were said to be lurking about on such occasions.

Many people have superstitions and fears. In the west, breaking a mirror, seeing a black cat, walking under a ladder and, depending on where you are, Tuesday the 13th or Friday the 13th are all seen as omens foreboding something evil. In the east, the Japanese wear their kimonos with the left side folded over the right, for the other way is reserved for corpses. Their houses are built with no windows or doors facing the northeast so that the demons, which are said to come from that direction, will not find the entrance. In the Philippines, people remove the shoes of the dead and place them beside the legs of the deceased before the burial so that Saint Peter will welcome them. Old folks tell youngsters to behave by pointing out that the figure on the moon is Saint Michael, watching and writing down their deeds.

Q. What should Christians do about such ideas?

A. No Christian should ever visit astrologers, psychic readers, fortune-tellers, or other kinds of soothsayers to inquire about the future or to obtain help in making a decision. The Christian should realize that the void filled by these superstitions is a place that is reserved only for God.

## Chapter Endnotes

2-1  The cabala (sometimes cabbala) was an esoteric system of interpretation of the Scriptures based on the assumption that every word, letter, number, and even accent in them had an occult meaning. It was popular among Jews, but was also used by Christians.  It borrowed from the scholastic influence of Plato which was mixed with Jewish theology.  It said that God is the source from which comes the entire objective world.  Evil is the result of the distance of certain of the emanations from their divine source, the distance causing them to lose their divine qualities.  It represented the soul as having existed from eternity and as being independent of the body.

## Chapter Terms

| | | |
|---|---|---|
| antichrist | copyist | jinn |
| cabala | electors | Lilith |
| Charter of Liberties | Ghibellines | pantheism |
| concordat | feria | plantagenesta |
| Constitutions | Guelphs | Templars |
| of Clarendon | Hegira | Teutonic Knights |

# Chapter Review Questions/Exercises

1. How did medieval towns form? (44)
2. Name some of the more important towns of the medieval period. (44)
3. Who had to give permission in a medieval town to have a fair? (44)
4. Describe two organizations of knights in the twelfth century. (45)
5. How did the Templars get their name? (45)
6. Describe some of the superstitions of medieval man. (46)
7. Describe a medieval university. (47)
8. What important contribution to education did Abelard make? (47)
9. Discuss the oral tradition in the twelfth century. (48)
10. What was Sigebert of Gembloux noted for? (48)
11. Who was Snorri Sturluson? (48)
12. Who was Abenezra and why were his writings important? (48).
13. Why were the Jews disliked by both the Christians and the Moslems? Does it take courage to love those whose religion is different from yours? (49)
14. Who was Saint Bernard? (50)
15. Discuss the matter of the antichrist. (51)
16. What makes a church a cathedral? (52)
17. In what ways besides worship was the medieval cathedral used? (52)
18. What was the Concordat of Worms and what major controversy was settled there? (53)
19. Why was Becket murdered? (54)
20. Describe the Second Crusade. (55)
21. Describe the Third Crusade. (56)
22. What happened to delay the start of the Fourth Crusade? (57)
23. Describe some of the highlights in England under Henry II. (58)
24. How did Richard I's absence from England during the Crusades influence that country? (59)

# 3

# 1201-1300

## {4:48 a.m.-7:11 a.m.}

---

During the next two hours and twenty-three minutes, Alphonso the Learned (1221-1284) will be born. He will scorn Ptolemy's view of the universe with the following thought:

> Had I been (present) at the creation,
> I would have given some useful hints
> for the better ordering of the universe.

---

## Overview

### 61. Medieval Towns

In the small medieval towns, a new class of people came into being—a class of merchants and professional men who often were the most dependable and progressive citizens of a community. They arose from the burgesses who originally settled around castles and were granted special privileges that ordinary villeins were not, or they grew out of the privileges sold to them when a lord went off on a crusade. The French version of the word was *bourgeois*, from the French word *bourg*, meaning "town." This group came to form the great middle class of medieval society.

Town life, or any life in which trade and manufacture played an important part, did not leave much place for serfs or slaves. Medieval towns, therefore, soon became noted as centers of freedom. *Stadtluft macht frei*—"Town air makes free"—it was said and it was understood that anyone who lived in a city for a year and a day ceased to be subject to anyone else's authority as a serf or a slave. Yet even more progressive towns showed some features of feudal life. The entire town might have a high stone wall around it and a moat. Its gates might be closely guarded, especially at night. Streets in a medieval town were often unpaved, and if they were paved, the surface was not likely to be maintained very well. The holes in the roadways collected all kinds of filth, including some garbage that was typically thrown into streets for the dogs.

Unpaved streets became quagmires. There were no sewers or sanitary water systems. Houses were crowded together on both sides of the narrow streets and were often built several stories high, presenting an airless and gloomy setting. The dead were buried close by in crowded churchyard cemeteries. Such unsanitary conditions obviously promoted the great waves of sickness that came along upon occasion; these plagues often carried off thousands of city dwellers in a few weeks. Fires caused such calamities that very strict laws were eventually passed punishing people who allowed their own houses to catch fire. Many towns had curfew laws which required everybody to "cover" their fires (French, *couvre-feu*, "put out the fire"), and go to bed when the town bell rang at some specified hour at night. Since no one was expected to be out after that hour, streetlights were not considered necessary.

## 62. Manufacturing and the Guilds

Manufacturing became so important in the medieval towns that for some time those who were engaged in the various industries almost ran their communities. Merchants and other businessmen usually formed *guilds*, (from an Old Norse word which means "payment") which were chambers of commerce of sorts. These guilds tried to look after the welfare of the town and to prevent business from getting into the hands of outsiders.

The merchant guilds arose in the Middle Ages out of the spontaneous associations of merchants. They were intended for protection of commerce in the perilous times of feudal and insecure local governments for traders who were often in danger of losing their merchandise to robbers on land and pirates at sea. In Germany, where these associations were called leagues, many notable examples of these types of associations existed. There was the agreement between Lubeck and Hamburg (1241) and another between the company of German merchants in Gotland whose headquarters were at Wisby. Also, the privileges granted Cologne merchants in London were extended to other Germans there and a league of German merchants was formed which became the famous Merchants of the Steelyard in 1259. Temporary alliances such as these led to the formation of the powerful German Hanseatic League in the next century.

There were also numerous craft guilds. These had some characteristics of our modern trade unions, but differed from labor unions in that they included employers and employees alike. They frequently set aside funds for payment of sick benefits and also to maintain religious services for their members who passed away. The *guildhall*, a sort of headquarters for them, was often a striking building in the town.

In London the term livery company was used to classify both craft and merchant guilds. There the craft guilds controlled the product of the members and the trade guilds controlled the trade of the members.

## Other Disciplines and Institutions

### 63. The Alchemists

A popular belief of medieval times was that if one tried hard enough, one might be able to find a way to change other metals into gold. The *alchemists* [see figure 3-1] spent much time trying to do this. They were known to all parts of Europe and were chemists of a sort— or at least they thought they were. They labored usually in dungeon-like laboratories, surrounded by vials of odd-looking and even stranger-smelling potions and over flaming hot ovens. They accomplished very little, but their objective was noble.

Knowledge of metals was not sufficient at this time for the alchemist to understand gold's origin. There were many theories and

63

one of the popular ones was that gold resulted from copper or other metal being heated by the earth's molten gases. Such a notion seemed logical to inquiring minds unaware of the limitations of medieval science. Gold was similar in color to copper, yet it was softer and heavier. If alchemists could only duplicate the process going on in the earth's interior, surely they could change other metals into gold, or so they thought. Thus generations of alchemists wasted much time and energy putting copper into furnaces, waiting for it to become gold.

## 64. Scholasticism and the Universities

At the hands of Saint Thomas Aquinas (1225-1274), the Italian philosopher and Doctor of the Church, scholasticism reached new heights of maturity in this century, even though his ideas did not find wide acceptance at this time. Using Aristotle's logic to interpret Christianity, Saint Thomas became "Aristotle Christianized," and the schoolmen contemplated the universe not with their own eyes, but through the eyes of Aristotle.

Thomas believed that the form or the universal existed in three ways—in God, in things, and in the mind. It was by the knowledge of things, he said, that man could learn of God's existence but God could only be discovered by reason.

Roger Bacon (circa 1214-1294) {5:07 a.m.-7:02 a.m.} had one of the greatest scientific minds of the Middle Ages. At a time when Aristotle's influence was unbounded, Bacon was one of the first men to demand proof of theories through experiment, and thus he became one of the founders of modern science. He added much to what was then known of science and nature and gave the world new knowledge on light and vision. He also made several discoveries in chemistry, identified errors in the calendar, and established scientific methods of investigation.

Universities made meaningful strides during this period. Of note was the founding of the Sorbonne (1252) which became an important college of the University of Paris, named after its founder, Robert of Sorbon (1201-1274). This institution was declared "useful to religion" by Pope Alexander IV (1259), and a *bull* (a formal announcement or official order from the pope) authorizing and confirming the college was granted in 1263. At the close of this century the Sorbonne was organized into a full college of theology which conferred licenses and degrees. The thoroughness of its examinations gave exceptional value to its diplomas.

An important development in higher education was reached in this century by the English bishop Walter de Merton (died 1277) who founded Merton College, Oxford. In 1261 he obtained a charter from the Earl of Gloucester for the use of certain lands for the support of scholars, and in 1264 a regular charter of incorporation was made. The establishment of a corporate body to rule and control the scholars marked the beginning of the collegiate system of education, and Merton College became the model for other colleges at Oxford and Cambridge.

Those involved in higher education devoted themselves to shaking off the control of teaching and research by any power outside of the universities. The schools insisted that they could not discover the truth and teach what they believed if they were controlled by outside interests. Even to raise questions, they said, was a useful service.

## 65. Explorers

One of the great overland explorers of this century was Marco Polo (circa 1254-circa 1324) who is remembered for his journey to the Orient (1271-1295). Marco, the son of Niccolo' and the nephew of Maffeo Polo, came from Venice. The trading activities of the elder Polos had led them into long journeys to the Orient. On one of these trips they reached Cathay, the name they gave to China. There they were warmly received at the court of the Mongol conqueror Kublai Khan (circa 1216; reigned 1260-1294) in Peking (now Beijing).

Khan appointed Marco to many high offices which made it possible for him to travel in various parts of the kingdom. Two years before Kublai Khan died, the Polos set out for the long homeward trip. They returned to Venice again in 1295.

# Matters of Religion

## 66. The Abbey and the Life of the Monks and Friars

In the early days, especially in the east, some Christians who wished to live holy lives separated themselves from society and lived in isolation in forests or deserts where they spent time praying, fasting, and sometimes even abusing their bodies. These things, they thought, helped them to think lofty thoughts, and monks were certainly expected to be engaged in such meditation often.

Some of these *hermits* attracted a following. Some believers found it desirable to associate with a hermit of their choosing and live like him. Some of these communities eventually became highly organized and their adherents dedicated their lives to the fulfillment of selected worthy causes.

The head of an abbey was called an *abbot* (from Aramaic *abba*, "father"). He had to be a man who was worthy to rule over a monastery by remembering to live up to the name of "superior" in what he did. He was expected to guide his charges carefully and to give council to those who became discouraged so that there was no loss to the flock that was entrusted to him.

The women of the church also did their part. An *abbess* was the female superior of a convent of nuns. She could also be in charge of an abbot, whose duties hers generally paralleled. The office was elective, the abbess being chosen by the sisters of their particular order. The abbess was solemnly admitted to her office by *episcopal benediction* (a blessing by the bishop), together with the conferring of a staff and pectoral cross, and she held the position for life, assuming that her conduct was good. The Council of Trent later fixed the qualifying age for an abbess at forty. Eight years of experience were a prerequisite as well. Abbesses had a right to demand absolute obedience of their nuns, over whom they exercised discipline, extending even to the power of expulsion, subject, however, to the bishop. An abbess, being a woman, was not permitted to perform the spiritual function of the priesthood belonging to an abbot. She was not allowed to ordain, confer the veil, or excommunicate church members.

## 67. The Franciscans

An Italian named Francis (circa 1182-1226) {4:21 a.m.-5:24 a.m.} founded *The Franciscans* (1209), a brotherhood similar to the Benedictines. He was known as Saint Francis of Assisi because he was from Assisi, Italy. His group devoted their lives to helping those in need. Like some of the early followers of Christ (see Matt. 10:8-9), they took no money or extra provisions with them when they went out among the people. Since they depended on what people gave them, they were sometimes called "begging" friars (or mendicant friars).

Saint Francis is credited with the following *Prayer for Peace:*

> *Lord, make me an instrument of Your Peace.*
> *Where there is hatred, let me sow love;*
> *Where there is injury, pardon;*
> *Where there is doubt, faith;*
> *Where there is despair, hope;*
> *Where there is darkness, light;*
> *And where there is sickness, joy.*
> *O Divine Master, grant that I may not*
> *So much seek to be consoled as to console;*
> *To be understood as to understand;*
> *To be loved as to love;*
> *For it is in giving that we receive;*
> *It is in pardoning that we are pardoned;*
> *And it is in dying*
> *That we are born to eternal life.*
> *Amen*

## 68. The Dominicans

An order of preaching friars and nuns, called the *Dominican Order,* was founded (circa 1212) by a Spanish clergyman named Saint Dominic (1170-1221) {4:03 a.m.-5:17 a.m.} to oppose the teachings of the Albigenses (see section 71). Their zeal in opposing the Albigenses caused the order to grow rapidly which enabled them to broaden their objectives. Pope Honorius III (served 1216-1227) granted *full permission* (official recognition by the church as an organization) to the order in 1218. The Dominicans quickly found their place by working largely among the upper class of society. Many of them became teachers in the universities. Saint Thomas Aquinas (see section 64) was one of these.

## 69. The Christian Church in Europe

The monastic orders worked together with the church and though knighthood was in a state of general decline, the church still defined and supported the concept of chivalry with its lofty idealization of women. The church became very active in prevention and rescue of women who felt it necessary to work in the streets. Rescue missions were organized, convents were founded everywhere for the reception of penitents, and dowries were provided to procure husbands for the women.

In other matters, the *Jubilee Year* was organized (1300) as an official observance of the church. A rumor spread through Rome in 1299 that everyone visiting Saint Peter's on January 1, 1300, would receive full absolution from their sins. There was an enormous rush of pilgrims to Rome. This attracted Pope Boniface VIII's (circa 1235; served 1294-1303) attention. A papal bull was issued and the pilgrims became even more numerous. Later the privilege was extended to other churches outside of Rome and the frequency of the Jubilee Year was fixed at every twenty-five years.

At the Fourth Lateran Council in 1215, the church officially accepted the doctrine of transubstantiation (the passage of one substance into another). It was used to explain the official position of the church that, in the Eucharist, the bread actually became the body of Christ, and the wine became Christ's blood. Later Protestant denominations would, for the most part, adhere to the doctrine of consubstantiation—that Christ is present in the sacrament of Holy Communion, but the elements are not His actual body and blood.

## 70. The European Church and the Rebirth of Drama

When Rome became largely Christian (circa 200), the church fathers, especially Quintus Tertullian (also see reference to Tertullian in section 21), condemned what they perceived to be the evil of the Roman theater which was viewed as the work of the devil. After all, the Roman theater (in amphitheater performances), at its zenith, had seen early Christians sacrificed to the lions, partly for retribution and partly for spectacle and entertainment. This sadistic realism represented the ultimate decadence of theater anywhere. So in medieval Europe, the Roman dramas were almost forgotten (as were the Greek dramas, but for different reasons) and for nearly 800 years, the church endeavored to strangle theatric art and prevented its rebirth. Individual actors or small groups wandered around performing at festivals or fairs, or before feudal lords at their courts.

In view of the understandable disdain the medieval church had for the abuse of the early Christians in the Roman amphitheater in the name of drama, their view that drama was an instrument of the devil, and the prohibition of its use by the church, it might seem strange that the church itself eventually became the instrument through which the European theater had its rebirth. In the tenth century Catholic priests decided to insert into the Mass a song with the words apportioned to two or more singers or chanters. Their motive was to make their teaching more effective by way of visual portrayals. Through these approaches, they were able to picture a story by means of actors instead of the usual custom of letting one stationary singer tell about the incident in Latin words that few could understand.

The custom spread far and wide so that the Mass was divided into the read parts, the sung parts, and the acted parts. On special occasions, such as at Christmas, entire acted episodes were introduced. This paved the way for the *Mystery Plays,* the *Miracle Plays,* and the *Morality Plays* which, by this century, were popular.

*Mystery Plays* dealt strictly with scriptural events, their purpose being to set forth, with the aid of the prophetic history of the Old Testament, and more especially of the fulfilling events of the New Testament, the central mystery of the Redemption of the world, as accomplished by the Nativity, the Passion, and the Resurrection. The *Miracle Plays* were concerned with the legends of the saints of the church, though the term mystery was not actually used in England. The *Morality Plays* taught and illustrated the same truths, not by direct representation of scriptural or legendary events and personages, but allegorically, their characters being personified virtues or qualities.

Yet the church's definition of drama was a narrow one and its control over performances was tenuous at best. Abuses prevailed and this caused some clergy to write letters of complaints to the bishops. There was disagreement among the clergy as to what actually constituted abuses. In this century, the Bishop of Lincoln twice prohibited performances in certain churches. The increasing use of the comic element in the biblical plays seemed out of proportion to the serious nature of the religious teaching. Thus, the serious religious drama that arose out of the solemn performances of the Mass at the altar and on the church porch was slowly absorbed by more popular elements by way of realistic incidents and farces. Drama was thus

69

reintroduced into society by a clergy that had grown weary of its popularity and fearful of its vividness and humor. Soon the stage was given over to the guilds and fraternities.

## 71. The Inquisition and the Albigensian Crusade

The church was interested in preventing practices it considered heretical and referred to one of Saint Paul's letters (1 Timothy 1:20) as the historical basis for doing so. *Heretics* were loosely defined as anyone who had a belief different from the accepted belief of the church itself. They even pursued organizations that were not officially declared heretical (such as the Albigensians) but whose practices were offensive to the leaders of the church.

In this century the *Inquisition*, which had functioned in principle before but mostly randomly as popes, priests, bishops, and other members of the clergy discovered and punished heretics, was established as a definite organization. The church also became willing to use capital punishment to suppress heretics after the suggestion found in the Bible (Deut. 13:6-9). The idea to formalize this process had first been made by Saint Dominic, even before he founded the Dominican order (see section 68), for the express purpose of countering the activities of the Albigenses.

The Albigenses centered around Toulouse and neighboring Albi, France and it was for the latter location that the sect was named. They were not Christians but were subscribers to the great Manichaean dualistic system that had been popular in the Mediterranean basin for centuries. They believed in the existence of good and evil, represented by God and the evil one, but accepted the typically Gnostic idea that Jesus lived only in semblance. One of the most curious practices of this group was the custom of suicide by its leaders, usually by starvation. Their justification for this practice was that if life was essentially evil, its end should be hastened. Local bishops were ineffectual in dealing with them. While it is reasonably clear that the church never officially declared this group to be heretical, it is known that church leaders grew alarmed at the growing popularity of this group. When Peter de Castelnau, the *papal legate* (a representative of the pope), was murdered in 1208, probably by one of the chief Albigensian nobles, Innocent III proclaimed what became a protracted conflict known as the Albigensian Crusade (1208 to 1229).

It was these influences that caused the Council of Toulouse in 1229 to make the idea of the Inquisition official, but it was not formally established until 1233. In that year Gregory IX (1145; served 1227-1241) addressed a letter to the bishops in France wherein he asked the preaching friars to look for heresy. He also directed the Dominicans to lead an investigation into the centers of Albigensianism with the legal power to name and condemn. The church tribunal consisted of a priest and several laymen in every parish and it existed only for the purpose of bringing heretics before the bishops. The tribunal became known as the *Holy Office* or the *Holy Inquisition* and it did most of its work in Portugal, Spain, and part of Italy. It was immediately unwelcomed by Moslems, Jews, and by those accused of heresy. Later it was disliked by *Protestants* (see chapter endnote 3-1) and in Spain even by many Catholics because it was made a state tribunal under Ferdinand V and Isabella I of Castile (late fifteenth century). It was finally done away with (1834).

Another group, this one clearly identified as heretical, received the attention of the church. There appeared in Italy the *Order of the Apostles* or *Apostle Brethren* (circa 1260). It was founded by Gerard Segeralli (died 1300), who had been denied admission to the Franciscan order. In an effort to become more like Christ, he wrapped himself in swaddling clothes and laid in a cradle. Then he walked through the streets of Parma barefooted, wearing a white robe and shouting, "Repent!" He soon had a large following in spite of the fact that he required his followers to live in absolute poverty and chastity. They begged and preached penitence. When these followers spread to several other Christian countries, the pope condemned them to banishment and Segeralli was imprisoned.

## 72. European Church Architecture

One of the earliest systems of protecting buildings from rain was the system which employed *dripping eaves*. The simplest and earliest form of dripping eaves was the use of *thatch* (of straw or reeds) which protected the building well beyond the wall. Efforts were made to get the roof, whether made of straw, lead, or tiles, as far beyond the wall as possible. This system of dripping eaves was, however, objectionable for several reasons. The eaves could not be made to project very far, and with a strong wind blowing toward the wall, much of the rain falling from them was dashed against walls, windows, and doorways.

71

It had long been recognized that this system was not very effective when used in the design and building of cathedrals and it was in this century that system of gutter, *gargoyle,* and *parapet* (a low wall at the edge of a balcony or roof) was first used as a substitute for dripping eaves. This system remained in use until the end of Gothic architecture's dominance. Stone spouts were tried here and there, but their tendency to clog kept them out of use until modern days when spouts could be cast in iron. In the gutter system, the parapet prevented the rain from escaping over the edge of the wall. At intervals, the parapet was pierced with a hole, and in this was inserted a perforated block projecting sometimes three or four feet through which the contents of the gutter found the way to the ground; this perforated block was termed a *gargoyle,* which is a form of the French "gorge," the throat. The gargoyles were carved into all sorts of fantastic forms, such as masks or monsters. In France, where lead was scarce and expensive, the gutters were designed to dispense with the need for gargoyles, and were more elaborate than those of England. Eventually it proved to be sufficient to cover the sides and bottom of the gutter with a sheet of lead.

## 73. Religion in Asia

One of the greatest religious achievements of this century for the Buddhist religion came from Korea. Korean artisans carved nearly 80,000 blocks which contained the entire Buddhist *canon* (regulations, teachings, and dogma). This great effort was done in part because it was believed that this dedicated effort would repel the Mongols who invaded their country (1231-1260).

Another momentous event in the Buddhist religion came (1252) {6:01 a.m.} when the great Buddha at Kamakura, Japan, was cast. This sculpture was officially known as the *Dai Butsu,* the gigantic bronze image of Gautama Buddha. It was cast in plates about an inch thick, which were joined with great skill. The statue was over forty-nine-feet high, and the width of the face from ear to ear was over seventeen feet.

72

# Matters of Church and State

## 74. The Fourth Crusade (1202-1204) {4:49 a.m. - 4:52 a.m.}

As previously mentioned (see section 57), efforts by Henry VI to start a Fourth Crusade in the closing decade of the previous century ended with his death in 1197. The church, under Innocent III, associated itself with what was really a lay movement but was unable to turn it into a religious crusade. Even so, due to Innocent's efforts, preparations for the Fourth Crusade were in full progress by the spring of 1200, especially in France, where Fulk of Neuilly played the part once held by Peter the Hermit by going around preaching to the poor to join the Crusade.

Like the First Crusade, the Fourth Crusade was a French effort, but only in its personnel and not in its direction. Its leading members were French feudatories like Theobald of Champagne (who was chosen the leader of the Crusade), Baldwin of Flanders (the future emperor of Constantinople), and the Count of Blois. The objective, which these three original chiefs of the Fourth Crusade proposed to themselves, was Egypt because Egypt was perceived to be the center of Moslem power. Jerusalem was no longer seen to be the center. But the Fourth Crusade became stalled in a maelstrom of political motives and Constantinople become their objective instead.

The Crusaders took three years to take Constantinople, and the result of the Fourth Crusade was, on the whole, disastrous both for the church and for the crusading movement. The direction of the Crusade had been taken from the pope, and the Albigensian Crusade against the heretics of southern France, which followed soon afterwards, showed that the example could be repeated (see section 71).

## 75. The Children's Crusade

The Children's Crusade (1212) was a pathetic but well-intentioned effort on the part of a great number of European children to recover the Holy Land. Perhaps they could succeed in that objective where older, less faithful Christians had failed. This crusade, which did not have Innocent III's approval, was started in France where a shepherd boy named Stephen appeared. Armed with his charming, youthful

73

manners, he convinced thousands of other youths to follow his guidance. Backed by his youthful army, Stephen rode on a wagon southward to Marseilles, promising to lead his followers through the seas as Moses had crossed the Red Sea when the waters had parted. In Germany a child from Cologne, Nicolas, also obtained a great following of his peers, hoping to join Stephen's group.

Neither of these groups were successful in achieving their goal of freeing Jerusalem from the Moslems. Stephen's army was kidnapped by slave-dealers and sold into Egypt. This left Nicolas's group without the leadership it had hoped for in Stephen, and it disbanded.

## 76. The Fifth Crusade (1217-1221) {5:12 a.m. - 5:17 a.m.}

The Fifth Crusade was the last of the Crusades started by the church. It owed its origin to Innocent III's determination to recover Jerusalem, rather than to any pressing need in the Holy Land. During the forty years after the loss of Jerusalem, an almost unbroken peace reigned in the region. More peace was made when Malik-al-Adil (circa 1143; reigned 1201-1218), the brother of Saladin, succeeded to his brother's possessions, not only in Egypt but also in Syria, and he granted the Christians a series of truces. While the Holy Land was thus at peace, Crusaders were also being drawn elsewhere by the needs of the Latin empire of Constantinople. But Innocent was displeased that Jerusalem was still held by the Moslems and the pathos of the Children's Crusade (see above) seemed to make his efforts more urgent.

In the Fourth Lateran Council in 1215, Innocent III found his opportunity to gain new support for the effort. Before this great gathering of all Christian Europe, he proclaimed a Crusade (for 1217), and it was decided that a Truce of God (which made private war illegal) should reign for the next four years. The statesman-like beginning of the Crusade proved worthwhile. In Germany, a large body of Crusaders gathered. Andrew II (1175; reigned 1205-1235), the King of Hungary, came to the Holy Land in 1217. Another army came from the northwest and joined at Acre the forces of the previous year in 1218. Egypt had already been indicated as their objective by Innocent III in 1215. The Crusade started by laying siege to Damietta on the eastern delta of the Nile. This effort was rewarded with success in 1219. The capture of Damietta was a considerable feat, but strangely no further efforts were made to advance their position. When the armies marched on Cairo, they reached a fortress and encamped there in July of 1219. There the sultan reiterated terms which he had already offered several times before—the cession of most of the Kingdom of Jerusalem, the surrender of the cross (which had been captured by Saladin in 1187) and the restoration of all prisoners. King John (circa 1167; reigned 1199-1216) urged the acceptance of these terms but Pelagius, the pope's representative, insisted on a large indemnity in addition and the negotiations failed. The sultan went to war and the Crusaders were driven back towards Damietta. Pelagius had to make a treaty with Malik-al-Kamil (1180-1238) by which he gained a free retreat and the surrender of the Holy Cross at the price of the restoration of Damietta. The Crusaders left Egypt and the Fifth Crusade ended.

## 77. The Sixth Crusade (1228-1229) {5:27 a.m.-5:28 a.m.}

The Sixth Crusade was called a "diplomatic crusade" because Jerusalem was obtained through negotiation, not war. This Crusade was headed by German king Frederick II (1194; reigned 1212-1250) and Holy Roman Emperor (reigned 1220-1250), a Hohenstaufen and the grandson of Frederick I of Barbarossa. After a number of delays the Crusade started in 1228. The diplomatic success of this Crusade was deeply rooted in Frederick's marriage to Yolanda, the young heiress to the kingdom. Following her death in 1228, Frederick crowned himself king of Jerusalem.

## 78. The Seventh Crusade (1248-1254) {5:56 a.m.-6:04 a.m.}

Jerusalem was captured by Turkish and Egyptian Moslems in 1244. This pressured King Louis IX (1214; reigned 1226-1270) (later Saint Louis) of France, to launch a new Crusade against Egypt. Pope Innocent IV (circa 1190; served 1243-1254) supported this effort. Although the Crusaders captured Damietta (1249), they were severely defeated on their way to Cairo. King Louis was taken captive at Mansura. The Arabs demanded and received a huge ransom for the release of the king.

## 79. Results of the Crusades

The Crusades began when Europe was still in a period that is sometimes called the Dark Ages. They ended upon the eve of the Renaissance (see Chapter 4 Overview). Their part in changing the character of western Europe was by no means small. In many ways, in many different degrees, the Crusades shaped Europe's style of life and thinking.

The decline of feudalism also helped to change medieval thinking. The Crusades influenced this decline in western Europe. Death had come to thousands of feudal barons, and many baronial families lost all of their money because of the burden of debts they had accumulated in financing trips to and from the Holy Land. Instead of finding new wealth in the east, many noble families were forced to forfeit their estates in Europe to their creditors because they returned with deep debt and empty purses.

There were significant cultural exchanges that resulted from the interaction between the east and west. The Latin kingdom of Jerusalem became the meeting place of two civilizations. The culture that developed in the west during this century following the Crusades, was greatly influenced by them.

The greatest economic benefit of the Crusades went to the merchants and artisans of the Italian cities, for they amassed vast amounts of money in payment for the services they gave to the Crusaders. They were further enriched by the commercial rights they obtained throughout the Near East. Genoa, Pisa, and Venice had special monopolies throughout the eastern Mediterranean. Their merchants used these privileges to introduce into the western world such oriental luxuries as pearls, silks, and spices—the sale and transportation of which brought them great profits. The demand for such commodities was so great that it prompted a search for new and more direct routes to the east. This search eventually resulted in the discovery and early exploration of America.

# Matters of State

## 80. England Under John

Richard was succeeded by his brother John (circa 1167; reigned 1199 - 1216). The English people suffered from both internal and external problems during John's inept reign. External pressures came from different sources, as when King Philip Augustus of France took Normandy and Arthur I Duke of Brittany (1187-1203), tried to seize Poitou (1202). Arthur fell into the hands of John, who sent him as a prisoner to Falaise. In the following year he was transferred to Rouen where he suddenly disappeared. It was commonly believed that John murdered him. Afterwards, John was condemned by the Court of Peers of France, and stripped of the fiefs which he possessed in France. In spiritual matters, John's relationships with the church reached a low point when he entered into a lengthy struggle with Innocent III over the appointment of Stephen Langton (circa 1150; served 1207-1228) as Archbishop of Canterbury. The pope cut off the whole of England from the church and issued a bull deposing John. John showed contempt for his own people. An example may be found in his requirement that he had to approve the citizens chosen to become mayors of London.

The English barons, led by Langton, met John at Runnymede on the Thames and forced him to sign the famous *Magna Carta*, or "Great Charter," on June 15, 1215 {5:08 a.m.}, the same year that Saint Thomas Hospital was founded in England. It became clear, though, that he had no other reason for signing the charter except to appease the barons, for he often did not live up to the provisions it contained. He was even able to get the pope to declare the charter illegal. John also gathered an army and began war on the barons who asked the French Crown Prince Louis to help. John died before the struggle over the document was completed, but the fact it was signed, forever changed the relationship between the king and his people.

## 81. France Under Louis VIII

Louis VIII (1187; reigned 1223-1226), son of Philip Augustus (Philip II) and Isabella of Hainaut, succeeded his father to the French throne. While still a prince, he earned the reputation of being a skillful warrior and went on several campaigns for his father. His reputation even spread to England where Louis was asked by some English barons, to "pluck them out of the hand of this tyrant" (John) (autumn, 1215). They actually declared Louis to be king of England in 1216. These barons secured the aid of more than 7,000 French knights who engaged the English, yet it was only after twenty-four English hostages had arrived in Paris that Louis himself prepared to invade England. Three months later he had secured a stronghold in eastern England, and had laid siege to Dover and Windsor (July). He asserted his claim to the English throne on the basis that John had forfeited the crown by the murder of his nephew, Arthur of Brittany, and that the English barons had the right to dispose of the vacant throne. This claim, though, lost strength when John died and his infant son took the throne as Henry III. The church intervened and excommunicated the French troops and the English rebels.

## 82. Germany

During this century, Germany remained a disunited region while England, France, and Spain were becoming real national states with kings who wielded considerable political power. The Holy Roman Emperor continued to rule over Germany. In 1273 the electors chose Count Rudolph of Hapsburg (sometimes Habsburg) to that position (1218; reigned 1273-1291). Previously his domain had been a little district in Switzerland. They elected him because they thought he would not amount to much; and he accepted the office because it would enable him to add prestige to his family. Before long, the Hapsburgs had become the ruling family in Austria. Until the end of World War I, a member of the Hapsburg family held the throne in Austria—thus making it one of the longest European dynasties, though by no means the happiest. From the early part of the fifteenth century on, the Austrian ruler was regularly chosen to be Holy Roman Emperor. By marriages, the Hapsburgs extended their family influence into Bohemia, Hungary, the Netherlands, and even into Spain.

# God in History

Q. How did the Roman Church (West) change during the Middle Ages?

A. The pristine Christianity set forth in the New Testament gradually became distorted. With the reintroduction of Aristotle's teachings, a type of humanistic element was added (which loosely resembled the humanistic elements that were to come later in the Renaissance) and the authority of the church took precedence over the teaching of the Bible. There was an increasing emphasis on salvation as being dependent on man's earning the merit of Christ, instead of on Christ's work alone being accepted by faith.

Also, the church had long struggled with its responsibility as outlined by Jesus to be in the world and not of it. This challenged Christians in their attitude toward material possessions and their style of living. There was also the constant need, seen throughout most of the Middle Ages, to carefully guard what the church considered to be the correct balance between God's laws and the will of the state, especially when the two came into conflict.

# Chapter Endnotes

3-1  The term *Protestant* to identify those who opposed the doctrines of the Catholic Church was not actually used until 1529.

# Chapter Terms

| | | |
|---|---|---|
| abbess | Dai Butsu | Magna Carta |
| abbot | Dominicans | merchant guild |
| alchemist | Franciscans | Miracle Play |
| allegory | gargoyle | Morality Play |
| begging friars | Inquisition | Mystery Play |
| burgesses | Jubilee Year | parapet |
| bourg | legate | personify |
| craft guild | livery company | |
| curfew | | |

# Chapter Review Questions/Exercises

1. Who were the new class of people to emerge from the small medieval towns? (61)
2. What does the phrase Stadtluft macht frei mean? (61)
3. Describe the conditions in a typical medieval town. (61)
4. What were the guilds? What was a livery company? (62)
5. Who were the alchemists and what did they try to do? (63)
6. Why were they unsuccessful at their main objective? (63)
7. What did Aquinas do with Aristotle's ideas? (64)
8. What did Roger Bacon demand? (64)
9. Which two important schools were formed in the thirteenth century? (64)
10. Who was Walter de Merton and what is he remembered for? (64).
11. How did universities try to achieve academic freedom? (64)
12. Who was an important overland explorer in the thirteenth century? (65)
13. Describe the abbey and the life of the medieval monks and friars. (66)
14. What part did women have in the church? (66)
15. Who were the Franciscans and what famous prayer is credited to Saint Francis? (67)
16. Who were the Dominicans and why were they formed? (68)
17. What was the Jubilee Year? (69)
18. What was the doctrine of transubstantiation? (69)
19. Why did the early Christians dislike drama? (70)
20. Explain the irony in the fact that European drama was revived in the church. (70)
21. What were Mystery Plays, Miracle Plays, and Morality Plays? (70)
22. Who were the Albigenses and why did the church use the Inquisition against this sect? (71)
23. What was the Order of the Apostles and how did the church react to it? (71)
24. What was the major improvement in cathedral construction in the thirteenth century? (72)
25. What were two important accomplishments of the Buddhist religion in the thirteenth century? (73)

26. Discuss the Fourth Crusade. (74)
27. What was the Children's Crusade and how did it end? (75)
28. Discuss the Fifth, Sixth, and Seventh Crusades. (76 - 78)
29. What were the results of the Crusades? (79)
30. What was life like in England under John? (80)
31. Why was French King Louis VIII declared the King of England in 1216? (81)
32. Describe the disunited region of Germany in the thirteenth century. (82)

# 4

# 1301-1400

## {7:12 a.m.-9:35 a.m.}

During the next two hours and twenty-three minutes, Geoffrey Chaucer (circa 1340-1400) will be born. The phrase, "love is blind," will be found in his great work, *The Canterbury Tales.*

Thomas à Kempis, the pen name of Thomas Hamerken (circa 1380-1471), will be remembered for his saying, "And when he is out of sight, quickly also is he out of mind."

William Langland (circa 1332-circa 1400) will originate the saying, "As dead as a doornail."

The Ming Dynasty (1368-1644) will substantially rebuild the Great Wall of China (a defensive fortification about 1,500 miles long) which was built in the reign of the emperor Shih Huang-ti (246-209 B.C.).

## Overview

### 83. The Renaissance

A new kind of thinking arose in Europe that writers of the nineteenth century called the *Renaissance* (rebirth). This term is somewhat misleading, for while there was certainly a rebirth of the ancient knowledge of the Greeks and Romans, the acquisition of knowledge had not entirely disappeared during the Middle Ages as the term "Dark Ages" implies. Science and other forms of study and culture struggled to keep alive during the relatively unproductive medieval years.

The start of the fourteenth century, therefore, was like the coming of spring after a long, cold winter. However, in the dead of winter there is life. The spring brings it on anew. Overall, the Renaissance was a period of transition during which the medieval world grew into the modern world. At the beginning of this thousand years, man was very much medieval in his thinking and deeds (see below); later, by 1500, he became very much the prototype on which modern man was built.

To fully appreciate this transition, it is necessary to recall that medieval man did not commonly care to investigate matters related to nature because he felt that would be like questioning God. It was widely believed that such questioning was a sin. Thus, it was considered wrong for medical students to dissect the human body since the Bible identified it as the temple of the living God (2 Cor. 6:16). Because medieval man was not particularly critical of the institutions around him, he accepted them as they were. He believed he could do little to modify them.

These attitudes began to change during the Renaissance and intensified with the rise of the Reformation and the Enlightenment when a new individualism asserted itself. These new perspectives also changed the way man looked at art. Medieval man thought it was improper to enjoy art for its own sake. It was acceptable, though, to put statues of the saints on cathedrals, or to decorate church windows since those were religious acts and not purely artistic ones. Medieval man did not have the time or the opportunities to learn how to appreciate and enjoy such creative pursuits.

The true Renaissance began in Florence, Italy, early in this century partly because the political climate in this city allowed the necessary artistic freedom to experiment. This was a time when some nations were still struggling to attain that goal, and still others were so barbaric that they had not even considered such a concept. The accumulation of wealth that came from the services that had been rendered to the Crusaders also spurred these new interests. Therefore, the wealthy Italians had the time and money to get interested in art and other matters. The most famous of these wealthy Italians was

Giovanni di Bicci dé Medici (1360-1429), who acquired a fortune by trade and used that fortune to encourage writers, artists, and other talented men of the day. He is regarded as the founder of the Medici dynasty that played such an important role in the Renaissance.

Another reason why the Renaissance began in Italy was that the break between the old and the new civilization was not as complete in Italy as it had been in the other countries of western Europe. The Italians were closer in language and in blood to the old Romans than were the other newly-formed nations. They regarded themselves as the direct descendants and heirs of the conquerors of the ancient world. This consciousness of kinship with the men of a great past exerted an immense influence upon the imaginations of the Italians and tended not only to preserve the continuity of human development in the peninsula but it also set as the first task of the Italian scholars the recovery and appropriation of the culture of antiquity.

The last reason why the Renaissance began in Italy was that numerous monuments of the civilization and grandeur of ancient Rome were everywhere in the peninsula. The cities themselves were, in a real sense, fragments of the old empire. The ground was literally covered with ruins of the old Roman builders. The influence which these reminders of a glorious past exerted upon sensitive souls is well illustrated by the biographies of men such as Petrarch.

Petrarch (1304-1374) had high regard for the material monuments of classical antiquity and believed that they should be studied and preserved. Many others of his day had very little intelligent curiosity or feeling regarding the monuments and ruins of the ancient world until Petrarch brought his literary influence to bear on their ideas. During all the medieval centuries until the dawn of the intellectual revival, the ruins of Rome had been viewed merely as a quarry. The monuments of the Caesars were torn down for building material, and the sculptured marbles were burned into lime for mortar.

## 84. Contributors to the Literary Revival in Italy

The writings of Dante Alighieri (1265-1321) became part of the literary revival in Italy. His classic work, *The Divine Comedy* (1300), was an epic of medievalism which provided a summary of medieval thought. Dante's theology was the theology of the medieval church, his philosophy was the philosophy of the schoolmen, and his science

85

was the science of his time. Dante wrote his works in Italian instead of Latin and they had a much greater audience as a result. This also helped to give a permanent character to the Italian language. The poem reveals that Dante knew the works of Virgil and Homer, but it contained new thoughts which could have come only from the mind of one so talented as Dante. In the poem, Virgil guided Dante through the realms of the after-life, but only as far as human reason can go. It was at this point that divine love, represented by Beatrice, took over. Beatrice was the guide of Paradise, and she was named after a woman Dante admired, Beatrice Portinari (1266-1290).

Francesco Balducci Pegolotti (died 1340) also had a part in the literary revival. This Florentine merchant wrote about the trade routes for the benefit of other merchants. He described how to pack goods and how to assay gold and silver. He traveled extensively and described London and monasteries in Scotland and England. His writings reflected the growth of commerce in the rich cities where ideas could be exchanged.

The eminent Italian lawyer Bartolus de Saxoferrato (1314-1357) did much to arouse and stimulate interest in the ancient Roman law. He did this partly through his extensive commentaries on the *Corpus Juris Civilis* (Body of Civil Law) and through his excellent teaching skills at the University of Perugia (1343) where he was appointed to the chair of civil law.

As the influence of these men and others grew into a new intellectual movement in classical learning in Italy, this awakening light spread over the rest of western Europe and into England where it reached its climax during the Elizabethan Era.

## 85. Literature in England

In England the poet William Langland (circa 1332-circa 1400) made important contributions to English literature. One of the earliest known pieces of English poetry is attributed to him; it is called *Vision of Piers Plowman*. Some scholars believe it may have been the work of several men, including Langland. It advocated rights for the poor peasants of the feudal system. It also contained the oldest mention of Robin Hood, the legendary English hero who was certainly as popular as another legend, King Arthur.

Another important English work with disputed authorship was

a poem called *The Pearl* (circa 1360). An unproven but likely candidate for its authorship was Ralph Strode (1350-1400) who taught logic and philosophy at Oxford and who wrote books on these subjects. The poem itself was a lament for a lost child who died before she was two years old. In it, the poet imagined that the child had been transfigured as a queen of heaven and he saw her beneath "a crystal rock," beyond a stream. The poet wanted to cross the stream but could not. He saw that his Pearl had grown in wisdom and stature, and instructed him in lessons of faith and resignation. Then the heavenly city suddenly became filled with glorious maidens, dressed in white robes, moving in a long procession toward the throne. In his dream he jumped into the stream in an effort to be with his Pearl, but this woke him up. The main features of this poem are found in the Bible in the allegory of the merchant who sold his all to purchase one pearl of great price, and in the words, so full of comfort for the child-bereaved, "for of such (children) is the Kingdom of Heaven."

The poem known as *The Imitation of Christ*, provided additional insight (apart from *The Pearl* and Dante's writings) into how medieval man viewed religion. It emphasized the power of love and suggested that the Christian could find inner peace by acquiring self-knowledge, self-discipline, and by demonstrating love. The Augustinian monk Thomas Hamerken (circa 1380-1471), who wrote under the name of Thomas a Kempis, has been regarded as the most likely author of this work. The authorship has been disputed though, because Kempis spent much of his time as a copyist and could have found these ideas expressed in the works he copied. His contemporaries, Groote (Hugo Grotius) and Jean Charlier de Gerson, famous theologians, are also considered to be possible authors of this famous work.

The works of Geoffrey Chaucer (circa 1340-1400) helped to give a permanent character to the English language. His most outstanding work was *The Canterbury Tales,* a creative work of satirical caricatures couched in the form of stories told by a group of wayfarers who were bound for the shrine of the martyr Thomas a' Becket (see section 54). These Canterbury pilgrims agreed it would make their journey more enjoyable if each member of the group told two stories on the way to the shrine and two more on the way home. The best storyteller was rewarded with a free meal at the expense of the others at their journey's end.

## 86. Not for Everyone

These outstanding examples of literary achievement in England showed the degree of creativity the writers of this period brought to their works. But even the new writings and the important changes that came in education were not able to bring Renaissance thinking to all men. Medieval habits that were the product of generations prevented the revival from causing quick reform among the masses of Europe.

In this century, *witchcraft*, which had survived as a ritual from pagan religion, became elaborated into a complex system and the *witch* and *wizard* were universally believed to be malignant beings who practiced all forms of the black arts. The witch was believed to be able to change into a cat or to summon apparitions. Religious persecution of supposed witches was common in the fourteenth century. Trials, convictions, and executions (beginning in 1450) were common throughout Europe. If someone engaged in scientific experiment he might be accused of being a witch.

The church absolutely continued to accept as true the Ptolemaic view of the universe with its concept of concentric spheres, with the earth at the center. This belief was common and many religions had their own versions of what these spheres were like.

Among Christians, there was Dante's view of hell (from *The Divine Comedy—the Inferno*) in which he represented hell as being a funnel-shaped hollow, formed of gradually contracting circles, the lowest and smallest of which was the earth's center. The Catholic belief in Purgatory, as perceived by Dante, was a mountain rising from the ocean on the side of earth opposite from hell. Purgatory was divided into terraces and its top was the terrestrial Paradise. From this "top" the poet ascended through the seven planetary heavens, the fixed stars, and the "Premium Mobile," which was the seat of God.

Similarly, the Jewish Cabalists believed in the existence of seven heavens, each rising in happiness above the other, with the seventh being the abode of God and the highest class of angels.

The Moslems also had their seven heavens, but their belief in what these places were differed from the Christian and Jewish views.

Finally, astrologers divided the heavens into twelve portions by means of great circles crossing the northern and southern points of the horizon, through which the heavenly bodies passed every twenty-four hours (the zodiac).

The Renaissance basically eluded China, which remained a closed society during this time because it was dominated by political conservatism and the Confucian philosophy which emphasized order, continuity, and stability.

# The Decline of Feudalism

## 87. Changes in Warfare

The introduction from China of *gunpowder*, the knowledge that a compound of saltpeter (potassium nitrate), charcoal and sulfur could be used in weapons, took much of the glamour out of being a knight. A bullet could penetrate a knight's armor, permitting even a peasant with a gun to kill him. Gunpowder tended to make "all men equal" in warfare and its invention changed the course of military history.

The use of the bow and arrow, likewise, became still another obstacle to the continuance of the feudal system. The armed knight with his battle-ax and lance was no match either for the steel-tipped arrows of hundreds or even thousands of men kneeling at a distance with their bows firing arrows in rapid succession.

The great battle of Crecy in 1346, the first important battle of the Hundred Years' War (see section 94), was the first example of a skirmish in which gunpowder and arrows were used against the feudalistic knights. With the defeat by the English of 1,200 French knights, the flower of French chivalry was destroyed at the hand of the gunman and archer, and the military base upon which the feudal system had rested was suddenly gone.

A few years later (circa 1350), the introduction of the large cannon into warfare reduced the security and value of castles. Whereas before, the builders of castles had depended on clever construction and isolation for protection, these fortifications became little match against well-trained artillery forces. So the castle, the center of feudalism, in which it lived and moved and had its being, then became a useless thing.

## 88. The Black Death

Within a year of the battle of Crecy a great natural disaster came upon Europe and Asia which did more than anything else to bring the feudal system to its knees. The *Black Death*, the most virulent plague recorded in human history, spread over Europe (1347-1350). It was followed by successive outbursts for the next three centuries.

There were two types of plague. The first, the *bubonic* form, involved swollen lymph nodes (or buboes) in the neck, armpit, or groin. These rapidly broke down to form carbuncles. The second was the *pneumonic* form. It was characterized by the spitting of blood, extreme contagiousness and death in three days.

The bubonic type was less infectious than the *pneumonic*, ran a slower course, and was frequently less fatal than the pneumonic type. The name "Black Death" was first applied many years after the initial outbreak and may have referred to the dusky-blue color of the dying victim, the sinister quality of the malady, or the spots of blood which turned black under the skin. It was fought by fumigation and the burning of herbs, both of which were completely ineffective. Citizens were advised to flee from it immediately and to go as far as possible. This, of course, served only to spread it more rapidly. The physicians who treated it wore gowns and gloves for their own protection and they also wore nose bags that contained vinegar, cloves, and cinnamon. It was not until later in 1377 that quarantining was used to fight the disease. At the Italian port of Ragusa on the Adriatic, ships were quarantined for forty days if they came from infected areas.

The plague brought down the entire system of feudalism. More than one-fourth of the population of Europe was destroyed in the wake of the Black Death in the fourteenth century. It left its mark on the great feudalistic institutions of the manors, the church, the educational systems, and even on the architecture of the day.

Entire families were lost to the plague and estates were left without heirs. In such cases, ownership of such properties returned to the original grantor. Farms became overgrown with weeds. The plague so reduced the number of workers on feudal estates that those who survived demanded new conditions of work and pay. Some peasants even rose in revolt. The French Jacquerie Revolt in 1358 and Wat Tyler's Rebellion in 1381 were examples of these peasant uprisings.

The loss of many clergy affected the feudalistic church profoundly. To replace them, new priests were hurriedly ordained, without sufficient training. These poorly trained priests indirectly contributed to the Pre-Reformation movements of Wycliffe and Huss (see section 90).

Medieval education systems underwent tremendous challenges as a result of the loss of both students and teachers. Two-thirds of the Oxford student body perished. In Europe and elsewhere, many faculty members were quickly replaced by new teachers who had little or no education. This resulted in an increasing use of vernacular languages, causing Latin to become less and less the language of choice for instruction.

## 89. Knighthood Organizations

The death of feudalism as a system of government did not end its existence as a social organization. The nobles lost their power and authority to petty sovereigns but retained their titles, their privileges, their social distinction and, in some cases, their vast landed estates. Many of these found expression in the many orders that were established in this and other centuries. Two of these were The Order of Christ (1318) and The Order of the Collar (1362).

# Matters of the Church

In times of suffering and disorder, people naturally longed for better days, even if those better days awaited them only in another world. The hope of heaven expressed in such songs as "Jerusalem the Golden" was enough to attract people who longed for a happier, perhaps more prosperous life. The church taught that God, in His own good time, would straighten out all difficulties and relieve all troubles, and that He had sent His Son, Jesus, into the world to give everlasting life to all who believed in Him (see John 3:16).

## 90. Pre-Reformation Events

Under the feudalistic medieval church, nearly everyone had become its mental and spiritual slaves. Even with the breakdown of feudalism, which freed their bodies, medieval man continued to be dominated by the church which itself clung to medieval practices and beliefs, even amid the growing Renaissance. This traditional outlook had advantages and disadvantages. Medieval man was expected to concentrate only on what was approved of by the church fathers. Followers were taught that this life is merely a brief candle, a vale of tears, during which one must prepare for the more important heavenly life. Therefore, one should not inquire into nature, for that

91

was like questioning God, and one should accept suffering from whatever cause, because it must be God's will. One experienced earthly pleasures at the expense of spending eternity in hell. The church stressed that the emissaries of the devil and the angels of God were always present, trying to persuade men to their viewpoints. Spiritual warfare was a reality to them. The appeal of the demons of hell was deceptively attractive and only by following the rules of the church closely, by taking no chances of thinking new thoughts, could man be sure of salvation. The coming of the Renaissance opened up a new way of thinking in some men who sought more complete answers to their spiritual questions and who also began to question certain practices of the medieval church. This did not keep the church fathers from enforcing and maintaining their viewpoints, however.

Two important opponents of the practices and teachings of the medieval church were John Wycliffe (sometimes Wyclif, Wickliffe, or Wiclif) (circa 1328-1384) of England and John Huss (circa 1369-1415), of Bohemia. Wycliffe's followers were named after the *Lollards,* a sect that was organized in Holland in the early years of this century. The original Lollards were dedicated to helping the sick and burying the dead. The term became applied to Wycliffe's followers (circa 1387). They were also called "poor priests." They wore long gowns and carried staffs as they ministered in the small villages of England. They suggested that the Bible authorized priests and deacons to be officers in the church and urged the government to pay no more feudal dues to the pope. Wycliffe taught that the doctrine of transubstantiation was an error and that the Bible, not the church, should be the ultimate authority in matters of faith and practice.

Huss came under the scrutiny of the church after he praised Wycliffe's doctrine, though he did not fully agree with it. In his sermons, Huss attacked the abuses of the clergy. After a lengthy investigation into these and other matters that were not approved of by the church, he was burned at the stake.

## The Architecture of the Church

### 91. The Cathedral Window

In the previous century, the problem of lighting the interior of large buildings like cathedrals was solved by the narrowing of the walls. It was the use of stained glass that added a significantly new dimension to windows in the churches and cathedrals.

This period of window development could be accurately called the stained glass period; its special characteristic was that straight lines were the main features of *tracery* in the windows. In this period the stained-glass painter, with his humble mate, the glazier, was the great man to whom even the master mason bent his design. In the end he dominated the mason completely.

The new *tracery* of this century had its origin in the great value believers placed on saint and angel, prophet and martyr and all the hierarchy of heaven. A further merit it possessed was that it accommodated a far-larger number of personages. Therefore, the windows would often be vastly increased in area. The window could be made, and often was made as broad and lofty as nave or choir.

Certainly the largest stained glass window in all of England at this time was the one that was constructed in the east window of Gloucester Cathedral. The north transept was remodeled (1330-1337); the east window retained most of its original glass, and the design of the armorial bearing suggests a date of completion (circa 1350). This was the first window to have the new, larger tracery. Its purely rectilinear design was very effective in that it allowed vast amounts of light to enter the cathedral. Stained glass windows had, therefore, both practical and spiritual applications.

---

**Reflection:**

*Consider the psychology of the men and women who supported the building of the great cathedrals, with their splendid windows and the spires that seemed to reach up to heaven. What does such an obvious religious architectural statement say about the importance of religion to these Christians?*

---

# Matters of Church and State

Though the church was well-organized, it was ill-prepared for the changes wrought by the presence of the strong kings which came to power. In the time since Pope Innocent III, strong kings came to the throne who required people to feel respect for them and demanded patriotism for their country. As this nationalistic feeling grew stronger, men's reverence for a ruler outside of their own country lessened, even with regard to the pope, in spite of the fact that he was the head of their church. Kings especially did not like the idea of sending money to Rome. Besides, some greedy princes wanted to acquire the valuable lands that belonged to the church. Moreover, some churchmen in high positions did not very often practice what the church taught. Some lived immoral lives, and some took bribes for favors they could grant. Others bought their positions in the church.

## 92. The Popes and France

For one disastrous period in the life of the church, the popes were not particularly to blame. Pope Boniface VIII (see section 69) got into a controversy with French King Philip IV the Fair (1268; reigned 1285-1314). Philip sent soldiers into Italy and these troops captured Boniface and brought him to Avignon, in southern France. The poor old pope was so distressed by this insult that he died soon afterward (1303).

Then followed a brief reign by Benedict XI (1240; served 1303-1304). Next, Philip had a French churchman, Clement V (1264; served 1305-1314) chosen as pope and he moved the pope's residence to Avignon. For nearly seventy years (1309-1377) the popes were really controlled by the French kings. In comparison with the captivity of the Jews, this period has been called the "Babylonian captivity" of the popes.

## 93. The Abolition of the Order of the Templars

Another example of the influence the French kings had over the popes may be seen in what happened on one occasion between Philip IV and Clement. The financially strained rulers of Europe envied the wealth that the Knights Templars had built up since their founding (1119). Philip had the organization investigated and its members tortured until they confessed to false charges. Clement was "encouraged" to abolish the organization in 1312. Their leader, Jacques de Molay (circa 1243-1314), was burned at the stake. Philip appropriated the cash assets of the Templars and deeded most of their lands to the Knights of Saint John.

The abolition of the Order of the Knights of the Temple by Philip the Fair suggested in part a parallel to the suppression of the Catholic monasteries in England by Henry VIII in the sixteenth century (see section 119).

# Matters of State

### 94. The Hundred Years' War

England and France were rivals for several centuries. From the conquest of England by William of Normandy until the nineteenth century, England and France were on opposite sides of any war in which they both took part, and there were few wars on the continent which France kept out of. However, English kings for a long time dominated, and were kings of part of France. An especially contentious part of this long rivalry lasted (1337-1453), with intermissions, about a hundred years, and was therefore called the Hundred Years' War (also see sections 100-104).

This conflict began during the reigns of Edward III of England (1312; reigned 1327-1377) and Philip VI of France (1293; reigned 1328-1350). The portion that was fought during this century ended during the reign of King John II of France (1319; reigned 1350-1364), with Edward III still in power in England. Edward claimed that he was the King of France by right. His claim was derived through his mother, in spite of the so-called Salic law (see chapter endnote 4-1) prevailing in France, which declared that no woman, nor anyone whose claims depended solely upon a woman, could succeed to the throne. Even if Edward's claims had been better, though, the French would have objected to an Englishman as their king.

Other causes helped to bring on this conflict. England was then raising a great deal of wool, but not manufacturing it. She wanted to sell it in the district which today is called Belgium, but which for a long time was known as Flanders. The French interfered with this trade and also with the wine trade between England and southern France. Further, the French helped the Scots in their quarrels with England.

All the fighting of this long war was on French soil, and so France suffered worse from the devastation of land and interference with trade. Strangely enough, the English won almost all the notable victories, but their victories did little good. At Crecy in 1346 and at Poitiers in 1356, the English were extremely successful over much larger French armies. These victories gave proof that the old feudal warfare was out of date. Light-armed soldiers, carrying long bows, could do much more damage than feudal knights with their awkward and heavy armor. During this war, gunpowder was used for the first time in a fight in Europe, but its main purpose was to scare the other side. Firing a heavy cannon was about as dangerous to the people behind it as it was to the people in front. A peace treaty was made in 1360 {8:37 a.m.}. The peace lasted until Henry V of England revived the claim of the English kings to the throne of France, and invaded France with an army in 1415 {9:56 a.m.}.

# God in History

Q. What influence did Dante, the Italian poet and author, have on the way medieval man viewed heaven and hell? What was the vehicle for this influence?

A. Dante's primary work,*The Commedia* (the word Divine was added later), exercised great religious influence on medieval man. Although the discovery of the new world and the invention of printing were still far in the future, Dante's time was clearly one of great men, of free thought and free speech, of brilliant and daring action. Then, too, there was the dominance of the church over the medieval mind. The time was right for an epic of this magnitude to spread its influence.

Q. Was Dante a Christian at the time of this writing?

A. It is generally thought that Dante went through a conversion experience just before he wrote *The Divine Comedy*.

Q. What are some of the symbols and important parts in the work?

A. The action of *The Divine Comedy* opens in the early morning of the Thursday before Easter (1300). The poet found himself lost in a forest, with all paths blocked by a wolf, a lion, and a leopard. All this, like the rest of the poem, was highly symbolic. His efforts to free himself from the "forest" of worldly cares were impeded by the temptations of the world, which were symbolized by the three beasts. But Virgil (symbolic of philosophy and human reason) appeared and explained that he had a commission "from on high" to guide him. Virgil took him through the two lower realms of the next world, hell and Purgatory. There he found popes, kings, emperors, poets, and warriors, Florentine citizens of all degrees, some doomed to hopeless punishment, others expiating their offenses in milder torments and looking forward to deliverance in due time.

Hell was a vast cone that reached to the center of the earth. Lucifer was at the very bottom of the pit, immovably fixed in ice. Next, they visited Purgatory which was described as having seven layers, corresponding to the seven deadly sins. He was then taken on a tour of heaven (Paradise) which had levels that corresponded to the astronomy and theology of the time. The poem ended when, for one moment, Dante was granted a vision of God and the comprehension of all mysteries.

## Chapter Endnotes

4-1 It was called the Salic Law on the false idea that it was part of the Lex Salica, a Germanic code. Actually, that code contained no public law of any kind. The intent of the law seems to have been to prevent the loss of family lands by marriage of the female members.

## Chapter Terms

| | | |
|---|---|---|
| Black Death | Lollards | Renaissance |
| bubonic | Order of Christ | Salic law |
| *Commedia* | Order of the Collar | |
| Corpus Juris Civilis | pneumonic | |

## Chapter Review Questions/Exercises

1. How did the coming of the Renaissance influence the thinking of medieval man? (83)
2. Why did the Renaissance begin in Italy? (83)
3. What influence did de Medici and Petrarch have on the Renaissance? (83)
4. Name several contributors to the literary revival in Italy. (84)
5. Who were some of the important writers in England in the fourteenth century? (85)
6. What were some of the medieval attitudes that even the Renaissance was slow in overcoming? (86)
7. Discuss the decline of feudalism. How did the changes in warfare and the Black Death influence this trend? (87-88)
8. What were the two main types of plague? (88)
9. Name two knighthood organizations that were formed in the fourteenth century. (89)
10. What were some of the events of the fourteenth century that eventually contributed to the Reformation? (90)

11. What problem occurred between the popes and Philip of France? (92)
12. Why were the Templars abolished? (93)
13. How did the series of conflicts known as the Hundred Years' War start? List the important battles of this war that occurred in the fourteenth century. (94)
14. What happened in 1360 to end the fighting for a time? (94)

[Fig. 1-1] Assault on a Medieval castle. (From an original oil painting by Jack Connelly.)

[Fig. 1-2] A tilting match between two knights. (From an engraving in Myers.)

[Fig. 2-1] Beverly Saint Mary—west front. (From Bond.)

[Fig. 3-1] The Alchemist. (From an original ink drawing by
Kyle Bennick.)

[Fig. 5-1] Erasmus. (After a painting by Holbein in Myers.)

[Fig. 6-1] Martin Luther. (After the portrait by Lucas Cranach, the elder; Uffizi Gallery, Florence, in Myers.)

[Fig. 6-2] The Bubble Nebula today, the remnants of the supernova of 1572 that Brahe used to prove that the heavens are not immutable. (Copyright UC Regents; UCO/Lick Observatory image.)

[Fig. 8-1] Pilatre de Rozier's first ascension in a fire balloon (1783). (From Adams.)

[Fig. 8-2] Charles' balloon (1783). (From Adams.)

[Fig. 8-3] Aerial view of the Bastille. (From Adams.)

The largest order the U. S. GOVERNMENT ever placed for Writing Ma-chines was for the

# "National" Type Writer.

Irrespective of price, "the best and most complete Writing Machine made. Embodies every good quality found in other Writing Machines, and has many points of superiority, all its own. *Smallest and most comprehensive* double case finger key machine made. Writes eighty-one to eighty-five characters, including capitals, small letters, figures, punctuation marks, commercial signs, etc., with only twenty-nine keys to learn and manipulate. Entirely portable. Weighs about thirteen pounds. Occupies space of a Dictionary. Perfect Manifolder. More and better manifold copies than upon any machine made. Price, including portable office case—**$60**

*Every Machine Warranted.*

**NATIONAL TYPEWRITER CO., Manfrs. and Sole Agents,**
715, 717 and 719 Arch Street, Philadelphia, Pa., U. S. A.
Send for illustrated pamphlet, giving fac-simile of key-board.

[Fig. 9-1] Early typewriter. (Illustration: *Century Illustrated*.)

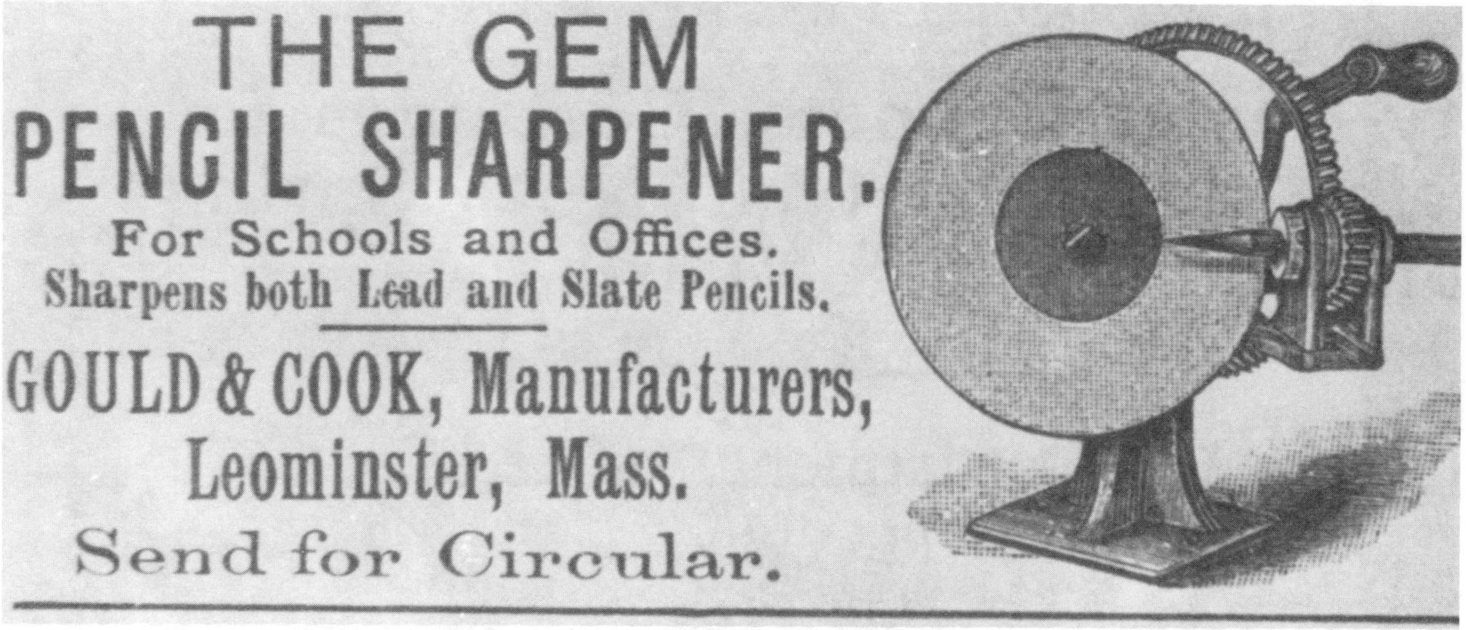

THE GEM
PENCIL SHARPENER.

For Schools and Offices.

Sharpens both Lead and Slate Pencils.

GOULD & COOK, Manufacturers,

Leominster, Mass.

Send for Circular.

[Fig. 9-2] Early pencil sharpener. (Illustration: *Century Illustrated*.)

[Fig. 9-3] Charles R. Darby. (Photo from the author.)

[Fig. 9-4] The Darby Double Shovel. (Photo from the author.)

[Fig. 9-5] Charles Martin Hall, founder of the
Pittsburgh Reduction Company (1888).
(Photo courtesy of the Aluminum Company of America.)

# 5

# 1401-1500

## {9:36 a.m.-11:59 a.m.}

During the next two hours and twenty-three minutes, John Skelton (circa 1460-1529) will be born. He will be remembered for his famous saying: "Spare the rod and spoil the child."

## Overview

The Renaissance was encouraged by the development of new ideas and discoveries. Astronomers became aware of a difference between true north (the direction of the North Pole) and magnetic north (the direction in which the compass needle points). The difference is called *magnetic declination* or *variation*. There were improvements in the compass, which was first used by the Chinese. Europeans knew about it (before 1200), though with them it was not much more than a needle attached to a straw. With improved compasses, mariners dared to venture farther from the sight of land on unknown waters. They also found useful the *astrolabe*, which provided a means of determining latitude. The mariner's astrolabe was adapted (from an instrument used by astronomers) by Martin Behaim (circa 1480); this was the instrument used by Columbus on his voyages of discovery. With the tables of the sun's declination then available, he could calculate his latitude by meridian altitudes of the sun taken with his astrolabe. *Portolani,* or mariners' charts, first used by the Portuguese, also became known during this century.

The Renaissance was encouraged by the sharing of new ideas. Some Italian scholars who felt the importance of meeting together to discuss their studies and ideas remembered that Plato's Academy (named after a park near Athens) had flourished from 387 B.C. to 529. The first such academy of the Renaissance was the *Accademia Pontaniana* established in 1433. Others soon followed.

Military campaigns other than the Crusades influenced the spread of the Renaissance by way of cross-pollination of cultures where these armies went. When Charles VIII (1470; reigned 1483-1498) of France crossed the Alps with a mighty army in an effort to take Naples in 1494, his returning men brought with them new ideas of the cultural achievements of the Italian Renaissance and introduced these into French society.

This century also saw the important changes that were on the horizon in education at all levels. The philosophy of the Dutch scholar Rudolphus Agricola (1443-1485), in many ways anticipated these changes. His ideas influenced Erasmus [see figure 5-1 and section 96] and other critics of the next generation, especially Francis Bacon (see section 129), who, like himself, sought to improve the scholastic philosophy of his day.

In medicine, the outbreak of certain epidemic diseases, which had been unknown to the ancients, had an important influence on the need for research in medicine. In previous centuries the plague had ravaged Europe and other parts of the world. In this century there was the "sweating sickness," or "English sweat," especially common in the country for which it was named, though it was not confined to England. It soon became painfully obvious that the medical knowledge left by Hippocrates and Galen was not adequate to meet these new threats.

Pope Nicholas V (1397; served 1447-1455), a founder of the Vatican Library, tried to help the medical community by publishing the writings of Celsus (born, circa 10 B.C.) which had been hidden for centuries. Celsus (see chapter endnote 5-1) had been a Roman medical writer, a native Roman citizen, and a member of the noble family of Cornelli. He has been called the "medical Cicero." In his works, Celsus summarized the best of all medical knowledge up to his day, describing many diseases accurately and prescribing sensible treatments for them. The real solution to dealing with the new diseases, though, was in the reestablishment of objective inquiry, an event soon to come about.

Another problem that had long plagued the medical establishment began to receive the attention it needed in this century. Medieval medical practice had long been hampered by the relatively low status of the surgeon. The common belief among doctors was that work with the hands was menial. This resulted in a division of work between the physician, who functioned only as an advisor in the operating room, to the surgeon or barber-surgeon, (see chapter endnote 5-2) who operated on the patient. It was in England in this century that these barriers began to come down when the barbers first received incorporation from Edward IV (1461).

Certainly the printing press, the greatest disseminator of information invented to this time, contributed to the spread of the Renaissance. It was not just that new books were written, but now they could be produced in such quantities that almost everyone could read them. This made the sharing of ideas much easier.

The Chinese were probably the first to fashion blocks that could be used to print multiple copies of something (circa 770). A foundry for casting movable metal type was established in Korea (circa 1403), but the printing press was not introduced into Europe from the east. Johannes Gutenberg (circa 1398-1468) of the German city of Mainz, received the credit for it (circa 1436 or circa 1450).

From Germany, the art of printing spread throughout the continent. There was a press in Italy (1464) and one in Venice (1469). Switzerland had a press (1472) and there was one in Spain (1475). The first press in England was established in 1476 {11:24 a.m.} by William Caxton (circa 1422-1491). Caxton's printing press in London caused a major change in English literature because it made it possible for books, such as Chaucer's *Canterbury Tales*, to be printed quickly and at relatively low cost.

The invention of printing also did away with the monopoly on learning that had been possessed by the monasteries, universities, and wealthy people. With it, books could be made much faster and cheaper than the best of the monks could make them by hand and they were far more accurate, since an entire edition was printed from the same type and mistakes in the different copies were thereby eliminated. Books came into the possession of many people and no longer remained the luxury of the few. All who could read now had books available to them, and by this means, the door to knowledge was opened to all. Printing also made possible popular education, public libraries and, eventually, inexpensive newspapers. These advances helped free mankind from the bondage of ignorance.

The Venetian printer Aldus Manutius (1450-1515) improved the printed word by devising "italic" type which was first used to print one of Virgil's books in 1501. He is also credited with the introduction of punctuation marks. Prior to his time, words were run together successively, without any indications of pauses or breaks in sentences.

# Other Renaissance Disciplines and Institutions

## 95. Art

Outstanding among all the Renaissance artists was Michelangelo Buonarotti (1475-1564), Italian architect, sculptor, painter, and poet of the Renaissance which he greatly transcended. He gave his entire life to his art—so completely, in fact, that his reputation became that of being an unfriendly man. Among his sculptures, the great statues of Moses and David are the most famous. Among his paintings, probably the Last Judgment is best known. He also painted frescoes on the ceiling of the Sistine Chapel in Rome.

Another Italian super-genius was Leonardo da Vinci (1452-1519) sculptor, painter, architect, musician, engineer and scientist. Two of his paintings are the Last Supper, painted in an abbey at Milan, and the Mona Lisa, who ever since has had people guessing as to the meaning of her smile.

The paintings of the Italian Baccio della Porta (circa 1475-1517), otherwise known as Fra Bartolommeo, were important. His technique was partially inspired by da Vinci but he also came under the influence of the great Dominican friar, Girolamo Savonarola (see section 99) who opposed the paganism of the court of Lorenzo de' Medici. At the famous "bonfire of the vanities," he burned all his paintings which were not religious in nature (1497).

Two German sculptors stood out during this period. Veit Stoss (circa 1445-1533), also a wood carver, created numerous religious works of note. Among his sculptures were *The Death of the Virgin, Christ on the Mount of Olives,* and *The Taking of Christ.* Because he was skilled in carving marble, he was commissioned to do several tombs, including one for Polish king Casimir IV (died 1492). This was placed in the cathedral in Cracow. Adam Kraft (circa 1455-1509), the German sculptor and architect of Nuremberg, completed a series of works known as *The Seven Stations.* They were made for the road to the Cemetery of Saint John there. His most celebrated work was the tabernacle for the Church of Saint Lawrence, also in Nuremberg. It was a pyramid over sixty feet high.

## 96. Humanism

The Renaissance saw the rise of a new type of thinking expressed in literature, an approach known as *humanism.* The greatest of the humanists was Desiderius Erasmus (circa 1466-1536) who was born in Rotterdam. One of his most famous works was *Praise of Folly.* It was a sort of ironical discussion of the evils of his time. He was disgusted with some practices of churchmen, though he was by no means an opponent of religion in general or the Roman Catholic Church in particular. He published a translation of the New Testament with the Greek and Latin versions side by side, in the hope that it might be more readily understood by people.

Erasmus and two of his friends are often called the "Oxford Reformers" because they were connected with Oxford University in England. One of them was John Colet (circa 1466-1519), who founded the famous Saint Paul's School in London. Still more prominent was Thomas More (1478-1535), canonized as a saint just 400 years later. He was best known for the writing of *Utopia.* This title came from Greek words meaning "nowhere." In this work he described what seemed to him to be an ideal community. Today we speak of a "utopia" as something too good to be true or an impossible ideal.

# Matters of the Christian Church

## 97. The Cathedral Window

The stained glass that gained such prominence in the last century achieved even greater notice in this one. Churches and glass windows

119

alike were commissioned and paid for by Christians for Christians.

What were Christians like in this century? In spite of the strides made by the medieval universities, except for a clerk here and there, nearly the whole world—certainly the Christian masses—were illiterate. This was a condition which not even the introduction of the printing press could immediately help to overcome. The whole Christian community needed instruction in the Old and New Testaments, the lives of the saints, and the doctors of the church as well as in the essentials of theological doctrines and theories. Thus, monk and priest set forth to communicate theological concepts, partly by wall paintings, partly by statued west fronts or redos, but mainly through the stained glass window. The attitude of the church towards glass was not the same attitude one would expect from an academy of artists, for the church's emphasis was not on art, but on the promotion of Christian knowledge. Windows were made primarily for edification, only secondarily for delight. Range after range of windows were utilized, just as the bosses (a raised ornament on a flat surface) of the vaults of Norwich Cathedral and Worcester Cloister were, to give lessons in scriptural history.

## 98. Fountains Abbey

The abbeys continued to play an important role in the architecture of medieval Europe. Fountains Abbey, the Cistercian establishment on the River Skell in England, founded during the twelfth century, underwent major changes during this one. Beginning in 1494, just two years after Columbus made his famous voyage, Abbot Huby (died 1526) started a tower there.

Flanking the west side of the cloister and extending across the Skell, there was a range of vaulted apartments, popularly called cloisters, which served as cellars and storehouses. These vaults had dormitories above them. The refectory flanked the cloisters upon the south; the chapter house with the monks' dormitory was located above, on the east.

The abbot's house, one of the largest and most elaborate in England, lay at the extreme eastern end of the compound, where much of the structure was suspended upon arches spanning the river. The great hall of this house was a splendid room, 170 feet long and seventy feet wide. It compared favorably with the great hall of feudal castles and the renowned Westminster Hall in London. It was divided into three aisles by two rows of nine piers bearing arches.

## 99. More Pre-Reformation Activities

The church was keenly aware of the growing discontent over its doctrines and practices, and it took certain measures to defend its position. The council at Oxford passed a provision forbidding the translation of the Bible into English without the consent of the bishop of the diocese or of a provincial synod. It also drafted documents in 1407 against the Lollards (the followers of John Wycliffe) which were published later in 1409. These documents were used by lower church officials to openly persecute the Lollards. English archbishop Henry Chicheley (1364-1443) persecuted a number of Lollards during 1428. The church even had the help of kings in their quest. Like his father before him, English king Henry IV (1367; reigned 1399-1413) continued persecuting the Lollards. He even had one of their leaders, Sir John Oldcastle (circa 1377-1417), killed.

In Italy the church faced impressive opposition from Girolamo Savonarola (1452-1498). For a time he lived as an ordinary Dominican friar, but after going to Florence in 1490, he began to preach with great effect. He attacked showiness and extravagance and urged people to give up their jewels and other expensive luxuries. For a time he was very popular and had great influence with the people of Florence and succeeded in ridding the city of the influence of the Medici court, which he considered evil. He even advocated that a monarchy be established in Florence and that Christ be proclaimed its king, with Savonarola as the interpreter of God's will. But some of the high church officials, including Pope Alexander VI (1431; served 1492-1503), resisted his efforts and forbade him to preach. Finally his enemies succeeded in getting him excommunicated and put to death.

But the murder of a few reformers didn't prevent the rapid spread of discontent that became increasingly evident during the latter part of the Renaissance. More and more people began to question the authority of the clergy in matters of doctrine. Whereas before, it was mostly kings who had objected to sending money to Rome, in this century even some peasants in England and Germany objected to the practice. The popes continued to argue that since Rome was the great center of Christianity, it was perfectly right to make the headquarters of the church attractive. Motives not religious were also mixed with the religious movements, as when German princes took advantage of the disturbed condition to shake off obligations to the Holy Roman Empire.

The Reformation was not far off.

# Matters of State

## 100. England, France, and the Hundred Years' War

As was shown earlier, sometimes the history of one country is so involved with another that it is best to speak of them together. Such is the case with England and France during the struggle known as the Hundred Years' War which began in 1337 (see section 94). It was renewed by Henry V (see below) and it was another period during which even the crowns of the two countries were intertwined.

## 101. England Under Henry V

Henry V (1387; reigned 1413-1422) of the House of Lancaster, was next crowned King of England. He resumed the dispute over French territory that caused what is now called the Hundred Years' War with the object of reclaiming the lands lost by England to France in other times. He went so far as to seek the crown of France itself.

After taking the town of Harfleur, Henry won a great victory at Agincourt (1415) {9:56 a.m.} in which the popular French soldier Ambroise de Lore participated (1396-1446). He succeeded in negotiating the Treaty of Troyes in 1420 with King Charles VI of France, which recognized Henry as heir to the French throne and by which it was agreed he would marry Catherine of Valois, the French king's daughter. Out of this marriage a son was born who became Henry VI. According to the treaty, the crown of France was to go to the English king on the death of Charles. War came again during 1422, but Henry died that same year.

## 102. England Under Henry VI

When Henry V died, his son and heir, Henry VI (1421; reigned 1422-1461, 1470-1471) was still less than one year old when he became King of England. The Duke of Gloucester assumed responsibility for governing England during Henry's minority. In addition, Charles VI of France (1368; reigned 1380-1422) died within a few weeks, and Henry VI became the French king. He was crowned in Paris by the terms of the Treaty of Troyes (see chapter endnote 5-3) which recognized Henry VI, and not Charles VII, as Charles VI's successor. In his place, his uncle, the Duke of Bedford, ruled for Henry VI in France, and held the northern part of that country until 1429. That year the English were defeated at Orleans by Jeanne d'Arc.

## 103. Charles VII and Joan of Arc

Jeanne d'Arc, recognized by her more popular name of Joan of Arc (circa 1411-1431), the "Maid of Orleans," was one of the most extraordinary characters in French history. Though she was born in the small country village of Domremy and lived the life of a peasant girl until she was eighteen, she had dreams and heard voices which she believed called her to attempt to rescue France from the English and to see that the French Prince Charles would be formally crowned at Reims as French kings regularly were.

Even though he was the son of Charles VI, Charles VII (1403-1461) had been denied the throne of France by the Treaty of Troyes, and although he called himself king after his father's death, his authority was restricted to the Loire country while the rest of France recognized Henry VI of England as their legitimate ruler. Things looked hopeless for Charles when Orleans was attacked by the English in 1428, but the appearance of Joan of Arc in Bourges changed everything. Her name attracted such fierce fighters as Arthur III (1393-1458) of Brittany, who fought at Orleans under her banner. There too was Jean Dunois (circa 1403-1468), one of France's best commanders at this time, who defended Orleans with the greatest of vigor which enabled them to hold out until Joan arrived. Under her leadership the French rescued the city of Orleans, and crowned the *Dauphin* (French for "prince"), in Reims (1429) as King Charles VII. (The word *Dauphin* has a similar significance to the French as the term "Prince of Wales" does to the English in connection with their royal family). The Treaty of Troyes was thus repudiated.

Joan met Charles on the grounds of the Chateau de Courdray (1429). The saddest part of the story was that Charles had little appreciation for what she had done for him. Though she thought her work was done, the French insisted that she keep on fighting. At length she fell into the hands of the English who put her on trial as a sorceress. She was burned at the stake in Rouen in 1431.

---

**Reflection:**

*The life of Joan of Arc can be described as one that was a product of a deeply religious attitude. Others viewed her accomplishments as being the result of witchcraft or demonism. The Bible urges Christians to be careful to objectively evaluate their leaders What are the dangers of relying only on superstition and unsubstantiated evidence in making such decisions?*

---

## 104. Other Battles in the Hundred Years' War

One of the strangest battles in the Hundred Years' War was the Battle of the Herrings in 1429. This was the name applied to the action at Rouvray between the French (and Scots) and the English who, under Sir John Falstolfe (also Fastolf or Falstaff), were convoying Lenten provisions, chiefly herrings, to the besiegers of Orleans. A sortie was launched by the men of Orleans in an effort to intercept the food, but the English repulsed them by using the barrels of herrings as a defense.

Other important battles of the Hundred Years' War followed. Jean Dunois raised the siege of Chartres and of Lagny in 1432 and engaged in a series of successful campaigns which ended in his triumphal entry into Paris (April, 1436). He continued to press the war against the English and gradually drove them to the north, though his work was to some extent interrupted by the civil disorders of the time in which he played an obvious part.

Both sides stopped fighting during 1453 and did not even bother to make a treaty about it. The English were by this time deeply involved with the Wars of the Roses (see section 105) and were unable to take the offensive against France anew. The English lost whatever territory their kings had claimed in France, except Calais.

## 105. The Wars of the Roses

The traditional name given to the intermittent struggle for the throne of England between the House of Lancaster (whose badge was a red rose) and the House of York (whose badge was a white rose) from 1455 to 1485 is the Wars of the Roses.

The three battles that were the landmarks of this struggle were the first battle of Saint Albans (1455), the battle of Towton Field (1461), and the battle of Bosworth Field (1485). The complex events leading up to the last battle involved the complex struggle between Edward IV's sons and Richard III and Henry Tudor.

## 106. England Under Edward V and Richard III

Edward IV died in 1483 before his sons reached their majority. His sons were Edward V (1470; reigned April-June, 1483), the rightful heir to the throne and Prince Richard (1472-1483), the Duke of York, who never served as king. Edward assumed the throne as Edward V at the age of thirteen but his uncle, Richard, duke of Gloucester (1452-1485), who had been appointed guardian over young Edward, acted as *Proctor* (someone employed to manage the affairs of another) of the Kingdom and intervened.

Edward's selection of a guardian had seemed logical. Richard was loyal to his brother, but after Edward died, he claimed that Edward's marriage had not been legal and that he, not Edward's son, was the rightful king. He ordered the arrest and execution of the most powerful relatives of the Queen Mother. Edward and his brother were put in the Tower of London and an intimidated Parliament, which probably preferred an experienced man to a boy-king anyway, declared the Proctor as the rightful ruler. He was crowned as King Richard III (1452; reigned 1483-1485).

These events called Richard's motives into question. He was seen by some as a wicked uncle who acted in his own interests and not those of his nephews. Shakespeare expressed such thoughts in his play "Richard III" (circa 1593). Others think the boys might have been

125

murdered by another individual or perhaps they just became ill and died. Almost 200 years later, the bones of two children were found buried in an old chest in the tower. These may have been the remains of the unfortunate children.

Richard III did not keep the crown long. It was taken from him by Henry Tudor, who claimed the right to be king based on his mother's relationship to John of Gaunt, founder of the House of Lancaster. He also had descended from Edward III. Henry returned from France in 1485 and invaded England. He defeated and killed Richard III at Bosworth Field, the last battle in the Wars of the Roses, and so became Henry VII, the first of the Tudor line.

## 107.  England Under Henry VII

Henry VII's long struggle for the English throne did not end when he became king (1457; reigned 1485-1509) even though he married Elizabeth, and united the houses of York and Lancaster. The early part of his reign was disturbed by the Yorkists, who tried twice to place impostors on the throne, both of which were unsuccessful.

Henry VII's reign was characterized by the gathering of a vast treasure, which he left to his successor. He also sought alliances with Spain and Scotland through the marriages of his children. The marriage of his daughter Margaret, who became the wife of James IV, king of that realm (1473; reigned 1488-1513), united the two countries under a single crown.

It was also during Henry VII's reign that the great geographical discoveries were made that broadened man's understanding of his world. Henry commissioned John Cabot, a Venetian navigator, and his sons to make explorations for England in the western and northern seas (see section 111).

## 108.  Scotland Under James I

When King Robert III died in 1406, his young son technically became King James I of Scotland but he was not actually crowned until eighteen years later (1394; reigned 1424-1437). On a trip to France in 1406, James fell into the hands of some English sailors who sent him to Henry IV. Henry refused to ask for a ransom for James but did confine him first to the tower, then to the castle at Nottingham, and finally at Evesham. Henry IV saw to it that the young lad was properly tutored.

When Henry V became king in 1413, James was again sent to the tower, but shortly thereafter he was taken to Windsor where he was treated with kindness. A treaty was signed at York in 1423 between Scotland and England and James was released upon the payment of a "maintenance fee," thus ending one of the strangest kidnapping-hostage stories of the millennium. Another term of this treaty permitted James to marry Jane Beaufort, daughter of John Beaufort, Earl of Somerset.

James returned to Scotland during April, 1424, and his coronation took place there in May of that year. James instituted a period of constitutional sovereignty in Scotland which reduced the power of the king and the nobles. During his absence, Robert, Duke of Albany, had ruled in Scotland as Regent until his death in 1420, when he was succeeded by his son Murdoch. James arrested Murdoch, his son Alexander, Albany's eldest son and Duncan, Earl of Lennox. They were put on trial and executed. Other efforts were made to bring order to the Highlands and many earldoms were forfeited. But this aggression aroused the anger of some of the nobles who sought revenge. James was killed by Sir Robert Graham (died 1437) who stabbed the king in 1437.

## 109. Spain and Portugal

While England and France were rising to leadership in western Europe, nation-building was also going on in the peninsula south of the Pyrenees. After the conquest of Spain by the Moors in 711, events in Spain did not have much part in the political story of Europe, but not all of Spain was conquered by the Moors. Certain districts in the northern part remained Christian. Little by little, these Christian principalities extended their territory at the expense of the Moors; and there was nothing left under Moorish control (circa 1400) except the district in the south, centering in the famed city of Granada.

Some of the Christian principalities united with others, until eventually two kingdoms in particular became notable— Castile in the central part and Aragon in the northeast. Ferdinand V (1452-1516), who became king of Aragon and Sicily (reigned 1479-1516), married (1469) Isabella I (1451-1504), heiress to the crown of Castile (reigned 1474-1504), and, therefore, these two kingdoms became one. The Kingdom of Spain then included almost all of the peninsula, except Portugal which had grown up separately.

One especially memorable year in Spanish history was 1492. This was the year of Columbus's famous voyage (see section 111). It was also the year when Spain's long-standing struggle with the Moors ended and the city of Granada was captured. These events added to the dominions of Ferdinand V and Isabella I after ten years of struggle. In its entirety, the peninsula belonged once more to the Christians.

The rule of Ferdinand and Isabella saw a reign of law and order and peace which had been unknown before. Efforts were made to put down robber barons who plundered travelers on the highways. Religious zeal, however, led the king and queen to one great mistake when Ferdinand (sometimes called "Ferdinand the Catholic") established the Inquisition in 1478. He attempted to expel the Jews (1492) and later tried to do the same with the Moors who would not convert to Christianity. These "heretics" were sometimes even put to death. In this way Spain lost some of her most active and brightest citizens. Tomas de Torquemada (1420-1498) became the Grand Inquisitor of Castile and Aragon in 1492 after having been appointed by Pope Alexander VI (1431; served 1492-1503). He was also very close to Ferdinand and Isabella and served as their confessor. Francisco Ximenes (1436-1517) later served in this capacity and was named Archbishop of Toledo by Isabella in 1495.

The end of this century, then, saw a third strong kingdom in western Europe—Spain—take its place beside France and England. Portugal for many years stood almost on a par with Spain, and both were the leading powers of Europe in discovery, trade, and conquest for a considerable period of time.

---

**Reflection:**

*In expelling the Jews and Moors from Spain, Ferdinand and Isabella followed a practice that had known before in other times and places and which would be repeated in later years in countries like Nazi Germany. How can religious and racial prejudices handicap rather than help a nation? Would Jesus have approved of such acts?*

---

## 110. The Ottoman Turks and the Fall of Constantinople

When the Mongols were on the move, some other peoples tried to get out of their way by going to the west. One band took its name from the name of its leader, Othman. These were the Ottoman Turks or Ottomans. Othman (circa 578; reigned 644-656) was the third Moslem caliph and the son-in-law of Mohammed. Without very much trouble, these Turks conquered nearly all of Asia Minor. Constantinople held out against them for a considerable time. Without waiting for its capture, the Turks pressed on into Europe. They were on the banks of the Danube in 1400 and still going. The Christian rulers of western Europe either could not or would not send help to the eastern emperor, and after a brave struggle, the famous city on the Bosporus had to surrender to the Turks. Some consider the year in which this happened (1453) as the dividing line between medieval and modern history.

## 111. The Discovery of the New World

During this century Spain and Portugal were ready to launch out for their share of the world trade. There was not much use in trying to get to Asia by way of Alexandria or Constantinople, because Venice and Genoa had these routes pretty well "sewed up." Besides, the Ottoman Turks made it less easy and less healthful for Christians to do business in the Near East. Why not try to find some other way to India? Suddenly the idea of reaching the east by sailing west seemed very logical.

Confidence that such voyages could be made came partly from the findings of Henry the Navigator (1394-1460) who for forty years had dedicated himself to exploration and the study of geography. He was the fifth son of King John I (circa 1357; reigned 1385-1433) of Portugal and he left the royal court when he was twenty-four years old to build himself a naval observatory near Cape Saint Vincent, the southwestern point of Portugal. There he surrounded himself with scholars and mapmakers. Henry planned expeditions, worked with compasses and other technical instruments, drew new maps, and talked to his sea captains. At that time, very little was known about the features of the world outside of Europe. The nearest continent, Africa, had been explored only along the Mediterranean coast. Prince Henry sent his ships down the west coast of Africa and out onto the Atlantic Ocean. Under Henry's direction, colonies were established on the islands of Madeira and the Azores. The Cape Verde Islands were discovered also.

The influence of Paolo dal Pozzo Toscanelli (1397-1482) must be

129

mentioned. He sent a chart of the world he had prepared to Columbus. This map agreed with Polo's data and logically refuted the Ptolemaic view of the world. This encouraged Columbus in his theory that he could reach India by sailing westward.

Christopher Columbus (circa 1451-1506) was the eldest son of Domenico Colombo (Italian form of "Columbus") and Suzanna Fontanarossa. He was born in Genoa, Italy, and in 1477 he settled in Lisbon, marrying the daughter of a Portuguese navigator and living in the atmosphere of the great period of Portuguese exploration. He was probably one of many men of his day who thought that it would be possible to reach the east by sailing west. The uniqueness of Columbus's position lies in the fact that he persisted in his efforts to find sponsorship for his dreams. Years later, he found himself at the court of Ferdinand and Isabella who agreed to sponsor him in his quest for a route to the east.

Columbus began his voyage in the *Santa Maria* on August 3, 1492, accompanied by the *Nina* and the *Pinta*. He set out thinking that he would reach India or China. When he did sight land in the Bahamas at 2:00 a.m. on October 12, 1492, he thought he had reached the East Indian Islands. In so doing, he found the opportunity to rename a whole race of people when he called them "Indians."

Portugal also got a share of the New World. Bartholomeu Dias (circa 1450-1500) rounded the cape (1487) which was soon named the Cape of Good Hope. Ten years later Vasco da Gama (circa 1460-1524) followed the same route but kept going toward the north and east, eventually reaching Calicut, India (1498). The explorer Pedro Alvares Cabral (circa 1460-circa 1526) reached Brazil in 1500 and claimed it for his king, Manuel I (1469; reigned 1495-1521). Thus, part of the New World came under the flag of Portugal.

The English explorer, John Cabot (1461-1498), discovered the North American coast at a point usually thought to be Cape Breton Island. In 1498 he again sailed for America to explore the coast. The English claims in North America were based on his discoveries.

Pope Alexander VI, in order to avert arguments between Spain and Portugal about their discoveries, set up a dividing line 300 miles west of the Azores (1493). All new lands found west of that line were to go to Spain; all that were located east of it were to go to Portugal. This was the famous Bull of Demarcation. A little later, the line was moved farther west and accepted by treaty between the two countries (1494). This treaty was called the Treaty of Tordesillas because it was signed in the Spanish town of the same name.

## God in History

Q.  What were some of the problems that beset the medieval church before  and during this century?  What great changes in history was  God getting ready to introduce to solve some of these problems?

A.  The real tragedy of the medieval church was that it did not adjust to the times.  Instead of being progressive and  providing a spiritual lead, it looked backward and became corrupt.  How did the popes, who claimed apostolic succession, fail even to provide the needed  spiritual leadership?  What was the cause of  these problems?

By  the  end  of this century, the  church,  with  parishes, monasteries, and convents throughout its domain, had  become  the largest  landholder in all Europe.  It owned as much as half  the land in France and Germany and a great deal in Sweden  and  England. To maintain this property, ecclesiastical appointees  were required to remit to the papal Curia (the administrative  bureaus  of  the papacy) half the income of their offices for  the  first year and annually therefore, a tenth or tithe.  A new  archbishop had  to  pay a substantial sum for the pallium (a band  of  white wool that served as the confirmation and insignia of his authority).   Whenever a church official died, his possessions  reverted to the papacy.  Things were so bad during this time that a common saying was: "If you want to ruin your son, make him a priest."

Even so, God was not ready to stand back  and  allow  this state of affairs to continue.  At the dawning of  the  sixteenth century, the Reformation and the Counter Reformation took place.

## Chapter Endnotes

5-1 The Celsus referred to here is not to be confused with the second century Roman philosopher by the same name whose writings opposed Christianity.

5-2  During the medieval period the barber was closely aligned with medicine and the practice of surgery. The barber's sign consisted of a striped pole, from which was suspended a basin. The use of these symbols, usually in modified form, could still be found commonly in America and Europe as late the middle of the last century in this millennium, and rarely, in its last decade. The separation of the barber from the practice of surgery had, of course, long been over by then.

5-3 The Treaty of Troyes (1420) was an agreement between Henry V of England, Charles VI of France, and Philip the Good of Burgundy, that was intended to settle the issues of the Hundred Years' War. Henry, who was to marry Charles's daughter Catherine, was recognized as "heir of France," while Charles was permitted to retain the royal title till his death. The dauphin, later Charles VII, did not honor the treaty.

## Chapter Terms

| | | |
|---|---|---|
| Academia Pontaniana | humanism | Proctor |
| barber-surgeon | italic type | sweating sickness |
| Bull of Demarcation | Maid of Orleans | utopia |
| Dauphin | portolani | |

## Chapter Review Questions/Exercises

1. List some of the accomplishments of man in the fifteenth century as related in the Overview to this chapter.
2. List some important Renaissance artists. (95)
3. Who was an important advocate of humanism? (96)
4. Who were the "Oxford Reformers?" and why were they called by that name? (96)
5. What was the main purpose of the stained glass window? (97)
6. Describe Fountains Abbey in the fifteenth century. (98)
7. Who was Abbot Huby? (98).
8. What were some important activities in this century that preceded the Reformation and who was involved in them? (99)
9. Why was the struggle known as the Hundred Years' War revived in the fifteenth century and who was mainly responsible for it? (100-101)

10. Discuss the details of the Hundred Years' War in the fifteenth century. Be sure to include Joan of Arc and Charles VII in your discussion. (100-104).
11. What were the Wars of the Roses? (105)
12. Discuss the matter of Edward IV's successor in England. (106)
13. What were some of the important accomplishments of Henry VII's reign in England? (107)
14. Discuss the matter of James I's rule of Scotland. (108)
15. What were some of the important accomplishments of Spain and Portugal in the fifteenth century? (109)
16. Why did Ferdinand and Isabella establish the Inquisition? How were the Jews and Moors treated? (109)
17. Describe the events that contributed to the downfall of Constantinople. Why is the year 1453 sometimes called the dividing line between medieval and modern history? (110)
18. Discuss the events leading up to the discovery of the New World. Name the important people who participated in this great adventure. (111)
19. What was the Bull of Demarcation? (111)

# 6

# 1501-1600

## {Noon - 2:23 p.m.}

---

It is noon. Our day is half over. The light of day shines on the Renaissance and the coming Reformation. Sometime during the next two hours and twenty-three minutes, Miguel de Cervantes (1547-1616) will pen the words "...honour is dearer to me than my life," in his work, *Don Quixote*.

John Heywood (circa 1497-1578), will write many wise sayings. Among them will be, "One good turn deserves another," "Give an inch (and they will) take a mile," and "Would you both eat your cake and have your cake?"

Nostradamus (1503-1566), the French astrologer and physician, will publish his controversial book *Centuries* (1555), which will contain his predictions for the future. It has been suggested that one of these predicts World War III (1999).

---

135

# Matters of the Christian Church

## 112. The Reformation

The movement which we call the Reformation, or the Protestant Revolt, began in part around the life and activities of Martin Luther (1483-1546) [see figure 6-1], a German monk. Luther was born to a peasant family in Saxony. His parents gave him a good education; and after some excellent preaching, he became professor of theology at the University of Wittenberg (1507). While there, he probably met George Burckhardt (1484-1545) who also was known by his assumed last name of Spalatin, after the town of his birth, Spalt, near Nuremberg. Spalatin exercised a vast influence over Luther and became his chief counselor in moral and religious matters.

Luther became upset over certain teachings of the church because he was convinced that the Bible teaches that salvation comes through faith rather than as a result of good works. He was aroused by the selling of *indulgences* in Germany by a friar named Johann Tetzel (circa 1465-1519). An *indulgence* was a grant of relief from some of the experiences which a soul might otherwise have to pass through in purgatory. It was intended to be given only in consideration of some pious deed or gift of money made by one who had repented of his wrongs. The sale of indulgences was strongly encouraged by Pope Leo X (served 1513-1521) who saw this as an acceptable means of raising money for the rebuilding of Saint Peter's Church in Rome, founded in 326, which had become unstable. Tetzel sold indulgences so freely that the matter of repentance could not get proper emphasis. Some who bought indulgences looked upon them virtually as permissions to keep on sinning.

Luther was so angered by the sale of indulgences, and other matters, that he nailed on the church door in Wittenberg his ninety-five "theses," or propositions (1517). These were written in Latin, and he challenged anybody to debate them with him. They were afterward translated into German and circulated generally all over the country. Luther soon went further and denied the authority of the pope, declaring that the Bible was the sole rule of faith and practice.

Luther was ordered to appear before a diet (a council) at the city of Worms in 1521. He was accompanied there by Justus Jonas

(1493-1555), the great German Protestant reformer. While there, Jonas aided the Reformation through his gifts as a translator, transcribing Luther's works into Latin. When Luther was asked to recant, he declared: "Unless I am proved wrong by Scripture or plain reason, I cannot and will not recant, because to act against conscience is unholy and unsafe. Here I stand. So help me God, I cannot do otherwise." The decision of the diet was against him, and he was proclaimed a heretic and an outlaw.

Frederick III the Wise, elector of Saxony (1463; served 1486-1525), insisted that Luther take refuge in one of the castles of Franz von Sickingen (1481-1523), the great German knight and strong supporter of the Reformation who offered his castles as places of refuge for harassed reformers. Luther went to Wartburg Castle (May, 1521), assumed the name of Junker Jorg, and stayed there for ten months while the excitement died down. There he translated the New Testament into German (1522) and began a translation of the Old Testament the next year (completed in 1534). These works had religious and literary importance since they helped to give the German language a definite literary form. Luther also wrote hymns and treatises on religious topics.

---

**Reflection:**

*Men are not often called of God to such greatness as was Luther. At a time when it was extremely dangerous to do so, he succeeded in forcing the pope into a position where he could not entirely prevent the preaching of God's Word. Consider how Christians should always monitor the institutions of religion and how they function in the light of God's will.*

---

## 113. Disagreement Among Protestant Leaders

Some German Protestants did not completely agree with Luther's teachings. There arose in Germany (1521) the Anabaptists who believed in withholding baptism until it could be preceded by a confession of faith in Jesus Christ after a person was old enough to understand its meaning. They also believed that Christians should renounce private possessions. They were persecuted by Catholics and Protestants alike, including Luther.

Disagreement among Protestants was also found outside of Germany where other Protestant organizations were formed. The Mennonites, an offshoot of the Anabaptists, took their name from Menno Simons (circa 1496-1561), the Dutch religious reformer. They did not believe in holding public office, refused to take oaths, and sought holiness by discipline.

The first notable Swiss reformer was Huldreich Zwingli (1484-1531), of Zurich. He declared that parish priests should be elected by the people of their parish, and said that every individual had the right to interpret the Bible for himself. An effort was made to bring Luther and Zwingli together, but Luther would not make any concessions on the points where their opinions differed. War broke out in Switzerland between Catholic and Protestant parties, and Zwingli was killed in battle.

The other great Swiss reformer was John Calvin (1509-1564). He was born in France. He believed that Luther's ideas were more nearly correct than the Catholic doctrines but, like Zwingli, did not entirely agree with Luther. Finding it dangerous to stay in France, he established himself in Geneva.

The Presbyterian Church can be traced back to Calvin's Reformed Church in Switzerland. For a number of years Calvin was the virtual ruler of the city. He set up high standards of conduct for the people. He insisted on a close observance of the Sabbath and allowed little in the way of amusement. He himself lived very plainly—in poverty—and opposed showy churches, believing that they distracted attention from the essentials of ministry. Geneva under his rule was a notable example of what came to be called Puritanism in England being carried into the everyday life of the people.

John Knox (circa 1505-1572), who was with Calvin in Geneva for some time, carried his teachings to Scotland where he gained the support of such zealous Reformationists as James Hamilton (circa 1515-1575). Presbyterianism became the established religion in that country. Some people in England also accepted Calvin's views, as did the majority of the Dutch. Many settlers in the English colonies of the New World who came to secure religious freedom for themselves brought Calvin's ideas along with them. In France, also, it was Calvin's variety of Protestantism that became popular instead of Luther's (the French Huguenots accepted his teachings).

# A Reformation in the Catholic Church

In the early years of the Protestant movement, the Roman Catholic Church tried to counteract the effects of the reformers chiefly by taking stern measures against the leaders of the Reformation. An important diet was held at Speyer, Germany (1529), which gave complete toleration to Catholics in Lutheran states, denied toleration to Lutherans in Catholic states, and refused toleration to Zwinglians and Anabaptists altogether. It was at this time that the term Protestant was first used by those who issued a formal protest against the closing of this meeting. The Inquisition was also used to suppress the Reformation.

Some Catholic leaders responded to the Reformation in milder ways. Pope Leo X, who had encouraged the sale of indulgences which were protested by Luther, was as interested in art as he was in the religious activities of the church. Others dedicated part of their efforts to promoting the interests of their relatives. Some Catholics may have felt that the reform movement would break up anyway.

## 114. The Society of Jesus

One of the first movements which helped to revive Catholic strength was the *Society of Jesus* or the *Jesuit Order.* A Spanish soldier named Inigo Lopez de Recalde (1491-1556), who was later made Saint Ignatius of Loyola, while lying wounded, was given several Christian books to read. He determined then to live the rest of his life on behalf of the church. He put away his military outfits and founded the Society of Jesus in 1534, which was organized somewhat like an army and made up of men who were just as willing to sacrifice themselves for the church as a soldier would be willing to sacrifice his life for a king or an emperor.

Jesuits soon became powerful. They founded schools in many countries which gave the people the best teaching then available. Some children of Protestant parents even attended such schools and often they became interested in Catholic religious teaching. Some Jesuits became advisers to kings and other prominent people. Jesuit missionaries went out to every part of the world.

The Jesuit Saint Francis Xavier (1506-1552), the "Apostle of the Indies" won thousands of converts in Asia. After the discovery of

Japan, he sailed there (1549) where he conducted valiant missionary efforts. Missionaries under Xavier first made converts in parts of Ceylon (1544). Other heroic Jesuits went to the New World and worked as missionaries in French Canada and in the Spanish colonies in Mexico and South America.

## 115. The Ursulines

Another institution formed to strengthen the Roman Catholic Church was the Ursulines, an order of nuns founded in 1535 by Saint Angela dei Merici (1470-1540). This order, named for Saint Ursula (found living circa fourth century), the virgin martyr of Cologne, was organized in order to nurse the sick, educate young women, attend to the wants of the poor, and sanctify the lives of its members. Pope Paul III confirmed the foundation of this order in 1544.

## 116. The Index

After the invention of the printing press it was easy for books to be circulated that contained teachings contrary to Roman Catholic beliefs. To prevent Catholics from reading them, the pope prepared a list of books which were forbidden to Catholics. This was known as the *Index Librorum Prohibitorum,* or simply the *Index.* The first such catalog had been published (400) long before the invention of the printing press, but the one mentioned here was completed at the direction of Pope Paul IV in 1557. The Index forbade the reading of the writings of Luther, Calvin, and the other reformers. Included also were a number of books relating to magic and some of the sciences, but bishops could allow educated people to read some of the works on the prohibited list when they thought it was appropriate.

# Matters of Church and State

## 117. Theories and Practices of the Monarchs of This Period

Almost any king or prince in Europe during this era would have avowed that he was the government of his country, that he had been put upon the throne by the will of God himself. This belief stemmed in part from Paul's statement in the Letter to Rome, "The powers that be are ordained of God." (See Romans 13). Kings, then, ruled by "divine right," and nobody had the privilege of questioning what a monarch might do.

To most people, this notion did not seem particularly out of place. A country had to have a leader. If not to their king, where would people look for leadership? A king was expected to stand up for the rights of his country, but it was not always easy to see the extent to which a king looked out for his own selfish interests as well.

Inexorably attached to this political philosophy was Niccolo Machiavelli (1469-1527), an Italian statesman and writer. He proved to be a very capable observer and spent much of his life studying men and political systems. He was the first true political scientist of the modern world. He began to study men, not according to some preconception, but as he found them. He drew his conclusions from the nature of mankind itself, noting a decided absence of conscience in some political leaders.

In addition Machiavelli held a profound concern for the citizens of Italy who were still largely steeped in and victimized by medieval political thinking (those who had not been touched by the Renaissance). Indeed the peninsula was generally divided into principalities and sovereign cities, each of which claimed autocratic jurisdiction. These separate despotisms had nothing of significance in common but were connected by a network of conflicting interests and ever-changing diplomatic combinations.

Machiavelli's theories, expressed in his best-known work, *The Prince* (1532), must be examined against this background. Italy had suffered much under the feudal system and Machiavelli believed that the people of Italy, to move out of these outmoded medieval ways of living, would have to submit to a powerful centralized gov- ernment. He thus predicted the rise of the absolute monarchs that were soon to come and he viewed it as the next logical step in European development. It was not so much that he was in favor of this development but his knowledge of politics enabled him to foresee it. He did not live long enough, of course, to see the absolute monarchs reach the point where they had outlived their purpose.

As he predicted, there soon arose rulers who had no higher ambition than to live in luxury and tyrannize a helpless people. These rulers were selfish, weak, and foolish. They were not generally given to making exceptions when dealing with religious matters either.

141

## 118. France Under Charles IX

It was during the reign of Charles IX (1550; reigned 1560-1574), second son of Henry II and Catherine de Medici, that the persecution of the Huguenots (as the French Protestants of the sixteenth and seventeenth centuries were called) reached a peak in what became known as the Saint Bartholomew's Day Massacre (August 24, 1572). The conflict continued for perhaps six weeks thereafter.

Prior to this (1569), the Huguenots and Catholics had met and made peace with each other. They agreed then that Prince Henry of Navarre, the Huguenot leader (who later became king Henry IV of France [1553; reigned 1589-1610]), would marry Margaret of Valois, the sister of King Charles IX. They were married in Paris a few days before the massacre.

One of the most important Huguenot leaders who attended the wedding was Admiral Gaspard de Coligny (1519-1572). Because of his influence with Charles (he was Charles's chief adviser), Catherine tried unsuccessfully to have him killed. So she tried, along with son Henry (who would soon reign as king Henry III (1551; reigned 1574-1589) to convince Charles that the Huguenots wanted to seize the throne. Charles then agreed to sign the death warrant of the supposed traitors but wanted to make sure there were no Protestants left to avenge the killing. Consequently armed men attacked Huguenots wherever they met them and murdered them without mercy. The massacre spread to so many French towns that thousands of Protestants were murdered within the weeks that followed. Catholic sympathizers, such as Philippe de Croy Arschot (1526-1595), who became governor-general of Flanders, expressed delight at the news of the event. Pope Gregory XIII (1502; served 1572-1585) himself was surprised by the massacre since he had long doubted Catherine's and Charles's devotion to the church—a fact that had been reinforced when Charles sanctioned his sister's marriage to a professed heretic. In celebration of the event, a mass was held in the Church of San Luigi de' Francesi and a high mass was held by Gregory (some sources say he had been told that the massacre was the suppression of a rebellion). A medal was also struck in honor of the event with Gregory's likeness on one side and an angel with a cross and a sword pursuing the heretics on the other side.

The conflict between the French kings and the Huguenots was part of a broader conflict which involved the struggle for power between the crown and the great nobles and the rivalry among the great nobles themselves for the control of the king. These conflicts continued until 1598. They were settled with the Edict of Nantes, which granted freedom of worship throughout France and established Protestantism in 200 towns, and with the Treaty of Vervins with Spain (both in 1598).

## 119. England Breaks Away From the Pope

Henry VIII (1491; reigned 1509-1547) followed his father, Henry VII to the throne. Soon after he was crowned, he married his brother Arthur's widow, Princess Catherine of Aragon (1485-1536), a dispensation having been obtained from Pope Julius II (served 1503-1513). During his first years as king, he left most of the affairs of state to his minister, Cardinal Thomas Wolsey (circa 1475-1530).

In religions matters, Henry gained the favor of the church when he wrote a pamphlet (1521) vigorously defending the Roman Catholic Church against Luther. Pope Leo X was so pleased with this defenses of the church that he gave Henry the title of "Defender of the Faith." English kings still include that as a part of their official title, though they no longer support the Roman Catholic Church (see below).

The church was also pleased by the persecution in England of certain reformers such as William Tyndale (1492-1536) who became very unpopular when he began translating the Bible and was forced to leave England for Germany. There he completed his work and had his translation published and circulated in England and other countries. His work, *The Obedience of a Christian Man* (1528), was not looked upon with favor in England either. There Tyndale was condemned for heresy, thrown in jail, and put to death for his efforts.

Though Henry gained favor with the Roman Catholic Church in attacking Protestantism, he was the first English monarch to break away from the church. Trouble started between Henry and Pope Clement VII (served 1523-1534) when he could not get the pope to set aside his marriage to Princess Catherine. Henry had become interested in a young lady of his court named Anne Boleyn (circa 1507-1536). The pope could not agree to this separation without offending the King of Spain, whose support was more important to the pope than Henry's. Besides, there was not sufficient reason under church laws for an annulment or a divorce.

Then there was the problem presented by Elizabeth Barton (circa

1506-1534) who, after an illness in 1525, began going into trances and uttering prophecies which were thought to be of divine origin. Also known as the "Maid of Kent," she began to foretell dire consequences to Henry if he should divorce Catherine and marry Anne Boleyn. Her correspondence with many notables made the maid's political importance great, and she was a serious obstacle to Henry.

To counter this and other types of opposition, Henry sent John Stokesley (circa 1475-1539) as ambassador to France (1529) and Italy (1530) to gain opinions from foreign universities in favor of the king's desired separation. Later, securing the goodwill of such important officials as Thomas Audley (circa 1488-1544), Lord Chancellor of England, he took things into his own hands. He disposed of the maid by having her arraigned after which she confessed herself to be an impostor. She was put to death for treason. He also had his marriage to Catherine set aside.

Anne Boleyn did not please Henry very long, and she was put to death on a charge of unfaithfulness. Her daughter, Princess Elizabeth, later became Queen Elizabeth I (see sections 121 -123), "Good Queen Bess," one of the most famous rulers of English history. Jane Seymour (circa 1509-1537), Henry's third wife (married 1536), was the mother of a prince who later ruled as Edward VI (1537; reigned 1547-1553).

Anne of Cleves (1515-1557), Henry's fourth wife, did not last long either because of her looks. "She was no better than a Flanders mare," Henry said, and the marriage was declared null and void by *convocation* (an assembly of clergymen and others to consider a matter).

Henry had six wives in all as a result of his quest for a wife who could bear him a son. Finally he married his last wife, Catherine Parr (1512-1548), who outlived him. How different would his life have been had he known of the discovery, made in the twentieth century, that the sex of a child is determined by its father?

As part of his break with the church, Henry persuaded Parliament to pass the Act of Supremacy (1534), which declared that Henry was the "only supreme head on earth of the Church of England." Thus originated the Great Schism of the West.

Henry did not call himself a Protestant and made only minor changes in the church rituals, such as the reinstatement of the use of ashes on Ash Wednesday (1538). This was a practice which had not survived the Reformation. He also had the Bible translated into English and used in church services but he did away with all the wealthy monasteries, keeping for himself as much of their property as he wanted. Henry dissolved the religious houses in England (1536-1540), closing more than 140 nunneries. The Anglican Church was left without sisterhoods for 300 years.

Henry's break with the Roman Catholic Church did not end religious persecution in England. It simply became wrong to speak against the English church. Anne Askew (born circa 1521) was first racked and then sent to the stake (1546) for questioning the doctrine of transubstantiation which had originally been a Roman Catholic belief. While she was in Newgate Prison, she composed a poem of fourteen stanzas which she called "The Fight of Faith." In the first stanza she compared herself to an "...armed Knighte," with faith as her shield. In stanza eleven she referred to Henry VIII in the following way:

> I sawe a royall throne,
> Where Justice shulde have sitte;
> But in her steade was One
> Of moody cruell witte.

---

**Reflection:**

*Some of the dangers involved with mixing church and state are revealed by these events. Consider how Christians should constantly monitor the involvement of government in the affairs of the church. What are the benefits of keeping these institutions separate?*

---

## 120. England Under Mary I

When Lady Grey's short reign (nine days) came to an end (see chapter endnote 6-2) she was followed by Edward's half-sister Mary I (1516; reigned 1553-1558) who was also known as Mary Tudor, the daughter of Henry VIII's first wife, Catherine of Aragon. She was a Roman Catholic because that was the religion of her mother, and she was as sincerely determined as the rulers of Spain were to root out Protestantism. Partly to get the help of Spain, she married the heir apparent to the throne, Philip II (1527; reigned 1556-1598) in 1554;

but though she loved him, he apparently did not care for her, and her reign proved to be an unhappy one. She so persecuted prominent English Protestants that they called her "Bloody Mary," and people turned away from her. In a war with France she lost the town of Calais, the last territory England held in France.

## 121. Elizabeth's Religious Policy

Next Elizabeth, the daughter of Anne Boleyn, came to the throne. Her long reign (1558-1603) {1:22 p.m.-2:27 p.m.} was a most notable one in the history of England. Because of the circumstances of her mother's marriage to Henry VIII, the pope refused to recognize her as Queen of England. She was, therefore, obliged to turn for support to the Protestants. A second Act of Supremacy was passed in 1559, which made the English ruler the titular (in name only) head of the Church of England. The so-called "Thirty-nine Articles" were adopted as the official covenant of the Anglican Church. Elizabeth found allies in such clergymen as Richard Hooker (circa 1554-1600) who authored the *Laws of Ecclesiastical Polity,* which became a formidable defense of the Church of England directed particularly against the Independents and Presbyterians.

There were some persecutions of Catholics under Elizabeth, but they were handled in such a way that little unfavorable feeling was aroused. Mary's persecutions of Protestants, however, aroused considerable unfavorable reactions. As time went on and England became involved in trouble with Spain, English people became so patriotic that even the leading Catholics of the country were loyal to Elizabeth as their queen.

# Matters of State

## 122. England and Scotland

Elizabeth was greatly embarrassed by the presence in England of her cousin Mary Stuart (sometimes Stewart) (1542-1587; reigned 1542-1567), Queen of Scotland, and popularly remembered as Mary, Queen of Scots. Mary also was descended from Henry VII, Elizabeth's grandfather, and she had a good claim to the throne of England whenever Elizabeth's claim might be set aside.

Mary's first husband was King Francis II of France (1544; reigned 1559-1560), son of Henry II and Catherine de Medici. She married him in April, 1558, and Francis became king upon his father's accidental death (July, 1559). But Francis himself died in 1560 in Orleans. He and Mary went there from Chenonceaux where Francis became violently ill from a malady in his ear which had tortured him for some time. The poor young king took to his bed, never to rise again. His mother, Catherine, followed him there, and at Mary's insistence the great barber-surgeon Ambrose Pare' (see section 128) was summoned. He wanted to operate but Catherine opposed the use of surgery. The unfortunate Francis lingered a few days in great pain, and finally died in the arms of his wife.

Mary's second husband, Lord Darnley, otherwise known as Henry Stuart (1545-1567), was murdered, but out of this marriage was born a son in 1566 who, while still a baby, became James VI of Scotland in 1567 on the forced abdication of his mother. He later reigned as king of Great Britain and Ireland as James I (see sections 137 and 140). Three months after Darnley was murdered Mary was wed to James Hepburn Bothwell (1535-1578), a man whom many suspected was the murderer of Darnley. Scottish leaders who were Presbyterians disliked Mary, a strong Catholic, and obliged her to give up the throne in favor of her young son James. Before leaving to take refuge in England, Mary nominated James Hamilton as one of her regents in an effort to regain favor there. Hamilton continued his unwelcome support of Mary until he acknowledged James's authority (February, 1573).

While in England, Elizabeth kept Mary virtually as a prisoner for nineteen years. Plots were made to get rid of Elizabeth in order to put Mary on the throne. Elizabeth, finally convinced that she was not safe as long as Mary lived, had her put to death in 1587.

James, at the age of twenty-one, behaved poorly in regards to his mother's execution. It has been suggested that he so longed to escape the poverty and insecurity of Scotland for the richer English throne, that he selfishly dared not to offend Elizabeth by objecting to her decision regarding his mother. Such selfishness characterized his reign over Scotland. He was obviously capable of trickery and deception. He made promises that he later did not keep and many that he was incapable of keeping under any circumstances. He reduced feudalism and enforced the superiority of the state over the church. When he came to power in England (1603), he was accepted as the alternative to a civil war, but he did not win the respect of the English people (see sections 137 and 140).

## 123. England and Spain

The unfriendliness between England and Spain, the chief defender of the Roman Catholic Church, soon became keen. Part of this unfriendliness grew out of the activities of the English navy. Until the days of Queen Elizabeth, Englishmen bothered very little with the New World, in spite of Cabot's exploration of North America during 1497. Now, however, such reckless, hardy seamen as Sir John Hawkins (1532-1595) and Sir Francis Drake (circa 1540-1596) came to the front. Hawkins was a slave trader—one who could hold religious services on ships carrying men to be sold as slaves. Hawkins, Drake, and others like them entered the harbors of Spanish colonies without permission from anybody, plundered Spanish merchant vessels, and made themselves general nuisances to the Spaniards.

Another conflict arose on the European continent at this time— the revolt of the Dutch against Spanish cruelty. Elizabeth secretly gave help to the Dutch and allowed Englishmen to go over and help them fight. Finally Philip II decided to punish England. He got together a fleet which the Spaniards called the "Invincible Armada." Under the leadership of Drake and Hawkins, the English assembled the best fleet they could by way of defense. As the Spanish fleet came through the English Channel, it was attacked by the English vessels. Then a tremendous storm assailed the Spanish vessels, and in desperation they tried to get back home by going north around Scotland. The battle, the storm, and the other dangers of the journey dealt great damage to the Spanish fleet. Only about one-third of the Armada ever returned to Spain.

The year in which the Armada met such a terrible disaster (1588), is one of the turning points in world history. Spain never again threatened England effectively. Englishmen planned for commerce and colonies in the New World without caring what Spain might do about it. Protestantism in Holland and England was safe. England had won the title of "Mistress of the Sea."

# Europe and the New World

## 124. Selecting a Name for the New World

The naming of the Americas came about in the following way. For a considerable time men continued to think that the new land seen by Columbus was projecting from the coast of Asia. Amerigo Vespucci (1454-1512), an Italian merchant, astronomer, and explorer, sailed on one expedition from Spain to the New World (1497), and returned to Spain a year later. He made a second voyage to America in 1499. Letters he wrote after he came back made a strong impression on some of their readers, including Martin Waldseemuller (circa 1470-circa 1522), a German geographer. The suggestion was offered that since he had seen probably a "fourth part" of the world, it should be named after him. And so the New World came to be called America after a man whose only service to the land that bears his name was in seeing it and writing about it.

## 125. Specific Involvement in the New World

The exploratory voyages of Columbus and others in the last decade of the previous century were quickly followed by others in this one. The Spaniard Vasco Balboa (circa 1475-1517) sailed to America in search of a fortune. He was the first European to reach the shores of the Pacific Ocean (September 25, 1513). There is some evidence to suggest that the Spanish explorer, Juan Gaetano sighted the Hawaiian Islands in 1542, but if he did, not much was made of it, and it was not until James Cook (1728-1779) first saw them in 1778, that the discovery received wide publicity.

The Portuguese navigator Ferdinand Magellan (circa 1480-1521) went farther and saw more than any explorer who preceded him. He started from Spain with an expedition in 1519 which followed south along the coast of South America and through the strait now named after him. He then continued north and west across the Pacific, only to lose his life in a fight with the natives in the Philippine Islands. One boat out of his fleet kept going, rounded the coast of Africa and finally reached home, three years after its embarkation. This epoch-making voyage put to rest many questions people had about the earth being round.

149

The Demarcation Line drawn by the pope in 1493 (see section 111), gave Central America and most of South America to Spain. Portugal received Brazil and was the first to get involved in the profitable trade with India and the East Indies. The King of France reacted to this by stating that he should like to see the clause in "Father Adam's will" that gave the world to Spain and Portugal. Later when Spain came into the Philippines, her claim to the country was not disputed by any other nation.

The Dutch turned their attention mainly to the east; and when they were at war with Spain, with which Portugal was united for a while, they helped themselves to a number of Portuguese colonies. The Dutch were the first to settle the Cape Colony at the southern end of Africa, and they occupied two regions in the western hemisphere at one time or another—Dutch Guyana in South America and what is now called New York, New Jersey, and Delaware in North America.

Seven nations thus laid claim to the New World lands. Spain, Portugal, and Holland have already been mentioned. Greenland and Iceland were held by Denmark. The Swedes lost their colony on the Delaware River to the Dutch. The greater part of North America, though, was left to the English and the French.

The French first came to the Saint Lawrence Valley in 1534 under Jacques Cartier (1491-1557) but it was sometime later before the French (or the English) actually occupied much land in the New World. They occupied large territories, the possession of which came to be challenged by the English in the conflict known in America as the French and Indian Wars (see section 139).

Sir Francis Drake was the first Englishman to undertake an expedition around the world, and it covered even more miles than the well-known voyage of Magellan. Going through what is now called Magellan's Strait, he sailed north along the western coast of the two continents as far as California. Then he turned west across the Pacific and came back to England after a thrilling three years' tour (1577-1580) {1:49 p.m.-1:54 p.m.}.

Yet England entered late in the race for colonies. Two knightly gentlemen, Humphrey Gilbert (circa 1539-1583) and Walter Raleigh (circa 1552-1618), were the first Englishmen to become involved. Gilbert tried to found a colony in Newfoundland, without success. Raleigh sent a company to settle in a district which he named Virginia, after England's Queen Elizabeth, "the Virgin Queen." Though greatly disappointed when the colony disappeared, he declared, "I shall yet live to see it an English nation." Before his death a permanent settlement had been started in 1607 at Jamestown {2:33 p.m.}. Raleigh is also remembered for having introduced both the potato and tobacco into England.

This Age of Exploration created a new interest in geography. Gerhardus Mercator (1512-1594) a Flemish geographer, became a mapmaker. He is noted most for his development of a map known as the Mercator Projection, which is a method of drawing maps with straight lines to show latitude and longitude.

### 126. Spain and Mexico

In this century Mexico was conquered by Spain. Hernando Cortes (1485-1547) landed at the site of the present city of Veracruz with about 600 men during 1519. To keep his men from returning to Spain, he set fire to his boats. He then led his soldiers on a march over the eastern mountain range of the central plateau.

During this time Montezuma II (sometimes Moctezuma) (circa 1480-1520) was the head war chief of the Aztecs. He had been made aware of the appearance of white men in America two years earlier, yet the Aztecs could not keep Cortes out of Tenochtitlan, the Aztec capital and present location of Mexico City. The Aztecs did succeed in driving out Cortes and his men but Cortes returned later in 1521 and brought Aztec power to its knees.

# Other Disciplines and Institutions

### 127. Literature and Drama in England

A most skillful English poet of his day was John Skelton (1460-1529), who became noted for his wit and humor. His poems were transitional with both medieval and modern qualities. For some time he served in the position of jester and poet laureate in the court of Henry VIII, after having served as Henry's tutor. Some of his writings included "The Garland of Laurel" and "The Tunnynge of Elynoure Rummynge." He wrote satirical verse against the great Wolsey such as "Why Come Ye Not to Courte" and "The Boke of Phyllyp Sparowe."

With the ascension of Elizabeth (reigned 1558-1603) to the throne, came one of the most glorious periods in English literary history. It is commonly known as the Elizabethan Age. Drama had, by this time, made a complete separation from the church, and secular plays were performed regularly. The writers of this age had new and daring ideas. One was Roger Ascham (circa 1515-1568) who published *On the Art of Shooting* (circa 1544), a book on how to use the long bow. John Foxe (circa 1516-1587) was noted for his monumental work, *History of the Acts and Monuments of the Church* (1563), a defense especially of Protestant reformers. It became popularly known as *Foxe's Book of Martyrs*.

It was also a time for daring writers to emerge, such as Edmund Spenser (circa 1552-1599), author of the poem *The Faery* (sometimes *Faerie*) *Queene* (1590) out of which came a new form of verse appropriately named the "Spenserian Stanza." There was Francis Bacon (also see section 129), who was noted for his political essays and the works of John Stow (circa 1525-1605), the famous historian. Stow's most famous work was his *Survay* (Sic) *of London* (1598) which described the buildings, social conditions, and customs of London during the time of Elizabeth. Nicholas Breton (circa 1555- circa 1626), became famous for his religious poems, including "I Would I Were an Excellent Divine." Then there was William Shakespeare (circa 1564-1616) {1:31 p.m.-2:46 p.m.}, clearly the most famous of all English writers of this era and quite possibly the greatest English writer of all time.

Much has been written about Shakespeare, the great poet, actor, and playwright. He was baptized in the parish church of Stratford-upon-Avon in Warwickshire (April 26, 1564). He was a glover but he also appears to have dealt from time to time in various kinds of agricultural produce. His skills as a playwright began to emerge when he was twenty-eight, when his play *Henry VI* was first performed (1592). Other performances in this century included *The Taming of the Shrew* (1594), *A Midsummer Night's Dream* (1595), and *Julius Caesar* (1599).

Because the public theaters attracted large audiences from all levels of society, pickpockets and other criminals were drawn to performances. As the Puritan influence grew in England, more and more complaints were made about the "godlessness" of the theaters, and they were occasionally closed because of the crimes, as well as for the plague. At such times the acting companies went on tour. The theaters were closed for riot and plague from June to December, 1592. The plague alone was the next cause of the closings (February-December, 1593, and February-December, 1594). They were again closed for misdemeanor crimes (July-October, 1597).

## 128. Medicine

The foundations of modern medicine were laid during this century, especially by the introduction of clinical instruction in hospitals. In Italy Giovanni de Monte (1498-1552) offered clinical lectures on the patients in the hospital of Saint Francis, which had wide influence. There was also an interest in the inspections of the dead to establish cause of death and to better study disease, though this was achieved with some difficulty against the superstitions regarding the dead.

The disease of *syphilis* was discovered in this century by the Italian physician Girolamo Fracastoro (1483-1553). He wrote an epic poem describing it and the disease takes its name from the title of that poem. Fracastoro was also the first man to describe *typhus* fever and wrote about other epidemic diseases. Indeed, he proposed the theory of rapidly multiplying invisible "seeds" of disease, centuries before bacteria (that really are such "seeds") were discovered.

In this century meaningful decisions were made in England regarding the different branches of the medical profession. Thomas Linacre (sometimes Lynaker) (circa 1460-1524) of Canterbury, became an important physician. He was disappointed by the lack of any proper regulation of medical practices in London. In 1518 he obtained from Henry VIII a charter for a group of physicians to examine and license practitioners of medicine. Except for graduates of Oxford and Cambridge, who were exempt from the examination, this group decided who was fit to practice medicine in the city of London and its surrounding territory. The organization that Linacre founded became the famous Royal College of Physicians of London (1551). It was also decided that the barbers, who had been similarly incorporated in 1540, should confine themselves to the minor operations of blood-letting and the drawing of teeth, while the surgeons were prohibited from "barbery or shaving." It was not until the nineteenth century that the practice of dentistry was regarded as a separate profession.

In addition to the physicians and surgeons there were many irregular practitioners who were harassed by the establishment which felt that these unlicensed practitioners improperly intruded into their area of responsibility. Thus it became necessary to pass an act for their protection and toleration in 1543. Since many of these practitioners were in the business of preparing medicines, the term apothecary was used to distinguish them from the others. This was a logical designation for this class of practitioners since the term had been used by Galen to denote the place where he kept his medicines.

The establishment was represented by men such as Ambroise Pare' (circa 1510-1590), the man who has been called the "father of surgery." He lived during the reigns of seven French kings, and during one of the most troubled periods of European history. A succession of devastating wars was underway (the Italian Wars raged between 1494-1559 and between 1562-1598 there was a series of civil wars in France), and it was on the field of battle that Pare' gained his knowledge of surgery. He learned how to "dress wounds that God might better heal them." He also learned how to stop bleeding after amputation by the use of the *ligature* (the practice of binding or tying a wound) rather than by *cautery* (the practice of burning a wound with a hot iron to prevent bleeding or infection) and he invented workable artificial limbs.

Important contributions to anatomy were made by Andreas Vesalius (1514-1564). He published his first book at the age of twenty-eight and it quickly become one of the greatest medical books of this century. It was much better than Galen's book on anatomy.

In this century the first book published in England by a physician on the care of children was Thomas Phaer's (circa 1510-1560) work entitled *The Boke of Children*. It demonstrated clearly that the medical professionals were exploring new fields worthy of their attention.

The development of the first crude compound microscope (circa 1590) {2:08 p.m.} by two Dutchmen, Hans and Zacharias Janssen (sometimes Jansen), opened new vistas in the study of medicine. In this primitive instrument two simple lenses were used for the lower lens and eyepiece. It provided higher magnification and sharper images than a magnifying glass could offer.

## 129. Science

It was in this century that much scientific advance was made (in spite of the obstacles imposed by the church) with credible refutations to the inaccurate theories of the classic Greek philosophers, especially Ptolemy and Aristotle, whose theories of the universe and nature were regarded as law. The leader in this rethinking of Aristotelian logic was Francis Bacon.

Francis Bacon (1561-1626), the English philosopher and statesman, did much to advance scientific progress with the formation of a new kind of logic. In so doing he further displaced the influence of scholasticism which continued to decline in this century. During his studies at Trinity College in Cambridge (he had enrolled there in 1573), Bacon became dissatisfied with the schoolmen and the Aristotelian logic that they were teaching. Aristotle's logic was a type of *deductive reasoning* (reasoning from the general to the particular) based on what he called the *syllogism*. It was a method of argument in which certain things being established as true, something else must follow from this truth. As an example, we might say that all animals are bodies (major premise). Then we might say that all men are animals (minor premise). The conclusion from these two statements would then be that all men are bodies. Bacon felt that this kind of reasoning was nonproductive and lent itself mostly to pointless argumentation. So Bacon eventually developed what became known as the *inductive method of reasoning* (reasoning from the particular to the general). Many facts are collected, experiment reveals what is common to all of them, and a general rule is formed which is probably true.

Nicholas Copernicus (1473-1543), the founder of modern astronomy, is best remembered for his book, *Concerning the Revolutions of the Heavenly Bodies.* In it he detailed his proof that the earth is not the center of the universe around which moves the sun, moon, and stars. Earth, he showed, is one of several heavenly bodies which, turning on their axes, all revolve around the sun, thus disproving the Ptolemy theory of the universe. Although the writing was probably completed sometime between 1531 and 1533, it was not published until the year of Copernicus's death because he feared that the church would persecute him for suggesting that the earth was not the center of the universe as it had long believed.

155

The Danish nobleman Tycho Brahe (1546-1601) also contributed to this new thinking in astronomy. This persuasive researcher obtained funding from King Frederick II of Denmark (reigned 1559-1588) to build an observatory, which he named *Star Castle,* on *Hven* (a small island in the Baltic between Denmark and Sweden now known as Ven). In 1572 he observed what today we call a *supernova* (a star that suddenly becomes brighter and then gradually dims). Then, though, it had no such technical name and was simply regarded as a star that became bright enough to be seen in broad daylight. Brahe carefully followed this curious celestial object (it could be seen for about six months) and wrote a detailed account of it which refuted the church's belief that the "celestial spheres" (as they called them), were immutable and perfect. The nebula the explosion left behind is still visible today. Astronomers call it the *Bubble Nebula* [see figure 6-2]. Also, his work on the great comet of 1577 showed that such objects travel in space and are not atmospheric phenomena as Aristotle had believed. Brahe is also noted for his thousands of accurate positional measurements of the planets and stars which he made between 1576 and 1596. These measurements became the material from which Kepler later deduced the laws of planetary motions.

Johannes Kepler (1571-1630), a German commoner, had a background much different from that of Brahe's. Kepler's father was shiftless and irresponsible. His mother had occult leanings and was once accused of practicing witchcraft, but she is credited with having interested him in astronomy. One evening, in 1577, she took Kepler outside to show him a bright comet (the one which Tycho saw), and from that moment on the boy was excited about astronomy. He went to the University of Tubingen in South Wurttemberg in 1589 to study theology. While there, he became convinced that Copernicus was correct in his views of the universe. From 1593 to 1598 he was professor of mathematics at Graz in Austria where he wrote his *Mysterium Cosmographicum* (1596). This work caught the attention of Brahe, who had abandoned his observatory at Hven in March of that year and moved to Prague, where he became Imperial Mathematician to the Holy Roman Emperor Rudolph II (1552; reigned 1576-1612). Brahe invited Kepler to join him in Prague. When Brahe died, his observations came into the possession of Kepler who used them to formulate his three Laws of Planetary Motion. He proved that the planets move around the sun, not in circles as might be expected, but in ellipses (an ellipse is an oval having both ends alike).

Incidentally, Rudolph II is remembered for his passionate, though often misguided, interest in science and some of his behavior was probably motivated by an undetermined metal illness. In Golden Lane, a street in Prague, he locked up alchemists, and commanded them to transmute base metals to gold. These alchemists, like their associates before (see section 63) and after them, were unable to succeed in this endeavor.

Galileo Galilei (1564-1642) is still another name that is closely associated with Renaissance science and with all the technological revolution that followed in the new age of awakening. By his persistent investigation of natural laws, he laid the foundations of modern experimental science. His theories about the universe even went beyond those of Copernicus, Brahe, and Kepler. He is popularly remembered as the first person to use the telescope to study objects in space (1610—see section 132).

Galileo was born in Florence, the eldest of seven children, and his father had difficulty supporting them. He entered the University of Pisa in Tuscany, in 1581 where he began the study of medicine. He soon grew tired of this and became absorbed in mathematics. Four years later he was out of money and was forced to leave his studies at the university, but he continued research on his own. In 1586 he wrote an account of a hydrostatic balance (hydrostatics is that branch of science that deals with the balance and pressure of water and other liquids) which was accurate enough to have solved Archimedes's (287-212 B.C.) famous assay problem of testing the purity of a gold coronet (see chapter endnote 6-1). In 1589 Galileo returned to his old university, not as a student but as a lecturer in mathematics, where he stayed for two years. It was there that he began his experiments concerning the laws of bodies in motion, which brought results so contrary to the accepted teachings of Aristotle that strong antagonism was created. He found that bodies of different weights fall with equal velocities and with a uniform acceleration. He is said to have demonstrated this from the Leaning Tower of Pisa, but the story has been disputed. He also found that a projectile in flight (such as a cannon ball) moves in a parabola (a type of curve) instead of a straight line and he is credited with conclusions foreshadowing Newton's laws of motion (see section 132).

## 130. Results of the Renaissance

The Renaissance marked a new period in the life of the world. It was a time of rebirth, discovery, and growth. As we examine it today, life in the Renaissance may seem crude and backward, but then it was a new age—a springtime in the history of the world. The seed of almost every notable phase of modern life—in culture, industry, religion, and government—was planted in the Renaissance. Some specific results are listed below.

(1) The Renaissance acquainted men once more with the works of the masters of ancient learning and restored them to people's cultural life.

(2) It broadened men's interests and gave them a desire for greater variety in life.

(3) It gave to the world wonderful achievements in art and literature which will always be a part of our priceless possessions.

(4) It aroused in man a spirit of inquiry, leading many to try to find the truth about the world in which they lived.

(5) It brought mankind a much wider knowledge about the earth. New lands were discovered. Even a truer understanding of the place of the earth in the universe came about.

(6) It inspired the creation and use of many valuable inventions without which discoveries and conquests would have been impossible. The printing press spread the new knowledge more widely.

(7) It gave people a new confidence in themselves and the courage to think and do new things.

# God in History

Q. How did God use the Reformation to further the spread of the gospel?

A. With the rise of Protestantism in this century, a further schism developed in the church—this time represented by a split in the western church. The eastern church, which had achieved complete separation from the west (1054), remained apart in this century (as it does today) and, with characteristic oriental conservatism, it claimed the title of "Orthodoxy" and retained the simple but effective creed and organization of the early church.

In the Age of Awakening that became the Reformation, men were challenged to think for themselves in new ways and to investigate the gospel for themselves. The Bible became the infallible, inspired authority in faith and morals. Interpretations by the fathers of the church or by the councils were looked upon only as aids to its understanding. With the rise of individual liberty, Renaissance man read the sacred Scriptures and interpreted them for himself without the intervention of priests or church; and he entered by faith in Christ into communion with God, so that all believers became "priests" before God.

## Chapter Endnotes

6-1  Tradition suggests that Archimedes was asked by Hiero II (circa 306-215 B.C.) to decide whether a certain crown was pure gold or alloyed with silver. Archimedes was puzzled until one day in his bath he realized that gold and silver, being of different density, would displace different weights of water and that he could test the crown based on this idea. Archimedes's principle states that a solid body immersed in a liquid is buoyed up by a force equal to the weight of the liquid displaced. When a solid body heavier than water is immersed in water and weighed thus, it apparently looses weight (i.e., weighs less than when weighed in air). Furthermore, this apparent loss of weight is found to equal the weight of the water which has been displaced by the solid. As a result, then, it is said that the solid body is buoyed up by a force (in physics, forces are measured in units of weight) equal to the weight of the water displaced. A body lighter than water will float in water but with a certain portion of its volume beneath the surface, thus displacing a certain volume of the water. When the weight of this volume of water is determined, it is found to equal the total weight of the floating body itself. Therefore, it is said that a floating body displaces its own weight in a liquid. Archimedes's principle is applied in determining the displacement of ships, and in the laboratory, the specific gravity of substances. It is applied also to gases, especially with respect to the "lifting" force of balloons.

6-2 Lady Jane Grey was the daughter of Henry Grey, Earl of Dorset, and Frances Brandon, niece of Henry VIII. She was unwillingly proclaimed queen (July 10, 1553). The English people, however, favored Mary I and after nine days as nominal queen, Lady Jane was imprisoned.

## Chapter Terms

| | | |
|---|---|---|
| Anabaptists | Elizabethan Age | Protestant |
| apothecary | Index | Star Castle |
| Archimedes's principle | inductive reasoning | syllogism |
| Bubble Nebula | Jesuit Order | Saint Bartholomew's |
| deductive reasoning | Mennonites | Day Massacre |
| diet | Mercator Projection | Ursulines |
| Divine Right of Kings | Presbyterian | |

## Chapter Review Questions/Exercises

1. Discuss in detail the Reformation. Who were some of the most important people in this major event and why were they disappointed with the Roman Catholic Church? (112)
2. What kinds of disagreements occurred among Protestants themselves? (113)
3. What were some of the different Protestant denominations to come out of the Reformation in the sixteenth century? (113)
4. What two new organizations were formed in the sixteenth century to increase the strength of the Catholic Church? (114-115)

5. What was the Index? (116)
6. Discuss Machiavelli and the Doctrine of the Divine Right of Kings. (117)
7. Explain the details of the Saint Bartholomew's Day Massacre. (118)
8. Why did England break away from the pope under the reign of Henry VIII? (119)
9. What did Henry VIII do to gain support for his divorce from Princess Catherine? (119)
10. Who was Elizabeth Barton and why did Henry VIII have her killed? (119)
11. Who was Anne Askew and why did Henry VIII have her killed? (119)
12. What were Elizabeth's religious policies? (121)
13. What was Elizabeth's attitude toward Mary Stuart? (122)
14. List the different husbands that Mary Stuart had. (122)
15. How did James react to the killing of his mother? (122)
16. Why was there tension between England and Spain during the sixteenth century? (123)
17. How did America get its name? (124)
18. What nations were involved in the New World? (125)
19. List the important writers in England in the sixteenth century. (127)
20. What were some of the outstanding achievements in medicine in the sixteenth century? (128)
21. List some of the important scientists of the sixteenth century and some of their accomplishments. (129)
22. What were the results of the Renaissance? (130)

# 7

# 1601-1700

## {2:24 p.m.-4:47 p.m.}

Sometime during the next two hours and twenty-three minutes, Alexander Pope (1688-1744) will be born. He will be remembered for such sayings as "A little learning is a dangerous thing," and "...as the twig is bent the tree's inclined."

Edward Young (1683-1765) will be remembered for his remarks that "All men think all men mortal but themselves" and "Procrastination is the thief of time."

John Bunyan (1628-1688) will write his famous book *Pilgrim's Progress* in which he will suggest the steps a Christian passes through on his journey to maturity.

The Irish prelate and scholar Bishop James Usher (sometimes Ussher) (1581-1656), in his chronological study of the Bible (2 vols. 1650-1654), will work out a system of dates which set the creation at 4004 B.C.

# Overview

As the world moved into the first years of this century, men from all classes seemed to be sparked with new ideas and challenges.

English King James I (1566; reigned 1603-1625) directed the great English architect Inigo Jones (1573-1652) to examine the mysteries of Stonehenge to determine its origin (1620). Although his conclusion was faulty (he thought it was an ancient Roman temple!), it showed that there was an increasing scientific interest in monuments such as this.

The English mathematician, astronomer, and philosopher Isaac Newton formulated the laws of gravity, invented integral and differential calculus, made important contributions to the study of light, invented a new kind of telescope (called a reflector), and did many other impressive things (see section 132).

The French astronomer Jean Picard (1620-1682) calculated the equatorial diameter of the earth at 7,801 miles, which made it possible for a ship at sea to determine its location with extreme accuracy.

Balances (scales) were improved when Pierre Vernier (1580-1637), a French mathematician, invented a device for subdividing the divisions of scales into small parts (1631). From this came the name "Vernier Scales" which is used even today.

In this century Galileo and Sanctorius (1561-1636) developed thermometers that consisted of a bulb with a tubular projection, the open end of which was immersed in a liquid. Heating or cooling the bulbs affected the height of the column of liquid in the tube, on which a scale was marked. They were the forerunners of the more familiar type of thermometer, developed in the next century and which is still in use today, that contain a liquid in a sealed tube.

The English physician William Gilbert (circa 1540-1603) published a book on magnetism and gave electricity its name (from the Greek word *elektron*—"amber"), for he showed that amber can be electrified by friction, and he demonstrated that the earth, too, possesses magnetism.

The Anglo-Irish scientist Robert Boyle (1627-1691), who regarded the acquisition of knowledge as an end in itself, discovered that, at constant temperature, the volume of a given gaseous mass is inversely proportional to its pressure, a concept which was named "Boyle's Law."

164

An Italian, Evangelista Torricelli (1608-1647), invented the barometer (1643), an instrument for measuring atmospheric pressure.

The English physician John Mayow (circa 1645-1679) discovered that air contains a component that is involved in combustion and that it is present in saltpeter, an element in gunpowder. He thus determined the method by which gunpowder works.

The British collector and physician Sir Hans Sloane (1660-1753) made vital contributions to botany with the collections of plants he accumulated over a lifetime.

William Harvey (1578-1657), an English physician and anatomist, published his monumental work in Frankfurt, Germany (1628), explaining how the blood circulates in the human body, and the discovery of the capillary circulation that supplied its final link was made by Marcello Malpighi (1628-1694), in Italy. Some of the discoveries made by Malpighi and others of this century came from the use of the microscope which, although it had been invented in the previous century, underwent important improvements in this one by Leeuwenhoek (see section 133).

The first taxi business was opened in Paris by Nicholas Sauvage (1640) with a fleet of twenty coaches, but it ran only when there were passengers. Blaise Pascal (1623-1662), the French mathematician and philosopher, proposed a regular system of coaches that would move along predetermined routes in Paris regardless of the number of riders (1662).

The clarinet was invented by Johann Christian Denner (circa 1690).

The first practical submarine was built (circa 1620) by C. J. Drebbel (1572-1634), a Dutchman living in England. It was a rowboat completely covered with leather and propelled by twelve oarsmen, the oars protruding through both sides of the boat. The method used to renew the air in the submerged craft with oxygen (which he extracted from saltpeter) enabled the vessel to remain underwater for up to fifteen hours. Another submarine was built in 1653 at Rotterdam and was designed for use against the British fleet, but it never saw action.

In education, the most famous new English academy of this century was known as the "Invisible College," formed in London (1645). It became the College of the Royal Society of London by a charter granted by Charles II (1662). Among its early members were such original thinkers as Robert Boyle and Robert Hooke (1635-1703), two Oxford scientists who made their important discoveries of the blood that really took up where Harvey had left off.

The English philosopher John Locke (1632-1704) thought that the development of a healthy body and the learning of a trade were important if one were to be properly educated. He was much ahead of his time in asserting that "there are possibly scarce two children who can be educated by exactly the same method."

John Amos Comenius (1592-1670), also known as Johann Komensky, a Czech theologian and educator, believed that education should be made a pleasant process rather than be "forced into" or "beat into" one's mind. He was the first textbook writer to use pictures to make his books more interesting. All people, men, and women alike, regardless of rank or ability, he said, were entitled to such education as they were able to absorb. He proposed divisions in the organization of schools which corresponded in a general way to schools that have kindergarten, elementary, secondary, and college designations.

Izaak Walton (1593-1683) published his creative book called *The Compleat* (Sic) *Angler* (1653). The book not only described the technique of angling, but drew a picture of peace and simple virtue which was Walton's protest against the civil war taking place at that time (see section 141).

Yet even among the new advancements that were made in this century, some of the old superstitions remained. The fanaticism over witchcraft, which gripped Europe during this century, spread even to the American colonies of Massachusetts, Connecticut, and Virginia. The fanaticism was particularly active in Salem, Massachusetts, where a number of people were hanged in 1692 after having been put on trial for being accused of being witches.

# Other Disciplines and Institutions

## 131. Art

The most famous artist to appear in Holland during this century was Rembrandt van Rijn (1606-1669) who is most easily remembered by his first name. His success came from his rich imagination, his ability to understand his subjects, and his way of communicating visually through the use of proper light and shade. He was equally at home with landscapes as he was with portraits or religious subjects.

Of equal importance was the Dutch artist Sir Anthony Van Dyck (sometimes Vandyke) (1599-1641). He was easily the greatest portrait painter of the period and his diligence was sufficient to produce a large number of excellent portraits, several historical paintings, and a number of works inspired by classical mythology. His paintings included *Saint Augustine in Ecstasy, Samson and Delilah,* and *Elevation of the Cross.*

Another artist from Holland was David Teniers (1610-1690). He was revered for his scenes and incidents from rural life and was noted for his success in historical and landscape painting. His religious works included *The Prodigal Son.*

The works of Hans Asselijn (1610-1660) were noted for their innovative style in landscape paintings. His example was followed by other leading artists of Holland.

The Flemish painter Cornelis Janssen (1593-circa 1662) worked in England (1618-1643) where he received the patronage of James I. He was generally credited with the famous portrait of John Milton as a boy of ten (1618). In his retirement years he was drawn to the great centers of art in Holland where he worked at Middleburg, Amsterdam, the Hague, and Utrecht before his death. His works, mainly portraits, were distinguished by clear coloring, delicate touch, good taste, and careful finish.

George Jameson (circa 1587-1644), a Scottish painter, was schooled under Paul Rubens (1577-1640) at Antwerp. He was noted for his portraits and was employed to copy several portraits of the Scottish kings for presentation to Charles I on his first visit to Scotland in 1633. The king rewarded him with a diamond ring from his own finger.

## 132. Astronomy

There were many important developments and discoveries in astronomy during this century. The introduction of the telescope made it possible to observe things that had been previously invisible to the unaided eye. Galileo heard (1609) of the development of a spyglass by the Dutchman Hans Lippershey (1570-1619) and he constructed a telescope of his own (see chapter endnote 7-1). Using it, he became the first investigator to observe the solar system and the universe with that instrument (1610). He discovered craters and mountains on the moon, the four satellites of Jupiter, the changing phases of Venus, the countless stars of the Milky Way, spots on the sun, and many other things. His crude telescope was not powerful enough to clearly observe Saturn's rings so he thought that the planet had "ears" around it. His observations of objects in space confirmed his acceptance of the Copernican theory of the solar system and he published the results in his *Dialogue* (on the two chief systems of the world) (1632) {3:09 p.m.}. He was rewarded for his hard work by being tried by the Inquisition (1633) which forced him to recant his theories. He died under house arrest in Arcetri at age seventy-seven. Incredibly, it was not until 1979 that Pope John Paul II (1920; served 1978- ) opened an investigation of the astronomer's condemnation by the church, calling for its reversal. The inquiry formally closed on October 30, 1992, with an acknowledgment of the Vatican's error.

The Dutch mathematician and physicist Christiaan Huygens (1629-1695), improved telescope lenses through his skill as a lens grinder. He discovered (1655) a satellite of Saturn and the rings of Saturn, thus solving the mystery caused by Galileo's crude telescope which was not powerful enough to clearly observe Saturn's rings which looked like ears to him.

Telescopes became so important for astronomical research that even kings became interested in them. The Italian Giovanni Domenico Cassini (1625-1712) was appointed the first director of a new observatory built by French King Louis XIV. Cassini became a naturalized French citizen soon after assuming his duties there in 1671. While there Cassini discovered four of the satellites of Saturn, described the structure of Saturn's rings, and noted a division in them which now bears his name. He also determined the rotation period of Mars and, because he was able to obtain more precise values to the *parallax* (see chapter endnote 7-2) of Mars and the sun and their distance from the earth, he obtained a significantly better understanding of the size of the solar system than had been known before. Cassini's detailed observations of the eclipses of satellites of Jupiter, became the basis for Ole Romer's (sometimes Roemer) (1644-1710) discovery that light travels at a definite speed and does not move through space instantaneously.

An extraordinary achievement in astronomy, mathematics, and physics was the writing and publication of Isaac Newton's (1642-1727) *Principi* (1687). Some of the most-often-referred-to concepts in this work are Newton's three laws of motion:

(1) Every body continues in its state of rest, or of uniform motion in a straight line, unless acted upon by other forces.
(2) The change of motion on a body is proportional to the forces acting on it; and is made in the direction of the right line in which that force is impressed.
(3) To every action there is always an opposite but equal reaction.

These three laws at last gave astronomers a basis for astronomical computation. The first rule, which stated the concept of inertia, meant that a body would remain at rest or in motion, as long as no external force acted upon it. This startling concept meant that the imagined premium mobile (see section 86), that ultimate moving force which medieval astronomers had believed was a part of the natural universe, was no longer needed. All observations of the motions of the stars and planets were explainable by the interaction of inertia and gravity. A satellite orbited a planet (or star) because it received a force that set it in motion. If no other force acted on it, it moved in a straight line. But gravity, the attraction of the planet (or the star) the satellite was orbiting, bent the straight line into a curve.

The great English astronomer and mathematician Edmund Halley (1656-1742) became famous as the first astronomer to predict the return of a comet. He began his astronomical work when he sailed to the island of Saint Helena to set up instruments to observe the southern sky (1676). As a result he made a catalog of 341 stars. He also built an observatory at Islington (1682) and made more observations there, especially on the great comet that came along that year. He identified it as the one that had been observed in 1531 and 1607 and predicted the year of its return (1759). Although he did not live to see its return, the comet was named after him in recognition of the outstanding mathematical achievement his prediction represented.

Julius Schiller reworked the ancient constellations to represent biblical subjects (1627), though these did not find popular acceptance.

## 133. Medicine

It was at this time that the Italian Renaissance began to lose its lead in medicine and the center of medical education moved to the Dutch University of Leiden (sometimes Leyden). This university had been founded in 1575 by William I, Prince of Orange (1533-1584), who wanted to reward the town for its heroic and successful stand against the Spanish in the preceding year. He offered the citizens of Leiden the choice between a ten-year remission of taxes or the establishment of a university within the city. The citizens of Leiden chose the university. It became one of the greatest schools in Europe.

In this century the apothecary profession in London continued to be separate from the physicians and surgeons as it had been in the past (see section 128), but they were incorporated with the grocers by James I in 1606. When their charter was renewed two years later, they were founded as a separate corporation, under the title of the "Apothecaries of the City of London." At this time it seems that the apothecaries prescribed medicines in addition to dispensing them, and claimed an ancient right of acting in this double capacity. This renewed the conflict between these professions regarding who should prescribe medicines and who should not. It was not officially resolved until the next century (see section 133). During the conflict, the status of physicians and surgeons of this century increased significantly and they earned greater respect as they learned more about how to help their patients.

The Dutchman Anthony van Leeuwenhoek (1632-1723) became famous for his skills in making lenses. He spent much of his life as a merchant but made a hobby of experimenting with lenses and he eventually made the microscope into a true scientific instrument. In the course of his long life he made many interesting discoveries. He was the first to observe, draw, and describe bacteria which made possible the eventual realization that bacteria cause diseases, thus confirming the theories of men in prior years about the existence of germs.

## 134. Philosophy and Religion

Rene' Descartes (1596-1650) founded a new school of philosophy known as *Cartesianism* in France. It is said that he developed his habit of contemplation when, as a child at a Jesuit school, his frail health excused him from his morning duties and he spent his time "reflecting" in bed. Descartes was concerned with the relationship of the mind with matter and his famous axiom, *Cogito, ergo sum* ("I think, therefore I am") became the basis for his system of philosophy.

The Dutch philosopher Baruch (or Benedict) Spinoza (1632-1677) was a student of Descartes. His parents were Jewish emigrants who fled the Catholic persecution in Portugal and Spain. Because he learned Latin he was able to read the entirety of contemporary philosophy and science, both represented in his day by the writings of Descartes. He rejected Jewish orthodoxy though the leaders of the synagogue tried to persuade him to return to the services. Even their threats failed to retain him and he was excommunicated in 1656. Afterwards, he rejected the Hebrew name of Baruch, assuming instead the Latin equivalent, Benedictus. In exile he practiced his occupation of lens-grinding and became acquainted with Christiaan Huygens (see section 132), the great astronomer of the day. He became a *pantheist* who believed that God was the universe. He developed Descartes' idea that the universe is divided into mind and matter.

## 135. Matters of the Christian Church

The belief in the antichrist continued in this century. To defend the church against the antichrist, whose imminent rise was anticipated by some Italians, an organization known as the Knights of the Apocalypse was formed by Augustine Gabrino in 1693. On Palm Sunday of that year, when the choir of Saint Peter's was chanting *"Quis est iste Rex Gloriae"* ("Who is this King of Glory?"), Gabrino ran into the church with his sword drawn, shouting *"Ego sum Rex Gloriae"* ("I am the King of Glory!"). It may be wondered how a madman such as this could gain a following, but he did. His society grew until a member denounced it to the Inquisition and the knights were arrested.

In other religious matters, it is interesting to note that since the signing of the Peace of Westphalia in 1648 (see section 138) there have been few changes in the religious loyalties of the nations of western Europe. One reason for this was because a provision of the Treaty of Westphalia stated that a prince would forfeit his lands if he changed his religion. Thus, an obstacle was placed in the way of any further spread of the Reformation. But even without this provision, few changes have been seen.

Individual Christians have changed their memberships from one religious body to another and many still do, but as nations these allegiances seem somewhat fixed. France, Spain, Italy, as well as Hungary, Austria, and Poland were and are almost unanimously

Roman Catholic. England, Scotland, Holland, and the Scandinavian countries became Protestant to stay. Germany was divided, with its northern sections largely Protestant and its southern districts chiefly Catholic. Switzerland, also, was part Catholic and part Protestant. As some of these countries carried their flag and their trade into the New World, their prevailing religions went along with them. So, in South America almost everybody became Roman Catholic; in North America, people became Protestant or Catholic, depending in most cases, on where the original settlers came from.

The various non-Catholic denominations made progress during this century. There is a record of a Baptist church having been established in Amsterdam in 1609 and one in London in circa 1611. In the New World, Roger Williams (circa 1603-1683) organized a church at Providence, Rhode Island (1639), which was probably the first Baptist church in North America. The Baptists survived in spite of the opposition they received from the Puritans of New England. The Presbyterians, who can trace their origins to the previous century from the efforts of John Calvin, established churches in the American colonies in the first half of this century. Colonists coming to America from Scotland (1670-1690), strengthened the movement.

Another denomination of the Christian faith is one whose members are often called Quakers. Members of this society prefer to be called Friends, and the Society of Friends was founded in England (circa 1648). Its first members did not approve of the elaborate ceremonies of the Church of England and they also advocated simple and moderate living. They adopted many customs which made them seem "strange" to their English neighbors. The central belief of this Society centered around what became known as the "inner light." Quakers believe that the Spirit of God is present in everybody to guide them into the truth. They do not believe in violence in any form. William Penn (1644-1718), a Quaker leader, founded the colony of Pennsylvania (1681).

A movement in the Lutheran Church known as *Pietism* grew in the latter part of this century in Germany, especially in the North and central part. It even reached into Switzerland and other parts of Europe and lasted until the middle of the next century. Pietism was formed to combat a spreading intellectual type of religion that seemed to take the place of Bible rules and religion from the heart in the Lutheran Church. Philipp Jakob Spener (1635-1705) was the founder of this philosophy and he began to hold devotional meetings (1670). His many writings were designed to encourage Christian fellowship and Bible study. He also thought that lay members should have part in the spiritual control of the church and that Christian beliefs should be shown in everyday living. The orthodox Lutheran clergy disliked his teachings and the theological faculty at Wittenberg brought formal charges against him (1695), but these did not stop the spread of his ideas.

John Biddle (1615-1662), the founder of English *Unitarianism*, whose adherents were called Biddelians, Socinians, and Unitarians, faced persecution most of his life for his ideas. He denied belief in the doctrine of the Trinity and presented his conclusions in his work, *Twelve Arguments Drawn Out of Scripture*. After the publication of his *Two-fold Catechism* in 1654, he was tried for his life but received from Cromwell a sentence of banishment to the Scilly Islands. He returned to England in 1658 where he brought attention to himself by once again sharing his religious views with others. He was thrown into prison in 1662 where he died.

The Rosicrucians, a semi-religious group that claimed ancient origin but definite proof of their existence, can be placed in this century. In 1615 Johann Valentin Andrea published his work *Confessis rosae crucis* (*Confessions of the Rosy Cross*) which caused much debate. The followers of this sect were basically theosophists, a philosophical system related to mysticism and which claimed insight into the nature of God and the world either through direct knowledge, through philosophical speculation, or through some physical process.

## 136. The Jews

In this century a man by the name of Sabbatai Zevi (1626-1676) claimed to be the Messiah (circa 1650). Many Jews looked to Zevi, believing that his claim was genuine but became angry when he was forced to embrace Islam to save his life. They had looked to Zevi to lead them back to the Holy Land in victory and were disappointed in his failure to do so.

This was the first century in which a Jewish community was established in North America. It was founded at the Dutch colony of New Amsterdam (1654). It was followed by another at Newport, Rhode Island (1658).

# Matters of Church and State

## 137. Religious Problems in England Under James I

Soon after James I became king (see section 140), a group of Puritans met him in a conference at Hampton Court (1604), in the hope of inducing him to adopt some of their religious ideas. To their great disappointment, he told them that Puritanism agreed with monarchy as well as God agreed with the devil. If Puritans would not "conform," he would "harry them out of the land or else do worse."

As a result, these "Pilgrims" made a brave journey to Massachusetts on the Mayflower and were thankful that they arrived safely in 1620. During the voyage they drew up the *Mayflower Compact*, an agreement designed to unify the colonists by providing a temporary government based on the will of the majority. It was the basis of the original Plymouth government and all succeeding governments of the colony. It is because of the Pilgrims that Americans celebrate Thanksgiving Day which was first observed by these early settlers in gratitude for the harvest they reaped after the severe trials of their first year in America. Tradition requires that roasted turkey be served at Thanksgiving dinner, although venison was the meat that was served at the first Thanksgiving.

## 138. The Thirty Years' War

This war originated for religious reasons when the Austrian Hapsburgs attempted to rid their dominions of Protestantism, but it soon became caught up in political objectives as well. It broke out in central Europe and lasted for thirty years (1618-1648) {2:48 p.m.-3:32 p.m.}. It was also the first of the national wars since it ultimately involved almost all of the continental powers.

The struggle soon turned into a civil war because the Hapsburgs were also Holy Roman Emperors, becoming a war between Protestants and Catholics. It became a national war when outside states came in to support their factions, thus making permanent the split between Protestant and Catholic Europe which had originated in the Reformation.

Other considerations ultimately prevailed. Roman Catholic France came to support the Protestant powers against their traditional Hapsburg enemies and the modern European system of independent states emerged with France as the leader. Spain relinquished the military supremacy she had enjoyed for over 100 years. The peace negotiations were started in 1643 but were extended over protocol disputes. The Treaties of Westphalia were finally concluded at Onsabruck and Munster on October 24, 1648.

# Matters of State

### 139. The New World

The attempt of European countries to divide the New World resulted in two kinds of conflicts—first, between the invaders and the native Americans who were already there; and second, between one European nation and another which wanted the same territory.

The basis for the conflicts between the invaders of the New World and the Indians largely depended on the type of relationship that existed between them. The Dutch dealt with the native Americans mainly through trade and they usually got along peacefully with them. The English felt a sense of superiority to the Indians and showed it, so relations between the English and the native Americans were not always good. The Indians usually used every advantage to acknowledge their dislike of the English, and took English prisoners whenever the opportunity presented itself. The great English explorer and founder of Virginia, John Smith (1580-1631), was taken prisoner by Powhatan (died 1618) while he was in the Chickahominy region. There is a popular, unsubstantiated story that he was saved from execution by Powhatan's daughter, Pocahontas (circa 1595-1617).

Even when certain Indians showed themselves to be friendly to the English, it often resulted in a backlash against their own. The Pequot chief Uncas (circa 1588-circa 1683), who made treaties with the English colonists and always remained faithful to them, was the object of much criticism from his own brothers who more than once went to war as a result. Even the group of Christian Indians who lived in East Massachusetts and who were known as praying Indians, were attacked by their brothers who viewed them as traitors during King Philip's War (1675).

Yet the early settlers of Plymouth and other places learned much about planting and hunting from the Indians. William Penn and the Quakers tried hard to give the Indians a fair deal, and between them and the Indians there was very little trouble.

Roger Williams (circa 1603-1683), noted Puritan clergyman and founder of the colony of Rhode Island, made friends with the Indians after he established Providence in 1636. The colonists of New England and the Middle States even used the Indians' money, better known as *wampum*, as legal tender (1627-1661).

The French came more closely in contact with the Indians than any other European people. They traded much with them, and some actually lived the same life as the Indians themselves. The French also encountered and dealt with the Canadian Indians. They were not as inclined to make war against the settlers as were their counterparts in the lower regions of the continent. Among the French much was done to try to win the Indians to Christianity, but sometimes these efforts met with great resistance.

The harsh influence of the Spanish leaders had long been felt in the Americas, yet this did not prevent the intermarriage between the Spanish and the Indians. As a result, many people of the western hemisphere have part Indian and part Spanish ancestry. The word Hispanic is used to describe these people today. The Spanish priests also made efforts to convert the Indians to Christianity and the Americas are dotted with early Spanish missions which are a testimony to their conversion efforts.

The other type of conflict over the New World arose between European nations competing for the same territory. These colonial wars especially raged between Great Britain and France for a protracted period, beginning in the late part of the seventeenth century, and they have been classified as belonging to what are known as the French and Indian Wars (1689-1763). They were really campaigns in the growing struggle for empire and were more or less linked to the European wars of the same period. While the fighting in Europe had more effect on the outcome than the fighting in America did, the Americans were largely victimized by the raids of the French and the British and of the horrors of the accompanying Indian wars. From the American viewpoint, the conflict may be seen as a single war with interruptions. The ultimate objective of the war was domination of the eastern part of the continent. This was accomplished by capture of the seaboard strongholds and the little western forts and attacks on frontier settlements.

The first of these wars was known as King William's War (1689-1697) because it took place when William III (1650; reigned 1689-1702) was on the English throne. It roughly corresponded to the European War of the Grand Alliance (1688-1697). In America it was characterized mainly by frontier attacks on the British colonies and by the taking of Port Royal (now Annapolis Royal, Nova Scotia) by British colonial forces under Sir William Phips (1651-1695) in 1690. The British were unable to take Quebec and the French commander, Louis de Buade, Comte de Frontenac (1620-1698), attacked the British coast. The peace that followed the Treaty of Ryswick in 1697 did not last long and the colonies were soon plunged into war again (see section 159).

William Kidd (circa 1645-1701), a Scotsman who later became a pirate, fought against the French in King William's War and was granted a reward of $750.00 from the City of New York for it.

## 140. England Under James I

James I (1566; reigned 1603-1625) was not a popular king with the English people. His undignified personal appearance worked against him (he usually dressed in strange, green clothes). He enjoyed talking at length on all sorts of subjects which, spoken in his unwelcomed Scottish accent, served only to distance him from the common people even more. He was given to slovenliness, tolerated disorders in his court, and allowed incompetent personal friends to influence his policies.

James's desire for handsome male favorites, whom he loaded with gifts and openly caressed, was greatly disdained and none of his subjects appreciated the oath of allegiance he required from them. He was well educated for his time, but he showed very poor judgment in the use of his learning. Henry IV of France called him "the wisest fool in Christendom." One of his major accomplishments was the commissioning of the translation of the Bible into what became known as the King James Version.

A little sympathy was generated for James because of a conspiracy that came to be known as the Gunpowder Plot. Guy Fawkes (1570-1606) and some others succeeded in planting gunpowder under the Parliament buildings with the idea of blowing up the two houses of

Parliament at a time when the king was present (November 5, 1605). The idea was to avenge the persecution of Roman Catholics in England. The plot was discovered and several connected with it were put to death. This led to an increase in hostility toward Catholics in England. The memory of this event is today celebrated as Guy Fawkes Day in England.

## 141. England Under Cromwell

In 1649 Parliament declared England to be a Commonwealth without a king or House of Lords. In Ireland and Scotland, revolts occurred against the Commonwealth. Richard Cromwell (1626-1712) suppressed the revolt in Ireland (1650) with such terrible thoroughness that for a long time one of the worst things one Irishman could say to another was "the curse of Crumell (Sic) on you." Forces of Scotsmen supporting the son of Charles I, invaded England, but Cromwell defeated them in two great battles during 1650 and 1651.

In 1650 the Scottish and Irish Parliaments were abolished, representation was given to Scotland and Ireland in the English Parliament, and various legal and administrative reforms were enacted. In 1653 Cromwell dissolved the Rump Parliament, which had earned its name because its members were ineffective in that they just sat around "on their rumps." He attempted to replace it with the Barebone's Parliament but it was so weak and incompetent that it dissolved itself. He finally accepted the Instrument of Government which made him "Lord Protector" for life (1653).

For five years Cromwell ruled England with all the authority that any absolute monarch could have exercised. Cromwell accepted his task as simply being an unpleasant duty, partly because the people made fun of him. The people called him "Yankee Doodle" which was applied to his entry into Oxford:

> Yankee Doodle came to town
> Upon a Kentish pony;
> He stuck a feather in his hat,
> And called it Macaroni
> (see chapter endnote 7-3).

Through it all, however, Cromwell believed that he was following the will of God, but not like the "divine right" of the Stuarts

(England's royal house). He gave the country peace and order at home. Abroad, too, he made England's authority respected, defeating both the Dutch and the Spanish.

## 142. France Under Louis XIV

Louis XIV's (1638; reigned 1643-1715) reign became the longest of any ruler of a great country in history. He was only a boy when he came to the throne. England was going through its civil war between Charles I and Parliament. Cromwell, Charles II, James II, William of Orange (1650; reigned as William III 1689-1702), and Queen Anne (1665; queen of England, Scotland, and Ireland 1702-1707; later queen of Great Britain 1707-1714) came and went before Louis died. A year after George I became King of England in 1714, Louis passed his crown to his great-grandson.

Louis XIV enjoyed being called *"Le Grand Monarque"* (the Great Ruler). He really did have a regal bearing and in many ways acted like royalty is expected to act; he was always dignified. The expression, "I am the state," is often attributed to him. Whether he said it or not, he doubtless thought it. He adopted the sun as his symbol, and his standard showed him in the center of things, sending out rays of glory in all directions. He was known as the Sun King.

Not being satisfied with the quarters in which he had to live in Paris, Louis had a marvelous palace and court laid out at Versailles, a few miles from Paris. It was the most elaborate royal establishment Europe had yet seen. His life there became famous for its luxury, display, and immorality. His court was the center of fashion and culture of the time. Louis XIV furniture became a fad in his day. He encouraged dramatists, sculptors, and painters. French became the fashionable language of European courts. Perhaps Louis did not realize the burden of his government upon the masses. The nobles and other courtiers would not tell him anything unpleasant, and they would not have dared to do so even if they had wanted to. This led some, such as Jean Moliere (1622-1673), to employ satire in their plays and other writings.

One unfortunate prisoner of Louis XIV became known as the Man in the Iron Mask because his identity was a closely held secret. This prisoner always wore an iron mask. He was held for many years at Pinerolo and in other prisons. He died in the Bastille in 1703. There has been much speculation as to the identity of this man and many names have been offered. One of the most likely is that of Count Girolamo Mattioli, an Italian statesman. He had refused to give up the Fortress of Casale, in Mantua, Italy, in 1678, after having signed an agreement with Louis saying that he would. He was captured and imprisoned.

## 143. Russia Under Peter the Great

Peter the Great (1672; reigned 1682-1725) brought Russia into closer and more meaningful contact with western Europe, removing what had been a period of relative isolation for that country. About seven feet tall, he had a very striking appearance. He was utterly heartless, however, indulging in liquor and other excesses to a disgraceful extent; yet he was ambitious, quick to learn and in his way, he was progressive. He did not learn to read and write until after he was eleven years old, but there was little limit to the wide range of things that intrigued him.

After Peter became Czar, he decided to bring western civilization to Russia and to get for Russia a "window to the west," so he could look out on Europe. The idea was to give him a seaport that would permit him to carry on direct trade between Russia and western Europe instead of having to do it by way of other countries. To get first-hand contact with the western civilizations, he traveled (1697-1698) in disguise with a few associates in Prussia, Holland, and England, even working as a laborer in a shipyard in Holland. He liked to work with tools and to tinker with such things as watches.

When Peter returned to Russia after this educational tour, he brought with him European shipbuilders, miners, mechanics, and engineers to show Russia how to do the things that western Europe knew. He had roads and canals constructed, mines opened, and ships built like those he had seen in Holland. He set up a new postal system and police organization in his cities and he formed a new army like that of the Prussians.

For the upper classes Peter introduced schools. He took out of the Russian alphabet some letters that were not needed, though those that remained were in many cases more like the ancient Greek than like the Latin letters used by the nations of western Europe. He introduced the calendar which was then in use in western Europe, though he did not accept the changes that Pope Gregory XIII had already made (1582). For over 300 years (until 1918), dates in Russia were twelve or more days behind those observed by the western European nations and the New World.

Peter wanted his people to look and act like Europeans. So he made the Russians cut off their cherished beards or pay a heavy tax if they insisted on wearing them. They had to shorten their long robes and wear clothes that were like those worn by the Germans. Whether the men wanted to or not, they had to learn to smoke tobacco. Women were allowed to appear in the same public places with men. He tried to quickly change Russian habits and customs that had grown up through centuries. The upper classes took on a coating of western civilization which in some respects sank in, but the great peasant classes of Russia were not very much changed.

## 144. Prussia and the Hohenzollern Family

The story of Prussia is closely aligned with the rise of the Hohenzollern family. The name "Prussia" first appeared on the map of Europe as that of a district near the southwestern corner of the Baltic Sea, whose rulers in the course of time obtained the title of Duke of Prussia. But what we call Prussia today has Berlin as its capital, and the history of that part of Germany goes back to the district known as the Mark (medieval Germanic for frontier province) of Brandenburg. As a reward for lending money to a Holy Roman Emperor, Frederick William (1620; reigned 1640-1688), count of the little district of Hohenzollern in southern Germany, received the district of Brandenburg to rule over.

The Hohenzollerns were not satisfied with the titles they had the right to use. They wanted to be kings. The ruler of Brandenburg was one of the "electors" who chose the Holy Roman Emperor. When the last of the dukes of Prussia died in 1618, the ruling family of Brandenburg claimed, through some distant relationship, that the title and country belonged to them.

Brandenburg was somewhat prominent in the latter part of the Thirty Years' War, and was one of the few districts which seemed to profit by it. The rulers of Brandenburg also inherited several other titles. Thus the territory of Brandenburg and Prussia grew until it occupied considerable space on the map of Germany, though it was not all in one solid mass.

181

Frederick William did much to attract new people to his country. He invited to his dominions Huguenots who found things uncomfortable in France after Louis XIV revoked the Edict of Nantes in 1685. Frederick paid the traveling expenses of 20,000 skilled French Huguenots who made permanent settlements there and exempted them from taxation.

# God in History

Q. How did God use the life of John Bunyan for His glory?

A. This English religious writer had a profound experience when he was about seventeen years of age. He enlisted in the parliamentary army, where he served (1645) during a decisive campaign. One of his friends, who had marched with the attacking army instead of him, was killed by a shot. Bunyan ever after considered himself as having been saved from death by God's will. He also drew his characters from the friends he met in the military. After going through a time of doubts, he joined a Baptist church and began to preach. He had been five years a preacher when the Restoration put it in the power of the Cavalier gentlemen and clergymen all over the country to oppress those they considered to be dissenters. When he refused to stop preaching at their insistence, he was thrown in a Bedford jail (1660), where he remained for a number of years.

While in jail, he gave religious instruction to his fellow-captives and formed a little flock from among them, of which he himself was the pastor. He studied the few books he had, two of which were the Bible and *Foxe's Book of Martyrs.*

Prison life also gave him time to write and, in addition to several tracts and some verse, he authored *Grace Abounding to the Chief of Sinners,* the narrative of his own religious experiences. Before he was released from prison, he began the work that made his name immortal. *Pilgrim's Progress* was published (1678), a work which spoke of the states of a Christian's progress. The fame which this work brought him elevated his station in life so that he was later able to exercise much good influence for the church in the political affairs of his day.

# Chapter Notes

7-1   The Galilean telescope was a refractor having a convergent objective and a divergent eyepiece. It gave a slightly magnified upright image and had a limited field of view. Today this optical system is used in opera glasses and not telescopes.

7-2  In astronomy, parallax is the degree of change in the direction in which an object is seen, caused by a change in the position of the observer, as when two different measurements of the same planet or star are made at the same time from different locations on earth.

7-3  The origin of this rhyme was in the medieval period where it was sung by the harvesters in Holland (circa 1500).  During Shakespeare's time, mothers sang it to their small children.  In the seventeenth century the Cavaliers used it to make fun of Cromwell when he road down from Canterbury to take charge of the Puritan forces there.  The reference to macaroni is to the young men of London who dressed in an unusual Italian style of the day.

## Chapter Terms

| | |
|---|---|
| elektron | Quakers |
| Friends | refracting telescope |
| inertia | Rosicrucians |
| Knights of the Apocalypse | Stonehenge |
| parallax | Vernier Scales |
| Pietism | wampum |

## Chapter Review Questions/Exercises

1. Describe some of the interesting things that happened in the seventeenth century as mentioned in the Overview to this chapter.
2. Name some important artists of the seventeenth century. (131)
3. What were some the significant accomplishments in astronomy in the seventeenth century?  (132)
4. What was Leeuwenhoek's great contribution to medicine? (133)
5. What was the famous saying that Descartes is noted for? (134)
6. Who was Spinoza and what is he remembered for?  (134)
7. Who was Augustine Gabrino and what is he remembered for? (135)
8. What was important about the Peace of Westphalia? (135)
9. Who were the Quakers? (135)

10. What was Pietism? (135)
11. What is John Biddle remembered for? (135)
12. Who were the Rosicrucians? (135)
13. Who was Sabbatai Zevi? (136).
14. Describe how Americans came to celebrate Thanksgiving. (137)
15. What was the Mayflower Compact? (137)
16. What was the Thirty Years' War? (138)
17. What were the two main sources of conflicts in the New World? (139)
18. Describe the problems that the English had in the New World. (139)
19. Who were the praying Indians? (139)
20. Who was Roger Williams? (139)
21. Who got along the best with the Indians? (139).
22. Who are the Hispanic people? (139)
23. What is William Kidd remembered for? (139)
24. What problems did the English people experience under the reign of John? (140)
25. What was the Gunpowder Plot? (140)
26. Who was declared Lord Protector of England and why? (141)
27. Explain the meaning of the term "Macaroni" as it was used in the poem about Cromwell. (141)
28. Who was the Man in the Iron Mask? (142)
29. What were some of the things Peter the Great tried to do for Russia? (143)
30. Discuss the situation with Prussia and the Hohenzollern Family in the seventeenth century. (144)

# 8

# 1701-1800

## {4:47 p.m.-7:11 p.m.}

During the next two hours and twenty-three minutes, the great American statesman, printer, scientist, and writer Benjamin Franklin (1706-1790) will publish many famous sayings, some of which will appear in his *Pennsylvania Gazette* and *Poor Richard's Almanac*. Two of these will be:

"Fish and visitors smell after three days"

"A stitch in time saves nine."

This great genius will also invent bifocal spectacles, a harmonica, and dozens of other useful inventions. His attainments in the physical sciences will also earn him a place in history (see section 148).

In geology, the doctrine of *catastrophism*, the philosophy that at intervals in the earth's history all living things have been destroyed by cataclysms (floods or earthquakes) and replaced by an entirely different population, will come into question. James Hutton (1726-1797), will suggest that the earth's history must be explained by observing the forces at work within it.

# Overview

The frontiers of knowledge continued to expand during this century in what became known as the Age of Enlightenment.

French King Louis XV sent the mathematician and astronomer Pierre Louis Moreau de Maupertuis (1698-1759) into Lapland to measure the length of a degree of the meridian (1736). The great Swedish astronomer Anders Celsius (1701-1744) accompanied Maupertuis on this expedition.

In America two English astronomers and surveyors, Charles Mason (1730-1787) and Jeremiah Dixon (died 1777), surveyed the boundary between Pennsylvania and Maryland (1763-1767).

Sir Isaac Newton published his experiments and studies in color and light in his *Optics* (1704) and was knighted by Queen Anne in 1705 for his many contributions to science.

Chester Moor Hall invented a new kind of refracting telescope, called an achromatic telescope (circa 1728), which solved the problem of color distortion inherent in earlier refracting telescope designs.

The English surgeon William Cheselden (1688-1752), published his outstanding work, *Anatomy of the Human Body* (1713) and developed a successful artificial pupil for the treatment of certain forms of blindness (1728).

John Wilkinson (1728-1808), an English ironmaster, built an extremely accurate boring machine (1774) that contributed to the success of James Watt's steam engine (1769). He also determined that water is a compound substance and not an element.

Jacob Joseph Winterl was the first to examine petroleum chemically (1788), and Count Alessandro Volta (1745-1827) proved that explosive gases could be ignited by an electric spark (1776), thus marking a significant step toward the development of the internal combustion engine.

The German chemist Martin H. Klaproth (1743-1817) discovered a new element (1789) and, naming it after the planet which Herschel had discovered eight years before, called it "uranium."

The use of the submarine in war first occurred in this century. The American David Bushnell's craft, the Turtle, was a small egg-shaped affair constructed of oak planks and was operated by one man, who turned a propeller. Water was admitted to submerge the vessel, and it was surfaced by forcing out the water with a hand pump. Lead

188

ballast kept the vessel upright. Its use in an attempt to blow up a British warship in New York Harbor during the American Revolutionary War (1776) by boring a hole in its hull and placing a charge to be ignited by clockwork failed because the boring tool, operated from inside the Turtle, could not penetrate the copper sheathing of the warship.

Robert Blackwell devoted most of his life to improving the quality of farm animals. Instead of growing relatively small cattle and pigs, he introduced scientific breeding; in several years a considerable improvement was brought about in the general size and quality of farm animals.

George Berkeley, (1685-1753), the Irish philosopher and clergyman, believed that matter could not exist without perception. He believed that his arguments constituted a complete refutation of atheism. He showed that qualities, not things, are perceived and that the perception of qualities is relative to the one who perceives.

Joseph Butler (1692-1752), an English theologian, saw the universe as a system, made up of individual facts through which man made his way slowly and inductively. Complete knowledge, he said, was impossible without knowing the whole.

Francois Voltaire's (1694-1778) writings epitomized the Age of Enlightenment which often attacked injustice and intolerance.

David Hume's (1711-1776) moderate style of living reflected his belief in moderation generally and his intense intellectual activity was evident in his writings. He is most famous for his ideas on skepticism, a philosophic position which denied the ability of man to know all and the ability of his reason to understand everything.

Immanuel Kant (1724-1804), a German philosopher, borrowed from the works of earlier philosophers, particularly Descartes, Spinoza, and Locke, to form some interesting new ideas. He believed that before any knowledge could be developed concerning the object of cognition, it was necessary to acquire the faculty of cognition and clearly realize the sources of knowledge it contained. He believed that sense, understanding, and reason were the three original faculties by which one acquired knowledge.

The memoirs of Giovanni Casanova (1725-1798) the great Venetian adventurer who became famous throughout Europe for his gambling, spying, and especially for his power to seduce women, were published after his death and endeared him to succeeding generations.

# Other Disciplines and Institutions

## 145. Aeronautics

This was the century in which speculation about flying turned to reality as man took to the air for the first time in a hot-air balloon (1783) {6:46 p.m.}. Jacques Etienne Montgolfier (1745-1799) and Joseph Michel Montgolfier (1740-1810) are credited with being the first Europeans to make a balloon that successfully carried a man. Their experiments began in 1783 when, as paper makers, they noticed that the smoke from a fire caused charred pieces of paper to rise. Soon they started to experiment with paper bags which they held open-end downwards over a fire for a while before releasing them. These bags rose rapidly into the air in a more controlled manner than the pieces of paper had. Thus they discovered the lifting source which would-be flyers had long sought. They called their discovery "Montgolfier gas." On June 5, 1783, at Annonay, France, they sent up a large cloth bag, thirty-five feet in diameter, lined with paper [see figure 8-2].

Later that year, they sent up the first balloon which carried living beings. A duck, a rooster, and a sheep were placed in a basket beneath the bag and sent aloft for eight minutes before landing safely. Flights by people soon followed.

J. A. Charles (1746-1823) became the first person in history to use hydrogen gas in balloons. In this type of balloon, he made a flight in 1783 of almost two miles [see figure 8-2]. When his balloon came down in a French field, the peasants tore it apart, believing that the moon had landed on earth.

## 146. Explorations and Discoveries

The outburst of geographical discoveries which characterized the fifteenth, sixteenth, and early-seventeenth centuries opened up so much of the world that people were kept busy getting acquainted with the newly discovered regions. Central Asia, central South America, most of Africa, some of the islands of the Pacific, and the frozen regions around the poles had been mysteries to the rest of the world. Alaska was explored in this century. Vitus Bering (1681-1741), a Danish navigator who sailed for the Russians, passed through the strait that now bears his name (1728) and discovered the Bering Sea. Bering also landed at Cape Saint Elias (1741), but he died there from the extreme cold.

In the latter part of this century, Captain James Cook (1728-1779), an English navigator and explorer, made some notable voyages of discovery in the Pacific Ocean. He found the Hawaiian Islands (1778) and named them the Sandwich Islands after his patron John Montagu, Earl of Sandwich (1718-1792), but met his death there a year later. On that same voyage, he coasted along the shores of Oregon, Washington, and Alaska. Except in the regions around the poles, not much in the way of newly discovered land has been added to the map of the world since the time of Captain Cook.

### 147. Music

Some outstanding composers came from Germany during this century. One of the greatest of these was Ludwig van Beethoven (1770-1827). Though he was born in Bonn, he went to Vienna as a young man, and there he studied for a time with Austria's famous musician/composer, Franz Joseph Haydn (1732-1809). Haydn was employed by a well-to-do Hungarian nobleman as the director of his private orchestra. Haydn first worked out the arrangement of players and instruments which makes the symphony orchestra such a wonderful means of expression in music. The great Austrian composer Wolfgang Amadeus Mozart (1756-1791) was there too and he acknowledged Beethoven's genius. In his later years Beethoven lost his hearing and could not hear the music he continued to compose. Franz Peter Schubert (1797-1828) also wrote many songs and symphonies.

Another great German-born composer was George Frederick Handel (1685-1759). His greatest oratorio, *The Messiah*, was first performed in Dublin, Ireland (1742), with Handel himself conducting. He had been commissioned to write an oratorio for a benefit program of the Dublin Foundling Hospital, and had composed in less than twenty-five days what has since become one of the most noted masterpieces in music history. The first London performance occurred the next year. As the singers began the "Hallelujah Chorus," George II (1683; reigned 1727-1760) king of Great Britain and Ireland rose to his feet; some say he did this so he could see better, others believed it was because he was inspired to do so. The audience, too, stood and remained standing until the chorus ended, thus establishing a tradition that is still followed today.

Italy became famous for its violins. The city of Cremona made the greatest contribution to this type of musical instrument. A family named Amati did much to develop the violin into the instrument which contributes so much to the music of our own day. One of the greatest of the pupils of the Amati family was Antonio Stradivari (1644-1737). His violins could produce such wonderful music that his name still stands as the greatest of all violin makers.

## 148. Developments in the Physical Sciences

Alchemy had long been the "chemistry of the Middle Ages." The primary occupation of its adherents had been the vain search to find a way to turn copper or other metals into gold. There was something called the "Philosopher's Stone" which was believed to have the power to change baser metals into gold or silver. As man learned more and more about the world in which he lived, true chemists began to emerge who made significant contributions to their field. It should be remembered, though, that the effort to transform one metal into another was done in the spirit of investigative chemistry and thus preserved a discipline that later blossomed into the science of chemistry as it is known today.

Frenchman Antoine Laurent Lavoisier (1743-1794) is regarded as the founder of modern chemistry. He demonstrated the importance of oxygen to the living body and made the first accurate scientific explanation of the mystery of fire, among other things. His work was neither understood nor appreciated and he was executed on the guillotine during the French Revolution for political reasons.

Joseph Priestley (1733-1804), an English clergyman and chemist, made vital contributions to chemistry. He invented the lowly but important eraser in 1770. A friend of his in America sent him a ball of crude rubber that was made from the latex of a tree which grew in South America. Priestley found that lumps of this substance rubbed out lead-pencil marks much better than the bread crumbs that had before been used for this purpose. In view of this property of caoutchouc, Priestley gave it the name "rubber." Priestley also discovered ammonia, nitrogen and its oxides, and carbon monoxide.

192

He did not realize the importance of his discoveries and he drew inaccurate conclusions about them. Priestley, along with Joseph Black (1728-1799), conducted many experiments with gases. They discovered oxygen in the air. Priestley called the gas "dephlogisticated air," but it was renamed "oxygen" by Lavoisier. Black is credited with the discovery of carbon dioxide, which he called "fixed air." Black also explained the difference between the mild and the caustic alkalines, the relation of lime to limestone, and the distinction between lime and magnesia.

The Swiss physicist Daniel Bernoulli (1700-1782) believed that temperature, which measures the intensity of heat, was really a measure of "vibrations" in solids, liquids, and gases (1738). He thus conceived of heat as consisting essentially not of matter but of vibrations—that is, he considered it to be a form of motion. Fifty years later, the British-American scientist Benjamin Thompson (1753-1814), who became Count Rumford of the Holy Roman Empire, further developed the idea. In a study presented to the British Royal Society (1798) he defined heat as a mode of motion rather than a material substance. His classic experiment showed that in boring a cannon with a blunt borer it is possible to heat over twenty-five pounds of water to the boiling point in about two hours and a half (see also reference to Rumford in section 149).

Improvements were made in thermometers themselves during this century. The first was invented (circa 1714) by Gabriel Daniel Fahrenheit (1686-1736) in Danzig, and introduced the use of mercury as a heat-measuring medium. The thermometer of Rene Antoine Reaumur (1683-1757) (invented circa 1730) used alcohol; the centigrade, invented (circa 1742) by Anders Celsius at Uppsala, became the most popular thermometer for laboratory work. These measuring devices were essentially small vacuum tubes of glass that were closed on one end and connected at the other, with a chamber for the liquid, with one or two scales etched on the front of the instrument. When heat was applied, the liquid expanded and rose.

Benjamin Franklin created many inventions of value and his achievements in the physical sciences were no less spectacular. His amazing experiment of flying a kite in a thunderstorm, which proved that lightning and electricity were the same (1751) {6:00 p.m.}, was but one of a series of experiments that won him recognition from the leading scientists of Europe and in America.

The continued use in this century of what was called the electrical machine, first conceived of by Otto von Guericke (1602-1686) in the previous one, eventually led to the development of the battery. Alessandro Volta (1745-1827) used the electrical machine in an experiment in which he piled silver and zinc discs with cloths between them that had been soaked in salt water (1792). He thus succeeded in obtaining electricity from this pile of metal discs which came to be known as the "voltaic pile."

## 149. The Social Sciences

One of the first social scientists was Count Rumford (see section 148) who became interested in improving housing conditions and was instrumental in eliminating smoky chimneys. He introduced central heating, based on convection currents of water. He also invented the steam table, the casserole, the chafing dish, and the coffee percolator, and suggested improved means of preparing and keeping foods.

Another important social scientist of this century was Thomas Robert Malthus (1766-1834), an English economist who is known for his *Essay on Population* (1798). His doctrine, which came to be known as Malthusianism, was written to refute the idea held by some writers of his time that life on earth could be brought to perfection by improvements in the social order. This was not possible, he predicted, because of the persistent tendency of man to increase his numbers and thus to crowd ever more closely upon the means of subsistence. He contended that the population increased faster than the food supply and that wars and disease were, therefore, necessary to remove the extra population. This idea was known as the Law of Diminishing Returns.

# Matters of Religion

## 150. The Dunkards

The Dunkards (also called the Tunkers), was a German sect of anabaptists. Their popular name came from the German word "to dip," in description of their way of baptism. Dunkards baptized once for each person of the Trinity and they evolved from the Pietist movement in Germany. The first congregation of the sect was organized there in 1708 by Alexander Mack. Persecution drove them to America. There, under Peter Becker, they settled in 1719 in Germantown, Pennsylvania. From this and other settlements in Pennsylvania they spread westward and into Canada. They were opposed to war, oaths, alcohol, tobacco, and worldly amusements. The original group in the United States was organized as the Church of the Brethren (Conservative Dunkards). From this body there grew a separate church known as the Seventh-Day Baptists, German (1728). James Conrad Beissel (1690-1768) was the founder of a Seventh-Day Baptist community in Pennsylvania. He emigrated (1720) from Germany and settled with the German Baptists in Germantown, Pennsylvania. Beissel published (1728) a tract on his conviction that Saturday was the true Sabbath. With his followers he established (circa 1728-1733) a type of monastic religious community.

## 151. The Sunday School

English Protestants welcomed the introduction of Sunday schools in 1781. Robert Raikes (1735-1811), publisher of the *Gloucester Journal*, saw this as an opportunity to bring in the poor children who spent their Sundays in idleness and play after a hard work week at the factories. Teachers were at first employed for twenty-five cents a day and the children were kept in the Sunday school the entire day, except for the brief period when they attended church services. Some teachers were not paid.

Rowland Hill established the first Sunday school in London (1784), and about 300,000 Sunday school members were enlisted in Great Britain (1789). In America the Philadelphia Society for the Support of Sunday Schools was organized (1786) with the view of forming organizations whereby children could be gathered into Sunday training classes. Sunday schools were also started in Boston, New York, and other cities.

## 152. The Methodists

There developed a revival from within the Church of England led by John (1703-1791) and Charles Wesley (1707-1788) in 1729. From their determination to conduct their lives and religion by certain "rules and methods" they were called Methodists. The denomination spread rapidly after 1739 in England and North America and was formally separated from the Church of England in 1791.

## 153. The Congregation of the Most Holy Redeemer

The Congregation of the Most Holy Redeemer, a religious organization, was founded in Italy (1732) by Saint Alfonso Maria de Liguori (1696-1787). Its members, sometimes called Redemptorists, devoted themselves to the religious instruction of the poor. The author of several books, Liguori advocated the concept of *equiprobabilism* in the priests' interpretation and administration of church doctrine. This concept suggested that the more indulgent opinion should always be followed, whenever the advantages in its favor were as good, or nearly as good, as those on the other side. A priest could not forbid dancing on Sunday, for example, if the practice had won widespread acceptance among the members of his congregation. Yet the priest had to exercise sound judgment and not allow the opinions of a few to permit the whole congregation to go astray.

## 154. Moses Mendelssohn

The works of Moses Mendelssohn (1729-1786), a German philosopher, had a great impact on the attitude of other people about the Jews. He believed that the Christians were victims of "hereditary antipathy" and that reforms would follow if Christians were given the opportunity to objectively view what was happening. He further observed that the Jews had fallen into a degree of degeneration in this century following their disappointments in Sabbatai Zevi (1626-1676) who, in the previous century had claimed to be the Messiah (circa 1650) but who had embraced Islam to save his life (see section 136). As a result they turned inward and their children were taught without any regard to outside conditions. They spoke and wrote a special jargon and their whole training tended to produce isolation from their neighbors.

Mendelssohn, more than any other individual, both by his career and writings, put an end to these conditions. When he was fourteen, he went to Berlin where Frederick the Great (Frederick II, king of Prussia), who followed the writings of Voltaire, believed that "to oppress the Jews never brought prosperity to any government."

Mendelssohn's important work, *Phaedo*, wherein he argued for the immortality of the soul, gained him the title of the "Jewish Plato." It also brought him acceptance by the leaders of the Gentile society in Berlin. Mendelssohn also translated the *Pentateuch* (the first five books of the Bible) into German with a new commentary by himself and others, introduced new ways of thinking, and thus brought the Jews into contemporary ways of thinking.

Several important outcomes arose from Mendelssohn's works. Scholars began a new and more serious study of Judaism, but his pragmatic ideas of religion weakened the belief of certain thinkers in the absolute truth of Judaism. Thus his own grandchildren, including the famous German musician, Jacob Ludwig Felix Mendelssohn (1809-1847), turned to Christianity.

# The Industrial Revolution

## 155. The Industrial Revolution in England

It is impossible to set an exact date for the beginning of the Industrial Revolution, for it did not start all at once and it did not begin in all countries at the same time. It was well in motion in England, however, by the last quarter of the eighteenth century. It reached some other countries many decades later.

Why did it begin in England? One reason was that England was perhaps the most progressive country in Europe; certainly more inventors and businessmen who were willing to try new methods were found (after 1760) there than in any other country at the time. It was the country most prepared in the world to take advantage of new ideas. Industry in England was freer from restraint and heavy taxation at the hands of the government than in most other countries. Besides, many of the first changes were in the manufacture of textiles—that is, woolen, linen, and cotton goods—and there was something about England's climate that was especially favorable to the manufacture of such goods. In constructing the new machines, such as the lathe, and in operating them by steam power, much iron and coal were called for. England had both of these commodities.

Also, England had built up a large trade with her colonies and with other countries. She had merchant ships. She could sell her manufactured products abroad and buy in return the raw materials for her industries and food for her workers. For a long time no other country could compete with her in this respect. So, in England, the Industrial Revolution was firmly established before other countries took up the new methods.

## 156. The Industrial Revolution Outside of England

England at first tried to keep its new machinery for its own use and did not allow it to be exported. Neither did they permit any models or drawings of it to be carried out of the country. But Samuel Slater (1768-1835), an English-born industrialist in America, looked carefully at some of those machines and carried his observations in his head to Pawtucket, Rhode Island, where, in 1790, he built the first factory in the United States. Factories did not make much headway in the United States, however, until the war with Great Britain in 1812. The New Englanders, whose extensive merchant shipping was practically ruined by the commercial troubles of the time, began to turn their attention to manufacturing; and so by the close of that war a real start had been made toward a factory system in the United States.

The change went more slowly in the United States than in England, however, as the records of the United States Patent Office prove. The maximum number of patents issued for new inventions did not exceed eighty (before 1812). Even later (1860) the number was only 5,000. But when, after the Civil War, America really got its industrial development under way, it moved quickly and became one of the greatest manufacturing nations in the world.

On the continent of Europe, northern France and Belgium were most suited for the early introduction of the Industrial Revolution. Many people lived there in a comparatively small area. They could furnish the labor for factories, and coal mines and iron ore were handy. Early in the Industrial Revolution France earned a good reputation for the quality of her manufactured goods.

## 157. Changes Between Government and Industry

As the Industrial Revolution continued to grow, the question of the status of the relationship between government and industry began to emerge. Should the factory owners be subject to any restriction by the government? Adam Smith (1723-1790), the great Scottish economist, published his *Inquiry into the Nature and Causes of the Wealth of Nations* in 1776. It had an important influence upon the thinking of those times. No doubt he sincerely believed his theories and they certainly did fit in with the wishes and notions of most factory owners.

Smith advocated the doctrine of *laissez-faire* which meant "let things alone" or "let things take their own course." Smith said, "Every man, as long as he does not violate the laws of justice, is left perfectly free to pursue his own interests in his own way and to bring both his industry and capital into competition with those of any other man." Such a policy would give businessmen the best possible opportunity to run their industries so as to make all the money out of them they could. He also believed that labor, and not land or money, was the real source of a nation's wealth.

But how did the policy of laissez-faire work out? Very badly, if one thinks of the terrible conditions under which many men, women, and children were often forced to work, and the relentless competition which drove employers to do things that in their own hearts they often detested. So laissez-faire had to give way to the doctrine of government regulation. Governments, so it developed, not only told industry how long a working day could be and regulated the conditions under which all workers could be employed, they set up standards with which every employer had to comply.

## 158. The Industrial Revolution and the Workers

Factory owners often found themselves in desperate competition with rival owners. To make their businesses profitable, they employed workers for any price they would take—and the workers had to accept rather small wages, because there was competition among them as well as among the employers.

The hours of labor lasted from daylight until dark. Even children nine years old worked unbelievably long and hard. In the factories and in mines, children and women sometimes toiled twelve, fourteen, or fifteen hours a day. About the only time the workers could get a break was when the machinery broke down. Sometimes they would throw their wooden shoes, in France called *sabots*, into the gears to make the machinery break down. This is where the word sabotage came from.

**Reflection:**

*What obligations do Christians have when circumstances affect on people's lives so dramatically as they did during the Industrial Revolution? Should the Christian consciousness work to alleviate such hardships? How could a Christian minister to these needs?*

# Matters of State

The struggle between the European powers for territory in the Americas that began in the previous century (see section 139) continued in this one. The French persisted in their aggressive assertions to their claims in the New World but they were weakened by trying to hold a vast territory with relatively few people. Though they were not as organized, the English had a larger number of people holding onto a smaller amount of territory than the French.

## 159. Continuing Struggles for the New World

The struggle between the European powers for territories in the New World that began in the last century and which produced open conflict on the European continent itself, continued in this one. It will be recalled that the American aspect of this conflict has been broadly classified as the French and Indian Wars (see section 139).

Queen Anne's War (1701-1713), which was fought to combat the aggressions of the French, corresponded to the European War of the Spanish Succession (1701-1714). The colonists were, once again, caught in the bloody struggle. The French and Indian raid (1704) on Deerfield, Massachusetts, was especially tragic. An attempt on the part of the British to take Quebec failed. Port Royal, and with it Acadia, fell (1710) to the expedition under Francis Nicholson (1655-1728) and were acknowledged as Britain's in the Peace of Utrecht (1713).

Peace returned to the colonies for a time afterward but war returned when trouble between England and Spain led to the conflict known as the War of Jenkins' Ear (1739-1741), which merged into the War of Austrian Succession (1740-1748—see section 163). The American phase did not begin until 1745, and it was called King

George's War because George II (1683; reigned 1727-1760) was on the throne in England. It lasted until 1748.

The last struggle in this century over the disposition of colonial territory in America was known as the Seven Years' War (1756-1763— see section 164). The American events of this war are called the French and Indian War, after the broader title given to all of the wars fought on the American continent in the late seventeenth and eighteenth centuries for these territories.

One of the British objectives of this war was to take French forts in the West, including Duquesne, Frontenac, Niagara, and the posts at Ticonderoga and Crown Point. They also were determined to take Louisburg and the French cities on the Saint Lawrence, Quebec, and Montreal. Early efforts were unsuccessful. Edward Braddock's (1695-1755) expedition against Duquesne (1755) was a resounding failure as were attempts by Admiral Edward Boscawen (1711-1761) against Canada and the first expedition against Niagara. But when William Pitt (1708-1778) became English Secretary of State, a decided change for the better came in the American part of the struggle.

There were many English victories that followed in the wake of the new generals that Pitt sent to the North American continent. In 1758 Lord Jeffrey Amherst (1717-1797) took Louisburg and General John Forbes (1710-1759) took Fort Duquesne without a fight. The English renamed it Fort Pitt after their great statesman, and a little later the village around the fort became Pittsburgh. Yet the decisive struggle in the New World was for the possession of Quebec. The French cause was lost when General James Wolfe's (1727-1759) men took Quebec (1759). In 1760 Montreal also fell, and the war was over. The Treaty of Paris (1763) ended French control of Canada, and went with the West to Great Britain.

## 160. The American Revolution

The leaders of the English colonies along the Atlantic coast would have been leaders anywhere, whether in old England, New England, or Virginia. Probably there was a higher average of intelligence and more enterprise and independence among them than among the mass of the people at home. The people of other nationalities—Germans, French Huguenots, Irish, Dutch, and Swedes—who were fairly numerous in some sections of the English colonies, were also of good quality. Nevertheless, it was to England that the people mainly traced their government and their ideas of liberty; and because they were such high-grade Englishmen they were not willing to accept the low-grade leadership that prevailed in England for a while (after 1763).

The political leaders of England at that time, as well as King George III (1738; reigned 1760-1820), who did not intend to be a figurehead, did not realize how their American "subjects" felt about things. England had spent much money protecting the colonies from French and Indian attacks. Why should not the colonies pay some of the bills? The Englishmen of the colonies, however, did not take kindly to such ideas. When Parliament passed the Stamp Act requiring the use of stamped paper for legal documents, newspapers, and other purposes in 1765, violent objection was offered all through the colonies. A secret organization known as the Sons of Liberty was formed to protest this act in 1765. "Taxation without representation is tyranny" was the Americans' slogan.

An occurrence in Boston Harbor one night (December 16, 1773) was the spark which set off an explosion. A number of Bostonians, disguised as Indians, went on board ships of the East India Company and threw the cargoes of tea into the water. This enraged the English leaders. Parliament passed a series of laws, which the colonists termed the "Intolerable Acts," intended to enforce British authority in the colonies.

One thing quickly led to another. At the suggestion of Virginia and members of the Sons of Liberty, a Continental Congress, with representatives from twelve colonies, assembled in Philadelphia (1774) and drew up a declaration setting forth the rights which its members believed English colonists justly possessed.

The first actual clash in arms occurred at Lexington and Concord in Massachusetts on April 17, 1775. Colonial soldiers encamped around Boston, and in less than a year the British troops left that city. A second Continental Congress met at Philadelphia (May, 1775) and, because there was no one else to do it, proceeded to take charge of the general interests of the colonies. One of its early acts was to choose as commander of the colonial troops George Washington (1732-1799) of Virginia. Without Washington it is hard to see how the colonial cause could have been successful.

At first Americans claimed to be fighting simply for their rights as Englishmen. Nothing was said—publicly at least— about separating from England. But as the British leaders made no concessions, a feeling gradually grew among the colonists that independence was the only way to assure them of their rights. A Declaration of Independence, which had been written by Thomas Jefferson (1743-1826), was adopted on July 4, 1776 {6:36 p.m.} by the Continental Congress.

For a time things did not go very well with Washington and his American troops. The British, after leaving Boston, forced him out of New York (1776), and the next year, occupied Philadelphia. Later they also overran a part of the southern colonies. But suddenly the whole situation changed. The British general Charles Cornwallis (1738-1805) took his forces to Yorktown in Virginia. A French fleet blocked Chesapeake Bay, so that reinforcements Cornwallis wanted could not reach him. He surrendered to General Washington on October 17, 1781. This was enough. The English people were tired of the war and there was no desire to press it any further.

The British government agreed to surprisingly generous terms of peace. The independence of the United States was recognized, with a territory including all the land east of the Mississippi River and south of Canada, except for the province of Florida which was given to Spain. The final treaty of peace was signed in Paris during September, 1783. The United States of America, separated from their former British associations, were now "on their own."

## 161. France Under Louis XV (Background for Revolution)

Louis XIV handed a kingdom over to his great-grandson that was not only burdened with taxes but one that was under the control of as disreputable a gang of useless nobles and court followers as one could imagine. Louis XV (1710; reigned 1715-1774) and his associates did not do anything to improve France. A common saying among them was "After us the deluge." Many of the burdensome restrictions upon peasant workers which had been inherited from old feudal times were still in force. Taxes, at times, took as much as four-fifths of a peasant's earnings.

Practically all power was in the hands of the king and his ministers or associates. The Estates-General, which was supposed to represent the French people, did not meet once during the long reigns of Louis XIV and Louis XV. The French people had no way of letting the government know what they wished, and anyone who was brave enough to ask for reforms risked being sent to prison for his nerve. Secret orders, bearing the king's signature and known as *"letters de cachet,"* under which people could be put in prison without a trial, were sometimes sold or given away. It is said that 150,000 of these were issued during the reign of Louis XV.

The king lived in luxury at Versailles. Flocks of attendants looked after his slightest whim, and the public treasury supported soldiers and courtiers in luxury who did nothing at all to earn what was spent on them. Graft, inefficiency, and everything else one might think of in bad government went on almost uncontrolled.

## 162. The Attack on the Bastille

Six years after peasants attacked J. A. C. Charles's hydrogen balloon when it landed in the French countryside, believing it was the moon (see section 145), a mob set fire to and destroyed the royal prison on July 14, 1789, which was known as the Bastille [see figure 8-3]. It housed at the time only seven prisoners, most of whom deserved to be there. But to the masses, the Bastille stood as the grim symbol of all the tyranny and injustice of the "Old Regime." King Louis XVI (1754-1793; French king 1774-1792) was roused in the night and told the story of the attack on the Bastille. "This is a riot!" he exclaimed.

"No, sire," replied the messenger, "it is revolution." The French people today celebrate Bastille Day, much as Americans do their Independence Day (July 4).

Next, the Revolution broke out all over France. Mobs tried to tear down castles and destroy the records of feudal obligations. In place after place the old governments were broken down and new ones set up. Soon a "National Guard," with Lafayette (sometimes La Fayette) (1757-1834) at its head, was organized (1789-1792), both to keep order and to protect the revolutionists against any efforts on the part of the king to suppress them. The National Assembly adopted the Tricolor— the flag with three stripes: blue, white, and red, which Frenchmen revere today—in place of the white banner of the old Bourbon family.

The night the National Assembly met on August 4, 1789, is actually more significant to France than Bastille Day. On that night, as the National Assembly was in session, a young noble whose conscience told him that his class was largely to blame for the Revolution, rose and proposed to give up the feudal privileges that had belonged to him. A wave of emotion, in some respects magnificent, in others merely hysterical, surged through the whole assembly. Man after man arose and proposed to do away with the special privileges he had enjoyed. Each proposal was speedily adopted. Serfdom was ended, special rights to office were repealed, oppressive taxes were abolished, and all citizens were given the same rights before the law. In one night almost all the rights and privileges on which the entire feudal system of France had rested were done away with. Victor Mirabeau (1715-1789) called it "an orgy of sacrifice." A few days later, on August 21, 1789, the Assembly drew up a "Declaration of the Rights of Man."

## 163. The War of Austrian Succession

Almost immediately after Frederick II "the Great" (1712; reigned 1740-1786) came to the throne in Prussia, he committed his first act of international dishonor. He wanted the district of Silesia, which was under Austrian rule, and suddenly marched his troops into Silesia and took possession of it. Maria Theresa (sometimes Teresa) came to the throne in Austria (1717; reigned 1740-1780), the same year Frederick became King of Prussia. She declared Silesia to be "the jewel of her crown" and had no mind to lose it without a fight. So the "War of the Austrian Succession" (1740-1748) began. Frederick had France and some German states on his side, and the English and the Dutch sided with Austria because they did not like France. After eight years, Maria Theresa gave up the struggle for a time.

Frederick did not try to be popular with all his fellow monarchs. He said once that the troubles of Europe were due to three old cats, meaning Elizabeth of Russia, Maria Theresa, and Madame Jeanne Antoinette Pompadour (1721-1764), the mistress of Louis XV of France. Maria Theresa after a few years tried once more to regain Silesia. This time she even won France to her side, as well as Russia, Sweden, and some German states. Frederick's only strong ally was England, which stood with him because France was on the other side.

## 164. The Seven Years' War

The Seven Years' War (1756-1763) was a world-wide war fought in Europe, North America, and India between France, Austria, Russia,

Saxony, Sweden, and (after 1762) Spain on the one side and Prussia, Great Britain, and Hanover on the other. As mentioned earlier, the complex struggle partially originated in the colonial rivalry between France and England. It also involved the struggle for Austria and the rising kingdom of Prussia. It was precluded in America by the outbreak of the last of the French and Indian Wars (see section 159) and in India by fighting among native factions and the struggle between Joseph Dupleix (1697-1763) and Robert Clive (1725-1774).

The War of the Austrian Succession (see section 163) had left Austria humiliated. Seeking to recover Silesia from Prussia, Empress Maria Theresa, even before the conclusion of that war, had secured the alliance of Elizabeth of Russia (1709; reigned 1741-1762). By extension, therefore, the European phase of the War of Austrian Succession was commonly known as the Seven Years' War. At one time Frederick's chances of winning looked poor. England did not send soldiers over to the continent but helped Frederick with money. Russia, Austria, and France all invaded Prussian territory, but Frederick defeated his enemies in two great battles. When England finally was ready to quit after beating the French in America and India, luck again turned Frederick's way. Empress Elizabeth of Russia died, and Russia withdrew from the ranks of its enemies, for Elizabeth's successor was a great admirer of Frederick.

When peace was made in 1763, Frederick still had Silesia. Then he joined with Russia and Austria in dividing Poland and added considerably more territory in that way. His seeming success, through his military genius and acts of selfishness and trickery, set a bad example for later rulers of his own and of other countries.

## 165. Austria Under the Hapsburgs

No other family ruled for so many centuries over such an illogical mixture of peoples as did the Hapsburg rulers of Austria. Germans in Austria, Magyars in Hungary, Czechs in Bohemia, Italians in Italy, and Flemings and Walloons in the Netherlands were all to be found under Austrian rule at one time. Time after time, an Austrian was elected Holy Roman Emperor; and even though this was not much more than a name, it carried a sense of prestige in much of Germany also.

Holy Roman Emperor Charles VI (1685; reigned 1711-1740), who had no male heir, feared what might happen at his death. He worked out an arrangement known as the Pragmatic Sanction, by which it was agreed that Marie Theresa would peacefully inherit her father's territories.

Marie Theresa shared in the first of the partitions of Poland, but was the only one of the three rulers who showed any conscience about it. "She wept," it was said, when she thought of the injustice of it, "but she took," for she figured that Poland was going to lose out anyway, and Austria might as well have a share in the spoil.

# God in History

Q. What mistakes did the humanists make in their efforts to better mankind?

A. The humanistic Renaissance thinkers believed that they could perfect society without God. The French romantically held to this view even in the midst of the Reign of Terror (a period during the French Revolution when people who were seen as a menace to the state were executed [1793-1794]). These thinkers were deists. They saw God as a being who had created the world but who had no contact with it anymore. (Voltaire resented God's "silence" after the Lisbon earthquake of 1755). They also felt that God had not revealed truth to men. The men of the French Enlightenment had no foundation but their own finiteness. They looked across the channel to a Reformation England, tried to build without the Christian base, and ended with a massacre and with Napoleon as their authoritarian ruler (see sections 173-179).

The French changed their calendar and called "1792" the "year one," and destroyed many of the things of the past, even suggesting the destruction of the Cathedral at Chartres. They proclaimed the goddess of reason in Notre Dame Cathedral in Paris and in other churches in France, including Chartres.

In a contrasting belief, Benjamin Franklin remarked: "Whosoever shall introduce into public affairs the principles of Christianity will change the face of the world."

# Chapter Terms

achromatic telescope
dephlogisticated air
electrical machine
equiprobabilism
fixed air
law of diminishing returns
Malthusianism

"Messiah" (music)
Montgolfier gas
Philosopher's stone
Redemptorists
Reign of Terror
skepticism

# Chapter Review Questions/Exercises

1. Name some of the important developments as mentioned in the Overview to this chapter.
2. Who were the first men to fly? (145)
3. Name some of the important explorers of the eighteenth century. (146)
4. Name some of the outstanding musicians of the eighteenth century. (147)
5. What were some of the major events in the world of science in the eighteenth century and who were the people behind them? (148)
6. Name two important social scientists of the eighteenth century and tell what they did. (149)
7. Who were the Dunkards? (150)
8. Who were two important men who helped to establish the Sunday school? (151)
9. Who founded the Methodists? (152)
10. What was the Congregation of the Most Holy Redeemer? (153)
11. Explain some important things that happened in the life of Moses Mendelssohn. (154)
12. Discuss in detail the Industrial Revolution in England. (155)
13. What were some of the important aspects of the Industrial Revolution outside of England? (156)
14. How were the workers affected by the Industrial Revolution? (158)
15. How did the Industrial Revolution produce changes between government and industry? Be sure to include the doctrine of laissez-faire in your answer. (157)
16. What were some of the wars fought in the French and Indian Wars? What were some of their European counterparts? (159)
17. What were the important events of the American Revolution? (160)
18. What were some of the problems in France that caused the attack on the Bastille? (161)

19. Describe the attack on the Bastille and Louis XV's reaction to it. (162)
20. What was the War of Austrian Succession? (163)
21. Describe the Seven Years' War. (164)
22. What influence did the Hapsburgs have on Austria? (165)

# 9

# 1801-1900

## {7:12 p.m.-9:35 p.m.}

During the next two hours and twenty-three minutes, Charles Darwin (1809-1882) will say:

> I feel most deeply that this whole question of creation is too profound for human intellect. A dog might as well speculate on the mind of Newton! Let each man hope and believe what he can.

Matthew Arnold (1822-1888) will observe:

> To understand that the language of the Bible is fluid, passing, and literary, not rigid, fixed, and scientific, is the first step toward a right understanding of the Bible.

The American Horace Greeley (1811-1872) will popularize the following saying: "Go west, young man."

By international agreement in 1884 the Greenwich, England, meridian will be selected as the Prime Meridian from which other meridians are measured.

# Overview

This was the first century in which the growth in industry and many other fields depended on science. The spectacular advances in pure science gave rise to equally more impressive technological developments than before. Business demanded more sophisticated devices. Inventions such as the typewriter [see figure 9-1] and the pencil sharpener [see figure 9-2] were thoughtfully provided.

Farmers benefited from an invention of the American James B. Darby (1858-1898) [see figure 9-3], who patented (1892) a plow which doubled the work done behind a mule [see figure 9-4].

George Washington Carver (circa 1864-1943), an agricultural chemist, directed his research in agronomy to the improvement of the American south, convincing southern farmers to diversify their crops by planting soil-enriching peanuts (from which he derived a great number of products) and sweet potatoes.

The first voting machine was demonstrated in New York in 1892. This mechanical device automatically recorded and counted votes.

Another important development was that of practical photography by the Frenchman Louis Daguerre (1789-1851) who exhibited his method of making permanent pictures (which he called Daguerreotypes) at the exhibition in Paris in 1822 (see section 171).

New ways were found to make better weapons, including those developed by the German manufacturer Alfred Krupp (1812-1887) whose improved guns gave his government decisive advantages in the Franco-Prussian (Franco-German) War (1870-1871).

In England, Sir William Congreve's (1772-1828) rockets were used in naval warfare in an attack on Boulogne (1806) and later they were employed with effective results on land.

The experimental work of the Austrian Ernst Mach (1838-1916) in the field of ballistics (published in the late 1870s and 1880s), led to the discovery of the sound barrier and the use of the Mach number which is the ratio of the velocity of a body in a gas to the speed of sound in a gas.

A process for making nitroglycerin was developed (circa 1846) by Ascanio Sobrero (1812-1888), an Italian chemist, but it was not used widely as an explosive for many years because it could not be depended on to explode as readily as gunpowder.

Swedish chemist Alfred Nobel (1833-1896), experimented with nitroglycerin, looking for a way to explode it safely. He obtained a patent on a detonating cap made of mercury fulminate (1864), which proved ideal. Thus, he invented dynamite which became a safe and convenient means for the transportation and use of nitroglycerin, making dynamite very popular.

The English teacher and chemist John Dalton (1766-1844) published his atomic theory of matter (1803). His theories made it possible to understand how atoms of elements combine to make compounds and molecules.

An important milestone in physics was the now-classic experiment conducted in 1886 by Albert Michelson (1852-1931) and Edward Morley (1838-1923) wherein they attempted unsuccessfully to find the theorized "universal ether," which was believed to be a weightless, invisible substance which scientists thought permeated all the space surrounding the earth and all the space between the stars. The failure of their experiment to detect it was one influence that led Einstein to develop his theory of relativity in the next century.

French physicist Antoine H. Becquerel (1852-1908) discovered radioactivity when he accidentally exposed a photographic plate to uranium salts (1896). This clue, combined with others, led to the knowledge of nuclear physics and, fifty years later, to the atomic bomb (see section 240).

The industrial uses of aluminum were made possible by the American chemist Charles Martin Hall (1863-1914) [see figure 9-5]. He discovered the electrolytic process for producing aluminum economically (1886), which is still known as the Hall Process. In Pittsburgh, Hall found a group of young industrialists who were willing to risk some of their capital on promoting his new smelting process. They formed the Pittsburgh Reduction Company (1888), a name which was later changed to the Aluminum Company of America (Alcoa) (1907).

As iron and steel began to be manufactured on a large scale, charcoal as a fuel was no longer satisfactory. Coal largely took its place. The production of coal had been cheapened by improvements in methods of mining and made more humane by Sir Humphry Davy's (1778-1829) invention of the safety lamp (1815) in which a wire gauze enclosed the flame. This saved the lives of thousands of miners who might otherwise have been killed through explosions of deadly

213

gases. United States coal production reached a million tons a year during 1840 and by the end of the century, production was up to 370 million tons a year.

Then came the power of electricity. Innumerable discoveries and inventions have made it the servant of man. Working on the foundations laid in the previous century, Michael Faraday (1791-1867) learned how to make electric power move machinery (1831). Georg Simon Ohm (1787-1854) developed an equation which measured electrical resistance. It became known as Ohm's Law (1827).

Jobard of Brussels advanced the idea that a small piece of carbon incandesced in a vacuum by electricity might serve as a lamp (1838). The work of Thomas A. Edison (1847-1931) turned this idea into reality with the first successful electric incandescent light made with a filament of carbonized cotton thread (1879). Edison was, of course, the wizard of many inventions including a system of duplex telegraphy, the carbon telephone transmitter, and the phonograph.

Marchese Guglielmo Marconi (1874-1937) invented the wireless telegraph in 1897 and opened the door to the entire range of modern communications.

Elias Howe (1819-1867), an American inventor, developed a sewing machine which was eventually attached to an electric motor.

The Englishman Sir Charles Wheatstone (1802-1875) invented an electric alarm and authored several important scientific works, including *New Experiments in Sound* (1823), and *Experiments to Measure the Velocity of Electricity* (1834).

The Industrial Revolution called for better methods of transportation because coal and raw materials had to be carried from their places of origin to factories and the products of the factories had to be taken to market. Yet the methods of transportation of these goods had improved little between the beginning of this thousand years and the beginning of this century. The seagoing ships—merchantmen and men-of-war—were decidedly different in their design from the caravels and galleons of previous days, but they followed the same principles. They depended on the winds to drive their sails and these vessels were in complete subjection to the winds. On land, the fastest travel was by coach which, ideally, could make up to fifty miles daily.

The use of steam for power, instead of wind or muscle, revolutionized ocean shipping and changed water transportation on rivers and lakes. The initiative had been taken in the previous century

214

by such men as the Frenchman Denis Papin (1647-1712) who built a steam-powered boat in 1707, and the American James Rumsey (1743-1792) who demonstrated his steamboat on the Potomac River (1787) {6:52 p.m.}. Early steamboat designs of this century used both steam and sail. Later steamboats were designed well enough to permit the sails to be done away with completely.

Inland waterways called canals were also built to facilitate the increased need for transportation occasioned by the Industrial Revolution. Much canal-building took place on the continent of Europe, in England, and in the United States in the latter part of the eighteenth century and through most of the first half of this century. By building locks and dams, problems imposed by difficult topographical features could often be overcome.

The railroads reduced the importance of the canals. The British engineer Richard Trevithick (1771-1833) invented the high-pressure steam engine (1800) and later experimented with traveling engines driven by steam. The English Parliament, which did not have much foresight or imagination, put an end to some of these early enterprises by requiring that any such machine traversing the roads of England must be preceded by a man carrying a red flag. Englishman George Stephenson (1781-1848) in 1814 put steam to such a use, and he was credited with the invention of the locomotive. The first steam-driven passenger train was built in 1825.

In its turn, the automobile did to the railroad what the railroad once did to the canal. Men had talked about a "horseless carriage" for some time, but it was only toward the end of this century, during which a number of new developments came, that the dream became reality. The German Karl Benz (1844-1929) built his first gas engine in 1878 {9:03 p.m.}. Electricity provided the spark that ignited the gas, and steel made strong, light-weight housings possible for the engine. Benz next produced his first motor vehicle in 1885. Charles Goodyear's (1800-1860) patent on a rubber vulcanization process (1844), eventually made it possible for rubber to be used in innovative ways in the automobile, and John Dunlop (1840-1921) patented the first pneumatic tire in Ireland (1889).

Other developments came quickly. The first organized motor-sports event was held in Paris (1894) and was known as the Paris-Rouen Trial. Frank Duryea (1869-1967) won the first major United States auto race from Chicago to Evanston (1895) and in the same

215

year, the first road race organized by the Automobile Club of France was held. It was during this race that the first race accident took place when a driver on the Paris-Bordeaux-Paris run collided with a dog.

In America, Henry Ford (1863-1947) built his first car in 1892 and founded the Detroit Automobile Company in 1899. Ransom E. Olds (1864-1950) opened his first automobile factory in the United States in 1899 and the Renault company was founded in France in the same year.

These and other developments quickly influenced the lives of men. Many thought this century marked the beginning of an age of limitless progress toward an earthly paradise. Old industries grew and new ones appeared as a result of the research and practical applications of science.

There were some great achievements in exploration in this period but the icy regions around the North Pole and South Pole remained unreachable in this century. The Englishman Sir Robert MacClure (1807-1873) succeeded in making a "northwest passage" around North America to Asia (1853), which Europeans had been looking for ever since the sixteenth century, only to learn that it was a futile quest. Expedition after expedition got nearer to the North Pole but it was not until the next century that it was reached (1909).

# Other Disciplines and Institutions

## 166. Aeronautics

With the success of the Montgolfier brothers in France, ballooning became more popular as better and better balloons were made. In America, John Wise (1808-1879) ascended in a balloon during the Philadelphia Exposition (1835). For almost four decades after that, he continued to demonstrate his balloons.

During the American Civil War, tethered balloons were sometimes used by the Union armies to observe the southern troops. During the Siege of Paris in the Franco-Prussian War (1870-1871), many messages were sent out of the imprisoned city by balloons.

Yet ballooning did not make man the master of the air. His flights in them were subject to the will of the wind, and flying in a balloon in bad weather was extremely dangerous, if not impossible. Some innovative men tried to devise ways to steer balloons but with little success. Henri Giffard (1825-1852) installed a light steam engine in the gondola of a cigar-shaped balloon and achieved near Paris the first feeble flights against the wind (1852).

Others besides Giffard experimented with this elongated shape for balloons and achieved greater speed and steadiness. Even these, though, had a tendency to "buckle" in the middle when driven against the wind. The German Count Ferdinand von Zeppelin (1838-1917) conceived of the idea of placing a rigid framework of aluminum inside the balloon to protect it from the winds. He was also able to attach propellers to the framework instead of to the gondola itself. His first practical "Zeppelin" (1900) encouraged him to make additional machines.

Development of flight in heavier-than-air machines proceeded along pathways that were separate from those of the balloon in this century. Englishman George Cayley (1773-1857) realized that fixed wings, not flexible bird wings, would be required for a stable flying machine (1800). He flew unmanned gliders from hilltops (1804). There is some evidence to suggest that he even flew a manned glider at least on one occasion that same year. He further concluded that heavier-than-air flight would require a "prime mover," or a more powerful and efficient engine than the steam power plants of his day afforded. His design for a powered airplane (1837) called for the best steam engines of the time, but they were inadequate. It was not until after the development of the internal combustion engine that heavier-than-air flight became practical early in the next century.

## 167. Astronomy

New observations of Mars were made during this century and were at the root of a major controversy. The Italian astronomer Giovanni Schiaparelli (1835-1910) is best remembered for his observations, during 1877, of that planet when its orbit brought it about as close to earth as it ever gets. He observed what he described as long, straight lines crossing the red Martian deserts. Schiaparelli called them *canali*, or channels, but the term was translated into English as canals. He made detailed observations of Mars at its next closest approach in 1879 and believed that some of these canali had a strange ability to become double. It was not until later that they were reported by anyone else (1886), but not everyone who saw them

217

felt confident about determining what they might be.

The controversy was taken up by the American Percival Lowell (1855-1916) who built an observatory in Flagstaff, Arizona (1896). Lowell believed that the canali Schiaparelli had observed were artificial canals designed by intelligent beings as a planet-wide irrigation system to pump water from the icy polar caps to "the populated regions nearer" the equator. He expressed his view this way: "That Mars is inhabited by beings of some sort or other is as certain as it is uncertain what those beings may be."

We know today that Lowell was incorrect concerning his conclusions about life on Mars but his other contributions were worthy ones nonetheless. He was a brilliant speaker and writer and an excellent organizer. Some of his research eventually led to the finding of the ninth planet in the next century by Clyde Tombaugh (see section 213).

An important observer of this century was the American Edward Barnard (1857-1923). When a reward was offered by a wealthy American for the discovery of a new comet, Barnard bought a small telescope and spent his nights earning money. The sixteen comets he discovered in his career paid for the house he lived in. He became an observer at the new Lick Observatory (completed in 1888). Using the thirty-six-inch refractor there, he discovered a fifth moon of Jupiter, called Amalthea (1892). When he was assigned to the staff of the Yerkes Observatory in Williams Bay, Wisconsin, with what was then the world's largest refracting telescope, he was unable to confirm Lowell's observations of canals on Mars.

Conclusive evidence that the earth rotates on its axis was finally provided by Jean Bernard Leon Foucault (1819-1868), a French physicist, who conducted the now-famous pendulum experiment in 1851 (see chapter endnote 9-1). He offered more proof in 1852 by using a gyroscope that maintained its axis in a fixed direction while the earth turned relative to that direction.

The English astronomer Francis Baily (1774-1844) became, during the annular eclipse of the sun in 1836, the first to observe the phenomenon now known as "Baily's Beads" (see chapter endnote 9-2).

A more accurate determination of the position of many of the known stars was made in this era as well and astronomers became more knowledgeable about their apparent brightness, motions, and speed through space. The German astronomer Friedrich Wilhelm Bessel (1784-1846) succeeded in making the first measurements of the distance of the star, 61 Cygni (1838). He settled on a distance of about 8.2 light years, a figure fairly close to the value of 11.2 light years that we accept today as being accurate.

The spectroscope was first used in the century to determine the speed and direction of motion of the stars. Christian Johann Doppler (1803-1853), an Austrian physicist and mathematician, explained the effect of motion on the pitch of sound—the so-called Doppler Effect (1842) (see chapter endnote 9-3). This explanation was to serve astronomers well in explaining also the effect of motion on the "pitch," or wave length, of light.

The English astronomer Sir William Huggins (1824-1910) became the first person to observe the spectrum of the red stars, Betelgeuse and Aldebaran, learning that they showed dark lines similar to our own sun (1863). Huggins later observed in 1868 that Sirius, the brightest star in the sky, is moving away from us at over twenty-nine miles per second. He and his wife, Margaret Lindsay Murray (also known as Lady Huggins), jointly authored the classic *Atlas of Representative Stellar Spectra* in 1899.

## 168. Geology and Evolution

In this century scientists presented impressive new ideas about the development of man and the globe on which he lives. The discoveries of Mary Anning (1799-1847), the English fossil-collector who found the first specimen of Ichthyosaurus (1811) in the steep cliffs near Lyme Regis, prompted scientists to rethink their theories about the earth.

The doctrine of uniformism, the basic concept of which was first advanced by Hutton in the previous century (see opening references to chapter eight), was developed in detail in this one by the Scottish mathematician John Playfair (1748-1819) in his *Illustrations of the Huttonian Theory of the Earth* (1802). This theory was also advanced by the English scientist Sir Charles Lyell (1797-1875), who has often been called the founder of modern geology. In 1833 he published his *Principles of Geology* in which he set forth the opinion that the earth was infinitely older than most people had believed. If it always took as long as it now takes for winds, water, freezing and thawing, and other changes to alter the face of the earth, the earth must be millions instead of thousands of years old he theorized. This assertion was in direct contrast with the belief of Usher that the earth had been created in 4004 B.C. (See entry on Usher in opening reference to chapter seven). He accepted modern theories about the Ice Age and evolution and he wrote about prehistoric man and his environment in his book *The Antiquity of Man.*

Another Englishman, Charles Robert Darwin (1809-1882), a naturalist, wrote *On the Origin of Species by Means of Natural Selection* (1859) and *The Descent of Man* (1872). Instead of animals and plants having always had the same form in which we see them, he theorized, they actually developed out of simpler forms through a process which we usually refer to as evolution. Even human beings, he thought, have changed greatly in their physical appearance and ability to adapt themselves to their surroundings. Though it is not accurate to quote him as claiming that man descended directly from apes, it was popular to believe that he did.

Thomas Henry Huxley (1825-1895), the English naturalist and philosopher, embraced Darwin's theories and the English writer Mortimer Collins (1827-1876) composed the following rhyme about him which he affectionately named "Darwin:"

> There was an ape in the days that were earlier;
> Centuries passed, and his hair grew curlier;
> Centuries more gave a thumb to his wrist,
> Then he was a Man and a Positivist.

---

**Reflection:**

*An attempt was made to connect the theory of evolution with Christian beliefs by Henry Drummond (1851-1897), a Scottish evangelist. He is thus noted for his two books,* Natural Law in the Spiritual World *and* The Ascent of Man. *Is it possible for religion and science to have a common ground for understanding God's world? How do the theories of creation and evolution differ?*

---

## 169. Literature

The early years of the nineteenth century produced an exceptional number of poets in Europe. There was William Wordsworth (1770-1850), who in 1843 became England's poet laureate (an honorary title in recognition of great poetic achievement). He is remembered for many works including, "Tintern Abbey," and "Ode to Duty." The very talented George Gordon Byron (1788-1824) also wrote many poems. Two of his numerous works include *The Prisoner of Chillon* and *Don Juan.* Two poems that were written by John Keats (1795-1821) were, "Ode on a Grecian Urn" and "Ode to a Nightingale" (1820). Percy Bysshe Shelley (1792-1822) is noted for such poems as "Ode to the West Wind," "To a Skylark," and "The Indian Serenade."

Queen Victoria's long reign (1837-1901) saw the rise of many other great English literary figures. Elizabeth Barrett Browning (1806-1861) is remembered for her greatest work, *Sonnets from the Portuguese* (1850), and her husband Robert Browning (1812-1889), is recognized for such works as *Dramatic Romances and Lyrics* which contained some of his most striking shorter poems. Alfred Tennyson (1809-1892) left such memorable poems as "The Lady of Shalott" (1832), "The Charge of the Light Brigade" (1855), and "The Holy Grail" (1872). Rudyard Kipling (1865-1936), poet, novelist, and short-story writer, left many impressive poems, including "Mandalay" and "Gunga Din." (1897). His children's stories included *The Jungle Book* (1894) and *Second Jungle Book* (1895).

Other great writers of this era included the novelists William Makepeace Thackeray (1811-1863) whose first major novel was *Vanity Fair* (1848), Charles Dickens (1812-1870), George Eliot (1819-1880), the pen-name of Mary Ann (or Marian) Evans, and Kenneth Grahame (1859-1932), the author of many children's stories.

Dickens's novels brought to light many of the social conditions in England that needed correction. His titles such as *Oliver Twist* (1841), *David Copperfield* (1850), and *Great Expectations* (1861) are writings that shed light on the social and political problems of the time. Another of his important works, *A Tale of Two Cities* (1859), was set in the time of the French Revolution. Evans's novels included *Adam Bede* (1859), *The Mill on the Floss* (1860), and *Silas Marner* (1861). Charles Lutwidge Dodgson (1832-1898), better known by his pen name of Lewis Carroll, authored *Alice's Adventures in Wonderland*

221

(1865) and *Through the Looking Glass and What Alice Found There* (1872). His popular characters, the Mad Hatter, the March Hare, the White Rabbit, the Red Queen, and the White Queen, quickly became familiar figures to the many children who came to adore these excellent literary works. Grahame is remembered for his children's stories *The Golden Age* (1895) and *Dream Days* (1898). His most popular story, *The Wind in the Willows*, was not written until the next century (1905).

Sir Walter Scott (1771-1832), the Scottish novelist and poet, is recognized for his swinging narrative poems which were a form of verse tale. His lyrics and ballads, such as "Lochinvar" and "Proud Maisie," were masterly in feeling and technique. Another noted author of Scottish origin was Sir Arthur Conan Doyle (1859-1930), a British physician and novelist, creator of the famous character Sherlock Holmes, the skilled and amazing detective. His adventures were told in such noted stories as *The Adventures of Sherlock Holmes*, and *The Hound of the Baskervilles*.

The genre of science fiction received the attention of some notable writers during this century as well. *Frankenstein* was written (1818) by Mary Wollstonecraft Shelley (1797-1851). It was her first and best novel. This early science fiction story dealt with the rather common theme that there are some things that man has no business fooling with—namely "playing God" by trying to make life. A time-travel tale entitled *The Mummy!* was written by J. Webb (1827). It was a story of travel to the twenty-second century. The Frenchman Jules Verne (1828-1905) gave the world such momentous stories as *Five Weeks in a Balloon* (1863), *A Journey to the Center of the Earth* (1864), *From the Earth to the Moon* (1865), *Twenty-Thousand Leagues Under the Sea* (1870), and *The Mysterious Island* (1875).

In addition to Verne, there were other great names in nineteenth-century French literature. Victor Marie Hugo's (1802-1885) *Les Miserables* (1862), is one of the greatest literary classics ever written. Alexandre Dumas (1802-1870) vividly pictured French life in the seventeenth century in some of his works but also excelled in writing what might be called historical novels, specific in place and time. Such remarkable titles as *The Three Musketeers* (1844; English translation, 1846) and *The Count of Monte Cristo* (1844-1845; English translation, 1846) are examples of the latter type. Emile Zola (1840-1902) became acquainted with the numerous phases of life in Paris by visiting the huts and hovels of the poorer classes. This caused him to become a powerful delineator of character and a close student of conditions which he skillfully worked into his stories which sought to reform the ills he perceived in society. One of the best known of his social reform works was *L' Assommoir* (1877; English translation, *The Dram Shop*) on lower-class life in Paris. Guy de Maupassant (1850-1893), a student of Zola, perfected the short story in France (he wrote over 300 of them). Three of the most remembered of these included *"La Parure"* ("The Necklace"), *"Clair de lune"* ("Moonlight"), and *"La Ficelle"* ("The Piece of String"). He saw that all men were alike and seemed to be filled with the same instincts. He was obsessed with the dread of growing old, of ceasing to enjoy life, and the horror of death. The latter became a major theme of his writings. Honore' de Balzac (1799-1850) proved to be a prolific and popular writer. His works exercised a significant influence on later movements in realism and naturalism. His greatest works were a collection of writings he called *La Comedie Humaine* (*The Human Comedy*) (1831-1851).

Russia contributed several important authors during this period as well. One was Leo Tolstoy (1828-1910) whose writings, while they were not very important for their literary value, were noticed anyway because they called attention to many of the social ills in Russia at the time. Feodor M. Dostoyevsky (1821-1881) is largely remembered for his ability to find good in the most helpless members of society. *Crime and Punishment* (1866) became one of his most famous works as did his novel entitled *The Idiot* (1869).

America also produced numerous successful writers during this period including Ralph Waldo Emerson (1803-1882) who is remembered for his *Essays* (first series, 1841; second, 1844) which expressed some of his transcendental beliefs (a philosophy that explains matter and objective things as products of the mind that is thinking about them). "Self-Reliance" is perhaps the best known of these works. Henry Wadsworth Longfellow's (1807-1882) many works included *Ballads and Other Poems* (1841) which contained the famous poems "The Wreck of the Hesperus" and "The Village Blacksmith." He is also noted for his poem *The Song of Hiawatha* (1855) which was based on an Indian legend. Nathaniel Hawthorne (1804-1864) left us the powerful novels *The Scarlet Letter* (1850) and *The House of the Seven Gables* (1851).

Other talented American writers of this period included Edgar Allan Poe (1809-1849) who became the master of the short horror story with such ghastly titles as "The Masque of the Red Death" (1842) and "The Tell-Tale Heart" (1843). He was equally comfortable with poetry, having left such extraordinary examples as "The Raven" (1845), and shortly before his death, "The Bells" and "Annabel Lee" (1847). James Russell Lowell (1819-1891) poet and editor, published his first book of poetry, *A Year's Life* (1841). He also became the first editor of the *Atlantic Monthly* (1857-1861). James Fenimore Cooper (1789-1851) wrote such unforgettable novels as *The Last of the Mohicans* (1826) and *The Deerslayer* (1841). Samuel Langhorne Clemens (1835-1910), who wrote under the pen name of Mark Twain, is perhaps best remembered for his novels *Tom Sawyer* and *Huckleberry Finn*. Washington Irving (1783-1859), is noted for his essays "Rip Van Winkle" and "The Legend of Sleepy Hollow," which were first published in serial form in New York (1819-1820). Irving also had a role in fostering the American concept of Santa Claus, which originated from a combination of folk traditions from many European countries. Irving's portrayal of Saint Nicholas in his *Knickerbocker's History of New York* (1809) as a happy, fat little fellow who traveled through the air in a wagon, should sound familiar to all American children today. The idea was enhanced by the work of Clement C. Moore (1779-1863), a professor of Oriental and Greek literature at Columbia University in New York, with his poem "Twas the Night Before Christmas" (or "A Visit From Saint Nicholas") (1822).

The great American lexicographer, Noah Webster (1758-1843), made significant contributions to both language and literature when he published his complete dictionary, *The American Dictionary of the English Language* (1828), and an enlarged edition (1841). His most popular smaller book was *Webster's Spelling Book*.

## 170. Medicine

The two main scourges of surgery since the decline of Rome, had been the inability to prevent pain and the onset of infection. Certain of the Greek and Roman physicians had used opium, dittany, and mandrake to reduce pain and had been able to limit infection by certain cleansing processes. Yet even these somewhat limited remedies moved in and out of popularity in the medieval and Renaissance periods and they never received wide acceptance at any time. It was obviously the poor sanitary conditions in the crowded, dirty dwellings of the sick, and in the filthy medieval and Renaissance hospitals and the neglect of physicians in hand washing, that were the main contributors to the problem of infection. This, along with the surgeon's limited ability to deal with pain, meant that surgery was practiced only in desperate cases since the mortality rate was so high. It was only near the middle of the nineteenth century that these matters were at last addressed with success.

To prepare the way for the introduction of anesthetics (substances that cause entire or partial loss of the feeling of pain) and antiseptics (substances that prevent infection), man had to obtain a clearer understanding of the body's chemical processes. It had long been believed that a "vital force" influenced chemical changes in living things. In 1828 the German chemist, Friedrich Wohler (1800-1882), showed how a simple, inorganic chemical, ammonium cyanate, could be changed by chemical action into urea (a soluble crystalline solid present in the urine of mammals). His experiment showed that urea could be made by chemical action just as any other chemical could— by a union between the atoms of its constituent elements. The chemistry of living things was thus seen to obey the ordinary laws of chemistry itself and organic chemistry became a separate branch of chemistry.

Advances such as these encouraged creative investigation into the body's chemical processes which led to methods of pain prevention. Dr. John Collins Warren (1778-1856) demonstrated that sulfuric ether could relieve the sufferings of a patient with terminal lung disease. Thus, while doctors could not cure such patients at this time, they at least had found a way to make their last days more comfortable.

Further advances in pain prevention were made in strange ways. William Clarke, a student at Berkshire Medical College, accustomed to the sniffing of ether at parties, administered some on a towel to a young woman while a dentist extracted one of her teeth in 1842. This is the first known instance of ether being used to produce surgical anesthesia.

The Scottish physician Sir James Young Simpson (1811-1870) introduced the use of ether to produce general anesthesia in childbirth, but he soon discontinued its use in preference to chloroform in 1847. That same year he read a paper before the Medical Society of Edinburgh in which he advocated its use instead of ether.

The English surgeon Joseph Lister (1827-1912) developed the idea of antiseptic (germ-free) surgery. He wrote a paper on "The Early Stages of Inflammation" (1857) based on his experiences with gangrene and pyemia (a form of blood poisoning caused by bacteria that produce pus) in London. His earliest clinical efforts were devoted to cleaning the wounds but he soon learned that infection set in anyway. When he learned in 1865 of Pasteur's discovery that air-borne germs could spoil milk and cause meat to rot, Lister correctly reasoned that spoilage was not caused by the spontaneous generation of germs, nor by oxygen in the air (the two dominant theories of the day) and there was some chance of preventing it. His solution was to clean the wounds with carbolic acid. But as successful as this procedure was, it was the caustic action of carbolic acid by itself that prevented its use in general surgery. To this end, Lister spent many years researching this problem before a final solution was achieved. His achievements saved thousands of lives of patients who would otherwise have died from infection.

Diagnosis for many medical problems became much easier after the discovery of the X-ray in this century. Wilhelm Conrad Rontgen (sometimes Roentgen) (1845-1923), a German scientist at the University of Wurzburg, Bavaria, found that rays could be produced which could shine through human flesh under certain conditions (1895). This new discovery enabled doctors to actually see inside the body of a patient. This gave surgeons a valuable new tool in their fight against sickness, pain, injury, and disease.

Considerable advances in the field of nursing occurred during this century also and two wars, the American Civil War and the Crimean War, served as backgrounds for these advances. Mary Ann Ball Bickerdyke (1817-1901) was a Union nurse in the American Civil War. Known as Mother Bickerdyke, she served throughout the war in the West where she worked for the improvement of care for the wounded enlisted men. Clara (Clarissa Harlowe) Barton (1821-1912) became a nurse in the same war. She founded the American National Committee (1877) which later became the American Red Cross. Florence Nightingale (1820-1910), an English hospital administrator, was influential in modernizing training for nursing. Her skills for administration were demonstrated when, in 1854, she organized a hospital unit of thirty-eight nurses for the Crimean War and established a new type of war hospital at Scutari and Balaklava.

## 171. Photography

Meaningful steps in the development of photography took place in this century when Sir Humphry Davy, the great English chemist, and Thomas Wedgwood, published their findings on how they produced silhouettes of subjects by soaking paper and leather in silver nitrate and exposing them to sunlight (1802).

Joseph N. Niepce (1765-1833) made the first negative by placing a piece of sensitized paper into a camera (1816). Louis J. M. Daguerre (1789-1851) devised an image-recording system whose glass plate was coated with silver iodine (1829). Light falling on the plate made the silver iodine go dark so the plate could be used to record the pattern of light and shade forming an image in a camera obscura (see chapter endnote 9-4). They were able to make the image permanent by exposing the plate to mercury vapor. This invention was called the Daguerreotype.

A decade later this process was improved upon by the work of William Henry Fox Talbot (1800-1877) who developed (1839) the "calotype" process in England. In his process an image was recorded on paper that was saturated with silver chloride and then "fixed" by chemical treatment.

It was George Eastman (1854-1932), an American inventor and industrialist, who made it possible for most people to be able to readily afford to make photographs at home. His first camera contained a roll of film which was returned after exposure while it was still inside the camera (1888). Later Eastman's company, the Kodak Corporation, marketed a camera that sold for a dollar (1900).

## 172. Matters of Religion

The missionary efforts of the various churches continued to grow in this century. Walter H. Medhurst (1796-1857) was an English Congregationalist missionary to China. He spent many years there preaching about Jesus, and he was also a member of a committee of delegates for the revision of the Chinese versions of the Bible.

Eli Smith (1801-1857) became an American missionary to Malta (1827) but he also traveled as a missionary in Syria, Greece, and Armenia. He went to Leipzig, Germany as well. The last ten years of his life were spent translating the Bible into the Arabic language. He is also noted for his book *Missionary Researches in Armenia*. His wife,

Sarah Lanman Smith (1802-1836), accompanied him and rendered valuable assistance in his missionary work.

The great English Baptist clergyman Charles H. Spurgeon (1834-1892), accomplished many important achievements during his lifetime. He was appointed to preach at a small chapel in London (1853), but his great preaching abilities soon made an enlargement of the church necessary. Consequently he engaged Surrey Music Hall as a place to address his large congregations. He then promoted the building of the Metropolitan Tabernacle (1861), a structure capable of seating 6,000 persons. Eventually he began publishing his sermons (1885) and the collection eventually reached 2,188 (1891). He founded a library of 8,000 volumes for indigent ministers and established a training school for evangelists. He also built numerous almshouses, an orphanage, and many chapels. His sermons were delivered with great force and he had them transcribed by a stenographer at the time of their delivery so they could be put into print. Among his most noted books were *Cheque-Book of the Bank of Faith*, *The Treasury of David*, and *Gospel of the Kingdom*.

Joseph Smith (1805-1844) was the founder of the Mormon Church (the Church of Jesus Christ of Latter-Day Saints). As a child he was troubled by the disagreements he observed among the religious denominations. He announced that he had received a vision in regard to a sacred book that he claimed was buried near Manchester, New York (1827), and later he allegedly received a volume known as *The Book of Mormon*. He gathered a few followers and moved to Ohio in 1831, where he failed in the management of his community and a storehouse. Soon after this he founded the city and temple of Zion near Independence, Missouri, and succeeded in attracting a large following.

One of Smith's followers was Brigham Young (1801-1877). He joined the settlement in Ohio (1832) and became one of their twelve apostles (1834). Later he became president and prophet after the death of Joseph Smith (1844). When the Mormons were forcibly expelled from Illinois, Young faced their difficulties with remarkable fortitude and led the larger part of the Mormons over the Great Plains and across the Rocky Mountains to Great Salt Lake, where he founded Salt Lake City in Utah (1847). Later he founded the beautiful Mormon Temple there.

# Matters of State

## 173. France

It did not take long for Napoleon Bonaparte (1769-1821) to make himself the real Emperor of France. Power was centralized under his rule and the early part of Napoleon's rule was a period of comparative prosperity for France. He favored a thorough system of education from the primary schools all the way through the higher grades to the University of France. Napoleon also tried to beautify the country, especially its capital city, Paris. In doing this he robbed the cities of Italy which were under his control of some of their most cherished works of art.

Napoleon's idea of rebuilding a colonial empire for France did not turn out so well. How did Napoleon dominate Spain? He forced Spain to hand over to him the American province of Louisiana (1800), and sent a French army over to conquer the island of Santo Domingo. Disease and an unexpected resistance of the natives (1801), under their leader Toussaint L'Ouverture (1743-1803), made Napoleon wonder whether the game was worth the gamble. So, when the United States government proposed to buy New Orleans, Napoleon astounded the American agents by offering to sell them the entire province of Louisiana. The bargain was made, and the United States acquired the western half of the Mississippi Valley (1803). No other country ever got more for its money than the United States did in paying $15,000,000 for this territory, though neither buyer nor seller knew much about its geography.

Though Napoleon had extended France to what Louis XIV had called its "natural boundaries" and seemed to have made permanent the good things that the revolution had brought to France, the country could not remain at peace under him. England, Austria, and other countries were either jealous of him or feared him.

Besides, under cover of extending the blessings of the French Revolution to the abused people of Europe, Napoleon attempted to bring almost the whole continent under his domination. He annexed part of Italy to France and set up puppet kingdoms elsewhere in Italy and in other parts of Europe. At various times he made his brother Louis (1778-1846) King of Holland (reigned 1806-1810) and his brother Joseph (1768-1844) King first in Naples (reigned 1806) and then in

229

Spain (reigned 1808-1813). The royal family of Portugal found it more comfortable to take a vacation, and went to their colony of Brazil, where they established a new Portuguese empire. Jerome Bonaparte (1784-1860) was made "King of Westphalia" (reigned 1807-1813), including under his rule considerable German territory. His sister Caroline (1782-1839) became queen in Naples (reigned 1808-1814). Wherever Napoleon's power was extended, serfdom and feudalism were done away with if they still existed and a much more efficient government was established.

When William Pitt, "the Younger," (1759-1806) became Prime Minister of England (served 1783-1801, 1804-1806), he formed a coalition of England and other powers against Napoleon (1804). Napoleon assembled a great army just across the English channel, as if he intended to invade England. Whether he ever actually meant to do so is a matter of debate. The death to any such hopes, if he did entertain them, came in the great naval battle off Cape Trafalgar (1805), when the entire French and Spanish fleets were almost wiped out by the English fleet under Lord Nelson (1758-1805), though Nelson himself died during his hour of victory.

Before this naval disaster, Napoleon had already turned his armies to the East. Austrian troops were defeated in two great battles, Ulm and Austerlitz (1805). Austerlitz is sometimes called the most brilliant of all Napoleon's victories. He turned against Prussia (1806), provoked that country into war, defeated the Prussian troops in the battle of Jena, and captured Berlin.

He went to war with Russia (1807) and defeated them in the battle of Friedland, but showed more sense in dealing with them this time than he did five years later. Instead of attempting to carry his campaigns into the heart of Russia, Napoleon met Czar Alexander I (1777; reigned 1801-circa 1825—see chapter endnote 9-5) on a raft in the Niemen River and dazzled him with the brilliant idea of dividing Europe into two great empires with each man at the head of one of them. Now most of the continent of Europe, except Turkey, was either under Napoleon's thumb or allied with him.

Napoleon's victories brought some lasting changes in the map of Europe. Many little German principalities and duchies were united under Napoleon's "protection" in what he called the Confederation of the Rhine or else they were annexed to other German states. Emperor Francis I of Austria (1768; reigned 1804-1835), who had been Francis II, Holy Roman Emperor (reigned 1792-1806), was forced to give up that rather barren title (1806). Thus disappeared from European politics a title which had been a trouble-maker for a thousand years or so. Napoleon had dreams of repeating Alexander the Great's (356-323 B.C.) conquests in Asia, but he was never able to get around to it.

## 174. France and the Resistance of Spain and Austria

Napoleon did not realize that though he might beat kings, it was not so easy to keep people down indefinitely. When he imposed his rule on other countries, he stirred up a spirit of national patriotism which had not been seen for many a year. Portugal refused to obey the continental system and turned to England for help. The English sent Sir Arthur Wellesley (1769-1852), also known as the Duke of Wellington, to assist her.

Then Spain rose in revolt against Joseph Bonaparte, whom Napoleon had put on the throne there and he had to get out. Though their own government had been nothing to brag about, the Spaniards were determined not to live under a foreign conqueror. Napoleon then took a big army into Spain (1808), carrying Joseph back to Madrid with him. But as soon as Napoleon left, rebellion broke out again. Wellesley and his English soldiers came into Spain through Portugal, and the long, dragged-out "Peninsular War" (fought by France against Great Britain, Portugal, and Spanish guerrillas in the Iberian Peninsula—1808-1814) followed which did not end until the French had been driven out of Spain.

## 175. Disaster to Napoleon

Though the Spanish Rebellion was the beginning of Napoleon's decline, Russia gave the blow which most directly caused his collapse. Czar Alexander I was utterly tired of the continental system. Russia was so far from France that it was hard for Napoleon to enforce his authority there; but when the Czar openly defied him by allowing English ships once more to come to Russia, Napoleon decided to punish him.

Napoleon assembled the largest army he ever had under his command at one time and led it to invade and conquer Russia; but

231

the invasion turned into one of the greatest disasters any ruler ever suffered. Napoleon failed to take the geography and topography of Russia into consideration. As his troops marched farther and farther toward the heart of that enormous country, the Russians made little effort to resist them in battle but laid waste the country and carried away all the food supplies they could. Napoleon finally captured Moscow, but soon after he occupied the city the Russians set it on fire. There he found himself in a burned city in the middle of a foreign land with the terrible Russian winter just coming on. He realized that disaster would face him if he stayed.

## 176. Napoleon's Retreat

Disaster followed him all the way as he tried to take his army back. The Russians again refused to enter into a decisive battle with him, but they followed close behind and made all the trouble they could. When Napoleon recrossed the western boundary of Russia, hardly 20,000 men were left of the 500,000 he had taken into the country. The rest had starved, frozen, or been killed during the ghastly retreat.

## 177. The Battle of the Nations

This Russian calamity broke the spell which Napoleon had held over Europe. The King of Prussia rose in open revolt against him. Austria rebelled once more. Sweden joined his foes. In desperation, Napoleon got together a new army made up chiefly of boys or of men who before had been thought to be too old to fight. Even with these he won two victories; but near Leipzig, in what he often called the Battle of the Nations (1813), Napoleon suffered his first bad defeat. Then he retreated into France, followed by the troops of his allied enemies. Holland, Bavaria, and Naples had also risen against him. Wellington crossed the Pyrenees into France from the south. It was over.

## 178. Napoleon Forced to Elba

Napoleon's enemies at first agreed to let him keep his throne in France if he would accept the Rhine as one of the boundaries of France and refrain from interfering in the affairs of other nations. But he indignantly refused this really generous offer. Then they told him that he would have to be satisfied with the little island of Elba as a principality which he might rule over (1814). He was not given a choice in this matter. The armies of his foes came into Paris, bringing "in their baggage," as Frenchmen said, the brother of Louis XVI, whom they put on the throne under the name of Louis XVIII (1755; reigned 1814-1824). He took the number XVIII in order to recognize the son of Louis VXI, who did live to take the throne himself.

## 179. Napoleon at Waterloo

Elba was too small for Napoleon and too near Europe for the safety of anybody else. While the "allies" were trying to get things worked out, Napoleon escaped from Elba and suddenly reappeared in France. The king sent troops to arrest him, but instead they deserted Louis XVIII and joined their "Little Corporal." Now the rulers of the other great European countries once more had to put armies in the field against him. For about 100 days he held his own with the help of troops whom the enthusiastic French supplied. The decisive battle came at Waterloo (June 18, 1815), not far from Brussels in Belgium. A British force under the Duke of Wellington, joined before the day was over by a Prussian army led by Gebhard L. von Blucher (1742-1819) proved to be too much for Napoleon. He was captured and sent to Saint Helena.

---

**Reflection:**

*Did Napoleon seem to resemble the kind of man Jesus referred to in Mark 8:36 "For what shall it profit a man, if he shall gain the whole world, and lose his own soul"? What made Napoleon so ambitious? How much better would the world have been had Napoleon never existed?*

---

## 180. The World After 1815

The story of much of the world after this time dealt with people, especially Europeans, who worked hard to pay the war debts and mend broken friendships. Politicians who wanted to forget the war found it easy to attain an office.

The Congress of Vienna (September, 1814 - June, 1815) marked the end of one period and the beginning of another. It was called to remake Europe after the defeat of Napoleon I. One cannot understand the cycle of events through which Europe passed (1789-1815) without knowing the main things that were accomplished at that congress. At the same time, the spirit of reaction that dictated the arrangements made there influenced strongly the history of Europe for the next half-century and more.

Nations had discovered that tyrants could be overthrown, and time after time during the nineteenth century the most courageous or reckless in many countries rose against despotism. In Great Britain changes came for the most part peacefully; step by step, the people of that kingdom gained more control over their government. So democracy—government by the people—began to grow in this century.

Another characteristic of the nineteenth century was the growth of nationalism. Nationalism often means a narrow kind of patriotism, though one can be patriotic without despising nations other than his own. Nationalism also may signify the coming together under a recognized government of people who are related by race. Some of this nationalistic spirit—though not too much—was needed by the Germans and Italians to help them develop for their own good. Other peoples, such as those under Austrian rule, wanted to be freed from rulers of another race so they could govern themselves.

These two forces, democracy and nationalism, along with a tremendous change in industry caused by the Industrial Revolution which began in the latter part of the eighteenth century, were the chief factors in transforming life in Europe and the rest of the world from what it was in 1815 to what it was destined to become.

Karl Marx (1818-1883), a significant figure in world history, was born during this time of ferment. He was a person whose ideas found a disturbing degree of acceptance. Marx was a German philosopher and socialist who believed that mankind's problems could be resolved through a socialistic form of government (see section 215). This German social philosopher and radical leader became the chief theorist of modern socialism. His ideas were expressed in his book, *The Communist Manifesto* (1848) which he published with Friedrich Engels (1820-1895), another German socialist. Another of Marx's works included *Das Kapital*, the first volume of which was published in 1867. Volumes II and III, were posthumously published by Engels (1885-1894).

## 181. Greece Wins Independence From Turkey

When the Greeks rose in rebellion against their Turkish tyrants they had the sympathy of most people in western Europe. The English poet, Lord Byron, not only wrote in behalf of Greek liberty but with reckless enthusiasm, he went to fight for Greece and died on Greek soil even before he had a chance to fight. The combined fleets of England, France, and Russia completely defeated the Turkish fleet in the Bay of Navarino in 1827. The independence of Greece was recognized in 1829, and Otto I (1815-1869; reigned 1832-1862), a Bavarian prince, was brought down to be king of the country.

## 182. Mexico Wins Independence From Spain

The Spanish provinces in Central and South America had gradually been winning a struggle for independence. A conspicuous example of this was Mexico which fought for and won its independence from Spain in this century.

Mexico's independence was made possible by several factors. France's invasion of Spain in 1808 caused Ferdinand VII (1784; reigned 1808-1833) to yield to Napoleon, which left the Spanish colonies without a recognized European ruler. Some of the more-educated citizens of Mexico read books on the American (1776) and French (1789) Revolutions and started thinking about how they could help Mexico with its own revolution. The struggle was not won easily, however.

It started with the efforts of Miguel Hidalgo (1753-1811), a priest of little renown who called on his Indian followers to revolt against their Spanish rulers (September 16, 1810). There was a certain logic in his decision to get involved in the struggle for independence. A significant amount of the conflict in Mexico centered on the differences between church and state. Ecclesiastics were often partners with the owners of the great estates and combined with leaders of the army. But Hidalgo was unique in that he saw what the government was doing to the lives of the common people he ministered to daily. His inexperienced group was soon defeated by government troops and Hidalgo was executed. Other priests took up his banner and a Declaration of Independence was formally proclaimed at Chilpancingo (1813).

## 183. France Under Napoleon III

Since the French constitution provided that after one term of four years a president could not immediately have another term, Louis Napoleon (1808-1873), the nephew of Napoleon I, tried unsuccessfully to get the constitution changed so that an incumbent president could be reelected at once. Then he decided to take the government into his own hands anyway. On the anniversary of the battle of Austerlitz, and the crowning of Napoleon I as Emperor on December 2, 1851, he put over a surprising *coup d'etat* (a sudden change of government by force). During the preceding night he had the political leaders who might have opposed the plan arrested, and in the morning people saw placards posted all over the city of Paris declaring that a new government had been set up with Louis Napoleon as its head. Soldiers kept Paris under control. Then he had a new constitution drawn up, making himself president for ten years. Louis Napoleon, just a year after this coup d'etat, proclaimed himself Emperor as Napoleon III (reigned 1852-1870); and just as in the case of his famous ancestor, the people voted for the new title by an overwhelming majority. So the Second Republic was even shorter-lived than the first one.

Louis Napoleon, as Napoleon III, was not very impressive. The only thing which could possibly play in his favor would be for him to achieve success in some important area. Louis Napoleon had his uncle's success to help him; but he was not entirely lacking in intelligence himself and he honestly wished well for his country.

He had roads, canals, schools, and churches built and encouraged trade in many ways. He made Paris the queen of European cities in appearance. He received the goodwill of workingmen by building houses for them to live in and arranging for them to have insurance against death and accident. For ten years or so France prospered so well under his rule that Frenchmen took him at his own estimate as a statesman.

## 184. France and Mexico

Napoleon III's first big mistake was an effort to set up an empire under French control in Mexico which had been in disorder for many years, and whose financial affairs were in bad shape. While the American Civil War was going on he induced Archduke Maximilian (1832-1867) of Austria to accept the title of Emperor of Mexico. By the time the War Between the States was over (1865) and the victorious Union government was able to do something about this violation of the Monroe Doctrine (see chapter endnote 9-6), Napoleon had already realized his mistake and called his French troops back home. Maximilian was then left to the "tender mercies" of the Mexicans who summarily shot him. Napoleon III guessed wrong as to the winner of the American Civil War; his sympathy with the Confederate states was no secret. In this matter he had for a time the cooperation of the British government but then "played safe" by not recognizing the Confederate states as being independent.

## 185. Prussia Becomes a Military Power

When Frederick William IV died in 1861, a new king came to the throne of Prussia. Already, William I (1797; reigned 1861-1888), the brother of Frederick William, was sixty-four years old; but there was nothing of the "sere and yellow leaf" about him. He had served as regent after his brother had gone insane (1857). He allowed the Prussian constitution (1850) to continue in operation, but he did not let it worry him much. He was somewhat more progressive than his brother had been, though he was still a believer in the divine right of kings. His chief of staff, Helmuth Karl von Moltke (1800-1891), was one of Europe's ablest soldiers.

Prince Otto von Bismarck (1815-1898) became William's chief minister. He had served his country in the diplomatic corps in France and Russia and he knew these countries well. He was forceful, determined, and willing to do anything that might put his program through, and he had nothing but contempt for any constitution that might stand in his way. He brought about German union.

King William and Bismarck had to get more money to maintain the Prussian army and to increase it as they desired. Year after year, for five years, the lower house of the Prussian Parliament refused to approve any additional military expenses. But Bismarck did not allow that to stop him. He advised his king to go ahead and collect the necessary taxes. Never mind the Prussian constitution.

Bismarck figured that if his program was successful, the people would not care how it was put through. He would not permit the newspapers or anyone else to criticize his policies openly though there was plenty of discontentment at first. He saw that the Prussian army was equipped with rifles of the best make then known and insisted upon three years of service (instead of two) for every enrolled young man. As the army steadily grew stronger, he had less and less to fear from any opposition.

Bismarck believed this was the natural way for a state to make itself strong. "Germany does not look to Prussia's liberalism but to her power," he said. "The great questions of the day are not decided by speeches and majority votes...but by blood and iron." "Blood and iron" was the keynote for everything that followed.

### 186. Bismarck's Three Wars to Unite Germany

To bring about a united Germany with Prussia at its head, Bismarck deliberately planned a program that was hardly equaled in history for its cunning, ruthlessness, and seeming success. Since there could be no real German unity with both Austria and Prussia included, he first had to find some way to get Austria out of German politics. A series of three wars—"blood and iron"—achieved everything he sought for.

### 187. Prussia and Austria Attack Denmark

The first of these three wars was with Denmark. The duchies of Schleswig and Holstein were united with Denmark by "personal union"—that is, the Danish king was also their king. When the King of Denmark mistakenly decided to make these duchies a part of Denmark, the Germans, who made up a majority of their population, objected. Bismarck then induced Austria to join Prussia in making war on Denmark to prevent the annexation of Schleswig and Holstein. These two strong powers beat Denmark (1863-1864) and the Danish king lost the two provinces.

## 188. The "Seven Weeks' War"

The next step was to "pick a quarrel" with Austria. It was easy to do so by raising an argument over what should be done with the districts that had been taken from Denmark. So the "Seven Weeks' War" broke out in 1866 between the two powers. To everyone's amazement, the Prussian army occupied some German states and then invaded Bohemia and completely defeated the Austrians in the battle of Sadowa. Austria then was forced to agree to withdraw from German affairs and to consent to a union of German states under the leadership of Prussia. To put additional pressure on Austria, Bismarck had induced the newly formed kingdom of Italy also to make war on her; and as a part of the peace arrangements, Austria had to give up most of Venetia to Italy.

## 189. Bismarck's Partial Success

Now, with Austria out of the picture, Bismarck went to work to unite the German states. Those in northern Germany came together in the North German Confederation (1867). It was a strong union under Prussian leadership, but four of the southern German states were still suspicious of Prussia and were not ready to join.

## 190. The Franco-Prussian (Franco-German) War

It took one more war to get them in. This was the war with France (1870-1871). Emperor Napoleon III of France, who had thought that Austria would probably beat Prussia, was sure he could achieve victory. History records what followed. The German victory, in which the armies of South Germany had joined with those of Prussia and the other northern states, produced great enthusiasm for German unity. All the states of Germany united to form a new empire and installed William I, king of Prussia (see section 185), as the German Emperor. Now a united Germany—a real German Empire—built by Bismarck and his Prussian king in ten years, had a place on the map of Europe. German nationalism, denied realization before (in 1815 and 1851), had succeeded.

239

## 191. Italy

France's Metternich observed that Italy was only a "geographical expression." The map of Italy, when the Congress of Vienna broke up (1815), showed the districts of Piedmont and Sardinia constituting one kingdom; Sicily and southern Italy under the king of Naples; the Papal States, or States of the Church, including Rome and running diagonally across the peninsula to the northeast; several duchies, large and small, north of the Papal States; and Lombardy and Venetia directly under the control of Austria.

Three possibilities of bringing about the unification of Italy had their advocates. One idea was that the pope might make himself the leader of such a movement. But the pope did not care to undertake this task. Even though most of the Italian people were Catholics, so also were most of the Austrians; and as the head of the church to which both nations belonged, what would happen if he championed Italy's cause against Austria?

Another dream was that of Giuseppe (Joseph) Mazzini (1805-1872) and those who shared his hope that Italy might become a republic. He organized a number of young men in a movement that was referred to as "Young Italy" (1831); but many people were either too afraid of Austrian vengeance or else they did not believe that a republican form of government was the right thing for Italy. Mazzini had more enthusiasm than practical leadership, and his hopes and ideals caused him to spend some of his life in prison. The authorities were suspicious of him because they could not understand young men who took solitary walks and refused to say what they were thinking.

When the revolutionary year (1848) opened, a rebellion had been started in Sicily and Naples. Then, as the overturn in France came on and Metternich was driven out of Vienna, the spirit of revolt flared up in almost every part of Italy. Mazzini attempted to set up a republic under a written constitution in Rome; but his republic (1849) lasted less than a year. French troops were sent by Louis Napoleon to restore the pope to his position. When the excitement died down, they returned home. Mazzini had to flee for his life, and like so many other refugees, he found safety in England. Even in exile, he was hopeful. "Our victory is certain," he said. "What matters the triumph of an hour?" But it was not to be Mazzini any more than the pope who was to unite Italy.

There remained another possibility. Charles Albert (1798; reigned 1831-1849), king of Sardinia and Piedmont, took the field against Austria when the revolutions broke out in 1848. He was defeated and had to abdicate his throne in favor of his son Victor Emmanuel II. But Sardinia was given a constitution, and that constitution later became the basis for a united Italy.

### 192. Cavour and the King of Sardinia

Sardinian king Victor Emmanuel II (1820-1878; reigned 1849-1861) was a thorough patriot and a fine man personally; but, like many other kings, he could not play the game of politics and international statesmanship as well as some who could not wear a crown. He was exceedingly fortunate in obtaining as his prime minister an extremely skillful statesman, Count Camillo de Cavour (1810; served 1852-1859, 1860-1861). When there seemed no chance of overthrowing Austrian power in Italy, Cavour had kept rather quiet, occupied with a country estate and travel. But he established the first newspaper in Italy that dared to favor liberal government (1847). After the Kingdom of Sardinia received a constitution, he quickly rose in prominence. He became a prime minister in 1852 and immediately set to work to establish a new day in his kingdom.

Farmers were advised as to improved methods of agriculture and manufacturers were also encouraged. The production of silk and cotton was notably increased. Railroads were planned and started; and even the construction of a tunnel through the Alps was undertaken. Education was promoted; and Italy certainly needed it, for seventy-five per cent of her people could not read or write.

But an unaided Sardinia could not unite Italy. So Cavour laid his plans to get help from somewhere else. When the Crimean War broke out (see section 195), though Sardinia had no particular reason to be interested in it, he offered to send troops to help France and England fight against Russia. When the time came to make peace, he sat with other leaders of nations in the Congress at Paris and had a fine chance to tell them about the needs of Italy and his ambitions to drive out Austria and unite the country.

## 193. How the Kingdom of Italy Was Formed

Cavour had some reason to expect help from Napoleon III, since the Emperor had professed his interest in peoples who wanted freedom, and probably was sincere about this interest. After a time, an Italian tried to kill Napoleon III, charging that he really was not a friend to liberty in France or any other place. This act made a deep impression on Napoleon. Soon afterward he gave Cavour his promise to help in driving the Austrians out of Italy—on two conditions: the war had to be seen as a defensive war on the part of Sardinia, and France had to receive the districts of Nice and Savoy—Napoleon's *pourboire*, or tip, as they were called.

Going ahead with his plans to invade Austria, Cavour caused the Sardinian armies to be enlarged and better organized. The Austrian ruler fell into the trap and declared war on Sardinia. Then Napoleon III kept his promise. He came into Italy with French troops and, joining the Sardinians, won two notable battles over the Austrians (Magenta, 1859 and Solferino, 1860).

Then a sad disappointment came to Cavour. Napoleon III, distressed at the suffering and loss of life that even victories caused, began to wonder how long the French people would stay with him in a war on behalf of somebody else. Besides, if Austria was weakened too much, Italy might become correspondingly strong. Would a strong Italy next door to France be in the best interests of France? So without any notice to Cavour, Napoleon arranged a peace with Austria in 1860. Lombardy was transferred from Austria to Sardinia; but Venetia, which the Italians had hoped to gain, was left under Austrian rule. For once, Cavour lost his head. He wanted the war to go on, even without Napoleon; but King Victor Emmanuel knew this was silly and he refused to risk what had been gained in a hopeless effort to get more. Savoy and Nice, both in southeast France, were turned over; and Cavour and his king waited for the next move.

Help came from a surprising source. Giuseppe Garibaldi (1807-1882) had taken part in some of the earlier revolutions in Italy and also had done some fighting in South America. He lived for a while on Staten Island as a candle maker and captain of a small ship. He got together a thousand men (1860), called "Redshirts," because of the outfits they wore, and they were as reckless as Garibaldi himself.

The destination of the "Thousand" was Sicily. In a few weeks,

Garibaldi and his Redshirts overran the whole island and then crossed to the mainland. Almost as easily, the throne of the King of Naples fell, and Garibaldi had the "Two Sicilies"—the island and the southern part of the mainland—under his control. Next they voted to join Sardinia. Garibaldi unselfishly asked for no honor of office for himself, but turned over his conquests to King Victor Emmanuel.

Meanwhile, several districts in north and central Italy, including the duchies of Parma, Modena, and Tuscany, and part of the Papal States, overthrew their own governments and voted to be annexed to Sardinia. A national parliament, made up of delegates from almost all of the peninsulas, met at Turin in 1861 and voted to call Victor Emmanuel II (served 1861-1878) as the King of Italy. He thus became the last King of Sardinia (see section 192) and the first King of Italy. Within a few weeks Cavour was dead, but he had lived long enough to see the accomplishment of the largest part of what he had set out to do. Only Rome and Venetia were still outside of Italy. Florence was for some years the capital of the country, though everybody expected that in time Rome would hold that honor.

## 194. Italy and the Pope

Outside of Austria, about the only people who regretted the day Italy had been brought together were the pope and those who thought it was wrong to take from him the territories over which he ruled. Although most of the people of Italy continued to be loyal Roman Catholics, the pope refused to recognize King Victor Emmanuel and his successors. Some said it was good for the pope to be freed of the burdens of being a political ruler and that he could be entirely independent of any government as long as he was simply the head of the Roman Catholic Church. Others argued, however, that the pope needed to have land to rule over in his own right in order to make sure of his independence from other monarchs.

After Rome became the capital of Italy, the Italian Parliament passed the Law of Papal Guarantees by which the pope was given a yearly payment to take the place of revenues he had been receiving from his former dominions. He was allowed to have entire freedom to send ambassadors to other governments and receive ambassadors from them. But the Italian government would not recognize him as a monarch. Pope Pius IX (1792; served 1846-1878), who was the one to lose Rome, refused to accept the money voted for him by the Italian government and shut himself up in the papal palace, calling himself "the Prisoner of the Vatican" (1870). As a "prison" it was a rather attractive place, for the palace and grounds covered about a quarter of a square mile, and nobody bothered the pope at all.

For a number of years this seemed to be a delicate situation, but it turned out to be very easily solved. The popes displayed excellent judgment at the time in not attempting to dictate what Catholic kings and governments should do in purely political affairs though this did not always remain so; after the dictator Benito Mussolini (1883-1945) came into power in Italy (1929), an arrangement was made by which the pope's palace and surrounding estates were recognized as Vatican City, and officially removed from the authority of the Italian government. A visitor to Rome enters and leaves Vatican City just as freely as one might cross the street, but the pope has his own coinage and postage stamps, and his Swiss guards, and he enjoys complete independence from the Italian government.

## 195. Russia and the Crimean War

Before the end of the reign of Czar Nicholas I (1796; reigned 1825-1855), Russia found itself involved in the Crimean War (1854-1856) which grew out of a set of problems, often referred to as "the Eastern Question," concerning what should be done with or about Turkey. Emperor Napoleon III claimed he had a treaty that allowed him to protect Roman Catholics under Turkish rule. Russia claimed to be the guardian of all the Greek Catholics in Turkish dominions. Great Britain did not want anything to happen that would leave Russia in control of Constantinople. Czar Nicholas I complicated the situation by making a remark to the British ambassador to Russia to the effect that the Sultan was "a sick man—a very sick man." The implication was that he might pass on before long and then his property would have to be distributed. Great Britain became suspicious when Russia, claiming the right to protect the holy places in Jerusalem, declared war on Turkey. Emperor Napoleon III and the British government intervened—not so much that they wanted to help Turkey as they wished to check Russia (1854).

Most of the fighting in the war was around the Russian port of

Sebastopol in the Crimea. Since Russia could not hold out against her four opponents, the war was soon over (1856). Russia had to give up her claim to the right to protect Christians in Turkish territory. The Sultan of Turkey promised to make some reforms and to grant religious freedom in his possessions. Few people believed that his promises really meant anything; the fact was, they did not.

## 196. Reforms in England Under Victoria

William IV was followed on the throne by his eighteen-year-old niece, Victoria (1819; reigned 1837-1901). Her reign, the longest in English history, was largely one of progress and prosperity in England. It is known as the Victorian Age.

Reform after reform in industrial and social conditions were put through after England was once fairly started on the process, sometimes by one political party, sometimes by the other. Improving the form of local government in the cities was one of the first of these changes. Better police departments, better streets, and sanitary sewer systems were brought into being. In 1833 slavery was abolished throughout the British Empire. Laws were passed restricting the labor of women and children in factories and mines.

Another serious question came up in connection with what England called the Corn Laws. The English at this time used the word corn in the same way that people in the United States used the word grain. Taxes were put on imported wheat to make it cost enough to permit owners of farmland in England to raise wheat profitably. Such taxes made the cost of grain and flour made out of grain to increase, and thus the cost of living of factory workers and townspeople was raised generally. Some people asked if it would not be better to do away with this tariff and let the grain come in freely from countries that produced it easily so that the town and city workers might get their flour more cheaply. A terrible potato famine in Ireland (1846-1847) made their case stronger than ever, for nothing could take the place of potatoes except imported grain sold at impossible prices.

## 197. The United States of America

This was a century during which the United States acquired much new land. The speed with which the United States reached through to the Pacific coast would have amazed President Thomas Jefferson

(1743-1826; served 1801-1809). Once he said that it might take 1,000 years before the region as far west as the Mississippi would be fully occupied. Yet it was in his own presidency (1803) that the United States purchased the vast Louisiana Province.

Just fifty years later, the main body of the territory of the United States (except for Alaska and Hawaii) was wholly under the Stars and Stripes. The peninsula of Florida was annexed in 1819; and Texas, which had separated itself from Mexico (1836) and set up an independent republic, was added in 1845. Then came the settlement of a dispute with Great Britain over Oregon in 1846 and the war with Mexico over California in 1848. Another part of Arizona and New Mexico—the so-called Gadsden Purchase—was obtained from Mexico in 1853.

Settlers moved rapidly from the states near the Atlantic coast, into the Ohio and Mississippi valleys. When gold was discovered in California in 1848, there was a jump to the Pacific coast, but the region between the Great Plains and the coast filled slowly. The native Americans (known as Indians) presented some difficulties for the early western pioneers who went to California in wagon trains. Settlers often treated the natives as unfairly as Europeans had done with the inhabitants of the lands they forced under their control earlier. During the administration of President Andrew Johnson (1808-1875; served 1865-1869), America purchased Alaska from Russia (1867) under the direction of William Henry Seward (1801-1872), Secretary of State. This was the last acquisition of the United States on the American contient. His foresight was not generally acknowledged, however, and Alaska was long popularly called "Seward's folly."

In expanding beyond the continent, the United States had to face problems much like those which European countries found in their distant possessions. Hawaii was annexed in 1898 and was made a territory. A war with Spain in 1898 added Puerto Rico, a few other little islands in the West Indies, the island of Guam, and the Philippines. Most of these possessions were already fairly thickly settled, inhabited by people who spoke mostly Spanish.

Some American statesmen, such as Benjamin Franklin (1706-1790), George Washington (1732-1799), Andrew Jackson (1767-1845), Abraham Lincoln (see section 198), Jefferson Davis (1808-1889), Theodore Roosevelt (1858-1919), and secretaries of state, like John

Quincy Adams (1767-1848), who also served as president (1825-1829), Daniel Webster (1782-1852), William Henry Seward (see above), and John Hay (1838-1905), were at least as well known to the people of western Europe as European leaders were to the people of the United States.

Toward the end of the nineteenth century, changes in methods of voting were brought about in America as they were in Great Britain. Voting was made a secret proceeding instead of being done in the open, and a system of balloting introduced from the British colony of Australia came to be accepted by most of the states.

## 198. The American Civil War

There was the same rivalry in the United States over the spirit of nationalism as there was in Europe. Eleven southern states attempted to leave the Union over states' rights (see chapter endnote 9-7) and set themselves up as the Confederate States of America. Following the Confederate attack on Fort Sumter, in the harbor of Charleston, South Carolina (April 12, 1861), a Civil War greater than anything of the kind that had yet occurred anywhere, went on for four years (1861-1865). Confederate general Robert Edward Lee's (1807-1870) surrender marked the defeat of the southern states and the triumph of nationalism, just days before John Wilkes Booth (circa 1838-1865) assassinated Lincoln (born 1809) in Ford's Theater in Washington on April 14, 1865.

Important names of this period included William Lloyd Garrison (1805-1879), an editor opposed to slavery, and Horace Greeley (1811-1872), a journalist who was noted for his anti-slavery activities. Another well-known figure was John Brown (1800-1859) who attempted to incite a rebellion of the slaves but was captured at Harper's Ferry, Virginia (now in West Virginia) and hanged at Charles Town, Virginia (December 2), thus becoming a martyr in the cause of abolition. Harriet Tubman (circa 1820-1913), an escaped slave, became one of the most successful "conductors" on the Underground Railroad, leading over 300 slaves to freedom.

Other decisive personalities of this era included Ulysses Simpson Grant (1822-1885), a general for the Union Army who eventually became the eighteenth president of the United States. General William Tecumseh Sherman's (1820-1891) march through Georgia, during which he destroyed and burned many southern homes, farms and plantations, helped defeat the South.

A type of ship known as the ironclad took to the waters during this war, but it was not the first use of such vessels. The first recorded use of iron-clad naval vessels was in the sixteenth century (1598). The iron-clad ship was a wooden boat that was covered with iron. The Confederates had the Merrimack, a United States frigate the Union had scuttled when they abandoned the Norfolk Navy Yard at Portsmouth, Virginia. The Confederates raised it and converted it into a formidable ironclad and renamed the Virginia. The Union had an ironclad ship called the Monitor. It had a low hull topped by a revolving turret for its guns. They engaged in a duel at the battle of Hampton Roads (March, 1862) but it was a draw since neither ship could damage the other very much. In December, the Monitor foundered (filled with water) and sank in heavy seas off Cape Hatteras.

The first successful submarine attack of the Civil War was made by the Confederate vessel Hunley while it was engaged in a battle in the port of Charleston, South Carolina (February 17, 1863). The Confederate submarine David damaged the Union ironclad Ironsides. Both vessels were lost in these engagements.

During the period following the Civil War, sometimes called the era of Reconstruction, northerners went to the South to get unfair political gain or other advantages. These opportunists were called carpetbaggers because some carried all of their belongings in a suitcase made from a strip of carpet. The Ku Klux Klan, founded in Tennessee (1866), often opposed reconstruction efforts and sometimes tried to prevent freedmen from voting. In some cases the blacks were persecuted, becoming the object of many acts of violence.

## 199. China

In this century, new efforts were made to increase trade with China. Not long after Vasco da Gama reached India by way of the Cape of Good Hope (1498), captains of trading vessels tried to get commercial privileges in China; but for centuries the Chinese allowed Europeans to trade only at the port of Canton where Portuguese, English, Dutch, and later even American commercial vessels found their way. The Chinese government, seeing what terrible harm was coming to its people from the use of opium brought in from India, tried to stop its importation. The British government then made war upon China (1839-1842) to compel the Chinese to let English merchants sell the deadly stuff to them. The English people as a whole did not realize just what was involved in this "Opium War," but it was one of the stains on British policy in Asia. The Chinese were defeated and were obliged to give up Hong Kong island to Great Britain (1841) and to open Shanghai and a few other ports to British trade.

Two years later (1844) the United States and France became involved. Their representatives made commercial treaties with China and opened trade with that country through the "treaty ports." China had another war (1856-1860), this time against England and France, growing out of matters affecting trade; and once more China lost. More ports were opened and China agreed to receive ambassadors and consuls from other countries. At about the same time, Russia took advantage of China's weakness to get a foothold in the province of Manchuria and to acquire Vladivostok. Near the end of this century, Germany began to compete with England, France, and the United States for Chinese trade. China was forced to let the European countries have certain ports as centers for their operations.

In 1898 an agreement was entered into whereby China leased to Great Britain for ninety-nine years the territory behind Kowloon Peninsula up to a line drawn from Mirs Bay to Deep Bay and the adjoining islands, including Lantao. The administrative center, officially named Victoria but more commonly called Hong Kong, is on the northern shore of the island.

## 200. Japan

Japan had been a "hermit" nation (a nation that prefers not to associate itself with other nations) after the shogun had expelled western influences from his country (1630s). It was the United States of America that began the opening of modern Japan to western civilization. After trade had been started with China, American seamen sometimes found it desirable to stop at Japanese ports for water and other things they needed, but the Japanese did not receive them well. President Millard Fillmore (1800-1874; served 1850-1853) decided to do something to open up relations with Japan by sending an expedition (1853) to Japan under the lead of Commodore Matthew C. Perry (1794-1858), brother of Oliver Hazard Perry (1785-1819), commander of the flagship Niagara and the victor in the famous naval battle of Lake Erie in the War of 1812. Commander Perry carried with him a miniature railroad, telegraph instruments, a telescope, and some other things it was hoped the rulers of Japan might like. Perry again visited Japan in 1854 with more ships and obtained an agreement for the opening up of two Japanese ports for trade with the United States. Soon European nations were getting trade rights to match those which had been granted to the United States, and more ports were opened. The Japanese finally concluded it was to their interest to pick out from western customs those things that seemed likely to enable them to get ahead.

## 201. Africa

For a long time Africa, except Egypt and the northern African coast, was considered to be the "Dark Continent." A few miles west of the Nile a vast desert—the Sahara—begins. The desert prevented easy exploration from the north. On the east and on the west, mountains follow closely along the shore a considerable part of the way. The only natural ways into the country are up the three great rivers—the Nile, Congo, and Zambezi—and there are falls in each of these which impede navigation. Clearly it would not be easy to explore Africa.

The earliest African explorers were David Livingstone (1813-1873) and Henry M. Stanley (1841-1904). Livingstone, a Scotch missionary, went into the continent northeast of the British possessions in South Africa. He was eager to carry Christianity to the natives and was deeply impressed with the need of getting rid of the African slave trade—"this open sore of the world," he called it. More than twenty years of his life were spent in Africa (1850-1873). He made friends with the native people and traveled 29,000 miles through regions that no white man had ever seen before.

When, for a number of years, no word came from Livingstone, James Gordon Bennett (1795-1872), founder of the *New York Herald*, ordered a reporter named Henry M. Stanley to go out and find him. Stanley nearly crossed the continent from west to east before locating him. Even then Livingstone decided to stay in Africa instead of going back with Stanley. Livingstone died the next year (1873), and his body rests in Westminster Abbey with many of the great men and women of England. Before it was carried away his native friends took out his heart and buried it under a tree in East Africa, for Africa, they thought, was the home of his heart's deepest interest.

Stanley found his way to Victoria Nyanza, one of the largest lakes in the world, visited other African waters, and went back to the western coast by following the Congo River to its mouth. His book, *Through the Dark Continent* (1878), relates some of the most extraordinary experiences that have ever been written. Stanley's last African journey was undertaken (1887-1889) and was reported in his *In Darkest Africa* (1890).

## 202. Latin America

For some time there had been a move in Latin America toward independence and in this century Spanish authority was overthrown in a considerable part of the continent. As in the revolution in North America, there was considerable doubt at first as to whether a majority of the people really cared much about independence. Considerably more damage to property and life resulted from the South American revolutions than from the struggle on the North American continent. The upper social classes would have been very satisfied to stay under Spanish rule. The movement for independence was not limited to South America. Central America and Mexico were drawn into it as well. Mexico obtained her independence in 1821 (see section 182).

Without intending to, Napoleon Bonaparte gave Latin America a push toward freedom. By putting his brother Joseph on the throne of Spain, he gave some of the discontented South Americans an excuse for revolting against the new government. Simon Bolivar (1783-1830) became the foremost leader in the struggle for independence. He was most active in the northwestern part of South America—in the countries now known as Venezuela, Colombia, Ecuador, Bolivia (named after him), and Peru. In the southern part of the continent the revolutionary movement was headed by Jose de San Martin (1778-1850). This movement started in Buenos Aires (1810). Under San Martin, Argentina and Chile successfully rose against their Spanish rulers, and San Martin also helped in gaining control of Peru. So that jealousy would not be able to prevent the success of the struggle for independence, San Martin very unselfishly gave up his leadership in favor of Bolivar.

251

Brazil passed through an unusual kind of change. When Napoleon took the Spanish royal family off the throne, he also put Portugal under his brother's rule. The royal family of that country thought the safest place for them was in their American colony; therefore, some of them went over to Brazil, and the son of the Portuguese king declared himself to be Emperor of Brazil as Pedro I (1789-1834; reigned 1822-1831). He was succeeded by his son Pedro II (1825-1891; reigned 1831-1889). During these two reigns, Brazil got along fairly well (Pedro II even abolished slavery in 1888) but political leaders who thought they would have more chance for office under a republic finally worked up a revolution, and Dom Pedro II was asked to leave; hence, a republic was established.

Twice in this century, the Monroe Doctrine (see chapter endnote 9-6) was invoked when the French tried to set up an empire in Mexico during the American Civil War (see section 198). But that empire "fell" when the French troops which supported it were called home (1867). It was also invoked (1895) when President Grover Cleveland (1837-1908; served 1885-1889, 1893-1897) declared that under the Monroe Doctrine the United States was interested in a boundary dispute between Great Britain and Venezuela. Long a subject of controversy, the subject became really interesting when it was learned that gold had been discovered in the disputed territory. The controversy was settled peacefully by referring it to a special board, whose decision was largely in favor of Great Britain.

## 203. Cuba and the Spanish-American War

The inefficient and ineffective government given Cuba by the Spanish authorities and the rebellion that started on the island (1895) made things awkward for Americans who had money invested in sugar and tobacco plantations. American public opinion, fueled largely by the newspapers of William Randolph Hearst (1863-1951), whose reporters had flocked to Cuba to report the cruel methods used in dealing with the problem, turned against the Cuban government. Then there was the sinking of the U.S.S. *Maine*, which had been sent to Havana Harbor on a friendly visit. The explosion (some sources say it could have been an implosion) killed 246 members of the crew and wounded sixty others. The United States Congress declared war on Spain in 1898.

The Philippines, Guam, and Puerto Rico were ceded by Spain to the United States through this short and one-sided war. Cuba was placed provisionally under American military occupation.

## 204. New World Republics

The republics of the New World share many common interests. The advancement of these common interests and the encouragement of friendly cooperation among the New World republics is often called Pan-Americanism. James G. Blaine (1830-1893), who twice served the United States as the Secretary of State, was largely responsible for the meeting in 1889 at the city of Washington of the first of a series of Pan-American Conferences, attended by representatives from the republics of the New World. Its most important achievement was the establishment of the Pan-American Union, first called the Bureau of American Republics (1890). It circulated information about the various countries in this union and provided means for cooperation among them.

## 205. Canada

Discontent with the government led (1837) to actual rebellion against British authority. To find out what was wrong and to recommend what should be done about it, the British government sent Lord Durham (1792-1840) to Canada. His wise report in 1839, which recommended a considerably larger share of self-government than Canada already had, was accepted by Parliament. Little by little earlier laws restricting trade and commerce were done away with, and Canada was allowed to make its own tariff laws and to get along without any British troops for protection.

One of the most notable pieces of legislation by the British Parliament was the act establishing the Dominion of Canada (1867). Ontario and Quebec were united with New Brunswick and Nova Scotia as provinces in a new, great general union. Other provinces which later joined the union in this century included Prince Edward Island (1873) in the east and Manitoba (1870), British Columbia (1871), and the Yukon (1898) in the west.

253

## 206. New Zealand

As far to the east from Australia as Boston is from Chicago, is New Zealand which became another British dominion. It consisted of two good-sized islands and several smaller ones. With a total area somewhat less than that of Great Britain and Ireland, and about equal to the state of Colorado, these islands stretched from north to south as far as the distance from Minneapolis to Memphis. It had been discovered in 1642 by the Dutch navigator A. J. Tasman (circa 1603-1659). Later the English took it over, and made it a separate colony (1840).

New Zealand became governed by a legislative council appointed by the dominion government and a house of representatives elected by the voters. Women finally obtained the vote in New Zealand in 1893.

## 207. England and the Boers in South Africa

Until after the Napoleonic Wars most of the people living in the Cape Colony (now Cape Province) at the southern end of Africa were Dutch, but when it was ceded to Britain (1814), Englishmen began to go there to settle. This immigration did not please the Boers, as the Dutch inhabitants were called, and they were further dissatisfied with some of the laws passed by the British, especially those affecting the slaves held by the Boers. Though the act of Parliament (1833) which abolished slavery throughout the British Empire gave slave owners part compensation for their slaves, the Boers were discontented.

The movement known as the "Great Trek" started in 1835. Thousands of Boer farmers with their families, farm wagons, and herds moved northward into country previously unsettled by Europeans. As a result of these movements, two Boer republics were established: the Orange Free State near the Orange River and the Republic of Transvaal, north of the Vaal River, which kept themselves practically independent for many years.

Rich gold fields were discovered (1884) in the Transvaal. Foreigners, chiefly British, flocked into the country in such numbers that they soon outnumbered the Boers. The newcomers, called Uitlanders, paid the greater part of the taxes of the Transvaal and demanded public improvements and reforms in government. The Boers refused to grant the demands of the Uitlanders and made it harder than ever for them to become citizens or to obtain the right to vote. The government of Cape Colony tried in vain to induce President Stephanus Johannes Paulus Kruger (1825-1904; served 1883-1900) of the Transvaal—"Oom Paul," his people called him—to permit changes in policy. The situation was made worse when a band of armed men from Cape Colony headed by a man named Sir Leander Starr Jameson (1853-1917) invaded the Transvaal. He was captured by the Boer army in 1895.

In 1899, the Boers under Kruger, declared war on Britain, beginning what became known as the Boer War. This conflict continued until 1902 when the Boers surrendered at Vereeniging. The republics later became the British Transvaal and Orange River colonies and were embodied in the Union of South Africa in 1910.

## 208. England and India

England came to India in the guise of neither trader nor conqueror. Here was a country with a known history older than that of England, with people perfectly satisfied with their habits and customs, however crude and dirty they sometimes seemed to westerners.

The year of the Sepoy Mutiny (1857) was a terrible but memorable one in India. It showed some of the very embarrassing problems—religious, racial, sanitary, and every other kind—with which the British have had to deal in India. About this time a kind of greased cartridge was introduced into the army in India, the end of which the soldiers had to bite off before it was put into a gun. Now by far the greater part of the soldiers in India were natives called Sepoys, who included both Hindus and Moslems. To the Hindu the cow is a sacred animal; to the Moslems the hog is an unclean thing. These soldiers (from both religions) thought that in touching the animal grease on this new cartridge they either would be disloyal to their religion or would defile themselves. With this as an excuse, much of the valley of the Ganges rose in revolt against the British. Terrible cruelties were imposed upon Britishers or British sympathizers who fell into their hands, and the British authorities retaliated with harsh punishments. At the cost of much money, distress, and life the British suppressed the mutiny; and when the rebellion was over, the British

255

were in a much stronger position than ever. All political control in India was taken away from the East India Company, and the British government became entirely responsible for the general administration of affairs in India (1858).

## 209. A Tower and a Statue

The story of the Eiffel Tower and the Statue of Liberty could have been placed under the section in this chapter labeled "Architecture" for they represent important engineering achievements. They have also been discussed under the section entitled "matters of state," since they originated from social and political activity, but these special monuments deserve their own section, brief though it is. Both had a French origin.

The Eiffel Tower was erected for the Paris Exposition (1889), in the Champ de Mars, Paris. It was the highest structure in the world, standing at 984 feet, making it 429 feet higher than the Washington Monument. Its height also exceeded Saint Paul's Cathedral by 580 feet. Its framework was composed of four uprights, which rose from the corners of a square measuring 300 feet on the side; thus the area it covered at its base was nearly 2.5 acres. These uprights were supported on big piers of masonry and concrete, the foundations for which reached to a depth of about forty-five feet on the side next to the Seine and about twenty-seven feet on the other side. Work was begun on this structure on January 28, 1887, and its full height was reached on March 13, 1889. The engineer, under whose direction the tower was built, was Alexandre Gustave Eiffel (1832-1923). Before he directed the work on the tower, he had already had a lot of experience in the construction of large metal bridges, and had designed the sluices for the Panama Canal when it was under the French Company.

The Statue of Liberty was a gift to the United States of America from France on the occasion of America's 100th birthday (1876). It was designed and constructed by the French sculptor, Frederic Auguste Bartholdi (1834-1904). Bartholdi was born in Colmar (sometimes Kolmar), Alsace, and was one of Garibaldi's soldiers (1870). The Statue of Liberty, which stands in New York Harbor, was partly his idea, and he helped collect the money to build it. A sonnet by Emma Lazarus (1849-1887) is engraved on a memorial tablet on the Statue of Liberty. The closing lines of "The New Colossus" read:

> ...Give me your tired, your poor,
> Your huddled masses yearning to breathe free,
> The wretched refuse of your teeming shore,
> Send these, the homeless, tempest-tost to me.
> I lift my lamp beside the golden door.

# God in History

Q. What was the greatest challenge to the Christian religion in this century?

A. The continued rise of the scientific method in this century presented many arguments about nature which seemed contrary to accepted religious teachings.

The strongest blow to religion in this century was the theory of evolution. The English naturalist Charles Darwin presented a direct challenge to the Bible's teaching of creation by God. How did the church respond? At first the clergy in England and other places denounced the theory. But opposition soon faded and there came a gradual acceptance of the theory in many places. Attacks on religion became bolder. Not satisfied with just criticizing the church, critics began to question the very foundation of religion. They asked such questions as: What is God? Why is there a need for God? How has belief in God affected human society? These doubts found expression in such statements as "Religion is the opiate of the people" and "God is dead."

Q. What can Christians do to deal with such criticisms?

A. Christians need to approach these problems in a mature way, keeping in mind that God is still in control of this world. Where scientific investigation seems to contradict the teachings of the Bible we need to understand that the same God who inspired the Bible also created the world. All of us need to realize that we may have an imperfect and incomplete scientific understanding of the world, but as scientists continue their investigations our understanding of God and nature will increase. We will do well to remember that God does not need Christians to validate His teachings any more than Christians need science to validate the teachings of the Bible.

# Chapter Endnotes

9-1 The rotation of the earth was accepted as fact by the scientific community when Copernicus's writings were published in 1543. The experimental proof of it, however, did not come until 1851 when

Foucault performed his important pendulum experiment at the Pantheon in Paris. A pendulum about 200 feet long, composed of a flexible wire carrying a heavy iron weight, was suspended so as to be free to oscillate in any direction. The weight was provided with a style which passed over a table strewn with fine sand, so that the style traced the direction in which the bob was swinging. It was found that the oscillating pendulum never retraced its path, but at each swing it was apparently deviated to the right, and moreover the deviations in equal times were themselves equal. This meant that the floor of the Pantheon was moving, and therefore the Earth was rotating. If the pendulum was swung in the southern hemisphere the deviation would be to the left; if at the equator it would not deviate, while at the poles the plane of the oscillation would traverse a complete circle in twenty-four hours.

9-2 Baily's Beads are a series of spots of light seen on one edge of the sun's disk prior to totality during an eclipse and again on the opposite edge just after totality. The effect is caused by light shining between elevations on the moon's surface.

9-3 The Doppler Principle states that, as the distance between a source of wave motion (such as sound or light) and an observer becomes less or greater, the frequency of the waves received by the observer increases or decreases respectively. This effect on the apparent frequency resulting from motion of source or observer is called the Doppler Effect. It is seen in the case of sound by the rise of pitch as the distance between source and observer decreases. In the case of light, the approach of source or observer causes a shift of color toward the violet end of the spectrum, while the receding of source or observer causes a shift toward the red end of the spectrum. This effect is of great importance in astronomy in measuring the motions of stars.

9-4 The camera obscura is a light-tight box or chamber with a convex lens at one end and a screen, on which an image is produced, at the other. It is sometimes used for making drawings and is the prototype of the modern photographic camera.

9-5 Alexander I was officially declared dead at Taganrog in 1825. There is reason to believe, though, that he secretly spent the rest of his life as a monk—possibly to be identified with Feodor Kuzmich, a hermit who died in Siberia in 1864.

9-6 The Monroe Doctrine originated out of a desire to prevent the European powers from taking a controlling share in the politics of the American continent. Though the idea was not originated by President Monroe, his declaration established the policy in concrete form and originated from the American apprehension that the combination of European powers known as the Holy Alliance would interfere in South America to restore the Spanish colonies, which had asserted their independence, to the crown of Spain. The precept was outlined in Monroe's message to Congress in December, 1823.

9-7 The issue of states' rights is an American issue as old as the beginnings of its national government. The Tenth Amendment to the U.S.Constitution, which went into effect in 1791, says: "The powers not delegated to the United States by the Constitution, nor prohibited by it to the States, are reserved to the States respectively, or to the people." There quickly arose a controversy as to how to interpret the enumerated powers granted the Federal government, which are not at all specific. Until the time of the American Civil War (and after), there were numerous cases which tested the matter. The strong feelings generated between the proslavery and antislavery forces led, by 1860, to secession. Eleven southern states seceded in 1860-1861 and formed the Confederacy. The American Civil War was on.

## Chapter Terms

| | | |
|---|---|---|
| anesthetic | electrolytic process | pourboire |
| antiseptics | evolution | radioactivity |
| Baily's Beads | Foucault's experiment | Reconstruction |
| Battle of the Nations | Great Trek | Redshirts |
| camera obscura | hermit nation | state's rights |
| canali | ironclad | universal ether |
| carpetbaggers | mandrake | urea |
| communism | Monroe Doctrine | Victorian Age |
| coup d'etat | Mormons | vital force |
| Daguerreotype | nationalism | Waterloo |
| dittany | Ohm's law | X-Ray |
| democracy | Oom Paul | |
| Doppler Principle | Pan-Americanism | |

260

# Chapter Review Questions/Exercises

1. From the Overview to this chapter, list some important events and discoveries of the nineteenth century.
2. What were some of the successes of aviators in the nineteenth century? Who were they? (166)
3. What was the error in translation from Italian to English that resulted in the mistaken belief that Schiaparelli thought there was life on Mars? (167)
4. What were some of the other important events in astronomy in the nineteenth century? (167)
5. Who were some of the people involved in the controversy over evolution? (168)
6. List at least ten outstanding writers of the nineteenth century and what they are remembered for. (169)
7. What were two problems that had plagued surgery since the decline of Rome? Who were some of the people who contributed to the solutions to these problems? (170)
8. What advances were made in nursing in the nineteenth century? (170)
9. Who were some of the people responsible for the developments in photography in the nineteenth century? (171)
10. Name some of the outstanding missionaries of the nineteenth century. (172)
11. What are some of the things Spurgeon is remembered for? (172)
12. What did Joseph Smith do? Who was Brigham Young? (172)
13. Discuss in detail the involvement of Napoleon and France, concentrating especially on the conflicts involved in Napoleon's rise to power. What was the battle that resulted in Napoleon's capture? (173-179)
14. Describe the political condition of the world after 1815, being sure to mention democracy, nationalism, and communism. (180)
15. How did Mexico win its independence from Spain? (182)
16. What happened in France under Napoleon III? (183)
17. What mistake did Napoleon III make in Mexico? (184)

261

18. Describe the emergence of Prussia as a military power. (185-190)
19. What were some of the events that happened in Italy in the nineteenth century? (191-193)
20. What happened in Italy in the nineteenth century concerning the pope? (194)
21. Describe the details of Russia's involvement in the Crimean War. (195)
22. What were some of the reforms in England under Victoria? (196)
23. List some of the important events that took place in America in the nineteenth century. (197-198)
24. What happened in China and Japan in the nineteenth century that increased their trade with other nations? (199-200)
25. Why did Livingstone and Stanley go to Africa? (201)
26. What were some of the important events in Latin America in the nineteenth century? (202)
27. List some of the important events that happened in the nineteenth century in Cuba, republics of the New World, Canada, and New Zealand. (203-207)
28. Describe the situation in South Africa between England and the Boers. (207)
29. What happened between England and India in the nineteenth century? (208)
30. List some important details regarding the Eiffel Tower and the Statue of Liberty. (209)

# 10

# 1901-2000

## {9:36 p.m.-11:59 p.m.}

Sometime during the next two hours and twenty-three minutes Pope Benedict XV (served 1914-1922), will ask the following question:

> "Is this civilized world to be turned into a field of death, and is Europe...to rush, as carried by a universal folly, to the abyss and take a hand in its own suicide?" (August 1, 1917).

Albert Einstein (1879-1955), a German-born American physicist, will astound everyone with his formula which describes how mass in the form of matter is equivalent to a certain amount of energy: Energy equals mass times the speed of light squared.

The American football coach Knute Rockne (1888-1931) will, while coaching for Notre Dame, revolutionize football by stressing offense and developing the backfield shift.

Rudyard Kipling, the great English poet, will write his famous poem "If," describing the qualities of a man (1910).

The American poet Joyce Kilmer (1886-1918) will pen these famous words: "I think that I shall never see a poem lovely as a tree," in his poem "Trees" (1914).

The great American Baptist preacher Kenneth Chafin (1926- ) will write his influential book on the family titled *Is There a Family in the House?* (1978).

# Overview

The technical and personal achievements that embodied the creativity, daring, and resourcefulness of man in the last century, as meaningful and contributory as they were, pale considerably in the light of the advances made in this, the last century of this thousand years.

This creativity, daring, and resourcefulness showed itself in the efforts of the Wright Brothers (Orville, 1871-1948 and Wilbur, 1867-1912) who finally solved the problems leading to successful flight in a heavier-than-air craft (America, 1903). Just sixty-six years later, the incredible blending of national will, science, engineering, and courage on the part of three brave men resulted in the realization of a trip to the moon (America, 1969). Neil Armstrong and "Buzz" Aldrin landed their rocket and got out to explore that alien world, while Michael Collins orbited overhead in the command module (see section 253).

Other explorers stood at the very top and bottom of our planet, climbed the highest mountains, and descended into the lowest ocean depths to discover many new things. The American Robert E. Peary (1856-1920) succeeded in reaching the North Pole (1909) and is credited with its discovery. The only thing he found there was a cold, howling wilderness. The South Pole was reached (1909) by Robert F. Scott (1868-1912), but this party of Englishmen did not survive. The American Richard E. Byrd (1888-1957) won the unique achievement of flying over the North Pole (1926) and the South Pole (1929).

The American Charles Lindbergh (1902-1974) became the first person to fly solo across the Atlantic, landing near Paris (1927). His success earned him the nickname of "Lucky Lindy."

The American aviator Amelia Earhart (1898-1937) became the first woman to cross the Atlantic in an airplane (1928) with others aboard. In 1932 she made a solo flight across the Atlantic, and in 1935 she flew across the Pacific, alone, from Honolulu to California. She was the first woman to make both flights alone. In 1937 she attempted, with Frederick J. Noonan (1893-1937), to fly around the world, but her plane was lost on the flight between New Guinea and Howland Island in the Pacific. Though there are those who have offered a reasonable solution to the mystery surrounding the disappearance of Earhart and Noonan, definitive proof is still lacking in the last decade of this millennium.

Frank Whittle (1907- ) patented a design for a jet-aircraft engine (England, 1930) and introduced a completely new way to fly (see section 245).

American physicists brought us the resources of atomic energy through the successful implementation of a controlled nuclear reaction (1942), the first atomic bomb (1945), and the first hydrogen bomb. Atomic submarines (1955), and nuclear-powered carriers also took their place in and on the oceans of the world. Controversial nuclear power plants first came on-line in the middle decade of this century.

Scientists and engineers opened incredible new vistas through the perfection of new means of communication. The English physicist and physician Oliver Heaviside (1850-1925) spoke of the existence of an atmospheric layer which aids the conduction of radio waves (1902). Wireless telegraphy was perfected (Marconi and others), as was radio and television (Sarnoff and others), and the motion picture was invented (Edison [see figure 10-1], and others). In the spirit of Jules Verne who said, "What one man envisions, another can do," even the ray gun predicted in the Buck Rogers comic strip (1930s), came true just two decades later in the form of the laser (America). This discovery alone has already been applied to hundreds of uses and its possibilities continue to expand. The introduction of the personal computer (late 1970s) caused further dramatic changes in the way knowledge is processed, information is stored, and work is accomplished.

Edison's invention in the last century of the phonograph became very popular in this one when the original cylindrical shape of Edison's machine was replaced with a disk. Three different kinds of disks, based on the number of times they turned in a minute, were successful. There was a disk that turned 78 times a minute, one that turned 45 times a minute, and one that turned 33.3 times a minute.

Other recording devices included the wire recorder, on which sound was preserved on a wire that moved through a magnetic head, the tape recorder, on which sound was placed on plastic tape, and a solid-state device with sound recorded on a chip. The eight-track tape player, on which many songs could be conveniently played back in a car, became popular. Later a small cassette tape replaced the eight-track technology and finally, the CD, with nearly perfect reproduction of sound, competed with the cassette tape technology in the last decade of this century.

It would be impractical to list here all of the thousands of entertainers who preserved their works on these various machines through the years of this century. It is a subject worthy of a work of encyclopedic length. Yet any such list certainly should include an American singer by the name of Elvis Presley and a group from England known as the Beatles (see section 248).

The proliferation of these inexpensive sound-recording devices along with the box camera and the movie and video cameras that came later, made this century the most recorded one in the history of the world. These records will allow future historians to understand life in our century to an unprecedented degree.

Educational systems of progressive countries worked to help children acquire necessary knowledge and skills, enabling them to become productive citizens. In America, some school districts worked to handle administrative matters in non-traditional ways by relegating the authority of the principal to a committee composed of representatives from the staff and different segments of the community. The unique problems associated with inner-city schools have also received special attention.

In America, Christian education was given a boost when Southwestern Baptist Theological Seminary was founded as an outgrowth of the theological department of Baylor University in Waco, Texas (1901). It moved to its present location in Fort Worth, Texas, in 1910. One of its founders was B. H. Carroll (1843-1914) who was one of the most outstanding Southern Baptists of his era. In the last decade of this millennium, the seminary was under the direction of Russell H. Dilday (1930- ) who exhibited an extraordinary degree of excellence and dedication in his position as president.

The first of the giant skyscrapers of this century was the Woolworth Building (sixty stories), completed (1913) in New York City. Other New York skyscrapers built in this century included the R.C.A. Building at Rockefeller Center (seventy stories) and the Empire State Building (102 stories). The Empire State Building was completed in 1931; it has 6,500 windows and ten million bricks. It stands 1,250 feet high, not including its television tower added in 1951. For forty years it was the tallest building in the world. Today Chicago's Sears Tower reaches 1,454 feet into the sky and the twin towers of the World Trade Center in New York are 1,368 feet high.

## 210. A Century of Energy

In the same way that coal fueled the Industrial Revolution, oil became the primary fuel for modern society. Large-scale production of oil began (1901) at a place called Spindletop, Texas. News of the Lucas Gusher (a well that produced huge quantities of oil) spread quickly and was followed by an enormous rush of the adventurous who quickly converged on the site to drill their own wells. Howard Hughes, Sr. (1869-1924) [see figure 10-3], lawyer, inventor, businessman, philanthropist, inventor of the Hughes Bit, and founder of the Hughes Tool Company, was in the vanguard of the rush.

Hughes wisely devoted his time to making an improved drill bit to replace the "fish-tail" bits in use at the time which were slow to penetrate hard rock formations. In collaboration with Walter Sharp, an associate, he constructed a small wooden model of a roller-type bit with two cone-shaped, toothed rollers (1906) {9:43 p.m.}. A patent was applied for and different designs were tried which resulted in the Sharp-Hughes Rock Bit [see figure 10-4]. This new bit became very successful and was the first in a series of designs that helped the world gain access to more oil.

## 211. Health and Medicine

Today's extensive knowledge about the causes and effects of diseases enables us to prevent many illnesses and to treat diseases that were previously fatal. By paying attention to what we have learned about good community health, we have learned to enact and enforce laws that require communities to furnish pure drinking water (typhoid fever was conquered when community water supplies were required to be purified) and to inspect water or milk from private sources, forbidding the use of those which are contaminated. Standards are also set for food products other than milk. The quality of our air has also been seen as important in maintaining good health and there are laws relating to this as well. Cities may try to do away with slums and try to prevent, by proper housing laws, the development of conditions that are dangerous to health and safety. Of course our great modern cities would be impractical without the sanitary sewer systems in place. Quarantine laws restrain the spread of many contagious diseases. Hospitals and special homes for the ill are provided by public or private support. Occasionally we still get reminded of how far we have yet to go in conquering disease when new diseases such as AIDS are identified. The spread of AIDS has been moderated somewhat through the monitoring of blood supplies and through the practice of a monogamous life-style, but it is still not curable and is the number one killer of men between the ages of twenty-five and forty-four.

Along with the Red Cross, founded in the previous century (see section 170), the United Nations started agencies which reached out to help the poor, hungry, and homeless. Small pox was eradicated in 1970 through the World Health Organization's efforts. These agencies continue to provide relief against the spread of ignorance, poverty, and disease, as does the Peace Corps which was founded during the administration of President John F. Kennedy (1917-1963; served 1961-1963) of the United States.

The discovery by Dr. Walter Reed (1851-1902) in 1900 that yellow fever is caused by a virus transmitted by the bite of a female mosquito, enabled man to bring this disease under control by reducing mosquito populations. By 1904 the Panama Canal Zone became an important successful example of how this could be done. This greatly aided the builders of the Panama Canal who had a difficult enough job before them without having also to contend with yellow fever. An American medical scientist, Dr. W. A. Sawyer (1879-1951), developed the first successful vaccine against the disease in 1938.

Doctors were given a powerful tool when penicillin was discovered in 1928 by the English bacteriologist Sir Alexander Fleming (1881-1955). It was not until the 1940s that the drug became wildly available but since then it has saved the lives of millions of people.

In 1908 Karl Landsteiner (1868-1943) showed that polio is caused by a virus. This and other related achievements led to the development of a dead-virus vaccine in 1947 by Dr. Jonas E. Salk (1914- ). His research was further developed by Dr. Albert Sabin

(1906-1993) whose live-virus oral vaccine largely replaced Salk's.

This century saw a much greater understanding than before of the causes of various forms of cancer. Much better methods were developed to detect and treat the disease.

Amazing improvements in the use of artificial body parts made life more convenient and comfortable for many. The use of the artificial heart was among the most startling of these innovations.

The development of the X-ray in the last decade of the previous century, and its perfection in this one, promoted improved versions [see figure 10-5] which could peer deeper and more effectively into the body. The development of even better devices (1970s and 1980s), using magnetic fields and computers, provided still additional tools for use in medicine.

## 212. Gains for Women and Children

Advances for women were made, but even early in this century women were considered to be "weak" and "frail" in advertisements of the day [see figure 10-6]. As more and more women took jobs outside their homes, they naturally began to feel they should have the right to own property; little by little, therefore, they acquired that right along with the right to vote in many places.

In progressive countries the law endeavored to give more consideration to children than it once did. People assumed that a child had a right to be educated, and many governments compelled children to be in school even when they did not want to be. Child labor laws imposed limits on the kinds of employment children could be given and the hours or conditions under which they could work. Abused children were taken away from their homes and put into foster homes or schools where they would at least be free from the wrong kind of parental authority. Special attention was also given to children who broke the law. Juvenile courts or judges tried to deal with these youngsters in such a way as to encourage them to do right, and to keep them from contact with hardened criminals.

## 213. Astronomy

A complete list of astronomical achievements that have come in this century clearly extends beyond the scope of this book, but a few of the most important ones certainly deserve mention. The new knowledge gained from this discipline has significantly altered the way we understand the universe.

One of the many worthy achievements was the measurement in 1916 by Edward Barnard, the comet-hunter from the previous century, of the proper motion of a faint red star. He determined that the star took 180 years to cross the sky by a distance equal to the apparent diameter of the full moon (a lot for a star!). Barnard's Star, as it came to be called, is relatively close to earth at six light years away. By observing the irregularities in its movements, it is believed that it has at least two planets in orbit about it.

The American astronomer George Ellery Hale (1868-1938) is remembered for his organization of three great observatories, Yerkes Observatory (which he directed, 1895-1905), Mount Wilson Observatory (director, 1904-1923), and Mount Palomar Observatory. He was also the inventor of the spectroheliograph, a device used to study the sun in one element only.

The concept of the *black hole* (see chapter endnote 10-1), was first discussed by a German astronomer named Karl Schwarzschild. His untimely death in World War I cut short any other contributions he made have made to astronomy.

The Estonian Bernhard Schmidt's (1879-1935) major contribution to astronomy was in his design of a new type of telescope. It used a spherical mirror combined with a special glass plate placed in the upper part of the telescope tube to correct the errors caused by the spherical shape of the mirror. These "Schmidt telescopes" (or Schmidt cameras) made it possible to photograph wide areas of the sky with a single plate, with the definition remaining sharp right up to the end of the field.

The American Harold Shapley (1885- 1972) became the first astronomer to make an accurate measurement of the diameter of the Milky Way Galaxy. He determined that it is approximately 100,000 light years wide.

The ninth planet in our solar system was discovered (1930) in this century by the American astronomer Clyde Tombaugh (1906- ) when he was affiliated with the Lowell Observatory in Flagstaff, Arizona. He is also noted for his discovery of a number of star clusters, variable stars, asteroids, and nebulae.

Radio astronomy, the study of radio waves from space, was

discovered by Karl Jansky (1905-1950) in 1931 when he worked at the Bell Telephone Company in New Jersey on a project that was designed to detect the origin of static, which was then a mysterious irritant to radio listeners. Much of the static was from thunderstorms, but Jansky quickly learned that there was a weak, steady hiss in his receiver which seemed to come from a definite region of the sky which moved steadily from day to day. He eventually determined that the hiss came from the Milky Way.

An astronomer from Missouri, Edwin Hubble (1899-1953), made an important contribution to man's understanding of our place in the universe when he proved that the so-called "starry nebulae," including the spirals, are independent galaxies. He made this determination with observations made with the Mount Wilson 100-inch reflector, at that time the most powerful in the world. In 1923 he arrived at a distance for the Andromeda spiral at 900,000 light years, a number slightly under the one we acknowledge today as correct, but he was the first to bring this kind of scale to our understanding of space and the distances between galaxies. He also measured the distances to many other galaxies, and he divided the systems into definite classes according to their shapes. It is for Hubble that America's first space telescope was named.

The launching of America's Hubble Space Telescope (HST) in 1990 was not the first time that astronomers and NASA had worked together. Different types of scanners and sensors had been put in space before, but the new space telescope was the first time that a truly large optical instrument had been placed in earth orbit. What are the advantages of doing this? Astronomers have long known that the most effective place for a telescope is as far above the earth's atmosphere as possible. That is why the large telescopes on this planet are built on the tops of mountains. After the initial difficulties with the HST were resolved with a visit by NASA astronauts in December, 1993, astronomers announced that it performed as planned. Hubble's new camera gave the telescope the ability to see faint distant objects with many times the resolution of any telescope on earth.

## 214. Matters of Church and State

There are many religions in the world. The foremost of these are Buddhism, Christianity, Hinduism, Islam, Judaism, Taoism, and various "primitive religions." In religion as well as in every other phase of human interest the pulse of change has been felt during the twentieth century. Much has happened since the Treaty of Westphalia allowed a ruler of a German state three choices in the religious field instead of two. The relationship between church and state can be handled in three different ways:

(1) There can be a state church supported by public taxation, with everybody expected to conform to it.

(2) There can be a state church recognized by the government and given a degree of government support while other religious bodies are perfectly free to worship as they please—this is known as religious toleration.

(3) Any religious group may be allowed to worship as it pleases so long as it does not offend public order or decency, with no group receiving any special recognition or aid from the government—this is known as religious freedom.

In the last 350 years there has been a tendency around the world to pass from the first of these approaches sometimes through the second, directly to the third. England still keeps the Church of England (the Anglican Church) as its established church, but members of any other religious faiths are entirely free to worship as they please. The English church has been "disestablished" in Ireland and Wales, where the great mass of people never were in sympathy with it.

In many countries—France, Italy, and the South American republics, for example—most of the people are Roman Catholics; yet other religions are not forbidden, and in some cases political leaders have not hesitated to get into lively arguments with the pope. There have been times in this century when some South American governments have tried to weaken the power of the Roman Catholic Church by causing open breaks between the church and the government, although most of the people still remain Catholics. In 1905 France set aside the Concordat made by Napoleon with the pope just 100 years earlier, so that now all the churches in France depend upon the contributions of the people for their support.

The concept of the separation of church and state is one of the characteristics of life in America. The United States Constitution specifies that Congress shall not make any laws respecting the establishment of a religion or prohibiting its free exercise. The matter of prayer in public schools, with the United States Supreme Court ruling that no school official can tell a student what to pray, became a major issue in the sixth and seventh decades of this century.

Religious persecutions "returned to fashion" early in this century. Rumania, for example, treated members of other religious bodies than the one favored by the government very harshly. Hitler's condemnable record with regard to his treatment of the Jews and other religious bodies is another vivid example of this trend. In Russia, the leaders tried to get their people to turn against all religion, until Mikhail S. Gorbachev (1931- ; served 1985-1991) came to power.

## 215. Socialism and Communism

Not all political changes in this century were positive ones. Socialist parties made considerable headway in the first half of this century in some countries. Chancellor Otto von Bismarck tried both directly and indirectly to suppress socialism in Germany, and socialists were blamed for many of the difficulties of Italy after World War I and of Germany later. In England, the Labor Party advocated the increased trend toward socialism in the thirties and later. Government ownership and operation of railroads and other public utilities became fairly common in Europe during this century.

Communism called for much greater changes than socialism did. Under communism, the state became everything. This is how it was in the Soviet Union after the Revolution (1917). From its inception, the Soviet Union denied individual citizens any right at all against the state (see section 222).

Communism suffered some setbacks when the citizens of East Germany demanded democratic reforms against the communistic form of government that had been prevalent there for so long. The Berlin Wall came down (December, 1989) and citizens of East and West Germany passed freely back and forth across the line. Germany became officially united in 1991. Similar reforms came to the Soviet Union itself where communism gave way to a democratic form of government. The Soviet Union no longer exists; a loosely formed confederation of independent states took its place.

# Matters of State

## 216. World War I

Earlier in the century, some students of international affairs believed there would never be another great war. It would be too destructive, they said, and no nation would take the responsibility of forcing the world into such a conflict. Their belief was only partially correct; as it turned out, no nation did accept the responsibility for what was called the "Great War" (World War I), but several nations were willing to let it happen, with the expectation of blaming somebody else for it. These nations had worked themselves into positions from which they were not brave or wise enough to back down.

Militarism became a crushing load on Europe. Preparedness for war, it was asserted, was the surest way to preserve peace, since a country is not likely to be attacked if it is able to defend itself. Here was another principle that sounded plausible, but in practice it meant that nations could jump into a war so quickly that nothing could keep them out. Nobody dared to stop building navies and organizing greater armies unless others would also stop. An example of a pre-war battleship may be seen in figure 10-7.

The Balkan Peninsula contained all the "makings" for a great explosion. In southeastern Europe there were several small nations—Rumania, Bulgaria, Serbia, Montenegro, and Greece—which at one time or another had been free from Turkish rule but did not love one another much more than they did the Turks. The Archduke Franz Ferdinand (1863-1914), heir to the throne of Austria, with his wife, Sophie Chotek, made a visit to the town of Sarajevo in Bosnia. While riding through the streets of this town they were shot and killed on June 28, 1914 {9:55 p.m.} by a young Serbian. This act set in motion the whole train of disasters that followed.

Austria declared war on Serbia (July 28, 1914). Russia mobilized in support of Serbia (July 29). Germany declared war against Russia (August 1) and against France (August 3). Germany, invoking the Schlieffen Plan (a military movement named after Alfred Schlieffen (1833-1913), invaded Belgium. This violation of Belgian neutrality led Britain to declare war on Germany (August 4). Austria declared war on Russia (August 6). Germany and Austria were joined by Turkey

274

(October 30, 1914) and Bulgaria (October 5, 1915). The Allies were joined by Japan (August 23, 1914), Italy (May 23, 1915), and the United States (April 6, 1917).

There had never been a war like this one. All forces displayed a great deal of heroism, but never before did an individual life count for so little. Military operations were viewed as one mass against another mass. In the west, both the Allies and the Germans "dug themselves in" with trenches almost 600 miles long, protected with concrete and equipped with rooms underground as if these bunkers were intended to be permanent homes. Instead of the open charge of one line against another, an attack might be opened with a tremendous barrage from hundreds of cannons. When it was thought that this barrage had gone on long enough, men would come out "over the top" of their trenches and move, sometimes slowly, through "no man's land" between the two lines until there seemed to be a good place for them to stop. Hand-to-hand fighting was much less common than in any previous war. The machine gun, such as the 30-caliber Browning machine gun, was used during these charges.

Germany made use of spies during this war. One of the most famous was Margaretha Geertruida Zelle, otherwise known as Mata Hari (1876-1917), the Dutch dancer and spy. She was captured in 1917 after which she was found guilty of having betrayed important military secrets confided to her by the many high Allied officers who were on intimate terms with her. Her execution by the French quickly followed.

The fragile craft first flown by the Wrights in 1903 had, by this time, evolved into a sturdy machine that rapidly found practical uses in war. For the first time in any war a considerable part of the fighting occurred in the air. Both sides had fighting planes, observation planes, and other kinds of aircraft. There were the Sopwith Camels and the Bristol fighters from Great Britain. The Camels were named after the English aviator and aircraft manufacturer Thomas Sopwith (1888-1989). Germany had planes called Fokkers and France flew planes called Spads. The Fokkers were named after the American airplane constructor Anton Fokker (1890-1939). Early in the war these planes were used primarily as scouts, and pilots could send radio messages indicating the position of enemy forces or direct artillery fire. Base stations equipped with the best radio gear of the day were used in France [see figure 10-8], Germany, and Britain to send and receive messages.

275

The role of the airplane in the war changed dramatically and quickly when they became platforms for guns. At first pilots used handguns to fire at each other but these were ineffective. There is record of only one plane being shot down during the entire war with a handgun. The machine gun changed this. With more rapid fire and with larger bullets, more and more planes fell from the skies. The French mounted double-barrel machine guns on the aft positions of their Spads [see figure 10-9] later in the war, with the man in the rear doing the shooting. Some early Fokker D-7s had the guns mounted toward the front. These were single-seat planes.

Bombs were dropped from airplanes during this war. Like the guns, these were at first small, hand-held devices which could do little damage. Eventually larger bombs were mounted under the wings which could be released by the pilot whenever his judgment suggested the time was right. It is not surprising, therefore, that bombing runs by World War I aircraft were seldom accurate.

The Lafayette Escadrille was a group of American volunteer aviators in the this war, created as Escadrille Americaine in the French air service (1916). This outfit saw much front-line action and heavy casualties. In 1918 the Lafayette Escadrille was recognized in the U.S. Army as the 103rd Pursuit Squadron.

The German aviator Baron von Richthofen (1892-1918) distinguished himself during the war. He is credited with shooting down eighty planes before he was killed in action.

The American Edward Rickenbacker (1890- 1973) was the commander of the 94th Aero Pursuit Squadron in France. He is credited with bringing down twenty-five German planes and for his heroism in action was awarded the Congressional Medal of Honor and the *Croix de Guerre* (a French award).

Before the airplane became a threat to them, the Germans used dirigibles to observe the enemy and drop bombs. But as airplanes became more powerful and were able to fly higher, the effectiveness of the dirigible diminished quickly. The first German dirigible to be forced down over France was the LZ-49 (October, 1917). This enormous craft came to rest with its nose in the trees.

The Germany navy's surface ships accomplished little during the war. A few ships, notably the Emden, performed some extraordinary exploits in capturing Allied merchantmen, but this vessel was finally sent to its fate by an Australian cruiser. A small German fleet won a victory over British ships in Pacific waters west of Chile, but was in turn completely destroyed by a British fleet near the Falkland Islands (1914). Most of Germany's big battleships were at home when the war broke out and they were speedily blockaded by the British fleet. Germany's merchant vessels were also blockaded or took refuge in neutral harbors. The British blockade of Germany turned out to be one of the determining factors in the war, and from the British point of view the navy fully justified all it cost.

On the sea the war took on a new character because of the submarine. The Germans used it in a brutal way that was in complete disregard of one of the long-recognized principles of international law, which required a warship attacking a merchant or passenger vessel to save the lives of non-combatants before sinking the ship. Instead, the German submarines shot their torpedoes and hurried away, leaving the ship and its passengers to their fates. Germany explained that the submarine could not take a chance on being hit by cannon that even a merchant vessel might carry; and besides, submarines could not accommodate captives anyway.

The most serious disaster from submarine activities occurred (May 7, 1915) {9:56 p.m.} when the British liner Lusitania was sunk off the coast of Ireland. It sank to the bottom with nearly 1,200 passengers, over 100 of whom were citizens of the United States. This event and the invasion of Belgium convinced many that the German war leaders were determined to win at any cost. They were important factors in America's decision to enter the war.

There was also the famous Zimmermann Note which convinced many Americans to enter the war. A secret coded telegram sent from Germany on January 16, 1917, to its ambassador to Mexico, Arthur Zimmermann (1864-1940), promised concessions to Mexico if it would come into the war against the United States. Finally President Woodrow Wilson (1856-1924; served 1913-1921) asked Congress to declare war against Germany which it did (April, 1917).

The nation responded to the president's war message with enthusiasm. Since the United States had only a small army, far-reaching draft laws were passed through which over four million men went to camp. About half of them went across the Atlantic into the A.E.F. (American Expeditionary Forces) before the war was over. General John J. "Black Jack" Pershing (1860-1948), was put in charge of the American troops in France, and he joined British Field Marshal

277

Douglas Haig (1861-1928) and General Henri P. Petain (1856-1951) who was then in command of the French troops.

During this time a great change came to Russia (see section 222). A party known as the Bolsheviki had been demanding far-reaching changes in Russia. The Germans, guessing what was going to happen, allowed a Bolshevist leader, Vladimir Ilyich Lenin (1870-1924) (sometimes inaccurately referred to as Nikolai Lenin) to come back from exile through Germany to Russia. Under the direction of Lenin and his associate Leon Trotsky (1879-1940), the Bolshevists soon obtained control of affairs in Russia. They set up an immediate demand for peace, intending as soon as this had been brought about to start an entirely new system of society and industry in Russia.

The people of Russia were ready for peace at any price. The Bolshevist leaders signed the treaty of Brest-Litovsk with the Germans (March, 1918). By this treaty, dictated by the Germans, it was agreed that a vast area which had been in the Russian Empire, including Poland and the smaller districts to the north, should be given up, thus laying open to the Germans all the natural resources, the factories and the farms of some of the best-developed sections of Russia. A similar treaty had put Rumania completely at the mercy of the Germans and Austrians. Their victory on the eastern front seemed to be complete.

When Russia fell apart, Germany and Austria seemed entirely free to give their attention to affairs on the western fronts. Vast bodies of troops were transferred from the east to the Italian front and the so-called Hindenburg Line in France. The Austrians inflicted a bad defeat on the Italians (October, 1917), pushing them back as far as the Piave River (a river in northeastern Italy flowing from the eastern Alps to the Adriatic above Venice). The Germans waited until the next spring before trying to break through the Allied line in the West (March, 1918). Hoping to push the Allies apart, they smashed heavily at the point where the British troops and the French met. The Allied line was bent back, but not broken.

Then the Allies selected Marshal Ferdinand Foch (1851-1929) of France as commander-in-chief of the entire Allied army, thus making possible a unity of command that had been lacking (March, 1918). When the Germans made their last drive, they pushed forward a little too far for their own good and left a weak spot which Foch discovered. Promptly he attacked and the Germans had to retreat.

Germany's three allies were forced out of the war in about one month. The Allied troops moved northward from Saloniki (sometimes Salonica) against the Bulgarians (September) and defeated them so badly that Bulgaria wanted to quit and signed an agreement to give up fighting. Turkey also signed an armistice (October). Next came Austria. In that same month the Italians mounted an ambitious drive against the Austrians and routed the Austrian army. In desperation, the new Austrian Emperor Charles I (1887-1922; reigned 1916-1918), nephew of Franz Joseph I (1830-1916) whose place he took on the throne, accepted what was almost a surrender to the Allies.

By this time the spirit of the German people was broken. The German government proposed an armistice, with the understanding that peace would be finally made on the basis of President Wilson's Fourteen Points. Kaiser William II took refuge in Holland, leaving his country to look out for itself. The Allied leaders made the armistice a pretty severe affair, but the Germans accepted it and the guns stopped firing all along the Western Front (at 11:00 a.m., November 11, 1918) {10:00 p.m.}. The peace treaty was signed at Versailles on June 28, 1919.

## Matters of State After World War I

The world was transformed in significant ways because of World War I. The Czar and his family had been murdered; the Kaiser and his family went into seclusion in Holland; kings who had ruled over parts of the German Empire retired; Emperor Franz Joseph of Austria died and his successor had to go into exile; the Sultan of Turkey lost his job. Russia came to be ruled by a small group of men with a tyranny at least equal to that of the Czar. Germany tried a republic, but became so uncomfortable during the process that it allowed Adolf Hitler to set himself up as dictator (1933) (see section 219). Austria, too, had an unhappy time as a republic. Turkey set up what was called a republic but became dominated by the enlightened purposes of one man—Mustapha (sometimes Mustafa) Kemal Ataturk (1880-1938). Italy, which before World War I seemed to have been a constitutional monarchy, also fell into the hands of a dictator (see section 220).

The League of Nations got under way (December, 1920) when representatives from many countries that had signed the peace treaty and some that had not, including the United States, assembled at Geneva, Switzerland, and started the machinery of the league. Some nations had held off several months before organizing the league in the hope that something would happen to induce the United States Senate to ratify the Versailles Treaty or accept the league. But that did not happen. President Wilson, without whom there probably would not have been a league, had antagonized some of the Republican leaders to such a degree that they would not permit the treaty to be ratified without "reservations," which the president in turn would not accept.

## 217. Prohibition of Alcoholic Beverages

In the twentieth century, Finland, most of Canada, and the United States tried by changing laws to prohibit the sale of intoxicating liquors. In America it was the Volstead Act (1919) which defined alcoholic liquor and provided for the enforcement of Prohibition. It received its name from its promoter, Joseph Volstead (1860-1947). It was the violation of this national law, along with certain state laws as well, that added aggravating and enduring features to the large-scale crime racket in America in the years following World War I. Law officers, such as Elliot Ness (1908-1957), had to deal with shrewdly managed *speakeasies*, highly organized syndicates of bootleggers, and rum runners (see chapter endnote 10-2). Gangs of hijackers competed for illegal business and turned modern weapons against each other as well as against the authorities.

The gangs engaged in the business of making, transporting, and selling liquor and became closely linked with bribery, gambling, underworld vice, and organized racketeering which successfully extracted tribute from labor groups, contractors, restaurants, and other types of legitimate businesses, especially in New York and Chicago. There was the "protection racket," for example, wherein thugs would promise not to bust up a place of business as long as the owner periodically paid them a certain sum of money.

Whole cities were divided into sections, each run by local "bosses." Chicago gangster Al "Scarface" Capone (1899-1947), who emerged as the top Chicago gangster, rode around in an armored car and headed a syndicate that grossed millions from beer and liquor sales, gambling establishments, dog tracks, dance halls, "roadhouses" (nightclubs located outside the city limits), and other sources. Drive-by shootings, which sprayed bullets wildly on public streets, injured and killed many innocent bystanders. In Chicago hundreds of persons were murdered in gang warfare (1920-1929). These murders reached a climax in the mass murder which became known as the Saint Valentine's Day Massacre (February 14, 1929). Five members of one gang (probably Capone's), some dressed as policemen, entered a garage on Chicago's North Side, and murdered seven members of the rival gang of George "Bugs" Moran (1893-1957) with machine guns. Many gangster killers escaped official detection or punishment. Capone himself was indicted by a Federal Grand Jury for evasion of income-tax payments (1931), the only charge against him that could be proved, and was sentenced to eleven years in prison.

In 1929 President Herbert C. Hoover (1874-1964; served 1929-1933) appointed a National Commission on Law Observance and Law Enforcement. It resulted in no changes. The enforcement of prohibition proved so difficult that it was gradually given up. The Canadian provinces were the first, followed by Finland. The United States repealed the prohibition amendment in its Constitution in 1933 {10:22 p.m.}.

Most countries contented themselves with lessening the opportunity to get liquor by having bars and stores closed at definite hours and on certain days. Some laws place a limit upon the amount of liquor that could be sold to any person.

## 218. The Great Depression

The decade after World War I proved to be prosperous for the industrialized countries least influenced by the Great War. In America Harry Houdini, whose real name was Erich Weiss (1874-1926), startled the world with his escapes from bonds of every sort—locks, handcuffs, strait jackets, and sealed chests under water. Flappers (young women who were considered bold and unconventional) danced to the Charleston while Walt Disney's (1901-1966) Mickey Mouse starred in the first talking cartoon, "Steamboat Willie" (1927) {10:13 p.m.} and "Lucky Lindy" flew solo across the Atlantic. The proliferating "everyman's" automobile—Henry Ford's Model T—gave America and the world new mobility and the need for improved roads. It seemed like this period, later characterized as an "economic drunk" by Will Rogers (1879-1935), would never end. Fourteen years after the Great War ended, however, prosperity was hard to find in Europe and America.

An economic paralysis came over the world. People who were out of work were not earning money and, therefore, they could not buy products (there was no Social Security or unemployment insurance at this time). Producers had little or no market for their goods. Not only within nations but among the nations, trade went down to distressingly low points. The first signs came from Europe and elsewhere. Great Britain was one of the first countries to be hit hard. France felt the depression later than some countries, perhaps because it had so much work involved with reconstructing the regions that had been devastated during World War I. Interest rates were raised to over six percent in Britain to obtain needed capital. There was also a rapid unloading of investments from European governments which caused a further fall in stocks. The United States thought it was having the best time ever for a while, but suddenly even America was startled with the Great Stock Market Crash (1929).

Although speculation in stocks and bonds was characteristic of the era of prosperity America experienced (1920s), it developed to great extremes during the final three years of the decade. While hundreds of thousands of people invested their savings in the stocks and bonds of corporations—most of which had been watered in the expectation of increased earnings or for less worthy motives—millions bought or sold stocks on margins. Such purchasers put up a sufficient sum to cover normal fluctuations and when the price had risen or fallen as far as they cared or dared to risk it, they would sell and realize a profit—or a loss. People from all walks of life played the market and borrowed money from banks on inflated collateral for this purpose. Some 8.5 billion dollars in loans for speculation were outstanding (October, 1929) {10:16 p.m.} as compared with 3.5 billion two years before. The rise in the price level of stocks (1927-1929) frequently had little or no relation to real value as judged by the earning power of the stock. Indeed some shares which had never paid any dividends at all climbed to amazing heights.

When loans became more difficult to obtain, private investors quickly unloaded their investments and the stock market continued to drop. Prices on the New York Stock Exchange fell rapidly (October 24) and more than twelve million shares were exchanged—the wildest day in the history of the exchange up to that time. Leading bankers tried unsuccessfully to stem the tide and the financial storm struck with full force (October 29). On that "Black Tuesday," over sixteen million shares changed hands. The next day Hoover said, "The fundamental business of the country...is on a sound and prosperous basis." The reality, though, was that the Great Depression had begun. The value of leading stocks was cut in half between October 1 and November 13. Additional declines followed so that the average value of stocks declined to little more than one-fifth of their peak value by 1932.

In the United States, the Farm Board was unable to stabilize agricultural prices with its half-billion-dollar revolving fund, and these prices moved downward to an average of about fifty percent of their previous (1929) value, whereas surplus farm products accumulated in warehouses. Farmers were unable to pay their debts or even meet interest payments and wholesale foreclosures resulted. Farmers in Iowa acted in groups to prevent the effective sales of farms under mortgage foreclosures, sometimes by preventing potential bidders from participating. Yet there was generally little relief from the state governments.

A bank panic shook America. With none of today's economic safety features such as the Federal Deposit Insurance Corporation to insure against such problems, 305 banks closed (September, 1931) and 522 were shut down (October). Fear that the country would go off the gold standard led to widespread hoarding of the metal. The national income in terms of dollars fell from slightly over eighty-two million (1929) to about half that (1932), with the physical production of goods declining more than one-third from the peak. In the United States alone, there were some twelve million workers who were unemployed (1932). Men stood on streets to sell apples while bread lines and soup kitchens were set up in cities to prevent starvation. Thousands of young men rode freight trains over the nation in a vain search for work.

Of all the books written about the Great Depression, it was perhaps John Steinbeck's (1902-1968) novel, *The Grapes of Wrath* (1939), that was one of the most accurate in depicting the problems of the "Arkies" (farmers from Arkansas) and the "Okies" (farmers from Oklahoma). He described the difficulties of these farmers who came from the "dust bowl" in the Midwest that resulted from the erosion of soil due to dry weather, strong winds, and the depletion of vegetation (1930s). The "dust bowl" aggravated the effects of the Great Depression and caused thousands of farmers to seek other jobs. Many headed to California seeking jobs as fruit pickers, only to find that there were so many pickers there that they had to work for almost nothing to get a job. Many had to live out of their cars [see figure 10-10] and trucks and they suffered untold hardships.

The financial resources of even the wealthiest cities and states of America neared depletion (December, 1930). It became obvious to city and state officials that only the great resources of the Federal Government itself could prevent mass starvation and save the national economy from total disintegration. President Hoover was, however, not in favor of direct federal aid to individuals at that time. He did sign the Smoot-Hawley Tariff Act (1930), a bill that he had seen as a method of raising tariffs primarily on agriculture products. By the time Congress finished with it, however, it included some of the highest rates in history on manufactured products. Within two years twenty-five nations retaliated by raising duties on U.S. goods. Even Great Britain abandoned its free-trade policy and levied import duties on many American articles. Such a process reduced trade between nations still further. The economic nationalism triggered by this legislation was blamed for deepening the worldwide depression.

On top of all this, and sometimes contributing to it, the money systems of some countries collapsed. Austria and Hungary received help from the League of Nations in rebuilding their finances. Germany and Russia were among the nations that tried to supply money by the means of simply printing it. This kind of "inflation" ultimately ruined them; but in almost any country there are those who believe it is possible to make people rich by merely printing paper money. German paper *deutsche marks* went down in value to such an extent that it took millions of them to equal a United States paper dollar or an English paper pound; and Russia's rubles devalued so completely that westerners would not even look at them except by way of curiosity.

Germany finally did start a money system all over again, borrowing gold from western Europe and the United States to do so. Italy and France "stabilized" their currency at a point about one-fifth of where it had been before World War I. Other countries, such as Great Britain (1931) and the United States (1933), finally went off the gold standard as many who had hoarded gold had feared.

284

## 219. Hitler and the Third Reich

A sour and dispirited Germany turned to new leadership in the 1930s. Adolf Hitler (1889-1945) had been a corporal in the Austrian Army in World War I. A would-be artist who supported himself by painting houses, he spent a few months in prison for trying to stir up a revolution in Bavaria (1923). While incarcerated he wrote *Mein Kampf* ("My Struggle"), wherein he detailed his theories of the racial superiority of the Aryans and his hatred of the Jews, among other things.

The economic crisis (1929-1930) and the conditions of the Treaty of Versailles proved to be an opportunity for him to pursue leadership goals. Hitler began to preach that he and his associates were the ones who could get Germany out of its distress. They called themselves National Socialists, but they were usually referred to as Nazis. Wearing brown shirts and using the swastika as a symbol, they "hypnotized" the Germans en masse, who, thinking that nobody else had accomplished much for Germany, were willing to try Hitler.

Hitler and his crowd talked about regaining for Germany the glories she had lost, promised to get work for Germany's unemployed, attacked the Jews as being responsible for most of Germany's difficulties and thus by appeals to all kinds of discontent, gained more followers.

In the presidential election (1932) Hitler was a candidate; he came in second to President Paul von Hindenburg (1847-1934; served 1925-1933). To keep Hitler quiet, he was offered a place in the cabinet, but he would accept nothing but the chancellorship. Finally, Hindenburg gave in and appointed Hitler as Chancellor (1933). Hitler soon secured from the Reichstag (the lower chamber of the German Parliament—1871-1945) a vote practically giving up all its own powers and making him a dictator for a four-year period.

Hitler was an excellent orator, partly because of his conviction and dedication to his cause and partly because of the persuasive appeal of his promises and the emotional effects of his rhetoric. Making full use of the radio, still then a relatively new communications medium, he appealed mainly to the middle class who had lost their property, to farmers who could not sell their crops, to laborers who were unemployed, to young men for whom there were neither jobs nor careers, and to all Germans who had been humiliated by the loss of the Great War and the drastic provisions of the Treaty of Versailles.

Hitler called his regime the Third Reich and predicted that it would last a thousand years. The First Reich had been the Holy Roman Empire (962-1806) and the Second the German Empire (1871-1918). But the Third Reich did not last for a thousand years; it lasted only for twelve (see section 238).

Once Hitler became Chancellor, he proceeded to unify the German people in thought and action. The German word was *gleichgeschalten*— literally to "make alike." To achieve this end, all political parties, except the National Socialists, were disbanded and outlawed; the separate states (Prussia, Bavaria, Saxony, etc.) of which the Republic was controlled, were abolished; freedom of teaching and the press were suppressed; and the full rights of citizenship were denied to Jews and others who were not regarded as of true German or of "Aryan" (Nordic) descent.

Many communists, socialists, and Jews were deprived of their properties, confined and brutally tortured in concentration camps or executed. Many of the foremost German writers and scholars, including Thomas Mann (1875-1955), a famous German novelist, and Albert Einstein (1879-1955), the world's foremost mathematician and physicist, were forced into exile. Hundreds of books not approved by the Nazis were taken from the libraries and publicly burned. Newspapers, schools and universities, and publishers of books were strictly supervised by the Ministry of Propaganda whose function it was to determine what Germans should think and say. No adverse criticism of the government was permitted. These were some of the measures used to create a "like-minded and like-acting" Germany.

---

**Reflection:**

*Among all the religious groups in history, the Jews have had the most varied and unpleasant experiences. Anti-Semitic movements in Germany saw Jewish officials in the government and universities forced out of their positions. Jewish people were hounded in their professions and places of business and turned into outcasts in their communities, because of the charge that the Jews were to blame for much of the distress from which Germany was suffering and that they held too many places of importance in German life. Later they were murdered by the millions in concentration camps. Would a truly conscientious person ever encourage religious persecution today? Is there any disadvantage in religious toleration as a definite policy if all faiths are allowed to worship as they please? What lessons did the Nazi Holocaust teach the world?*

When Hitler could not get other countries to agree that Germany might have a larger army and navy than the Versailles Treaty allowed, he refused to take any further part in the conference at Geneva and announced that Germany would withdraw from the League of Nations. Hindenburg's death (1934) gave Hitler another chance to enlarge his authority. No one was allowed to take office as president, but Hitler now called himself Reichschancellor and "Fuhrer" (literally, "leader"). He announced that he would create an army of 600,000 men (1935). He sent troops into the "demilitarized" Rhinelands (1936). If he had been opposed, he would have retreated. The famous "war guilt" clause of the Versailles Treaty (which declared that Germany alone was responsible for the war) was officially repudiated (1937). Thus Hitler scrapped the Treaty of Versailles and Germany was once more the strongest military state in Europe (1938).

Hitler used this new state to adopt a policy of expansion. He entered into an understanding with the Italian dictator Benito Mussolini (1883-1945). The agreement between the two dictators came to be known as the "Berlin-Rome Axis". Hitler joined Mussolini in giving aid to the Spanish rebels (see section 221), demanded as a right and as a necessity the return of the German colonies, and declared that German influence must be extended in eastern Europe. He insisted that Nazi Germany was the chief bulwark of Europe against communism, and his purpose seemed to be to form a central European "bloc" of fascist states to oppose the Soviets. Thus, Hitler revived the old German policy of a *Drang nach Osten*— "Drive to the East." The first crucial steps in this drive were the annexation of Austria and Czechoslovakia (see sections 225 and 226).

One of the important propaganda devices Germany had during the 1930s was the great airship Hindenburg. In a day when airplanes were still relatively primitive, travel by airship was a luxury. The Hindenburg flew passengers on a regular schedule around the world where its great tail fins, that had been painted with swastikas, could be clearly seen.

One of the disadvantages that the designers and builders of the Hindenburg had to contend with was the understandable reluctance of the government of the United States to sell helium to Hitler's Germany (the U.S. had a monopoly on the gas). The great airship was, therefore, filled with the lighter but highly explosive gas hydrogen which was plentiful in Germany. On the evening of May 6, 1937, when the airship was landing at Lakehurst, New Jersey in America, it caught fire and exploded. Hitler's traveling propaganda device was suddenly destroyed. The cause of the explosion was never determined.

## 220. Italy

Italy was in bad shape at the end of World War I. Industry was seriously upset. Extreme socialistic ideas had gained much favor among Italian workers, and some thought of setting up a system like Russia's. Factory workmen frequently went on strike and sometimes even demanded the right to run factories to suit themselves. There was general disrespect for law and order.

While this state of affairs was almost at its height, Benito Mussolini, who had himself once been a socialist, organized a new group called the Fascists. Somewhat similar to Garibaldi's "Red Shirts" (1860), this fascist (see chapter endnote 10-3) group wore black shirts. One night in October, 1922, armed bands of Black Shirts from all parts of Italy headed for Rome and camped outside the city. King Victor Emmanuel III (1869-1947; reigned 1900-1946) of Italy, knowing that if he tried to suppress this movement there would surely be civil war, decided to yield to it. He summoned Mussolini and asked him to serve as the Prime Minister.

From that time until the end of World War II, Italy was under the complete control of *Il Duce* ("the leader") as Mussolini was often called. He had no use for democracy. The only political party allowed was his Fascist Party. The power of the king and royal family was taken away and even local governments lost their right to govern themselves. Rome, the capital city, was administered by a "governor" appointed by Mussolini. Some communities had a *"podesta"* appointed by the central government to whom they were responsible.

## 221. The Spanish Civil War

Spain's great military strength of the previous century had declined, so that by this century she was no longer one of the great European powers.

The dictatorship of Miguel Primo de Rivera (1870; ruled 1923-

1930) was overthrown and a democratic republic was established. There followed a bitter struggle between the conservative parties on the right (the landowners, the church, and the army) and the liberal and radical parties on the left (the lower middle classes, intellectuals, peasants, and workers). In elections the left gained control of the government (1936) and initiated a drastic socialistic program designed to limit the privileges of the church, break up the great estates, and make a more equitable distribution of wealth among the people. The elections were followed by strikes, seizures of land by the peasants, and sporadic fighting in many places. The army threatened to take control and some regiments started a rebellion against the government. This resulted in what is known as the Spanish Civil War (1936-1939) {10:26 p.m.-10:31 p.m.}.

Except for the involvement of the outside world, the civil war would probably have been only another Spanish civil war. The Soviet Union sent aid to the loyalists; Italy and Germany helped the rebels. People in the democratic countries were divided among those who regarded communism as the greatest threat and those who regarded fascism as the greater danger. Also, Italy and Germany wanted to secure control of the mineral resources in Spain. It was estimated (December, 1936) that there were 50,000 foreigners of twelve nationalities who were fighting in Spain.

The rebel forces won decisive advantages (March and April, 1938). The war continued, though, until the fall of Barcelona (January, 1939) virtually ended resistance to General Francisco Franco (1892-1975). The surrender of Madrid (March 28, 1939) ended the long conflict. The new government, with General Franco as its leader, aligned itself with Italy and Germany.

## 222. Russia

After World War I, the Bolshevist leaders, Vladimir Lenin and Leon Trotsky, were so eager to try out their extreme ideas in government and economics (communism) that they made peace on German terms. The new Russian leaders had no easy time in gaining a solid foothold in Russia, but in 1922 the Russia Socialist Federated Soviet Republic (R.S.F.S.R.) became the official name for the country which before had called itself Russia. Officially it was a federation made up of different republics. But the words federation and republic as used in the Soviet Union, did not mean local self-rule and democratic government, as they do in free countries such as the United States. The government of the Soviet Union became a strict, centralized dictatorship with complete control vested in the Communist Party. The actions of their leaders in setting up this system and of maintaining it are reminiscent of some events that occurred during the French Revolution.

The Russian leaders set up what they called the "red terror," after the fashion of the French radicals, except that the Russians did it on a tremendously wider scale. Anybody who dared to disagree with the new policy might be executed or imprisoned. A villainous secret police might dodge any man's footsteps or listen at any keyhole. Bolshevist leaders bragged about putting to death over a million people in establishing their authority.

Most other governments did not look kindly on Soviet Russia. People detested the brutal methods used by the Bolsheviks to gain power and they were afraid of harm that might come from Russian threats to overthrow all capitalistic governments. Several Russian leaders were connected with the Third Internationale, a movement to unite workers from all over the world under communist leadership. The desire to carry on trade with Russia finally caused a change of heart on the part of many governments, especially when Russians had less to say about upsetting things in other parts of the world. The United States was the last of the great powers to recognize the government of Russia (1933).

One thing which antagonized people in other countries was Russia's attack upon religion under Stalin. The old Russian Orthodox Church had been so closely tied up with the government under the Czars as to be virtually a part of it. When the new leaders came into power they wiped out every vestige of connection between the Russian church and the government. They also harshly repressed other religious bodies, though at first they encouraged them. The teaching of religion in any form to anybody under the age of eighteen was forbidden. Disgusting posters were put up in public, attacking beliefs in God, Jesus Christ, or any teaching of a distinctly religious nature. There was to be nothing for the people to depend on except their government.

## 223. Japan (Road to Empire)

For years Japan had looked to China with conquest in mind. After the Boxer Rebellion (1900-1901) a reform movement developed in China, the object of which was to establish a government strong enough to defend the country against the aggression of foreign states. The result was the overthrow of the Manchu Dynasty and the creation of the Chinese Republic (1912). But the new government was hardly more efficient than the former had been. China proved to be an easy target for Japanese aggression both during and after World War I.

Japan gained control of Korea after the Russo-Japanese War and certain privileges in the Chinese province of Manchuria, including the right to build a railroad there. Manchuria had been controlled by two influential men. Chang Tso-lin, (known as the "Old Marshall"), and his son, Chang Huseh-liang who cast his lot with the new national government of China, under the leadership of Chiang Kai-shek (1887-1975). Encouraged by a division between the Chinese authorities in Canton and Nanking, the Japanese made a conquest of Manchuria (1931) and set up a puppet state of Manchukuo there under the minimal rule of the former boy-emperor of China, Hsuan Tung (reigned 1932-1945).

The Japanese fought the Chinese at Shanghai (1932) and occupied the city. In the city itself, the Japanese were equipped to carry out their plans. It was also during this period that the United States maintained an interest in this area as evidenced by the intermittent presence of the U.S. carrier Houston off the coast of Shanghai (1930s).

Japan continued its conquest of China with the resumption of the conquest of Manchukuo (1937). Their objective was to take possession of the main cities and ports on the coast and to control the main highways and railways and strategic points of the adjacent interior. The Japanese were in possession of Shanghai (China's richest city) and Nanking, the capital (winter, 1938). They also controlled the principal port cities north of Shanghai, Peiping (Beijing), the former capital, and the main highways and railroads north of the Yellow River.

This Japanese aggression intensified international friction in Europe and throughout the world. Japan was unquestionably the strongest power in Asia (1941). Germany and Italy were friendly to Japan, while France, England, the United States, the smaller democratic countries, and the Soviets were hostile. There was also the mounting aggression from Germany. The threat of the most serious international crisis since the beginning of World War I loomed like storm clouds over the entire world.

# World War II

## 224. Background and Causes

The responsibility for this war rested with three nations. Most of the civilized nations of the world had agreed to settle international disputes by peaceful methods, thereby renouncing war. Japan, Italy, and Germany, however, chose to reach their goals through the use of force. The League of Nations proved ineffective in dealing with these uncooperative nations.

None of the peaceful nations were willing to use force to preserve peace. The smaller nations put their security in a policy of neutrality. The larger nations adopted a policy of appeasement.

Stalin urged other nations to join Russia in suppressing German aggression. But some countries feared communist Russia more than Nazi Germany and they believed Hitler when he said that a strong Germany would prevent the spread of Bolshevism to the west. The Germans, it was believed, would be satisfied if they regained the territory which had been taken from them after World War I. France and Britain made no effort to enforce the Treaty of Versailles. Thus, Hitler worked unhindered toward his "drive to the East."

## 225. Hitler Moves Into Austria

The Nazi Movement increased in strength and Hitler took the first step toward open intervention by forcing the Austrian government to appoint certain Nazis to high office (1938). Hoping to maintain its independence, the Austrian government suddenly announced that a plebiscite (a vote for or against a proposal) would be held to determine whether the Austrian people desired to be united with Germany. It is probable that a vote would have resulted in a majority against the union, and to prevent the vote from being held Hitler marched troops into Austria, took charge of the government and announced that Austria was part of the German Empire (March,

1938). Hitler himself announced a vote, the result of which was all but unanimous in favor of annexation (April, 1938).

## 226. Hitler and Czechoslovakia

England and France protested this action. They were very concerned with Hitler's intention regarding Czechoslovakia, the last democratic country in eastern Europe. Czechoslovakia was completely surrounded by fascist states. This country, set within the circle of the Sudeten Mountains, was a serious obstacle to Hitler's "drive to the east." Its chief political defense was its alliance with Russia and France; its main military defense was the strongly fortified mountain range. Hitler's main aims were to gain control of the range and to force Czechoslovakia to renounce its alliance with Russia and France.

To Hitler's advantage, there were in these mountain areas some two to three million Sudeten Germans who were subject to Czechoslovakian rule. These Germans were treated better than any other minority group in eastern Europe. But there was some discontent among them and Hitler made use of it to promote the Nazi Movement there. The leader of the movement was Konrad Henlein who demanded complete local autonomy for the Sudetens. Though concessions were made, disturbances increased (summer, 1938). Hitler stated that the situation was intolerable and must be settled immediately (September).

With the prospect of war very likely, British Prime Minister Neville Chamberlain (1869-1940) took the unusual step of flying to Germany to have a personal interview with Hitler at Berchtesgaden (September 15). Appalled at the prospect of another European war, he believed that even a successful war against Germany would neither save democracy in Czechoslovakia nor restore it in Germany. Rather, he thought it would allow communism to establish itself in central and eastern Europe. With the approval of France, Chamberlain informed Czechoslovakia that she must cede some of the Sudeten lands (sometimes Sudetenlands) to Germany, otherwise neither France nor Great Britain could promise to support her. At Berchtesgaden the terms of the transfer were tentatively agreed upon by Chamberlain and Hitler.

Hitler later made additional demands which Chamberlain could not accept. Hitler stated that if his demands were not met quickly (October 1, 1938), his troops would march into Czechoslovakia. At this point Mussolini suggested a conference involving himself, Hitler, Chamberlain, and the French premier, Edouard Daladier (1884-1970). The conference was held at Munich (September 29) where it was agreed that:

(1) the Sudeten regions containing a majority of Germans according to the last census before World War I should be ceded to Germany.

(2) that in certain other regions votes should be held to determine whether or not these regions should be ceded to Germany.

These territories were transferred to Germany, giving Hitler a stunning diplomatic victory. He encouraged Slovakia (the eastern region of Czechoslovakia) to declare its independence, and forcibly annexed Bohemia to Germany and the greater part of Moravia (March, 1939), thus destroying the independent state of Czecho-slovakia. Shortly afterwards, he began to demand the city of Danzig and the Polish Corridor.

## 227. Other Matters Leading to War

At about the same time, Mussolini suddenly sent troops into the little kingdom of Albania on the Adriatic coast. Without encountering much resistance, he successfully conquered that country.

These aggressive acts prompted a change in French and British policy. France and England had made an agreement with Poland to help her with all their forces if Poland ever had to use force to repel a German invasion. They also tried to bring Rumania, Greece, Turkey, and Russia into a general alliance with themselves and Poland against Germany and Italy. These negotiations were still in progress when Germany and Russia signed a friendly non-aggression pact (August, 1939). Hitler did this to prevent Russia from joining France and Great Britain, and to obtain needed supplies. Stalin signed it in order to strengthen his frontier against Germany. Having succeeded in removing Russia from the western powers' alliance, Hitler renewed his demands with vigor.

## 228. Germany and Russia Enter Poland

As the crisis became more intense, all four powers prepared for war by partial or complete mobilization. Without declaring war, Germany began military operations against Poland (September 1). After an ultimatum to Germany to withdraw its troops from Poland, both Great Britain and France declared war against Germany (September 3).

After German armies had conquered western Poland, Russian armies invaded Poland from the east (September 17) , and within a short time Poland was divided between Germany and Russia. Russia then demanded, and was given the right to establish military and naval bases in Estonia, Latvia, and Lithuania. Similar demands upon Finland were rejected, but after heroic resistance Finland was forced to cede to Russia her fortified frontier north of Leningrad, control of the harbor of Petsamo, and the right to build a railroad across northern Finland to Sweden.

## 229. Germany Invades Norway and France

German armies invaded Norway (April 9, 1940) {10:32 p.m.}, occupied Oslo (formerly called Christiania, 1624-1925;—see chapter endnote 10-4), the capital, and within a few weeks were in control of Norway's chief western ports, including Trondheim, where the establishment of airports and submarine bases enabled the Germans to operate more efficiently against the British blockade.

Hitler realized that his best chance of winning the war was to risk everything on a *Blitzkrieg* ("lightning war"), a sudden and tremendous smash through Belgium into France. He hoped for a decisive victory before the Allies could bring to bear their superior reserves. Without warning, German armies invaded Luxembourg, Belgium, and the Netherlands (Holland) on May 10. They employed the same tactics as in Poland. Largely ignoring fortified places, they drove a kind of flying-wedge of heavily armored tanks, supported by bombers, into enemy country. In this way they blasted a path for the infantry.

Five days later the Netherlands were conquered and the Allied lines were pushed back into western Belgium and northern France. Steadily the French were forced to retreat toward Soissons and

Amiens. Within a few weeks the Allied line was broken. One German army occupied several of the channel ports in France and attempted to surround the English and Belgian armies. The unplanned and unconditional surrender by King Leopold III (1901-1983; reigned 1934-1951) of the entire Belgian army left the English armies in a desperate situation. A masterly retreat enabled them to reach Dunkirk, where, in spite of heavy German bombing, most of them were rescued by English and French boats. They reached England with the main part of their forces intact but with the loss of all their equipment.

The Germans quickly drove the French armies south beyond Paris. The French government surrendered, signing an armistice (June 22). The armistice provided that France should be divided into two parts. The larger part—northern France, including all of the northern and western seaboard—was to be occupied and governed directly by Germany; the smaller part—southern France—was permitted to have its own government, but only with many restrictions which made it dependent on Germany.

Three identifiable errors may be cited which contributed to France's demise. First, there was too much reliance on the Maginot Line. The Maginot Line, named after war minister Andre Maginot (1877-1932), was a series of French fortifications built (1927-1936) along France's eastern frontier from Switzerland to Belgium. It was designed to repel an invasion—but it did not accomplish this because the Germans invaded France through Belgium and the guns were pointed in the wrong direction.

Second, they either did not expect the Germans to strike through Belgium or, if they did, had made no adequate preparations for defense on the Belgian frontier.

Third, they failed to consider the new German methods of attack. They were unprepared to resist the technique of "lightning war."

The rapid fall of France astounded everyone, including the Germans. This event also brought the United States much nearer to war than was suggested by the reassuring slogans of the candidates in the United States national elections (1940). Isolationists increasingly were afraid that their country was headed toward war. Interventionists, that is pro-Allied elements, feared that American aid might be too little and too late to save England from a German invasion.

## 230. England's Finest Hour

At this frightful hour, England stood alone. The feeling was that England could not long resist the superior German military and air force. Mussolini was so sure of German victory that, twelve days before the French signed the Armistice (June 10), he entered the war, expecting to get something for it. Hitler believed that after a little bombing the English would ask for peace. He would invade and conquer the country if they did not. As a preparation for invasion, he started a terrible and nearly continuous bombing of English cities (August, 1940). He predicted that the English would submit (mid-September). This was his first serious mistake.

In this, "their finest hour," as Prime Minister Winston Churchill (1874-1965) said, the English people proved that they were at their best when everything seemed lost. Day after day, they endured the bombing with its heartless destruction of their cities. The bombing did not destroy their morale; actually, it improved it. The Royal Air Force of England, assisted partly by the invention and use of a new weapon known as radar (an instrument for determining the distance and direction of unseen objects by the reflection of radio waves), achieved an heroic status in defending their island. With the coming of cloudy weather and long nights, the bombing became less effective and it began to look as though the concept of "lightning war" could not be applied in a conquest of England (early 1941). The amazing resistance of the British became one of the turning points in the war.

## 231. Hitler Invades Russia

Hitler unexpectedly invaded Russia on a 2,000-mile front from Leningrad to Bessarabia (June 22, 1941) but Russia was not prepared. Even though the Russian armies retreated in the initial German attack, they destroyed or removed everything that could be of use to the Germans; and the Germans were not able to take Leningrad, Moscow, or Sevastopol before the cold Russian winter came. Expecting to win the war quickly, the Germans were not prepared for winter fighting but the Russians were. The Germans retreated, and although they still held a little territory, they suffered heavy losses in men and equipment. Hitler had to warn his people that the war might last another winter.

## 232. The Japanese Attack Pearl Harbor

The Americans were strongly divided concerning how much involvement in the European conflict would be necessary to ensure the safety of democracy when (December 7, 1941) {10:34 p.m.}, the Japanese decided it for them by a sudden, treacherous attack on Pearl Harbor, Hawaii. The next day, at the request of President Franklin Roosevelt (1882; served 1933-1945), Congress declared war on Japan. Three days later, Congress declared war on the other Axis powers (Bulgaria, Finland, Germany, Hungary, Italy, and Rumania) (December 11).

The attack on Pearl Harbor showed that the war was really one that affected the vital interests of all countries. It removed any doubt that the war was a conflict on a world-wide scale between radically different ideals of life and human rights. It showed that the war had to be fought for the preservation of a world in which nations could be reasonably secure against unprovoked military conquest and destruction, and could be free to live according to the ideas and institutions it preferred.

The United States' entry into the war was good news for Great Britain in more ways than one. The British armies had a desperate shortage of tanks at that time and a heavy, eight-wheel-drive armored car was built (called the Mark VI) from components which were originally found on typical construction equipment in use at the time. It was to have been used in North Africa (1942), but by that time the United States was in the war and everyone knew that miracles of production in the United States would ensue, thus greatly reducing the need for vehicles like the Mark VI. Only two of the armored cars were completed.

## 233. Japanese Objectives in the War

The object of Japan was not only the conquest of China, but the conquest of the entire Far East—China, the Netherlands East Indies (now Indonesia), India, Australia, the Philippines, Hawaii, and Russia's Siberia. To further this aim, the Japanese had signed a ten-year "Axis Pact" with Germany and Italy (September 27, 1940). After the fall of France, they took the first step by occupying the French possessions in Indo-China (October, 1940).

By destroying British and American power in the Far East, the Japanese opened the way for the conquest of the Netherlands East Indies and India, and cut off the supplies from Britain and America to the Chinese. If Germany could conquer the Near East, they reasoned, Japan and the Germans could unite for the mastery of Europe, Africa, and Asia. The center of British power in the Far East was the great naval base at Singapore. This could not be easily taken from the sea, and the British thought it could not be taken from the land because of the jungles of lower Burma. But jungles were not unknown to the Japanese who chose the jungle route to achieve their objective. Singapore was taken (February, 1942).

The fall of Singapore opened the way for the conquest of the Dutch islands of Sumatra and Java (April). The Americans were forced to surrender Corregidor (May), their last stronghold in the Philippines, even though the American and Filipino forces under General Douglas MacArthur (1880-1964) had resisted heroically. General MacArthur had already been transferred to take command in Australia, which was, aside from India, the one remaining base for the operations of the Allies in the Far East. As a prelude for an invasion of Australia, the Japanese landed forces on New Guinea and New Britain, and occupied the Solomon Islands and the New Hebrides.

## 234. America Responds Directly

The Americans, led by James H. Doolittle (1896-1993), bombed Tokyo with B-25 bombers launched from a carrier (April, 1942). Although her strength in the Pacific had been greatly weakened by the loss sustained at Pearl Harbor, America sent aid to the Australians as quickly as possible. By May, an American naval force was able to win a victory in the Coral Sea.

A month later, a large Japanese fleet, headed for the Hawaiian Islands, was turned back with heavy losses in the Battle of Midway (June 4-6, 1942). American Marines captured three small islands and made a landing on Guadalcanal in the Solomons, and took Henderson Airfield (August). The Japanese made desperate efforts to hold Guadalcanal, and only after much hard fighting on land and sea, with heavy losses, did they yield it to the Americans.

Americans and Australians launched a counterattack on the Japanese in New Guinea (September), driving the invaders back

299

across the Owen Stanley Mountains and fighting them one-by-one in the jungles. Americans fought in swamps with Jeeps (small but powerful, general-purpose automobiles with a four-wheel drive) and artillery to overwhelm the enemy, and General MacArthur announced his victory (January 23, 1943) {10:36 p.m.}.

## 235. The "Second Front"

The decision to create a "second front" to reduce German strength in Russia was another factor that led to the defeat of Hitler. General George C. Marshall (1880-1959; served 1939-1945), Chief of Staff of the United States Army, favored a much earlier drive into France without the delay of a diversionary activity and before the Germans could expand defense forces and fortifications. This step would have suited the Russians who were urgently calling for a "second front" in the west. But Churchill, for England's benefit, opposed this, partly because a possible failure would be disastrous to British morale and power. He preferred to make an attack on the Mediterranean front through the "soft underbelly of Europe," move through the Balkans and into Poland and defeat Germany there. Marshall opposed this strategy because he did not consider the area to be "soft." It was thus decided to invade Europe first from the south, in Italy. Before this could happen, the Axis forces had to be driven from North Africa and the Mediterranean had to be secured. As plans for the African invasion developed, the American General Dwight D. Eisenhower (1890-1969) was chosen to be its commander instead of General George C. Marshall.

There was a sense of urgency regarding the proposed invasion. The British had lost Tobruk and thousands of captives to Rommel's forces. The German Field Marshal Erwin Rommel (1891-1944) pushed eastward almost into Egypt. The Russians had lost the Black Sea stronghold of Sevastopol. There was fear that a consolidated German drive to the east might connect with a westward sweep of the Japanese who were in Burma and threatening the borders of India. Allied victory would be postponed perhaps forever unless the course of war could be changed.

The United States War Department in Washington announced (November 7, 1942) that the United States Army, Navy, and Air Force started landing operations during the hours of darkness at numerous points on the shores of North Africa. It was explained that the action was necessary because of an Axis menace to that area. The expedition consisted primarily of American and British forces, with contingents from other countries.

This was an amphibious operation of unprecedented magnitude, utilizing 500 transports and 350 warships of varying sizes. The German intelligence had been aware of the movement, but was not good at guessing its destination. In four days 1,500 miles of coastline had been occupied, and all of French North Africa, except Tunisia, was brought under the control of the United Nations.

The immediate effect of the African invasion was to stir the Germans to redoubled action. They committed troops to Tunisia and they moved into "unoccupied" southeastern France. Just before they took over Toulon, where the bulk of the French fleet lay idle, the French scuttled the fleet.

## 236. The Fall of Italy to the Allies

Sicily was the next objective in the planned invasion of Italy. After weeks of air bombardment of the island, the amphibious assault was launched (July 10, 1943). Partly because of stormy weather, the defending Italian forces were completely surprised. In the hasty action that followed there were cases of Italian naval and land forces firing on their own planes. Eighth Army British First Viscount Field Marshal Bernard Montgomery (1887-1976) headed a British force, while American Generals Omar N. Bradley (1893-1981), George S. Patton, Jr. (1885-1945), and others led Americans in the undertaking which brought Sicily into Allied control just nine months after the landings in North Africa.

One important effect of the invasion of Sicily was that it precipitated the fall of Mussolini from power in Italy. The king announced the resignation of the Duce (July 25, 1943). The new premier, General Pietro Badoglio (1871-1956), contacted General Eisenhower in an effort to negotiate a surrender without the knowledge of the Germans who dominated Italy virtually as conquerors. The day before American troops invaded the Italian mainland, the surrender was announced (September 8, 1943). The Italian fleet units came over to the Allies on the ninth and succeeding days. Mussolini was put into captivity, rescued by a band of Germans, and then was recaptured when Germany fell. He was later executed by Italian partisans.

Even after the fall of Italy, the Germans offered strong opposition

301

to the invasion which was frequently slowed down by the conditions of terrain and weather. American forces under General Mark Clark (1896-1984), as well as British and Canadian troops, engaged in stubborn fighting in the landing areas south of Naples. Rome was not taken until later (June 4, 1944). The Germans finally quit Italy (May 2, 1945) {10:39 p.m.}.

### 237. The Invasion of France

It was decided that France should be invaded by the Allies (1944). It was thought that this would shorten the war by facilitating the westward advance of Russian troops and also by denying Germany needed time for dangerous technological advances in methods of destruction as seen in such developments of the first jet fighter, the V-1 and V-2 rockets (see section 242), and possibly the atomic bomb.

The D-day armada included a total of some 4,000 ships of all kinds and approximately 500,000 men, counting those who manned the ships. Preceding the landing were two American airborne divisions and British airborne troops whose objective was to seize vital areas in the rear of German coastal defenses. The assault troops hit the beaches between Cherbourg and Caen shortly after midnight (June 6, 1944) {10:38 p.m.}. They met formidable resistance, but several divisions were landed by the first day. By the second morning the beachhead was secure.

The landing of more troops and supplies made it possible to break out of the beachhead (end of July and early August). General Patton broke through with the American Third Army and made a speedy and sweeping movement around the southern wing of the Germans, cut off the enemy forces in Brittany, and then turned northward, almost joining other Allied forces and sealing the German forces in Normandy from escape. A French division of the United States First Army entered Paris (August 25). There was much optimism that victory over Germany was near.

### 238. Germany Surrenders

Evidence suggests that Hitler decided he did not want to be captured. As the Russians moved into what was left of Berlin, Hitler and his mistress, Eva Braun (born 1912), went through a marriage ceremony (April 29, 1945). He then made his last will and testament to the German people in which he blamed the war on "the poisoner of all peoples, international Jewry." The next day he poisoned Eva and took his own life. He thus avoided the humiliation that was visited upon Mussolini and his mistress who had been killed by a mob. All German forces in Austria surrendered unconditionally (May 6).

With Admiral Karl Doenitz (1891-1980) taking over the role of Hitler, the German emissaries surrendered all land, sea, and air forces to the Allies (May 7), at General Eisenhower's headquarters in a schoolhouse in Reims, France. To meet Russian wishes, a virtually identical surrender was signed at Berlin the next day. The tasks of war in Europe yielded to the tasks of occupation.

American President Franklin Roosevelt died (April 12, 1945) {10:39 p.m.} before he could effectively enjoy the fruits of the hard-won victory. His death came about three weeks before the German surrender. His successor, Vice-President Harry S. Truman (1884-1972; served 1945-1953), was to lead the American people through victory over Japan (see section 240) and into the vital post-war period.

## 239. The Air War

In World War I the airplane had played an important part in the spreading of information gleaned from aerial reconnaissance but, compared to World War II aircraft, scored few points in terms of damage inflicted from bullets shot or bombs dropped from these machines. Airplanes of World War II were far superior in every way to those used in World War I and their use in battle often produced practical, effective benefits.

The first important American bomber of the war was the Boeing B-17 [see figure 10-12]. It was, in fact, a fleet of these bombers that was caught in the attack on Pearl Harbor (see section 232). The new bombers were being delivered to Hawaii and were low on fuel and carried no ammunition. Some were shot down before they could land and others crashed as they landed.

General Curtis LeMay (1906-1990) was selected to command the Eighth Air Force in Britain and the B-17 was used for the daring daylight raids against the enemy.

To combat the bombers, fierce fighter planes invaded the skies. The Germans had such planes as the Messerschmitt 109E which could speed up to 354 miles per hour and had a range of 412 miles. The

303

British had such planes as their Spitfire I which could fly at 365 miles per hour and had a range of 575 miles.

Fighters did, of course, accompany bombers as far as their range would allow them to do so. But frequently bombers had to fly far beyond the range of even the best fighters of the day, and their protection for the entire mission was not possible. There was also the danger from the ground from anti-aircraft fire or flak, which came from the German abbreviation Fl.A.K., (*Fliegerabwehrkanonen*) which meant anti-aircraft cannon.

Bombers based in Britain attacked German railroad centers, factories, and submarine bases on the continent. The British bombers attacked by night and the Americans attacked by day in their B-17s. As the number of bombers in England steadily increased, bomber attacks on Germany became more frequent. Big air raids, made by a thousand or more planes, were really battles, in which 4,000 or 5,000 men in planes dropped tons of explosives on the enemy who fought back with fighter planes and guns on the ground. Germany's industrial cities were bombed again and again and were steadily reduced to ruins. Germany's capacity to make war materials was thus reduced.

The American Boeing B-29 Superfortress was the best-protected bomber of the war. Its defensive armament comprised twelve large caliber machine guns mounted in five low-silhouette, power-operated turrets. The guns were fired by remote control and were linked to a unique central gunfire control system. Gunners had primary control of certain turrets and secondary control of others. The gunner with primary control of a turret had first call on its services which he could relinquish to gunners with secondary control. Thus, in the event of a concentrated attack on the bomber from one direction, the gunner whose vision covered the point of attack, could borrow a second turret to double his firepower. The Boeing B-29 could also climb higher than most of the fighters of the war. This aided "Bocks Car" [see figure 10-13] when it flew over Japan to drop the second atomic bomb. The Japanese Zero could not climb to the 30,000-plus feet at which the B-29 flew.

## 240. The Atomic Bomb

The dropping of two atomic bombs on Japan (1945) climaxed the wartime expansion and technological application of what American and European scientists had learned about nuclear energy. The theories advanced by Albert Einstein and the advances made by other scientists made it clear that nuclear energy offered a source of almost unbelievable destructive power. The Axis powers were concerned with the problem, but the United States took the lead in the actual development.

The Manhattan Project was the official name of the American effort to develop the atomic bomb. Major Leslie R. Groves (1896-1970) was made military chief of the project. His advisers included Harvard's President J. B. Conant (1893-1978) and Dr. Vannevar Bush (1890-1974), an American electrical engineer. Hundreds of scientists were assigned to the project. The work embraced experimental research at leading universities and technical activity at special engineering establishments, particularly at Oak Ridge, Tennessee. A self-maintaining nuclear chain reaction was initiated for the first time in a uranium graphite pile at the University of Chicago (December 2, 1942).

The first atomic bomb used plutonium (a radioactive element derived from neptunium) for its energy and was exploded on the desert near Los Alamos (July 16, 1945) {10:39 p.m.}. The plutonium was arranged in the form of a sphere which was blown inward at the moment of detonation (implosion). This brought the plutonium close enough together to form what is called a critical mass. It thus formed a chain reaction which resulted in an immediate release of energy which produced the nuclear explosion. The yield was equal to approximately 16,000 tons of TNT. The detonation formed an enormous mushroom cloud.

It was Secretary of War Henry Lewis Stimson (1867-1950) who recommended that the atomic bomb be directed toward Japan to shorten the war. Officials had estimated that a land invasion would cost at least a million lives. Some of the American atomic scientists were violently against Stimson's idea because the bomb would be dropped on civilian populations as well as military targets. They suggested that a "demonstration" on a forest target would accomplish the same results. President Truman, however, sided with Stimson.

The news of the successful test in New Mexico reached Truman while he was in Berlin at the Potsdam Conference with the Russian and British leaders. General Carl Spaatz (1891-1974) received instructions from Potsdam to drop an atomic bomb on the industrial installations of any one of four cities.

305

This led to the destruction of Hiroshima (August 6, 1945), a city with a population of 343,000. The B-29 aircraft known as the "Enola Gay," based in the Marianas Islands, dropped a uranium-235 bomb of approximately 16-kiloton yield (estimates vary) [see figure 10-14]. The city was composed mainly of light wooden houses along with many reinforced buildings. The bomb fell near the center of the city and exploded 1,850 feet above the ground. It devastated an area of forty-seven square miles in the central part of the city. It destroyed nearly all wooden buildings and damaged even the strongest of the reinforced buildings. It killed or injured 140,000 people.

Because the Japanese did not subsequently make any clear steps toward surrender, a second atomic bomb was dropped on Nagasaki (August 9). The plane that dropped this bomb may be seen in figure 10-13. This bomb convinced Emperor Hirohito (1901-1991) that Japan should surrender. Japan surrendered (August 14, 1945) {10:39 p.m.}, and the formal document of surrender was signed (September 1) on the United States battleship *Missouri* in Tokyo Bay, with General MacArthur representing the United States and taking over the command of occupation. Although victory celebrations were over, President Truman officially assigned a date to V-J Day (September 2).

## 241. The Propaganda War

This was the first war in which the use of the radio played a significant role in the development of public opinion. Through broadcasting a politician could speak to thousands of his countrymen at the same time. Hitler used this medium to aid his rise to power in Germany. Politicians in other countries took advantage of the medium to communicate their views as well. President Franklin Roosevelt's "Fireside Chats" (radio addresses to calm the public) became very popular. Important speeches were made during the war to inform the citizens of all countries. Some countries, such as Japan, used the radio to broadcast propaganda to enemy troops. Their spokesperson was known as Tokyo Rose but her real name was Iva Togori (1916- ) and she had been born in Los Angeles, California. She had gone to Japan in 1941 and, after the Japanese attack on Pearl Harbor, she was recruited by Tokyo radio for propaganda purposes.

## 242. The Background of the V-2 Rocket and World War II

The rocket became a major weapon in World War II. Important advances in rocketry had been made earlier in this century with the efforts of Robert H. Goddard (1882-1945) in the United States who launched the world's first rocket propelled by liquid fuel at Auburn, Massachusetts (1926). He had published his theories on rocketry (1919). Hermann Oberth (1894-1989), who was of German descent but was born in the Transylvanian Alps, read about it in a newspaper and requested a copy of the report directly from Goddard (1922). Oberth later made important contributions to the field as well.

The German Society for Space Travel was formed in 1927. For the rocket enthusiasts it was a time when small amateur groups could still make important contributions by building and firing rockets. This organization launched a rocket to an altitude of 3,000 feet (1931). The rocket was recovered by parachute.

If more progress was to be made in the field of rocketry, it was evident that some kind of government support was needed. Wernher von Braun (1912-1977) and his associates set up a demonstration for the German Army near Kummersdorf (1932). It was good timing for them. Hitler was coming to power and the army recognized that rockets were outside the scope of the Versailles Treaty which forbade the manufacture of aircraft in Germany. By the end of the year the German government had taken over the operations of the society and von Braun had received an invitation to conduct experimental work for his doctor's thesis on rocket combustion at the army's proving grounds. Most of his work was based on the ideas of the American Robert Goddard.

From the new rocket base at Peenemunde, the rocket designated as the A-4, later called the V-2, made a perfect flight and reached a maximum height of fifty-three miles before splashing into the Baltic Sea some 118 miles from its launch pad (October, 1942). World War II had already been underway for three years. Before adequate trials could be carried out, Hitler ordered the A-4 into large-scale production as a means of bombarding London and the surrounding area.

The A-4 attack on London began (September 8, 1944) from a site near the Hague in Holland. There was no known defense against it. Some 4,320 V-2s were launched (September 6, 1944, to March 27,

307

1945). Of these, some 1,120 were directed against London, killing 2,511 people and seriously injuring nearly 6,000 more.

When the war in Europe ended, the full extent of the V-2 operation was discovered. The great facilities from which the V-2 and the smaller V-1 rockets had been made and launched were inspected. The principals at Peenemunde, in the face of the Russian advance, fled westward, preferring to place themselves in the hands of the western Allies. General Walter Dornberger (1895-1980) and von Braun surrendered to the U.S. 7th Army in May, 1945.

Wernher von Braun's interrogation report showed the depth of progress that had been achieved by the work of his team. It had kept alive the space-flight ideal in spite of the pressure of the military. Dr. von Braun showed the U.S. Army his plans for a rocket in which a pressure cabin replaced the warhead so that a man could fly in space. He talked of a coming era where multi-stage rockets would launch artificial satellites, and make possible trips to the moon (see sections 253 and 254).

# The World After World War II

## 243. The United Nations and NATO

The League of Nations was replaced by the United Nations (June 25, 1945). This international organization was dedicated to world peace and also to national self-interest. Its charter was signed by fifty-one nations, weary of war and aware that the League of Nations, which had been inoperative (since 1939), was in dire need of replacement. Essentially, the principles that formed the basis of the United Nations Charter, which recognized the sovereignty and equality of all nations, evolved from the Atlantic Charter, an unofficial document of Allied intent that had been issued jointly by U.S. President Franklin D. Roosevelt and English Prime Minister Winston Churchill on August 14, 1941.

Efforts of the United Nations have been met with various degrees of success. The United Nations was not so effectual during the Hungarian rebellion of 1956 since the Soviets refused to admit neutral observers. After the Congo (now Zaire) was declared to be an independent republic (1960) the U.N. was not immediately successful in ending the fighting and establishing permanent peace. The War in Vietnam (see section 250) and the crisis in the Dominican Republic were other matters where the United Nations was not able to be very effective. But the record is full of success stories also. The United Nations acted decisively in such international crises as the Korean Conflict (see section 247) and in the Suez Crisis after Egypt nationalized the Suez canal (1956). Britain and France adhered to the U.N. resolution that their hostilities with Egypt should cease. Increased unity and effectiveness were evidenced in the final decade of this millennium with the various political changes in the world and there was obvious unity in the matter of the invasion of Iraq and Operation Desert Storm (1991). And for all its efforts, if the U.N. has prevented World War III even once, who can put a price on that obvious benefit to mankind?

Another organization, this one limited to certain non-communist nations, was formed in 1949. Known as the North Atlantic Treaty Organization (NATO), it was a defensive alliance signed by the United States, Canada, Great Britain, France, the Netherlands, Belgium, Luxembourg, Italy, Norway, Denmark, Iceland, and Portugal. These nations reaffirmed their adherence to the Charter of the United Nations and pledged to "unite their efforts for collective defense and for the preservation of peace and security" and to consider an armed attack on any of them an attack against all. It was just one event in the waging of something called the Cold War.

## 244. The Cold War

A new kind of peace crept over the world following World War II. The noise of hot bullets and bombs was quickly replaced with a new type of conflict known as the Cold War. It was characterized by a state of diplomatic tension between nations, especially between the East and the West (communism versus democracy), particularly between the Russians and the Americans. It was deliberately maintained for the winning of political and economic advantages without fighting, and efforts were made to influence nations not committed to either side, including those of the Third World. Occasionally this cold war turned into a hot one as in Korea, Vietnam, and the many guerrilla wars in countries such as Africa and South America. It is generally recognized that the Cold War was officially over with the downfall of communism in the former Soviet Union and the aging of the communist leaders in China and Cuba.

309

## 245. America After World War II

A technological revolution had taken place during the war. The developments in the field of rocketry and nuclear weapons have already been mentioned. Significant changes also took place in other fields. Before World War II, fighter planes were biplanes, although the monoplane was replacing them in some places. The main armament for air-to-air-combat was a battery of small-caliber machine guns. By the end of the war, some fighters were powered by jet propulsion and they had swept-back wings for reduced drag at their high operational speeds. The main armament was a battery of heavy, rapid-firing artillery weapons.

American research on the jet engine had been going strong during the war based partly on Whittle's work in England. General Electric received a license from Britain to build the Whittle engine. America's first jet plane flew (1942). By the Korean War, the F-86 Saber was ruling the skies in jet dogfights launched from carriers.

American skies became filled with a profusion of daring and innovative experimental aircraft. Convair put four of the new General Electric TG-180 jets into a traditional airframe to produce the XB-46 bomber (1947). Far more dramatic was Northrop's XB-35 all-wing bomber, which was called the "Flying Wing." It was the late-forties version of today's Stealth Bomber. Convair's B-36 bomber [see figure 10-16] served as a test-bed for many experiments and as an instrument for the Strategic Air Command. It was replaced by Boeing's all-jet B-52 bomber (1950s). Convair's XF2Y-1 Sea Dart was a daring effort to produce a jet that could land and take off on water. It was discontinued after stability problems were encountered on takeoff.

## 246. The Development of Television

An important figure in the development of television was David Sarnoff (1891-1971) of R.C.A. who had been the wireless operator (1912) who received the first news of the Titanic's disastrous collision with an iceberg. He remained at his post for seventy-two hours during that tragedy and from this came his belief in wireless impulses as essential modes of communication. He also moved up the corporate ladder of the American Marconi Company and its successor, R.C.A. He dreamed of a plan which would make radio a household utility (1916). He described a system which would bring music into the home by wireless in the form of a simple "radio music box." He also added that this device could be used to announce events of national interest such as baseball scores and election results.

R.C.A. and the National Broadcasting Company worked on making television practical (1920s). Felix the Cat and later Mickey Mouse were placed on a phonograph turntable. Under bright lights and before test-pattern backgrounds, Felix spun for days and weeks while engineers in the field made reception tests. Felix offered many advantages because he worked cheaper than actors and was all black which made for a sharper image. These field tests continued for a full decade.

At the New York World's Fair (1939), R.C.A. demonstrated its see-through television receiver with an 8-x-10-inch screen [see figure 10-17]. U. S. President Franklin Roosevelt made a speech before the cameras while he was at the fair, and R.C.A. executives also made speeches before the cameras.

Within the decade, there were 170,000 television sets in the United States (1947) which gave U.S. President Harry S. Truman a sizable television audience for his State of the Union message that year. To increase the size of the audience even more, R.C.A. offered to share its technology with rival manufacturers in order to speed up the sale of television sets.

Early American television programs included shows which were basically vaudeville on television. Slapstick comedy, built on unsophisticated premises and stage settings, were just right for the television medium which added the dimension of visual humor. There was also the use of live drama and comedy on the intimate set. Close-in settings were ideal for the early limitations of television. The "soap operas" made their transition from radio to television. These shows, aimed at the housewife, were often sponsored by soap companies. Television also became an important source for news.

R.C.A. put its first home color television set on the market (1954). Though the screen was smaller than comparable black-and-white models of the period, they were welcomed in homes across America (1950s).

Television was important in other countries too. Germany used television to televise the Berlin Olympic Games (1936), and regular broadcasts were conducted in Britain before they were in the United States.

## 247. The Korean Conflict

After the surrender of Japan and the end of World War II, Korea was divided at the 38th parallel into two zones of occupation (1945). The U.S.S.R. controlled the north and the United States controlled the south. Elections were held in the south (1948); a democratic constitution was promoted and the Republic of Korea, with Syngman Rhee (1875-1965; served 1948-1960) as its first president, was announced (July 17). In the north, a people's republic, the Democratic People's Republic of Korea was proclaimed (September 9, 1948). It was not, however, a republic as is generally thought of when the word is seen, but a Soviet-style dictatorship. Many incidents between these two governments culminated in the Korean War (1950-1953).

The North Koreans launched a powerful offensive across the 38th parallel against the Republic of Korea (early morning hours of June 25, 1950) {10:47 p.m.}. A force of Russian-built tanks was followed by some 80,000 or more North Korean troops armed from Soviet arsenals. Since the Republic of Korea was not a member of the United Nations, the United States government immediately brought the aggression to the attention of the United Nations Security Council, branding the assault across the thirty-eighth parallel as aggression and a clear threat to international peace and security.

Within a year the Korean Conflict involved more than a million United Nations troops, including actual or token forces from nineteen nations. The total casualties of all United Nations forces, including those of South Korea, were estimated at about 250,000 for the first year, as compared with several times that number for the North Korean and Chinese enemies.

The age of jet aerial warfare was ushered in during this war. Dogfights between the Soviet MIG-15s and the American F-86 Saberjets were common. The area from the Yalu River to Pyongyang in northwestern Korea where most of the dogfights took place became known as "MIG Alley." During the early part of the war, as many as 150 planes took part in a single engagement.

Because of problems associated with the war and because of Commander MacArthur's outspoken views on how the Korean conflict should be fought (he wanted to widen the war against

Truman's wishes), President Truman relieved him (April 11, 1951) and General Matthew B. Ridgway (1895-1993) replaced MacArthur.

With the war limited to Korean soil to avert a global conflict, warfare in the peninsula turned into a back-and-forth battle for control of key terrain features along positions near the 38th Parallel. Such names as "Pork Chop Hill" and "Old Baldy" became commonly known.

The negotiators reached an agreement (July 19, 1953) {10:51 p.m.}. The armistice was signed eight days later. With the opposing forces still facing each other across a no-man's land that roughly follows the 38th parallel, the thirty-seven months of fighting came to an end, though the basic issues that divided Korea remained unresolved even in the last decade of this millennium.

## 248. Rock and Roll

A great social phenomena known as "rock and roll" swept America, beginning in the 1950s, and eventually its influence spread to other nations as well. It was fueled largely by the economic interests of teenagers who, by 1958, were buying seventy percent of all phonograph records sold. They were interested in the new music that was pounding from their new transistor radios which was a combination of country-western music with rhythm and blues, and were anxious to take these new sounds home so they could play them on their record players. The fact that their parents generally disliked the music didn't keep the teenagers, especially the girls, from loving it. They made national idols of previously unknown guitar-bangers and in so doing made them wealthy.

The man who is most remembered for his success with this new type of music was a twenty-one-year old truck driver from Memphis, Tennessee, named Elvis Presley (1935-1977). It was his style, characterized by a series of wild arm movements, pelvic gyrations, and a voice that trembled and shouted in unpredictable ways, that were his appeal. With such song titles as "Heartbreak Hotel," "Don't Be Cruel," and "Love Me Tender," $120 million worth of his records, sheet music, movie tickets (he made several movies), and merchandise had been sold.

A group from England became part of the music scene even in America. The Beatles formed a rock music group that consisted of John

313

Lennon (1940-1980), Paul McCartney (1942-), George Harrison (1943- ), and Ringo Starr (1940- ). Their style and success set the standards for music from the 1960s through the rest of the century. Their hits included "Love Me Do" (1962) and "I Want to Hold Your Hand" (1964) and the albums "Sargent Pepper's Lonely Hearts Club Band" (1967) and "Let It Be" (1970). They also made films, including "A Hard Day's Night" (1964) and "Help" (1965). In the 1970s the group disbanded but their influence will be felt far into the next century.

## 249. On the Brink

The world came close to nuclear war in America's confrontation with Russia during Kennedy's administration in what has been called the Cuban Missile Crisis (1962). Cuba had been a thorn in the side of the U.S. ever since Fidel Castro (1927- ) took power (January, 1959) {11:00 p.m.} and established a communist state. The United States broke diplomatic relations with Cuba, encouraged and supplied revolutionists (during the presidency of Eisenhower), and then failed to support an invasion by exiles (April, 1961) under the new Kennedy administration.

The failed invasion, which became known as the Bay of Pigs fiasco, loosed an avalanche of arms from Cuba's new protector, the Soviet Union. Following a visit to Russia by Raul Castro (1931- ), then Minister of Defense (July, 1962), there was a noticeable upturn in the volume of shipping reaching Cuba. The harbors of Havana and Mariel were crowded.

An American reconnaissance mission over Cuba (August 29, 1962) brought back the first photographic evidence of missile sites there. At least two were positively identified and six others looked like anti-aircraft missile batteries. Flights made (October) revealed the presence of missiles with nuclear warheads on Cuban soil.

President Kennedy spoke to the nation about the Cuban situation (October 22) and detailed the measures to be taken against it: a quarantine of the island, increased surveillance, and a readiness to retaliate. After one U-2 was shot down over Cuba (October 27) and many diplomatic exchanges, the Russians, under Nikita Khrushchev (1894-1971; served 1958-1964), agreed to remove their missiles from Cuba. Moscow Radio broadcast a statement that the Soviet Union was dismantling them (October 28). They were removed the next day.

## 250. The Vietnam War

The assassination of President John F. Kennedy (November 22, 1963) {11:05 p.m.} caused Vice-President Lyndon B. Johnson (1908-1973; served 1963-1969) to become president. It was under his presidency that the United States involvement in Vietnam increased to the point of war. On June 23, 1968, {11:12 p.m.} it became the longest war in United States history.

Vietnam is a country in southeast Asia that is bordered by the South China Sea on the south, the Gulf of Tonkin on the east, the People's Republic of China on the north, Laos on the west, and Cambodia on the southwest. The political differences and conflicts in these regions served as a hotbed of strife.

In the previous century, the conflict between the Vietnamese monarchy and Catholic missionaries from Europe allowed the French to conquer the region (1858-1883). After the Japanese occupation (1940-1945), the French were unable to regain control even though they waged war to reclaim it (1946-1954). The French were defeated at Dien Bien Phu (1954). A conference in Geneva divided the country at the seventeenth parallel, into North and South Vietnam. Under the presidency of Ho Chi Minh (1890-1969), guerrilla troops from North Vietnam began to invade South Vietnam (1958) and fierce fighting developed which eventually involved the United States.

The United States, under the direction of President Lyndon Johnson, steadily increased its military involvement in support of South Vietnam which reached a peak of 550,000 men (July, 1969). Hopes of a military victory in Vietnam were dashed after North Vietnam's Tet Offensive (February, 1968). Discouraged by the growing anti-war movement in America, President Johnson declared that he would not seek reelection as president (April, 1968). Richard M. Nixon (1913- 1994; served 1969-1974) was elected president on a promise of ending the war. The peace agreement was signed in Paris (January 22, 1973) {11:20 p.m.} and U.S. troops were withdrawn. Two years later the South Vietnam government collapsed. The country was officially reunited (July 2, 1976).

## 251. Africa

After World War II, Africa experienced political struggles against European powers over Algeria, Suez, and Angola, and much international conflict in Kenya, the Congo, South Africa, and between Israel and Egypt. This period of time was also characterized by rapid economic development and increasing nationalism which led to political independence for much of the continent. Egypt was evacuated by the British (1956) and Tunisia, Morocco, and the Sudan became independent. Ghana obtained independence (1957), followed by Guinea (1958), Mali (1959), Nigeria, the Congo, Somaliland, and twelve former French colonies (1960), Tanganyika (1961), Algeria, Uganda, Rwanda, and Burundi (1962). The United Arab Republic of Egypt and Syria was established (1958) but Syria withdrew (1961). Katanga seceded from the Congo (1960) and was reintegrated (1963). The Republic of South Africa left the British Commonwealth (1961). The Central African Federation, which had been set up (1951), was dissolved (1963) and Kenya became independent. Zanzibar gained independence (1963) and joined Tanganyika to form Tanzania (1964). Nyasaland became independent under the name of Malawi, and Northern Rhodesia became Zambia (1964). Gambia became independent (1966) and changed its name to Botswana. Basutoland took the name of Lesotho when it obtained independence (1966). Equatorial Guinea and Swaziland became independent (1968), as did the French Comoros (1975). In the face of opposition from most other African countries, Britain and the Commonwealth, white-ruled Rhodesia made a unilateral declaration of independence (1965) and later became independent Zimbabwe under black rule (1980). Upper Volta changed its name to Burkina Faso (1984). Western Sahara, given up by Spain (1976) and divided between Morocco and Mauritania, was fought over by Morocco and the Polisario, an armed independence movement (1980s). Unrest over the white government's traditional policy of apartheid in South Africa invited much international attention.

## 252. The Space Age

The rockets that von Braun and his team brought with him to the United States (see section 242) were taken first to the U.S. Army's White Sands Missile Range in New Mexico, a facility which had been especially established for that purpose. As mentioned earlier, it was discovered that the Germans had relied largely on Robert Goddard's ideas in the design of their rockets. The rocket launchings made at White Sands provided valuable data for the construction of better and larger rockets. Before the decade ended (1940s), a two-stage rocket was launched to an altitude of some 250 miles. The second rocket, designed entirely in America, was released from the first when its maximum speed was reached (not maximum altitude). The second stage, known as the W.A.C. Corporal, was recovered by parachute.

The United States Air Force moved its operations from White Sands, New Mexico, to Cape Canaveral (Spanish for a place of tall cane), Florida (1950). There they turned a hunting and fishing area into the great Atlantic Missile Range. In his book, *From the Earth to the Moon*, Jules Verne used the cape area as the site for his "lift-off" to the moon. Even though his technology was not sound (he shot his astronauts from a cannon), his geography was good. The Kennedy Space Center, named in honor of U.S. President John F. Kennedy, is located at Cape Canaveral. Shuttle launchings are from adjacent Merit Island.

### 253. Early Artificial Satellites and Manned Space Flight

Automated satellites and animals went into orbit before men did. The first artificial earth satellite was launched by the Soviet Union (October 4, 1957) {10:57 p.m.}. Named Sputnik I, it weighed 184 pounds and transmitted a signal for twenty-one days. The Soviets launched Sputnik II (November 3). This satellite weighed 1,120 pounds and carried a dog as a passenger.

The United States launched its first artificial earth satellite, Explorer 1 (February 1, 1958) {10:58 p.m.}. This satellite discovered the inner *Van Allen radiation belts* (named after Dr. J. A. Van Allen (1914- ) who designed the detector) and provided micrometeorite impact data. The satellite was launched by the Army's Jupiter-C rocket which had been developed (early 1950s) as an outgrowth of the research on the captured German V-2 rockets.

The U.S. Navy had tried to launch a satellite of its own, *Project Vanguard* (late 1957), but the first rocket exploded on take-off. The Navy's satellite, *Vanguard 1*, successfully achieved orbit (March 17, 1958). It provided refined data on the shape and size of the "pear-shaped" earth. The first communications satellite was placed in orbit by the U.S. (December 18, 1958). It weighed 8,700 pounds (an entire Atlas missile was put into orbit) and relayed a taped message of U.S. President Eisenhower's voice for thirteen days.

To reduce competition between the branches of America's military, the National Aeronautics and Space Administration (N.A.S.A.) was founded (1958) and was placed in charge of all manned and unmanned U.S. launches. They were further charged with conducting research on flight within and outside the earth's atmosphere, and conducting activities required for the exploration of space with manned and unmanned space vehicles.

In a speech at Houston's Rice University Stadium shortly after his election as U.S. President (November, 1960), John F. Kennedy called for a national effort aimed at landing a man on the moon and safely returning him before the decade was over. The space agency had already been working on Project Mercury, the name of the first U.S. manned space program. NASA used the Atlas Intercontinental Ballistic Missile (I.C.B.M.) as the primary launch vehicle for this spacecraft. But the first American to go into space in a rocket was sent there atop a Redstone Rocket (Mercury-Redstone 3) (May 5, 1961) {11:02 p.m.}. Astronaut Alan B. Shepard Jr. (1923- ), went into a sub-orbital flight in his spacecraft *Freedom 7*. It attained a maximum speed of 5,100 miles per hour, reached an altitude of 116.5 statute miles and landed 302 statute miles down range.

The United States space agency developed its moon program in stages. *Project Gemini,* a two-man space capsule, followed Project Mercury. It provided for orbital flights of up to fourteen days with exercises in rendezvous and docking. The *Titan II* rocket was used as the prime lifter for the Gemini spacecraft. The Gemini program placed Americans in orbit for up to eight days and allowed its astronauts to go on "space walks" (1965). The first American to do this was Edward H. White II (1930-1967). He stayed outside his *Gemini 4* capsule for twenty minutes (June 3, 1965) {11:08 p.m.}.

There were unmanned programs designed to augment the Apollo program. *Ranger* was sent to gather data on the moon's constitution and surface. Many important lunar photographs as well as television views were transmitted to earth as a result of the *Ranger* project. The Surveyor project placed laboratories on the lunar surface to provide data for possible landing sites. Some of the other programs included the *Explorer* probes, the *Mariner* spacecraft, and the *Orbiting Solar Observatory*.

The rocket that finally took Americans to the moon was called the *Saturn V.* At launch it stood 364 feet above the pad, weighed 6.1 million pounds and developed 7.5 million pounds of thrust. In the twilight of the seventh decade of the final century of this millennium, the *Apollo 11 Saturn V* space vehicle lifted off for the moon at 9:32 A.M. Eastern Daylight Time on July 16, 1969 {11:14 p.m.} [see figure 10-18].

The *Apollo 11* crew consisted of Neil Armstrong (1930- ), "Buzz" Aldrin, Jr. (1930- ), and Michael Collins (1930- ). It was the first time men ever landed on the moon. Armstrong and Aldrin landed their rocket on the Sea of Tranquility. They stayed on the moon for 21 hours, thirty-six minutes and twenty-one seconds before returning to earth. Their total flight time was 195 hours, eighteen minutes,and thirty-five seconds.

The second manned landing on the moon was made during the flight of *Apollo 12*, (November 14-24, 1969). The crew consisted of Charles Conrad, Jr. (1930- ), Alan Bean (1932- ), and Richard Gordon, Jr. (1929- ). Conrad and Bean landed their rocket on the Ocean of Storms and their stay on the moon lasted approximately thirty-one hours and thirty-one minutes.

The third manned landing on the moon came during the flight of *Apollo 14* (*Apollo 13* had failed) which left earth January 31, 1971, and returned February 9. The crew members were Alan Shepard, Jr. (1923-), Edgar Mitchell (1930- ) and Stuart Roosa (1933- ). Shepard and Mitchell landed at Fra Mauro.

The fourth lunar landing was made by the *Apollo 15* crew of David Scott (1932- ), James Irwin (1930-1991) and Alfred Worden (1932-) between July 26-August 7, 1971. The objective of Scott and Irwin was the Hadley-Apennine region. This was the first time the Lunar Rover (an electric powered car with four wheels) was used to drive on the moon (July 31).

The fifth lunar landing was made during the flight of *Apollo 16* (April 16-27, 1972). The crew consisted of John Young (1930-), Charles Duke, Jr. (1935- ) and Thomas Mattingly II (1936- ). Young and Duke set up the moon's first astronomical observatory in the Descartes region.

The last moon landing of the Apollo series came in the flight of *Apollo 17* (December 7-10, 1972). The crew consisted of Eugene Cernan (1934- ), Harrison Schmitt (1935- ) and Ronald Evans (1933-1990). Cernan and Schmitt drove the Lunar Rover in the Taurus Littrow region.

Americans began to experiment with space stations with the launching of *Skylab* (a temporary space station made from a portion

319

of a Saturn rocket body) (May 14, 1973). The first crew to board *Skylab* consisted of Charles Conrad, Jr., Joseph Kerwin (1932- ) and Paul Weitz (1932- ). Their stay in America's first space station lasted May 25-June 22, 1973. The second crew to board *Skylab* consisted of Alan Bean, Jack Lousma (1936- ), and Owen Garriott (1930- ). Their stay in space started July 28 and ended September 25, 1973. The third and final crew to board the station consisted of Gerald Carr (1932- ), Edward Gibson (1936- ) and William Pogue (1930- ). This mission started November 16, 1973, and ended February 8, 1974.

As the final decade of the millennium passes, NASA is continuing work on a permanent space station. Other plans have been made to return to the moon (this time to stay), and from there to launch a mission to Mars.

Russian manned space flights (1970s) involved visits to their *Saluyt 5* spacelab. One such flight involved a two-manned *Soyuz* launch vehicle (February 7-15, 1977). The flight lasted 424 hours and forty-eight minutes.

## 254. Deep Space and Planetary Probes

Efforts to learn more about the mysteries of space beyond the vicinity of the earth resulted in unique unmanned probes. Some early efforts included the U.S. *Pioneer I* which went into space (October 11, 1958) to study the moon. It reached an altitude of 70,717 miles and it returned radiation, magnetic field, and micrometeorite impact data.

Russia's unmanned spacecraft *Luna 16* landed on the moon (September 12, 1970), collected soil samples, took off under remote control, and was recovered successfully (September 24).

Two American *Viking* spacecraft landed on the surface of Mars to provide the world with its first glimpses of Mars from Mars (1976). While there, the spacecraft sampled soil and analyzed the contents, beaming the information back to earth. While the landers produced no evidence of life on Mars, it provided scientists with a wealth of information about the planet's geology, atmosphere, and composition.

The most comprehensive deep-space-probe program ever undertaken was begun in 1972 and dubbed "The Grand Tour" because it took advantage of the alignment of the planets in our solar system to give the spacecraft involved additional velocity as they sped past certain planets. There were two types of spacecraft involved in this mission. The *Pioneers* (10 and 11) were precursors to later missions by larger spacecraft which were called *Voyagers* (1 and 2).

*Pioneers* 10 and 11 became the first man-made objects to leave the solar system. They headed out of the solar system in nearly opposite directions after completing their missions. They now seek evidence of perturbations from possible remote planets beyond Neptune and Pluto, and from gravity waves originating outside the solar system. They continue to map the heliosphere, observing the changes and characteristics of the solar wind, and are gradually accumulating data over a complete cycle of solar activity in the far reaches of space.

The United States launched two unmanned *Voyager* spacecraft on "The Grand Tour" (1977). Like the *Pioneer* spacecraft before them, they headed toward the outer planets. The first encounter was with the giant Jovian planetary system, 400 million miles away. Passing by Jupiter and its complex satellite system (1979), the *Voyager* spacecraft collected and returned an enormous amount of data and information. One of the most astonishing findings at Jupiter was the discovery of a ring around the planet. Also, an active volcano was found on Jupiter's moon Io.

*Voyager 1's* Saturn encounter period began August 22, 1980, at a range of sixty-eight million miles from the planet. Even at this great distance, Voyager's images were better than any from earth-based telescopes. Before the long encounter ended on December 19, 1980, continuous observations of Saturn's realm were carried out by Voyager's instruments.

At Saturn, *Voyager I* returned amazing images of the rings that Galileo first saw (1610) {2:37 a.m.}. The rings were found to be only a few kilometers thick and the ring particles—from a few microns to a meter in size—have been described as icy snowballs or ice-covered rock.

From Earth to Saturn, *Voyager 1* traveled in the ecliptic plane, the plane in which the major planets orbit. Having completed its final planetary fly-by, *Voyager 1* rose above this plane on a trajectory that will eventually carry it out of the solar system, probably before the end of this millennium. In 1990, *Voyager 1* completed its final photographic mission when its cameras were turned to look back at the earth and some of the other planets in our solar system. After this the cameras were turned off to conserve power. Instruments designed to gather data on charged particles and electromagnetic fields remained on, however, and scientists expect to listen to the spacecraft until about 2015. It is headed toward the stars.

*Voyager 2*, which followed a similar path to that of *Voyager 1*, is also headed toward the stars.

Our imaginary day is over. It's been an exciting thousand years!

## 255. The End-of-the-Millennium Party

During the years 1999 and 2000 let the entire world be joined as one in an END-OF-THE-MILLENNIUM-PARTY. Unlike the year 1001 when only a few knowledgeable persons kept track of the progress of the Christian millennium, today we have the means to invite nearly everyone on the planet to the party. We will even have some help from a natural event in space. During the night of November 17, 1999, the comet Temple-Tuttle will shed whatever debris encounters the earth's orbit. Periodically it provides a spectacular show as these "shooting stars" burn up in our atmosphere. This celestial spectacle may permit us to say farewell in a glorious way to this thousand years and welcome the next with hope—for, after all, how often do we get to celebrate the arrival of a new year, decade, century, and millennium all at once? Once every thousand years!

# God in History

Q. What should be the mission of the Christian Church in this new "age of achievement"? Can Christianity meet the spiritual needs of the new intellectuals who deal in information with computers and a society that is fast moving into space?

A. Man still needs God as much today as he ever did. The Atonement for man's sins which Jesus made on the cross forever altered man's relationship with God. The infinite grace of God stands waiting for men everywhere. Christian astronauts will want to live responsible lives as a testimony to others. Chaplains will one day give devotionals in the space station and the day may not be far off when the first sermon will reverberate from the walls of a lunar cathedral. On earth the Church should continue to reach out to help the needy, the poor, and the disadvantaged. We should use our technology to preach the gospel to all of earth's citizens. And if we should ever meet "Them (out there)," we should tell them about Jesus too. Dr. Billy Graham (1918- ), among others, believes this will be our mission at some time in the future.

## Chapter Endnotes

10-1  A black hole is an object in space that is really a collapsed star as might be left over after a super nova explosion. Because of its gravity, the star becomes more and more compressed. The theory developed by Schwarzschild, based on Einstein's theory of relativity, predicted that even light will be bent so much by the strong gravity of such a star, that the light will no longer be able to escape. Such a star is called a *black hole*.

10-2  "Speakeasy" was a slang term for a place where illegal liquors were sold. "Bootleggers" was a slang term for someone who sold, transported, or made illegal liquor, and "rum runner" was a slang term for someone who transported illegal liquor.

10-3  *Fascism* is a system of government in which property is privately owned, but all industry and business is regulated by a strong national government.

10-4 Christian IV, King of Denmark and Norway (1577; reigned 1588-1648), rebuilt Oslo and renamed it Christiana in 1624. Its name was changed back to Oslo in 1925.

# Chapter Terms

| | | |
|---|---|---|
| Allies | Grand Tour | Rock and Roll |
| Apollo | Great Depression | rum runner |
| Bay of Pigs | Hubble Space | Saint Valentine's |
| Berlin-Rome Axis | Telescope | Day Massacre |
| black hole | League of Nations | Saturn V |
| Blitzkrieg | Lunar Rover | Schmidt camera |
| Bolsheviki | Manhattan Project | Skylab |
| bootlegger | militarism | socialism |
| Cold War | N.A.S.A. | Space Age |
| communism | Nazis | speakeasy |
| D-Day | Peenemunde | spectroheliograph |
| Drang nach Osten | Pioneer I | Third Reich |
| Explorer I | plutonium | Treaty of Versailles |

# Chapter Review Questions/Exercises

1. From the Overview of this chapter, list some of the outstanding events of the twentieth century.
2. What improvements did Howard Hughes, Sr. make in the "fish-tail" drill bits that were used in the early part of the twentieth century? (210)
3. List the important accomplishments made in health and medicine in the twentieth century. (211)
4. How have attitudes towards women and children changed in this century? (212)
5. What were some of the outstanding accomplishments in the field of astronomy in this century? (213)
6. Describe some of the situations regarding religion that are typical of this century. (214)
7. Describe the negative effects of socialism and communism. (215)

8. What were some of the factors that contributed to World War I? (216)
9. What happened to Archduke Ferdinand and his wife? (216)
10. Discuss in detail the events of World War I. Be sure to mention the role of the airplane and the submarine in this war. When did America become involve? Describe the defeat of Germany. (216)
11. What was the world like after World War I?
12. Discuss Prohibition and the rise of the gangs in America. When did Prohibition end? Why? (217)
13. What was the Great Depression? Why did it happen and what steps were taken (both effective and ineffective) to end it? When did it finally end? (218)
14. Describe in detail Hitler's rise to power in Germany. What part did the Nazis and Hindenburg play in this matter? Why were Jews not welcome in Germany during this time? Why did Hitler send troops into the Rhinelands? (219)
15. What were conditions like in Italy after World War I? (220)
16. Discuss the events of the Spanish Civil War. (221)
17. Who were the leaders of Russia after World War I and what new form of government did they put in place there? (222)
18. List some of the important things that happened in Japan between 1900 and 1941. (223)
19. Discuss the background and causes of World War II. (224-228)
20. Describe the fall of Norway and France to Germany. (229)
21. What was Hitler's mistake regarding his plans to conquer England? (230)
22. What happened in Russia that kept Germany from taking England? (231)
23. When and why did the Japanese attack Pearl Harbor? (232)
24. What were the Japanese objectives in World War II? (233)
25. What were some of the first things America did in the war? (234)
26. What was the "second front?" and what was its objective? Describe the invasion of Africa by the Allies. (235)
27. How did Italy fall to the Allies? (236)
28. Describe the Allied invasion of France. (237)
29. What happened to Hitler at the end of the war? (238)
30. Discuss the role of the airplane in World War II. (239)

325

31. What was the Manhattan Project and how was the atomic bomb built? What use of it was made to bring the war to an end? (240)
32. How was the radio used by politicians in this century? (241)
33. Discuss the background of the V-2 rocket and how the Germans used it in the war. (242)
34. Describe the origin of the United Nations and some of its successes and failures. What was NATO? (243)
35. What was the Cold War? (244)
36. What were some of the new aviation experiments that took place in America after the war? (245)
37. Discuss the development of television. (246)
38. What was the Korean Conflict? (247)
39. What was "rock and roll," and how did it influence American culture? (248)
40. What was the Cuban Missile Crisis? (249)
41. What was the Vietnam War? (250)
42. Discuss the origin of the Space Age. (252)
43. List some of the early rocket launches. (253)
44. Why was the National Aeronautics and Space Administration formed? (253)
45. Discuss America's decision to send men to the moon. Who were some of the important figures in that decision? Who were the first and second men on the moon? Who were the third and fourth men on the moon? (253).
46. Name some planetary and deep space probes that have been launched by America. (254)

[Fig. 10-1] Thomas Alva Edison (circa 1904). (Photo courtesy of Con Edison, New York.)

[Fig. 10-2] Steam-powered tractor. (Photo courtesy of Judy Vestel and Toni Harrison.)

[Fig. 10-3] Howard Hughes, Sr. (Photo courtesy of
Hughes Tool Company.)

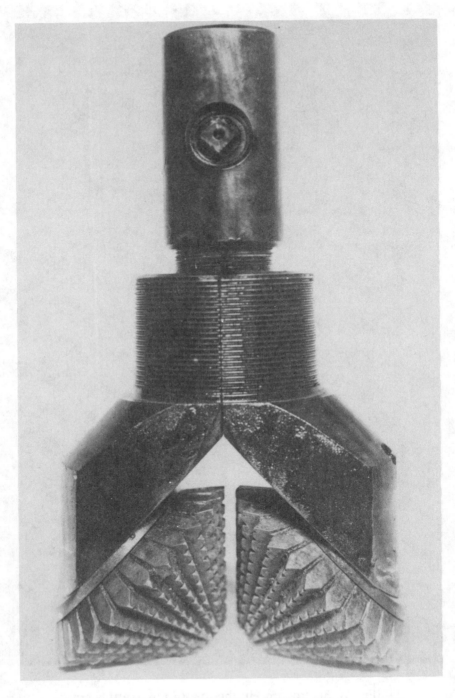

[Fig. 10-4] The Hughes Two-Cone Bit. (Photo courtesy of the
Hughes Tool Company.)

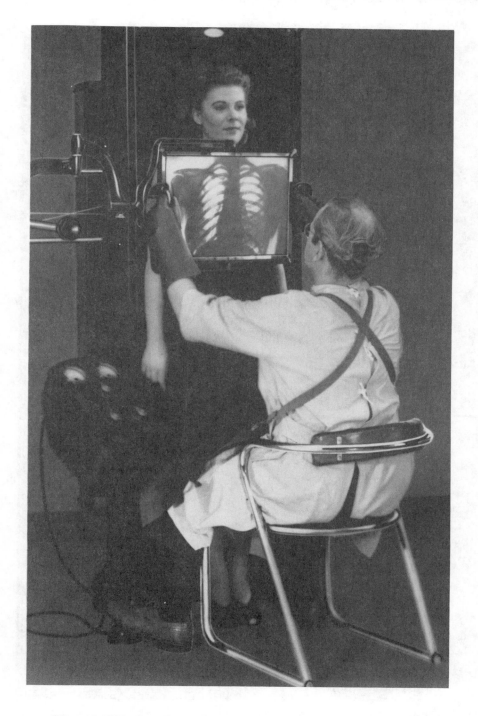

[Fig. 10-5] Early G.E. Diagnostic X-ray Imaging Device. (Photo courtesy of the General Electric Company.)

[Fig. 10-6] Advertisement for a Rauch and Lang Electric Car, Cleveland, Ohio (1910). (From Funk.)

[Fig. 10-7] The Hoche, a pre-World War I battleship (circa 1895.)

[Fig. 10-8] A radio operator with equipment in France.
(Photo from the author.)

[Fig. 10-9] A Spad in the clouds over France.
(Photo from the author.)

[Fig. 10-10] Oakies living in their cars in California during the Great Depression. (Photo courtesy of Weber's Supply.)

[Fig. 10-11] Typical American food market (circa 1935).
(Photo from the author.)

[Fig. 10-12] Boeing B-17. (Photo courtesy of the Boeing Company Archives.)

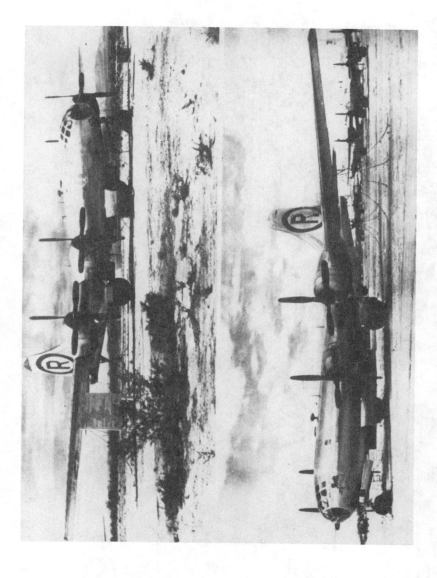

[Fig. 10-13] "Bocks Car." This B-29 dropped the second atomic bomb on Japan. (Photo courtesy of the U.S. National Archives and Records Administration.)

[Fig. 10-14] Fat Man atomic bomb. (Photo courtesy of the U.S. National Archives and Records Administration.)

[Fig. 10-15] An American soldier's memorabilia from World War II. (Photo from the author.)

[Fig. 10-16] A B-36. (Photo courtesy of General Dynamics Convair Division.)

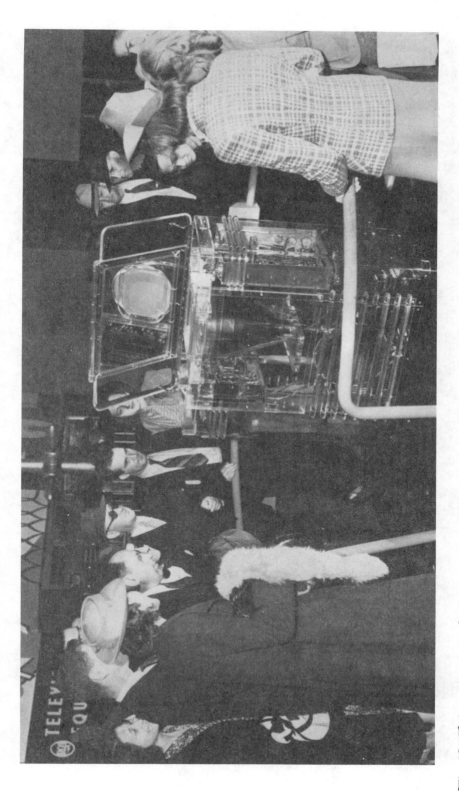

[Fig. 10-17] A transparent television receiver. This was demonstrated at the New York World's Fair (1939). (Photo courtesy of RCA.)

[Fig. 10-18] Apollo 11 lifts-off for the moon. (Photo courtesy of
NASA.)

# 11

# The Next Thousand Years

For I dipt into the future, far as human eye could see,
Saw the vision of the world, and all the wonder that would
be ....

*Alfred Tennyson (1809-1892)*

You better live your best and act your best and think your
best today; for today is the sure preparation for tomorrow
and all the other tomorrows that follow.

*Harriet Martineau (1802-1876)*

If the stars should appear one night in a thousand years,
how men would believe and adore, and preserve for many
generations the remembrance of the City of God which had
been shown?

*Ralph Waldo Emerson (1803-1882)*

# Preview

It was Mark Twain who wished the twentieth century "well." Let us do the same to the next thousand years for whatever good it will or will not do. Let us also remember the importance our intercessory prayer will have for generations yet to come.

The present time is to the year 3001 as A.D. 1001 was to now. We are at a mid-point in history between these two dates, and like the medieval monk of a thousand years ago who may have endeavored to look forward to this present age, we look to that distant year (3001) and imagine what the world might be like then. What can we know about the future? The following generalizations about tomorrow seem logical:

1. The nature of man will continue to influence the shaping of the future.

2. Our institutions, customs, and traditions will continue to influence people's lives.

3. One "wild card" of tomorrow is the vast unknown of the universe. What we find or do not find "out there" will have significant impact on the future.

## 1. The nature of mankind will continue to play a part in the shaping of the future.

The nature of mankind has long been of interest to theologians, scientists, educators, politicians, artists, poets, and more recently to psychologists. Sigmund Freud (1856-1939), an Austrian neurologist who founded psychoanalysis, postulated the existence of the id, that collection of man's instinctive drives which function below the conscious level. These instincts, he said, are moderated by many things, including man's higher mental capacities which in turn are influenced by external factors in the developing child. Both Freud and Carl Jung (1875-1961) studied the importance of social environment in a person's development. More recently the importance of heredity has been the subject of much investigation in relation to these matters.

If we are truly interested in improving the quality of life, more should be done to strengthen the family unit which underwent enormous changes during the twentieth century. In some industrialized countries, the number of single-parent families rose alarmingly as did the rise in the number of unwed mothers. The number of families in which both the mother and father worked also sharply increased. Many children, called "latch key children," because they used their key to open the door to an empty house or apartment, found themselves without guidance from meaningful caretakers who were either not there because of a divorce or separation, or who were at work.

---

**Reflection:**

*Jesus reminded Christians that they should be sensitive to human need wherever it is found. We should feed the hungry, give drink to the thirsty, welcome strangers, give clothes to those who do not have them, and visit prisoners and the sick. This is a high calling for we are reminded that the King himself said, "Inasmuch as ye have done it unto the least of these...ye, have done it unto me" (Matt. 25:40).*

---

## 2. Our institutions, customs, and traditions will continue to influence people's lives.

### 256. Matters of Religion

The differences between some of the many religions on this small planet have long been a source of conflict, with the Crusades being an important but hardly isolated example of wars fought in the name of religion. The very nature of religion, with its deep personal commitment to what is often a narrowly-focused belief system, can produce intolerance and hostility to different belief systems. Whether these feelings arise out of insecurity or out of a sincere dedication and belief that there is only one religious truth, is a matter of conjecture.

One thing is sure. Millions have died in religious conflicts and man himself has frequently placed God at the head of all excuses for them. Can God honestly sanction so many wars to defend so many divergent belief systems, or is the cry "God wills it" often a matter of man denying responsibility for his own actions and claiming that God sanctions something that no man is capable of? If so, this says more about the nature of man than it does about the nature of God. Our role as Christians is to reach the world with the redeeming Gospel of Jesus Christ who loves us and gave himself for us.

The Great Commission is so important, not only to ensure future peace on earth, but in space also since man will take his religion with him into space. Hopefully in the new millennium and in the new environment of space, there will not be time nor occasion for the old problems to arise.

On the positive side of all this, the day is not far off when the first sermon will be preached from a small chapel aboard a space station. The day will also come when men and women will gather in a modest but splendid lunar cathedral to sing praises to God and hear His messengers speak. What a glorious day that will be. Perhaps the cathedral will feature a stained glass window with a clear central circle large enough to frame the earth which hangs motionless in the lunar sky.

## 257. Matters of Education

The speed at which new knowledge is acquired will continue to increase, with the computer being an important influence in this process. Advances in chip technology and biology may one day allow the human brain to access data banks on chips implanted in the skin which would represent a new way of learning. These libraries on a chip (what is a library, after all, but an extension of man's mind?) might work in the same way our short-term memories do so that our brains would be unable to distinguish information received electronically from knowledge acquired in conventional ways. The brain would likely become most familiar with the information accessed most frequently, but the other information would still be just a thought away. Students so equipped would not have to spend years in college acquiring knowledge in their majors, but would instead spend their time between matriculation and graduation by

348

learning how to use the knowledge on the chip and in acquiring the social parameters required for their profession. Through such advanced technologies universities could produce more effective graduates in less time than they can do now.

## 258. Developments in Science

Our descendants will do things on a scale that might be difficult for us to imagine. They may construct machines as large as the moon or as small as microbes and they may be able to conduct their business at the ends of our solar system. Perhaps they will even be able to influence time in some way.

With the placing of artificial satellites in earth orbit man's ability to predict the weather has improved significantly. Efforts have also been made at controlling the weather. Sometime during the next thousand years our descendants will, in all probability, develop an increased influence over weather systems that cover our planet.

Weather-control machines may dot our planet to cooperate with satellites in space. There may come a time when weather might even be used as a weapon in war or as a threat to prevent one. If mankind were to develop the ability to start a hurricane at any time, in any place and of any size and duration in order to send winds of 200 miles per hour over enemy territory for an extended period of time, we would certainly have a formidable weapon to use in warfare. Is such a development possible for the future?

## 259. Medicine and Aging

The average life-span of thirty years in 1001 is now approaching eighty years in certain countries. If it more than doubles again in the next thousand years, prompted by innovations such as "intensive healing" centers in hospitals and genetic research, then the average life span will be nearly 160 years by 3001. This has startling implications for society which will change significantly as a result. War, for instance, has traditionally been fought by young people in response to the politics of their elders. Such a traditional expectation may radically change in the next millennium.

## 260. Manipulating DNA

We have recently acquired a rudimentary ability to splice DNA into differing species. These early experiments represent promising tools that we will use in helping to improve the human condition. Genetic defects may become a thing of the past. Expediency may dictate that we apply this skill to other life forms as well. Scientists have already taken DNA from one life form and placed it into another. For example, have seen tobacco plants that glow in the dark from firefly DNA.

# 3. One "wild card" of tomorrow is the vast unknown of the universe. What we find or do not find "out there" will have a significant impact on the future.

## 261. Man's Future in Space

We are no longer an earth-bound species dependent on the welfare of only one planet for our survival. We have begun a quest from which there is no retreat. As we soar into space in mighty rockets, we challenge this new frontier. The brave and daring "space knights" who war against acceleration, weightlessness, and long days in space are making it possible for what was begun in the twentieth century to be done in a bigger and better way during the next thousand years.

America's space station will finally take its place in earth orbit and Americans (along with citizens from other countries) will return to the moon, this time to make man's presence permanent there. To give the Congress a greater incentive for funding the space program, *perhaps America should declare the six Apollo landing sites to be American territory.* Since NASA is the agency of choice for America's access to space and return to the moon, senators and congressmen might feel better about allocating money to that agency if we include this new, significant objective in NASA's agenda. Part of the money allocated to NASA would be spent on projects, the ultimate objective of which would include developing new American territory. "Lunamerica," as these new acquisitions might be called, would seem like logical places to begin permanent colonization of the moon and could function as support bases for a manned mission to Mars.

A manned mission to Mars, though a challenge to our technology, will eventually be undertaken. Such a journey would logically precede the colonization of the red planet. These Martian colonies, small and remote, will be subject to the successes and hardships that colonies everywhere have experienced. Their remoteness will require that they make the most of whatever natural resources they find. They may be so remote, based on the present state of our rocket power, that Martian colonists will prefer to call themselves Martians instead of earthlings. The humans on all colonies in the solar system may grow differently in the various gravity fields of their environments. They may be thinner and taller than humans on earth or fatter and shorter, with distinctive facial features.

These colonies may become the sources for a new system of space commerce, not unlike the kind that caused cities to develop at strategic locations in the Middle Ages. There may be certain orbits or transfer points that are more desirable than others because of their convenience and economy. Asteroids located in favorable orbits might bring a premium price. There may be specific locations on the moon or Mars that are better than others for cities for the same reasons. Extraterrestrial materials may become part of such commerce and may become so plentiful that they might be used as building materials on earth. Glass might be made from lunar soil and tile might be made from the sand of Mars. Important works of art might be carved from extraterrestrial stones.

Not even the vastness of the New World that lay before post-Columbus explorers can in any way compare to what waits for us in space. Real estate beyond imagination glitters in billions of solar fires. A wealth of minerals beyond belief orbits constantly over our heads. There are worlds to conquer, planets to tame and transform. We will have to learn new skills, develop new tools, and new ways of doing things in the process.

The future looks bright for human exploration of the inner planets (Mars and Venus) even when we think of going to them in rockets based on our present technology. But it seems unlikely that humans will travel to the outer planets in the chemically powered "snails" we have now, and we will never go to even the nearest stars, which are in the Centauri group 4.3 light years away, in them. The distances are far too great.

Who among us really comprehends the enormous distances to the stars? Those of us who come closest probably are the astronomers who spend their lives studying the stars. But what about the rest of us? We have little practical experience to guide us. Efforts to help us understand this vastness take many forms. One of the most common is to compare the distances to the stars to a scale we are familiar with.

If we represent the average distance between the earth and the sun, something astronomers call an Astronomical Unit and which equals ninety-three million miles, by a line one-inch-long, Pluto, the ninth planet, would be a dot 39.4 inches away, but the nearest stars would be a dot 4.371 *miles* away. Using a speed with which many of us are familiar, fifty-five miles per hour (a speed common on American highways), it would take 192.8 years to reach the sun and over fifty-three million years to reach the nearest stars.

But let's be realistic. We do not send our astronauts into space at freeway speed; it's more like 25,500 miles per hour, or seven miles per second when they are headed to the moon. At that speed the sun could be reached in five months and one day. But to reach the nearest star at that speed would require a journey of approximately 120,000 years! We, who are accustomed to measuring our lives in decades, can have no direct experience with such time frames and we must content ourselves with simply imagining them.

Yet even if we succeed in developing new rocket technologies, there is another problem to contend with. When Einstein advanced his ideas about relativity, one of his most profound statements was that there is a natural speed limit in the universe that prohibits any object from exceeding the speed of light. Furthermore, he said that while we might build ships that move at a respectable fraction of the speed of light, we will never build ships that equal or exceed it. This limitation suggests that during the next thousand years our descendants will easily reach the outer planets of our solar system and probably a few of the nearest stars, but they will not be able to do much better than that.

It has been suggested that we might circumvent these limitations or work within them in various ways. We could build great space arks that would travel for thousands of years so that the remote descendants of the original crew and passengers could place humanity of other worlds. It has also been suggested that we might learn how to "warp space" so that travel from one distant point to another could be faster. Perhaps worm holes or even black holes offer travel advantages.

It may be that the final word is not in on this matter and that further modifications to our understanding of space will be forthcoming. After all, Einstein modified Newton's laws to explain the behavior of objects moving near the speed of light (something Newton could never have thought of). Stay tuned.

## 262. Extraterrestrials

One matter that is worth considering when thinking about space and the next thousand years is the burning, unanswered question as to whether or not life exists on worlds besides earth. It is certainly a question worthy of our attention as we extend ourselves more and more into the space beyond our own planet. The present inability of our science to either confirm or deny the matter places us in about the same relationship to the question as medieval man was to the matter of deciding what earth's place was in the universe. That is, was the earth the center of the universe as the Ptolemy theory suggested or not? The answer to the present question is no less important.

There is only one definitive answer to the question: either there is or there isn't life elsewhere. For the sake of discussion it seems appropriate to categorize these different schools of thought into two groups:

(1) The *homo singularis* theory (from the Latin words *homo* meaning "man" and *singularis* meaning "single"—hence unique) states that life on earth is the only life in the entire universe.

(2) The *homo communis* theory (from the Latin word *homo* meaning "man" and *communis* which means "shared by all or many") states that life is abundant in the universe.

From this second theory, a variation is possible:

(3) The *homo isolationist* theory (from the Latin word *homo* meaning "man" and *isolate,* meaning "island") states that other life exists in the universe but that the universe is so large that man is effectively isolated from it and contact with other life forms, if it ever comes, will be by radio or some other similar means. Physical contact can never occur, according to this view.

The *homo singularis* school of thought contends that man is alone in the universe. Its advocates can cite many reasons to support their view but they all center around the accurate claim that there has never been any known scientific confirmation of contact with extra-terrestrials.

Two types of contact are possible. There is physical contact, such as might result from the landing of an alien spacecraft on earth and there is what might be termed non-physical or remote contact, as might be experienced in the interception of a radio message from a civilization on a distant planet.

It is true that many persons have alleged physical contact with aliens through accidental encounters in isolated places, or by abduction during which some claim to have undergone physical examinations while they were under some hypnotic trance. It is also true that psychologists who have counseled some of these claimants contend that at least the people involved sincerely believe they had such experiences. Yet honest belief in the reality of an alleged experience does not constitute proof of its actuality.

What would constitute proof of physical contact with aliens from space? Minimal but compelling evidence could come from the presentation of an artifact that is beyond our present ability to fabricate or from a more familiar object, such as a navigational instrument that one might reasonably expect to find on a ship that travels through space and the atmosphere of a planet, but which is constructed of an unknown alloy or metal. Even knowledge of an advanced nature haphazardly obtained by an abuductee, such as a new mathematical formula or some special information about the universe that we presently do not know, would lend credence to stories of contact. Other more substantial evidence would come from the retrieval of a crashed spaceship, or the recovery of the body of a space alien. Yet, in all of this millennium, none of these preposterous things have happened.

354

There is also a compelling lack of evidence for indirect contact. The many hours that have been spent listening to the cosmos for artificial radio signals have ended in a big zero (see below).

So curious are we about this matter of other life in the universe that some of us have estimated the number of inhabited planets in the universe capable of having life as we know it. These estimates are based on our present understanding of how many stars there are in the universe and how many planets might be in orbit around them. But as intriguing and well-intentioned as these estimates are, they are just educated guesses.

If we turn to the Christian theologian for his views on this matter, he is likely to concentrate on the relationship between God and man for his answer. We know that God sent his Son, Jesus, to die for the sins of man. If we accept the view that there is life nowhere else in the universe, then we do not have to consider what, if any, relationship God may have with other sentient beings.

Yet if it is true, as the *homo communis* theory suggests, that there is other life in the universe, then theologians must seek new answers to the perplexing questions that such knowledge is likely to produce. Is it possible that there are multiple examples where the God of the universe has sent His Son to die for the sins of other sentient life forms? If the Incarnation on our planet is the only example, will earth's missionaries go and preach the gospel to citizens of other planets, thus repeating the example set by the post-Columbus missionaries who preached to the Indians of the Americas? Are these things possible?

The day will finally come, no matter how protracted its arrival, when man will either be able to confirm or deny the existence of extraterrestrials. Indeed, our presence may already be known to others out there. When man invented radio and started transmitting signals from one ground station to another, he had inadvertently constructed and was using a device that is capable of communicating over interplanetary and interstellar distances. These signals, later joined by those from radar and television, have been traveling into space, causing earth's radio spectrum to gradually brighten. Eventually our transmissions may pass an inhabited planet that is advanced enough to notice them. At that moment, our existence will no longer be a secret.

Once it was realized that radio signals could be used in this manner, the first reaction was to listen for messages that might be coming from other civilizations in space. Project Ozma (1959) was one of the first scientific efforts to do this. There have also been a few deliberate scientific efforts to transmit messages to the stars. One such transmission was sent from the thousand-foot radio telescope at Arecibo, Puerto Rico (1974). It was aimed at a cluster of stars known as M13 in the constellation of Hercules, 24,000 light-years away. But do not keep the light on. It will be A.D. 49,974 before we can even expect to hear a reply.

Such statements tend to create a feeling of security for those homo isolationists who believe that the universe is so vast that "we aren't going anywhere and they aren't either." Such an attitude carries a calculated risk. We have seen over the years how the discovery of scientific truth has altered our understanding of man's place in the universe. But even after astronomers proved that the earth was just a planet going around the sun with some others, there was a tendency to believe that the solar system was the center of the universe. We now know that our solar system is in a remote section of something we call a galaxy, which itself is part of a group of galaxies referred to as the local group. These in turn are part of the universe. We have also seen over the last thousand years how one generation accomplished things former generations could not. The fact that we have not learned how to cross thousands of light-years in a space ship quickly does not mean there is not a way. We also seem to believe that such more advanced "heavenly beings," should we ever meet them, would be benevolent, or at least benign and that contact with them would be to our advantage. This may be a dangerous assumption.

Will such aliens want to (or be able to) conquer us and make us their slaves? Will they have a religion? Will any of our religions be like theirs? Will their theologians, if they have them, want to convert us to their religion? Will humans want to intermarry with these beings? Do they exist at all?

---

### Reflection:

*If beings from space came to earth to preach a new religion would their missionaries be received any differently from the way non-Christian countries have received Christian missionaries? Would it be possible for us to find enough things in common to permit people of many different beliefs to live in harmony? Would we be able to convert them to Christianity?*

## 263. The Next Dark Ages

At home we must continue to manage our affairs so that we enhance the quality of life for all. We must control our appetite for war and should enlarge upon the Truce of God (see section 14) to include the entire world. At this moment there are thousands of nuclear weapons on our planet. Their combined release in a Third World War would have disastrous effects, possibly leading to a nuclear winter which could extinguish most of life on earth. This would make the Dark Ages seem insignificant by comparison. There would be no "Rome" to emulate. Mankind might find itself reverting to the Stone Age. Great floating cities (if we ever build them) could go unattended while gangs of men, with life-styles fashioned after the Stone Age, could plunder and destroy amid the efforts of a few "elite" scientists who would attempt to rebuild civilization [see illustration 11-2].

**Reflection:**

*How much like the first Dark Ages would a second Dark Ages be? Would Christians endeavor to maintain important Christian documents such as the Bible and other religious works? What responsibilities would Christians have toward their fellow men should such a terrible thing happen?*

# God in All of Our Tomorrows

As Christians look ahead to the next millennium many religious questions come to mind. One of the most important of these is whether or not Christ will return during that time and bring down the curtain of history, an event that would effect all of humanity, not just Christians. Such a consideration is not new and Jesus himself admonished us to always live as though this were the day of His return.

Will Christ return during the next millennium? Many people think the signs indicate His return may be very soon. We have seen more than 2,000 years (since the time of Christ) of nations rising against nations, of kingdoms against kingdoms, all of which were predicted by Christ to precede His return. The famines, pestilences, and earthquakes He predicted continue to leave their mark.

357

Our geologists have mapped the "Ring of Fire" that circles the Pacific Rim with its mighty volcanoes. Our seismologists continue to study the San Andreas Fault and others, trying to unlock the mysteries of earthquakes. The false prophets Jesus spoke of have come and gone and how like the days of Noah the present time is! But the most significant sign, some say, was the formation of the State of Israel (1948), which, according to one interpretation of Scripture (Matt. 24:32), will closely precede the return of Christ. Jesus himself said that "This generation shall not pass, till all these things be fulfilled" (Matt. 24:33). We may indeed be living in the end times with the Rapture and the Tribulation close at hand. These eschatalogical events will be followed by the thousand-year rule and reign of Christ. Will the next thousand years be the Millennium prophesied in the Revelation of John?

Science has addressed the question of when the world will end, but its conclusions are independent of man and religion since scientists deal with the breakdown of observed physical processes in earth and space in determining such matters. Do such considerations have a place alongside a theological question related to the return of Christ and the end of the world? We certainly do not require science to validate God. At the same time, science, in accepting God as the Creator of all things, need not be seen as being contrary to religion, either.

The physical processes that fuel our sun will eventually burn out, in an estimated fifty million years, some scientists say. This is a relatively short time in terms of the cosmos. But life on earth will have been extinguished before that when our sun goes through a period of instability and its expansion engulfs the earth in its heat. Also, it is possible that a massive meteorite could strike the earth, destroying civilization as we know it. Eventually the sun will be extinguished through a natural physical process (engineered by God) and the burnt, lifeless cinder of earth will orbit a dying star. If Christ does decide to return soon, it will be a decision made independently of these physical processes.

In the midst of all our speculation, however, one thing remains true. Jesus reminded us that, when it comes to determining the exact time of His return: "...of that day and hour knoweth no man..." (Matt. 24:36).

**Faith in God leads us to one inescapable conclusion: God is in control of the universe. He is working His purposes out. In light of this truth, no matter what happens, the next thousand years promises to be very exciting indeed.**

# Bibliography

The following sources were useful in the writing of this book:

Basu, Champak, *Know India Cuisine,* (Printwell, Bombay), 1986.

Boger, Forlaget Aktuelle, *Facts about Denmark,* (Ministry of Foreign Affairs of Denmark, Press and Cultural Department), 1987.

Bond, Francis, *Introduction to English Church Architecture from the Eleventh to the Sixteenth Century,* (London: Oxford Press, 1913).

Bowers, Verne L., official, Department of the Army ROTC Manual, Readings for "Evolution of Warfare and The Role of the Army in Support of National Objectives," (U.S. Government Printing Office, Washington, D.C.), 1971.

Boys, Don, Pilgrims, *Puritans & Patriots, Our Christian Heritage,* (Goodhope Press, Indianapolis, IN), 1983.

Bucher, Franz, etal, *Verkehrshaus,* (Mengis & Sticher A.G., Luzerm, Switzerland), 1987.

Bumpus, T. Francis, *The Cathedrals and Churches of Northern Italy*, (James Pott & Co., New York), 1907.

Butalia, Urvashi, *Know India Fairs & Festivals*, (Thomson Press, Ltd., India), 1986.

Collins, J. Lawton, ed., Korea—1950, (Department of the Army, U.S. Government Printing Office, Washington, D.C.), 1982.

Department of Science and Technology, Government of India, *Know India Science & Technology*, (Thomson Press, Ltd., India), 1986.

Finnegan, John Patrick, *Military Intelligence a Picture History*, (U.S. Government Printing Office, Washington, D.C.), 1984.

Grier, Thomas Graham, *On the Canal Zone*, (The Wagner & Hanson Co., Chicago), 1908.

Holme, Charles, ed., *Peasant Art in Sweden, Lapland and Iceland*, (The Studio, Ltd., London), 1910.

Holst, Bernhart P., ed., *The New Teachers' and Pupils' Cyclopaedia*, Vol. 3, (The Holst Publishing Company, Chicago), 1910.

Holst, Bernhart P., ed., *The New Teachers' and Pupils' Cyclopaedia*, Vol. 5, (The Holst Publishing Company, Chicago), 1910.

Hutton, Barbara, *Castles and Their Heroes*, (Griffith and Farran, London), 1868.

Mace, William H., *The Story of Old Europe and Young America*, (Rand McNally & Company, Chicago), 1915.

Masahide, Bito, and Watanabe, Akio, *A Chronological Outline of Japanese History*, (International Society for Educational Information, Inc., Tokyo, Japan), 1986.

Miltoun, Francis, *Castles and Chateaux of Old Touraine and the Loire Country*, (L. C. Page & Company), 1906.

NASA, *Voyager Encounters Jupiter,* (U.S. Government Printing Office, Washington, D.C.), July, 1979.

NASA, *Voyager 1 Encounters Saturn,* (U.S. Government Printing Office, Washington, D.C.), December, 1980.

Neely, F. Tennyson, *Fighting in the Philippines,* (F. Tennyson Neely, Publisher, London), 1899.

Otis Elevator Company, *Tell Me About Elevators,* (Communications Department, Otis Elevator Company, Farmington, Connecticut), 1974.

Ramlose, Terri, ed., *Beyond Earth's Boundaries, Human Exploration of the Solar System in the 21st Century, 1988 Annual Report to the Administrator, the Office of Exploration National Aeronautics and Space Administration,* (U.S. Government Printing Office, Washington, D.C.), 1988.

Rand, McNally, *Universal Atlas of the World,* (Rand, McNally & Company, Publishers, Chicago), 1898.

Rose, Elise Whitlock, *Cathedrals and Cloisters of Northern France,* Volume I, (G.P. Putnam and Sons, New York), 1914.

Rose, Elise Whitlock, *Cathedrals and Cloisters of Northern France,* Volume II, (G.P. Putnam and Sons, New York), 1914.

Rying, Bent, *Hans Christian Andersen,* (Bianco Luno, Copenhagen, Denmark), 1983.

Rying, Bent, *Niels Bohr,* (Bianco, Luno, Copenhagen, Denmark), 1985.

Rying, Bent, *Soren Aabye Kierkegaard* (1813-1855), (Bianco Luno, Copenhagen), 1983.

Shamir, Hitzhak, *Foreign Affairs: Israel at 40: Looking Back, Looking Ahead,* Vol. 66, No. 3, 1988 (Council on Foreign Relations, Inc., Israel), 1988.

Shim, Chong-supp, ed., *Introduction to Korean Studies,* (National Academy of Sciences, Republic of Korea), 1986.

Slutsky, Yehuda, etal, *History (of Israel) from 1880,* (Keter Books, Keter Publishing Houst Ltd., Jerusalem, Israel), 1973.

Smith, Roswell, ed., *The Century Illustrated Monthly Magazine,* Vol. 39, November 1889, to April 1890, (The Century Co., New York, New York).

Smith, Roswell, ed., *The Century Magazine,* Vol. XLI, No. 1, November, 1890, (The Century Co., New York, New York).

Smith, Roswell, ed., *The Century Magazine,* Vol. XLI, No. 6, April, 1891, (The Century Co., New York, New York).

Smith, Roswell, ed., *The Century Magazine,* Vol. XLII, No. 4, August, 1891, (The Century Co., New York, New York).

Tazawa, Yutaka, *Japan's Cultural History—a Perspective,* (Ministry of Foreign Affairs, Japan), 1985.

Wharton, Anne Hollingsworth, *In Chateau Land,* (J. B. Lippincott Company, Philadelphia), 1911.

# Picture Credits

Pictures and illustrations in the text without a credit are from the author's collection.

Illustrations attributable to the following sources are so indicated on the illustration:

Adams, Charles Kendall, Ed., *Johnson's Universal Cyclopaedia*, Vol. 1 (New York, D. Appleton and Company, 1896).

Adams, Charles Kendall, Ed., *Johnson's Universal Cyclopaedia*, Vol. V (New York, D. Appleton and Company, 1896).

Myers, Philip Van Ness, *Medieval and Modern History*, (Boston, Ginn and Company, 1905).

---

[2-1]. Bond, Francis, *An Introduction to English Church Architecture from the Eleventh Century to the Sixteenth Century*, (London: Humphrey Milford, Oxford University Press, 1913).

[9-1] and [9-2] (advertising section).
*Century Illustrated Monthly Magazine, The,* Vol. XLI, No. 6, April, 1891.


[10-7]. Funk, Isaac K., ed., *The Literary Digest* (New York: Funk &
Wagnalls Company, Vol. XL, No. 14, April 2, 1910).

# Annotated Index by Person

Abelard, Peter (1079-1142, French scholastic philosopher and theologian), 47

Abenezra (circa 1092-1167, Jewish writer), 48

Adams, John Quincy (1767-1848, American president 1825-1829), 246-247

Adelaide (931-999, Frankish regent 991-995), 26

Agricola, Rudolphus (1443-1485, Dutch scholar), 116

Albert, Charles (b. 1798, king of Sardinia and Piedmont 1831-1849), 241

Aldrin, "Buzz" Jr. (1930-, Apollo 11 astronaut), 264, 319

Alexander I (1777-1825, Russian Czar 1801-circa 1825), 230, 259-260

Alexander II (Pope 1061-1073), 24

Alexander III (Pope 1159-1181), 45

Alexander IV (Pope 1254-1261), 64

Alexander VI (b. 1431, Pope 1492-1503), 121, 128, 130

Alexander the Great (356-323 B.C., king of Macedonia), xii, 47

Alphonso the Learned (1221-1284), 61

Ambroise de Lore (1396-1446, French soldier), 122

Amherst, Lord Jeffrey (1717-1797, British commander), 201

Andrew II (b. 1175, king of Hungary 1205-1235), 74

Anne of Cleves (1515-1557, fourth wife of Henry VIII), 144

Anne (b. 1665, queen of England, Scotland, and Ireland 1702-1707, later of Great Britain 1707-1714), 179, 188, 200

Anning, Mary (1799-1847, English fossil-collector), 219

Anselm, Saint (b. 1033, Archbishop of Canterbury 1093-1109), 32

Antiochus IV Epiphanes (b. circa 215 B.C., king of Syria 175-circa 163 B.C.), 50

Aquinas, Saint Thomas. *See* Thomas Aquinas, Saint

Arcadius (b. circa 377, Roman emperor of the East 395-408), 21

Archimedes (287-212 B.C., Greek mathematician), 157, 159

Aristotle (384-322 B.C., Greek philosopher), 64, 79, 156

Armstrong, Neil (1930-, Apollo 11 astronaut, first man on the moon), 264, 319

Arnold, Mtthew (1822-1888, English poet), 211

Arschot, Philippe de Croy (1526-1595, governor general of Flanders), 142

Arthur I (1187-1203, duke of Brittany), 55, 76-78

Arthur III (1393-1458, duke of Brittany), 123

Ataturk, Kemal (Mustapha) (1880-1938, Turkish leader), 279

Ascham, Roger (circa 1515-1568, English author), 152

Askew, Anne (circa 1521-1546, religious martyr), 145

Asselijn, Hans (1610-1660, Dutch painter), 47

Athanasius, Saint (circa 296-373, patriarch of Alexandria), 20

Audley, Thomas (circa 1488-1544, Lord Chancellor of England), 144

Averroes, Rushd (1126-1198 Arab philosopher), 47

Bach, Johann Sebastian (1685-1750, German musician and composer), xii

Bacon, Francis (1561-1626, English philosopher and statesman), xii, 116, 152, 155

Bacon, Roger (circa 1214-1294, English scientist and philosopher), 64

Badoglio, Pietro (1871-1956, Italian marshal), 301

Baily, Francis (1774-1844, English astronomer), 218, 259

Balboa, Vasco (circa 1475-1517, Spanish conquistador, discoverer of the Pacific Ocean), 149

Baldwin I (b. circa 1058, king of Jerusalem 1100-1118), 36

Baldwin II (birth uncertain, king of Jerusalem 1118-1131), 45

Baldwin III, (b. 1130, king of Jerusalem 1143-1163), 53

Balzac, Honore' de (1799-1850 French novelist), 223

Barbarossa, Frederick. *See* Frederick I. Called *Barbarossa*

Barnard, Edward (1857-1923, American astronomer), 218, 270

Bartholdi, Frederic Auguste (1834-1904, French sculptor), 256-257

Bartolus de Saxoferrato (1314-1367, Italian lawyer), 86

Barton, Clara (Clarissa Harlowe) (1821-1912, American humanitarian and organizer of the American Red Cross), 226

Barton, Elizabeth (circa 1506-1534, "the Maid of Kent"), 143-144

Basil II (b. circa 957, Byzantine emperor 976-1025), 22

Bean, Alan (1932-; Apollo 12 astronaut (fourth man on the moon), Skylab astronaut, and space artist), 319, 320

Becket, Thomas á. *See* Thomas á Becket, Saint

Becquerel, Antoine H. (1852-1908 French physicist), 213

Bede (circa 673-735, English historian), 48

Beethoven, Ludwig van (1770-1827 German composer), 191

Beissel, James Conrad (1690-1768, founder of a Seventh-Day Baptist community in Pennsylvania), 195

Benedict XI (b. 1240, Pope 1303-1304), 94

Benedict XV (Pope 1914-1922), 263

Benedict, Saint (circa 480-547, founder of Western monasticism), 30

Bennett, James Gordon (1795-1872, American newspaper proprietor), 250

Benz, Karl (1844-1929, German engineer), 215

Bering, Vitus (1681-1741 Danish explorer), 190

Berkeley, George (1685-1753 Irish philosopher and clergyman), 189

Bernard of Clairvaux, Saint (circa 1090-1153, Cistercian monk), 49,52

Bernard of Morlaix (found living 1150, French Cluniac monk, of English parentage), 1

Bernoulli, Daniel (1700-1782, Swiss physicist), 193

Bessel, Friedrich Wilhelm (1784-1846, German astronomer), 218-219

Bickerdyke, Mary Ann Ball (1817-1901, Union nurse in the American Civil War), 226

Biddle, John (1615-1662, founder of English Unitarianism), 173

Bismarck, Otto von (1815-1898, German statesman), 237-239, 273

Black, Joseph (1728-1799, Swedish chemist and physicist), 193

Blaine, James G. (1830-1893, American Secretary of State), 253

Bloody Mary. *See* Mary I

Blucher, Gebhard von, (1742-1819, Prussian field marshal), 233

Boetius (circa 475-525, Roman philosopher and statesman), 16

Boleyn, Anne (circa 1507-1536, second wife of Henry VIII), 143-144

Bolivar, Simon (1783-1830, South American revolutionist, Called *the Liberator*), 251-252

Bonaparte (family name of Napoleon I, French emperor) Bonaparte, Caroline (1782-1839, queen of Naples 1808-1814), 230

Bonaparte, Jerome (1784-1860, "King of Westphalia" 1807-1813, youngest brother of Napoleon I), 230

Bonaparte, Joseph (1768-1844, king of Naples and Spain, brother of Napoleon I), 229-231, 251

Bonaparte, Louis (1778-1846, king of Holland 1806-1810, brother of Napoleon I), 229, 240

Bonaparte, Louis Napoleon. *See* Napoleon III

Bonaparte, Napoleon. *See* Napoleon I

Boniface VIII (b. circa 1235, Pope 1294-1303), 68, 94

Booth, John Wilkes (circa 1838-1865, American actor, the assassin of Abraham Lincoln), 247

Boscawen, Edward (1711-1761, British admiral), 201

Bothwell, James Hepburn (1535-1578, third husband of Mary Stuart), 147

Boyle, Robert (1627-1691, Anglo-Irish scientist),164, 165

Braddock, Edward (1695-1755, British general), 201

Bradley, Omar N. (1893-1981, American general), 301

Brahe, Tycho (1546-1601, Danish nobleman), 156

Braun, Eva (1912-1945, Hitler's mistress and wife), 302-303, 316

Breton, Nicholas (circa 1555-circa 1626, English poet), 152

Brown, John (1800-1859, American abolitionist), 247

Browning, Elizabeth Barrett (1806-1861, English poet), 221

Browning, Robert (1812-1889, English poet), 221

Bruno. *See* Gregory V

Bunyan, John (1628-1688, English author), 163, 183

Burckhardt, George (1484-1545, associate of Luther), 136

Bush, Vannevar (1890-1974, American electrical engineer), 305

Butler, Joseph (1692-1752, English theologian), 189

Byrd, Richard E. (1888-1957, American aviator and polar explorer), 264

Byron, George Gordon (1788-1824, English poet), 221

Cabot, John (found living 1461-1498, English explorer), 126, 130

Cabral, Pedro Alvares (circa 1460-circa 1526, Portuguese navigator), 130

Calixtus II (Pope, 1119-1124), 33

Calvin, John (1509-1564, French Protestant theologian of the Reformation), 138

Canute (b. circa 995, king of England, Norway, and Denmark 1016-1035), 23

Capet, Hugh. *See* Hugh Capet

Capone, Al. Called *Scarface* (1899-1947, Chicago gangster), 280-281

Carr, Gerald (1932-, Skylab astronaut), 320

Carroll, B. H. (1843-1914, founder of Southwestern Baptist Seminary), 266

Carroll, Lewis (1832-1898, English writer and mathematician), 221-222

Cartier, Jacques (1491-1557, French navigator), 150

Carver, George Washington (circa 1864-1943, American agricultural chemist), 212

Casanova, Giovanni (1725-1798 Venetian adventurer and author), 189

Cassini, Giovanni Domenico (1625-1712, French astronomer), 168

Castro, Fidel (1927-, Cuban communist dictator 1959-,), 314

Castro, Raul (1931-, Cuban Minister of Defense 1962-,), 314

Catherine of Aragon (1485-1536, first wife of Henry VIII), 143-145

Catherine Parr (1512-1548, sixth wife of Henry VIII), 144

Cavour, Camillo de (b. 1810, premier of Sardinia 1852-1859), 241-243

Caxton, William (circa 1422-1491, English printer), 117

Cayley, George (1773-1857, English aviation pioneer), 217

Celsius, Anders (1701-1744, Swedish astronomer), 188, 193

Cernan, Eugene (1934-, Apollo 17 astronaut), 319

Cervantes, Miguel de (1547-1616, Spanish novelist, dramatist, and poet), 135

Chafin, Kenneth (1926-, American Baptist preacher), 264

Chamberlain, Neville (1869-1940, English statesman), 293-294

Charlemagne (9th century emperor of the West and Frankish king), 15, 22, 24, 26, 47

Charles I (1887-1922, Austrian Emperor 1916-1918), 279

Charles VI (b. 1685, Holy Roman Emperor 1711-1740), 206

Charles VII (b. 1403, French king 1422-1461), 122-124

Charles VIII (b. 1470, French king 1483-1498), 116

Charles IX (b. 1550, French king 1560-1574), 142

Charles, J. A. C. (1746-1823 French physicist), 190-204

Charles the Bald (b. 823, French king, 843-877), 25

Chatham, William Pitt, first earl of (1708-1778, English statesman 1756-1760), 201

Chaucer, Geoffrey (circa 1340-1400, English poet), 83, 87

Cheselden, William (1688-1752 English surgeon), 188

Chiang Kai-shek (1887-1975, Chinese general and statesman), 291

Chicheley, Henry (1364-1443, English archbishop), 121

Christian IV (b. 1577, king of Denmark 1588-1648), 324

Churchill, Winston (1874-1965, British statesman, soldier, and author), 297, 300

Clark, Mark (1896-1984, American general), 301

Clemens, Samuel Langhorne. See Twain, Mark

Clement II (Pope 1046-1047), 33

Clement V (b. 1264, Pope 1305-1314), 94

Clement VII (Pope 1523-1534), 143

Cleveland, Grover (1837-1908, American president 1885-1889, 1893-1897), 252

Clive, Robert (1725-1774 British soldier and statesman), 206

Colet, John (circa 1466-1519, an Oxford Reformer), 119

Coligny, Admiral Gaspard de (1519-1572, Huguenot leader), 142

Collins, Michael (1930-, Apollo 11 astronaut), 264, 319

Columbus, Christopher (circa 1451-1506, discoverer of America), 116, 130

Comenius, John Amos (1592-1670, Czech theologian), 166

Comnenus, Alexius (b. 1048, Byzantine emperor 1081-1118), 22, 34

Conant, J. B. (1893-1978, president of Harvard and advisor on the Manhattan Project), 305

Congreve, Sir William (1772-1828, English rocket experimenter), 212

Conrad II (b. circa 990, German king 1024-1039), 25

Conrad III (b. circa 1093, German king 1138-1152), 52-53

Conrad, Charles Jr. (1930-, Apollo 12 astronaut), 319-320

Constantine I (b. circa 288, Byzantine emperor 306-337), 21, 29

Constantine the African (circa 1020-circa 1087, Benedictine monk), 19

Cook, James (1728-1779, English navigator and explorer), xii, 149, 191

Cooper, James Fenimore (1789-1851, American novelist), 224

Copernicus, Nicholas (1473-1543, Polish astronomer), 155, 258

Cornwallis, Charles (1738-1805, British general), 203

Cortes, Hernando (1485-1547, Spanish conquistador, conqueror of Mexico), 151

Cromwell, Richard (1626-1712, lord protector of England), 178-179

Daguerre, Louis J. M. (1789-1851, French physicist), 212, 227

Daladier, Edouard (1884-1970, French politician), 294

Dalton, John (1766-1844, English teacher and chemist), 213

Dante Alighieri (1265-1321, Italian writer), 85-88, 97

Darby, James B. (1858-1898, American inventor), 212

Darnely, Lord. *See* Stuart, Henry

Darwin, Charles (1809-1882, English naturalist), 211, 220,258

Davis, Jefferson (1808-1889, American statesman, President of the Southern Confederacy 1861-1865), 246

Davy, Sir Humphry (1778-1829, British scientist), 213, 227

Descartes, Rene' (1596-1650, French philosopher and scientist), 170

Dias, Bartholomeu (circa 1450-1500, Portuguese navigator), 130

Diaz, Rodrigo (circa 1030-1099), 21

Dickens, Charles (1812-1870, English novelist), 221

Dilday, Russell H. (1930-, Baptist seminary president), 226

Dionysius Exiguus (d. circa 545, Roman biblical scholar), 37

Disney, Walt (1901-1966, American motion picture cartoonist and producer), 281

Dixon, Jeremiah (birth uncertain-1777, English astronomer and surveyor), 188

Dodgson, Charles Lutwidge. *See* Carroll, Lewis,

Doenitz, Karl (1891-1980, German admiral), 303

Dominic, Saint (1170-1221, founder of the Dominicans), 67, 70

Doolittle, James H. (1896-1993, American general of the Army Air Forces), 299

Doppler, Christian Johann (1803-1853, Austrian physicist), 219, 259

Dornberger, Walter (1895-1980, German rocket scientist), 308

Dostoyevsky, Feodor M. (1821-1881, Russian novelist), 223

Doyle, Sir Arthur Conan (1859-1930, English author), 222

Drake, Francis (circa 1540-1596, English navigator and admiral), 148, 150

Drebble, C. J. (1572-1634, Dutch inventor), 165

Drummond, Henry (1851-1897, Scottish evangelist), 220

Duke, Charles Jr. (1935-, Apollo 16 astronaut), 319

Duke of Wellington, the. *See* Wellesley, Sir Arthur

Dumas, Alexandre (1802-1870, French novelist and dramatist), 222

Dunlop, John (1840-1921, Scottish inventor), 215

Dunois, Jean (circa 1403-1468, French commander), 123

Dupleix, Joseph (1697-1763, French colonial administrator), 206

Durham, John George (1792-1840, British statesman), 253

Duryea, Frank (1869-1967, American inventor and pioneer automobile manufacturer), 215

Earhart, Amelia (1898-1937, American aviator), 264

Eastman, George (1854-1932, American inventor and industrialist), 227

Edgar the Atheling (circa 1050-circa 1130, brother of Harold II), 23

Edison, Thomas A. (1847-1931, American inventor), 214

Edward III (b. 1312, English king 1327-1377), 95

Edward V (b. 1470, English king April-June, 1483), 125

Edward VI (b. 1537, English king 1547-1553), 144

Edward the Confessor (b. circa 1002, English king 1042-1066), 3, 24

Eiffel, Alexandre Gustave (1832-1923, French engineer), 256

Einstein, Albert (1879-1955, German-born American physicist), 263, 286, 305,352

Eisenhower, Dwight D. (1890-1969, American president 1953-1961), 300-301

Eleanor of Aquitaine (circa 1122-1204, queen of Henry II of England), 55

Eliot, George [pen name of Mary Ann (or Marian Evans)], (1819-1880, English novelist)], 221

Elizabeth (b. 1709, empress of Russia 1741-1762), 206

Elizabeth I (b. 1533, English queen 1558-1603), 144, 146, 148, 152

Emerson, Ralph Waldo (1803-1882, American novelist and essayist), 223, 345

Engels, Friedrich (1820-1895, German socialist), 234-235

Erasmus, (or Desiderius Erasmus) (circa 1466-1536, Dutch humanist), 119

Eric the Red (circa 950-circa 1010, Norwegian navigator), 28

Ericson, Leif (found living 1000, Norse mariner and adventurer), 28

Evans, Mary Ann (or Marian). See Eliot, George

Evans, Ronald (1933-1990, Apollo 17 astronaut), 319

Exiguus, Dionysius. See Dionysius Exiguus


Fahrenheit, Gabriel Daniel (1686-1736, German scientist), 193

Faraday, Michael (1791-1867, English physical scientist), 214

Fawkes, Guy (1570-1606, leader of the Gunpowder Plot), 177-178

Ferdinand V (1452-1516, king of Aragon and Sicily 1479-1516), 127, 128

Ferdinand VII (b. 1784, Spanish king 1808-1833), 235

Ferdinand, Franz. See Franz Ferdinand

Fillmore, Millard (1800-1874, American president 1850-1853), 249-250

Fleming, Sir Alexander (1881-1955, English bacteriologist), 268

Foch, Ferdinand (1851-1929, marshal of France), 278

Fokker, Anton (1890-1939, American airplane constructor), 275

Forbes, General John (1710-1759, British general), 201

Ford, Henry (1863-1947, American industrialist), 216

Foucault, Jean Bernard Leon (1819-1868, French physicists), 218, 259

Foxe, John (circa 1516-1587, English author and martyr), 152

Fra Bartolommeo. See Porta, Baccio della

Fracastoro, Girolamo (1483-1553, Italian physician), 16, 153

Francis I (b. 1768, Austrian king 1804-1835 and Holy Roman Emperor, 1792-1806), 230-231

Francis II (b. 1544, first husband of Mary Stuart and French king 1559-1560), 147

Francis, Saint (circa 1182-1226, founder of the Franciscans), 66-67

Francis of Assisi, Saint. See Francis, Saint

Franco, Francisco (1892-1975, Spanish general and head of state), 289

Franklin, Benjamin (1706-1790, American statesman, printer, scientist, and writer), 187, 193, 208, 246

Franz Ferdinand (1863-1914, heir to the throne Austria whose assassination sparked World War I), 274

Franz Joseph I. Francis Joseph (1810-1916, emperor of Austria 1830-1916, king of Hungary 1867-1916), 279

Frederick I called Barbarossa (circa 1122, German king 1152-1190), 45, 54

Frederick II (king of Denmark 1559-1588), 156

Frederick II (b. 1194, German king 1212-1250), 75

Frederick II (b. 1712, Prussian king 1740-1786), 196, 205, 206

Frederick III the Wise (b. 1463, elector of Saxony 1486-1525), 137

Frederick the Great. See Frederick II, king of Prussia

Frederick William (b. 1620, elector of Brandenburg 1640-1688), 181

Freud, Sigmund (1856-1939, Austrian neurologist), 346-347

Frontenac, Louis de Buade, Comte de (1620-1698, French governor of New France), 177


Galen, Claudius (circa 131-circa 200, physician and writer), 17

Galileo Galilei (1564-1642, Italian astronomer), 157, 164, 167

Gama, Vasco da (circa 1469-1524, Portuguese navigator), 130, 248

Garibaldi, Giuseppe (1807-1882, Italian patriot and soldier), 242-243

Garriott, Owen (1930-, Skylab astronaut), 320

Garrison, William Lloyd (1805-1879, American abolitionist), 247

Genghis Khan (circa 1162-1227, Mongol conqueror and emperor), xi

George II (b. 1683, English king 1727-1760), 191, 201

George III (b. 1738, English king 1820), 202

Gerbert of Aurillac. See Sylvester II

Gershom ben Jehuda (960-1028, Jewish scholar), 27

Gibson, Edward (1936-, Skylab astronaut), 320

Giffard, Henri (1825-1852, balloon aviator), 217

Gilbert, Humphrey (circa 1539-1583, English navigator), 150

Gilbert, William (circa 1540-1603, English physician), 164

Giovanni de Monte (1498-1552, Italian physician), 153

Goddard, Robert H. (1882-1945, pioneer American rocket designer), 307, 316-317

Godfrey of Bouillon (b. circa 1060, first ruler of Holy Land 1099-1100), 36

Godiva, Lady (found living 1040-circa 1080), 23

Godwin, Earl (d. 1053, English statesman), 23

Godwinson, Harold. See Harold II

Gogh, Vincent van. See van Gogh, Vincent

Goodyear, Charles (1800-1860, American inventor), 215

Gorbachev, Mikhail S. (1931-, Russian premier 1985-1991), 273

Gordon, Richard (1929-, Apollo 12 astronaut), 319

Graham, William "Billy" (1918-, American evangelist), 323

Grahame, Kenneth (1859-1932, Scottish author), 221

Grant, Ulysses Simpson (1822-1885, American president 1869-1877), 247

Greeley, Horace (1811-1872, American newspaper editor), 211, 247

Gregory I (b. circa 540, Pope 590-604), 20

Gregory V (Pope 996 and 998), 26

Gregory VII (b. circa 1021, Pope 1073-1085), 32, 33

Gregory IX (b. 1145, Pope 1227-1241), 71

Gregory XIII (b. 1502, Pope 1572-1585), 142, 180

Gregory of Tours, Saint (circa 538-circa 594, French historian), 17

Groves, Leslie R. (1896-1970, American major and military chief of the American atomic bomb project in World War II), 305

Guiscard, Robert. See Robert Guiscard

Gutenberg, Johannes (circa 1398-1468, German printer), 117

Haig, Douglas (1861-1928, British Field Marshal), 277-278

Hale, George Ellery (1868-1938, American astronomer), 270

Hall, Charles Martin (1863-1914, American chemist), 213

Halley, Edmund (1656-1742, English astronomer and mathematician), 169

Hamerken, Thomas (circa 1380-1471, German monk), 83, 87

Hamilton, James (circa 1515-1575, Protestant reformer of the Reformation), 138

Handel, George Frederick (1685-1759, German-English composer), 191

Hannibal (247-circa 182 B.C., Carthaginian general), xii

Hardecanute (reigned 1040-1042, English king), 23

Harding, Saint Stephen (d. 1134, founder of the Cistercians), 30

Harefoot. See Harold I

Harold I (English king 1037-1040), 23

Harold II (b. circa 1022, English king 1066), 23

Harrison, George (1943-, member of the Beatles singing group), 314

Harthacanute. *See* Hardecanute

Harvey, William (1578-1657, English physician and anatomist), 165-166

Hawkins, Sir John (1532-1595, English privateer), 148

Hawthorne, Nathaniel (1804-1864, American novelist and short story writer), 223

Hay, John (1838-1905, American secretary of state), 247

Haydn, Franz Joseph (1732-1809 Austrian composer), 191

Hearst, William Randolph (1863-1951, American journalist and publisher), 252

Heaviside, Oliver (1850-1925, English physicist), 265

Henry I (b. 1068, English king 1100-1135), 25, 32, 38, 55

Henry I (b. circa 1011, French king 1031-1060), 24

Henry II (b. 1133, English king 1154-1189), 48, 52, 54-56

Henry III (b. 1551, French king 1574-1589), 142

Henry III, the Black, (b. 1017, German king 1039-1056), 26

Henry IV (b. 1553, French king 1589-1610), 142, 177

Henry IV (b. 1367, English king 1399-1413), 121, 126

Henry IV (b. 1050, German king 1056-1105), 26, 32-33

Henry V (b. 1387, English king 1413-1422), 122-123, 126

Henry V (b. 1081, German king 1105-1125), 33, 96, 101-123

Henry VI (b. 1421, English king 1422-1461, 1470-1471), 96, 123

Henry VI (b. 1165, German king 1190-1197), 54, 73, 122

Henry VII (b. 1457, English king 1485-1509), 126, 143

Henry VIII (b. 1491, English king 1509-1547), 52, 95, 143, 151, 153

Henry the Navigator (1394-1460, prince of Portugal, patron of exploration), 129

Heywood, John (circa 1497-circa 1578, English dramatist), 135

Hidalgo, Miguel (1753-1811, Mexican priest and revolutionist), 235

Hiero II (circa 306-215 B.C., tyrant of Syracuse), 159

Hindenburg, Paul von (1847-1934, German president 1925-1933), 285

Hippocrates (circa 460-circa 370 B.C., Greek physician), 17

Hirohito (1901-1991, emperor of Japan), 306

Hitler, Adolf (1889-1945, German dictator, founder and leader of National Socialism), xi, 273, 285-287, 292-295, 297, 302-303

Ho Chi Minh (1890-, Communist leader and president of North Vietnam 1954-1969), 315

Honorius (b. 384, Roman emperor of the West 395-423), 21

Honorius II (Pope 1124-1130), 45

Honorius III (Pope 1216-1227), 67

Hooke, Robert (1635-1703, English scientist), 165

Hooker, Richard (circa 1554-1600 English theologian), 146

Hoover, Herbert C. (1874-1964, American president 1929-1933), 281-283

Howe, Elias (1819-1867, American inventor), 214

Hsuan Tung (1906-1967, boy emperor of China 1932-1945), 291

Hubble, Edwin (1899-1953, American astronomer), 271

Houdini, Harry. *See* Weiss, Erich

Huggins, Sir William (1824-1910, English astronomer), 219

Hugh Capet (b. circa 940, French king 987-996), 25

Hughes, Howard Sr. (1869-1924, American lawyer, inventor, businessman, and philanthropist), 267

Hugo, Victor Marie (1802-1885, French poet, dramatist, and novelist), 222

Hume, David (1711-1776 Scottish philosopher and historian), 189

Huss, John (circa 1369-1415, Czech religious reformer), 92

Hutton, James (1726-1797, Scottish geologist), 187
Huxley, Thomas Henry (1825-1895, English naturalist and philosopher), 220
Huygens, Christiaan (1629-1695, Dutch mathematician and physicist), 168, 171

Innocent III (b. circa 1160, Pope 1198-1216), 54, 70, 73-74, 93
Innocent IV (b. circa 1190, Pope 1243-1264), 75
Iron Mask, Man with the (mysterious French prisoner of state), 179, 180
Irving, Washington (1783-1859, American author and diplomat), 224
Irwin, James (1930-1991, Apollo 15 astronaut), 319
Isabella I (b. 1451, Spanish queen of Castile and Leon 1474-1504), 127-128

Jackson, Andrew (1767-1845, American president 1829-1837), 246
Jacques de Molay (circa 1243-1314, founder of the Order of the Templars) 94
James I (b. 1394, Scottish king 1424-1437), 126-127
James I (b. 1566, king of England and Ireland 1603-1625 and as James VI of Scotland 1567-1625), 126-127, 147, 164, 170, 177-178
James IV (b. 1473, Scottish king 1488-1513), 126
Jameson, George (circa 1587-1644, Scottish painter), 167
Jameson, Sir Leander Starr (1853-1917, British colonial administrator and statesman in South Africa), 255
Jane Seymour (1509-1537, third wife of Henry VIII), 144
Jansky, Karl (1905-1950, American physicist), 271
Janssen, Cornelis (1593-circa 1662, Flemish painter), 167
Jefferson, Thomas (1743-1826, American president 1801-1809), 203, 245-246

Jesus, 8, 18, 47, 91, 347, 355, 357-358
Joachim of Floris (circa 1130-1202, Cistercian monk), 80
Joan of Arc (circa 1411-1431), 123-124
John I (b. circa 1357, king of Portugal 1385-1433), 129
John II (b. 1319, French king 1350-1364), 95
John XV (Pope 985-996), 26
John (b. circa 1167, English king 1199 - 1216), 75-77
Johnson, Andrew (1808-1875, American president 1865-1869), 246
Johnson, Lyndon (1909-1973, American president 1963-1969), 315
Jonas, Justis (1493-1555, German Protestant reformer), 136
Jones, Inigo (1573-1652, English architect), 164
Jorg, Junker (assumed name of Martin Luther, 1521-1522), 137
Julius II (Pope 1503-1513), 143
Jung, Carl (1875-1961, Swiss psychiatrist), 346

Kant, Immanuel (1724-1804, German metaphysician), 189
Keats, John (1795-1821, English poet), 221
Kemal, Mustapha (or Mustafa) (1880-1938, "father of the Turks"), 279
Kempis, Thomas a. See Thomas a Kempis
Kennedy, John F. (1917-1963, American president 1961-1963), 268, 314-315, 318
Kent, Maid of. See Barton, Elizabeth
Kepler, Johannes (1571-1630, German astronomer), 156
Kerwin, Joseph (1932-, Skylab astronaut), 320
Khan, Genghis. See Genghis Khan
Khayyam, Omar. See Omar Khayyam
Khrushchev, Nikita (1894-1971, Russian statesman, premier of the Soviet Union 1958-1964), 314
Kidd, William (circa 1645-1701 pirate), 177
Kilmer, Joyce (1886-1918, American poet), 263

Kipling, Rudyard (1865-1936, English poet, novelist, and short story writer), 221, 263

Klaproth, Martin H. (1743-1817 German chemist), 188

Knox, John (circa 1505-1572, Scottish religious reformer), 138

Komensky, Johann *See* Comenius, John Amos

Kraft, Adam (circa 1455-1509, German sculptor and architect), 119

Kruger, Stephanus Johannes Paulus (1825-1904, South African Transvaal statesman 1883-1900), 255

Krupp, Alfred (1812-1887 armament industrialist), 212

Kublai Khan (b. circa 1216, Mongol emperor 1260-1294), 65

Lafayette (or La Fayette) (1757-1834, French soldier), 204

Landsteiner, Karl (1868-1943, American physician and pathologist), 268

Langland, William (circa 1332-circa 1400, English poet), 83, 86

Langton, Stephen (circa 1150, Archbishop of Canterbury 1207-1228), 77

Lavoisier, Antoine Laurent (1743-1794 French physicist), 192

Lazarus, Emma (1849-1887, American poet and essayist), 256-257

Lee, Robert E. (1807-1870, Confederate general of the American Civil War), 247

Lennon, John (1940-1980, member of the Beatles singing group), 313-314

Leeuwenhoek, Anthony van (1632-1723, Dutch student of natural history and maker of microscopes), 165

LeMay, Curtis (1906-1990, American general), 303

Lenin, Vladimir Ilyich (1870-1924, Russian revolutionist and statesman, founder of Bolshevism and of Soviet Russia), 278, 289

Leo IX (Pope 1049-1054), 29

Leo X (Pope 1513-1521), 136, 139

Leofric, Earl of Mercia and Lord of Coventry (husband of Lady Godiva), 23

Leonardo da Vinci (1452-1519, Italian sculptor, painter, architect, musician, and engineer), xii, 118

Leopold III (1901-1983, Belgian king 1934-1951), 296

Liguori, Saint Alfonso Maria de (1696-1787, founder of the Congregation of the Most Holy Redeemer), 196

Linacre (sometimes Lynaker), Thomas (circa 1460-1524, English physician), 153

Lincoln, Abraham (1809-1865, American president 1861-1865), 246

Lindbergh, Charles (1902-1974, American aviator), 264

Lippershey, Hans (1570-1619, developed spyglass), 167

Lister, Joseph (1827-1912, English surgeon), 225-226

Livingstone, David (1813-1873, Scottish missionary and explorer), 250-251

Locke, John (1632-1704, English philosopher)

Longfellow, Henry Wadsworth (1807-1882, American poet), 223

Louis I (b. 778, French and German king 814-140), 24

Louis VII (b. circa 1120, French king 1137-1180), 52-53, 55

Louis VIII (b. 1187, French king 1223-1226), 77

Louis IX (b. 1214, French king 1226-1270), 75

Louis XIV (b. 1638, French king 1643-1715), 168, 182, 203, 229

Louis XV (b. 1710, French king 1715-1774), 188, 203-204

Louis XVI (1754-1793, French king 1774-1792), 204, 233

Louis XVIII (b. 1755, French king 1814-1824)

Louis Napoleon *See* Napoleon III

Louis, Saint *See* Louis IX

Louis de Buade (1620-1698, French commander), 177

Lousma, Jack (1936-, Skylab astronaut), 320

Lowell, James Russell (1819-1891, American poet, editor, and diplomat), 224

Lowell, Percival (1855-1916, American astronomer), 218

Luther, Martin (1483-1546, German leader of the Reformation), 136-138

Lyell, Charles (1797-1875, English geologist), 219


MacArthur, Douglas (1880-1964, American general), 299-300, 306, 312-313

McCartney, Paul (1942- member of the Beatles singing group), 314

MacClure, Sir Robert (1807-1873, British arctic explorer), 216

Mach, Ernst (1838-1916, Austrian physicist), 212

Machiavelli, Niccolo (1469-1527, Italian statesman and writer), ix, 141

Magellan, Ferdinand (circa 1480-1521, Portuguese navigator), 149

Maginot, Andre (1877-1932, French minister of war 1929-1930), 296

Malik-al-Adil (b. circa 1143, brother of Saladin), 74, 75

Malpighi, Marcello (1628-1694, Italian physician), 165

Malthus, Thomas Robert (1766-1834, English economist), 194

Mann, Thomas (1875-1955, German novelist), 286

Manual I (b. 1469, Portuguese king 1495-1521), 130

Manutius, Aldus (1450-1515 Venetian printer), 188

Marco Polo. See Polo, Marco

Marconi, Marchese Guglielmo (1874-1937, Italian physicist), 214, 265

Marshall, George C. (1880-1959, American army officer and statesman), 300

Martel, Geoffrey, count of Anjou, 24

Martineau, Harriett (1802-1876, English journalist and traveler), 345

Marx, Karl (1818-1883, German social philosopher), 234-235

Mary I (b. 1516, English queen 1553-1558), 145, 160

Mary, Queen of Scots. See Mary Stuart

Mary Stuart (1542-1587, Scottish queen 1542-1567), 146

Mason, Charles (1730-1787 English astronomer and surveyor), 188

Mata Hari. See Zelle, Margaretha Geertruida

Mattingly II, Thomas (1936-, Apollo 16 astronaut), 319

Maupassant, Guy de (1850-1893, French novelist and short-story writer), 223

Maupertuis, Pierre Louis Moreau de (1698-1759, French mathematician and astronomer), 188

Maximilian (b. 1832, emperor of Mexico 1867), 237

Mayow, John (circa 1645-1679, English physician), 165

Mazzini, Giuseppe (Joseph) (1805-1872, Italian patriot and revolutionist), 240

Medhurst, Walter H. (1796-1857, English Congregationalist missionary to China), 227

Medici, Giovanni di Bicci de (1360-1429, founder of the Medici dynasty), 85

Mendelssohn, Jacob Ludwig Felix (1809-1847 German musician), 197

Mendelssohn, Moses (1729-1786 German philosopher), 196-197

Mercator, Gerhardus (1512-1594, Flemish geographer), 151

Merici, Saint Angela de (1470-1540, founder of the Ursulines), 140

Michelangelo Buonarotti (1475-1564, Italian architect, sculptor, painter, and poet), 118

Michelson, Albert (1852-1931, American physicist), 213

Mirabeau, Victor (1715-1789, French social philosopher and physiocrat), 205

Mitchell, Edgar (1930-, Apollo 14 astronaut), 319

Mohammed (circa 570-632, Prophet of Islam), 49

Mohammed II (conqueror of Byzantine Empire in 1453), 21

Molay, Jacques de (circa 1243-1314, last grand master of the Knights Templars), 94

Moliere, Jean (1622-1673 French dramatist, actor, and master of comedy), 179

Moltke, Helmuth Karl von (1800-1891, Prussian field marshal), 237

Montagu, John (1718-1792, Fourth Earl of Sandwich), 191

Monte, Giovanni de, (1498-1552, Italian physician), 153

Montgolfier, Jacques Etienne (1745-1799, co-inventor of first practical balloon), 190

Montgolfier, Joseph Michel (1740-1810, co-inventor of first practical balloon), 190

Montezuma II (or Moctezuma) (circa 1480-1520, Aztec emperor), 151

Monroe, James (1758-1831, American president 1817-1825), 260

Montgomery, Bernard (1887-1976, British field marshal), 301

Moore, Clement C. (1779-1863, American teacher and poet), 224

Moran, George "Bugs" (1893-1957, Chicago Gangster), 281

More, Thomas (1478-1535, an "Oxford Reformer"), 119

Moreau, Pierre Louis de Maupertuis (1698-1759, French mathematician and astronomer), 188

Morley, Edward (1838-1923, American scientist), 213

Mozart, Wolfgang Amadeus (1756-1791, Austrian composer), 191

Mussolini, Benito (1883-1945, Italian dictator, founder of Fascism), 244, 287-288, 301

Mustafa, Kemal See Ataturk Kemal

Napoleon III (Louis Napoleon Bonaparte) (b. 1808, nephew of Napoleon I and French emperor 1852-1870), 236-237, 239, 242

Napoleon Bonaparte (Napoleon I) (1769-1821, French emperor), xi, 229-234, 251

Nelson, Lord Horatio (1758-1805, English naval hero), 230

Newton, Isaac (1642-1727, English physicist and philosopher), xii, 164, 168, 188, 353

Nicholas I (b. 1796, Russian czar 1825-1855), 244

Nicholas V (b. 1397, Pope 1447-1455), 116

Nicholson, Francis (1665-1728, British colonial administrator), 200

Niepce, Joseph N. (1765-1833, French chemist), 227

Nightingale, Florence (1820-1910, English hospital administrator), 226

Nixon, Richard M. (1913-1994, American president 1969-1974), 315

Nobel, Alfred (1833-1896 Swedish chemist), 213

Nostradamus (1503-1566, French astrologer and physician), 135

Noonan, Frederick J. (1893-1937, Earhart's navigator), 264-265

Oberth, Hermann (1894-1989, German rocket scientist), 307

Ohm, Georg Simon (1787-1854, German physicist), 214

Olaf I (b. circa 963, king of Norway 995-1000), 37

Oldcastle, John (circa 1377-1417, Lollard leader), 121

Olds, Ransom E. (1864-1950 American automobile manufacturer), 216

Omar Khayyam (circa 1050-circa 1123, Persian poet), 43

Othman (b. circa 578, third Moslem caliph 644-656 and son-in-law of Mohammed), 129

Otto I (b. 912, German king 936-973), 32, 235

Otto III (b. 980, German king 983-1002), 26

Otto of Freising (d. 1158, German chronicler), 43

Papin, Denis (b. 1647-circa 1712, French physicist), 215

Pare', Ambroise (circa 1510-1590, French army surgeon), 147, 154

Pascal, Blaise (1623-1662, French mathematician), 165

Pasteur, Louis (1822-1895, French chemist and biologist), xii

Patton, George S. Jr. (1885-1945, American general), 301

Paul, Saint (d. circa 67, Apostle to the
Gentiles), 57, 70, 140
Paul IV (Pope 1555-1559), 140
Paul, John (b. 1920, Pope 1978-), 168
Peary, Robert E. (1856-1920, American arctic
explorer), 264
Pedro I (1789-1834, Brazilian emperor 1822-
1831), 252
Pedro II (1825-1891, Brazilian emperor
1831-1889), 252
Penn, William (1644-1718, English Quaker,
founder of Pennsylvania), 172, 176
Peppin III (b. circa 714, Frankish king 751-
768), 26
Perry, Matthew C. (1794-1858, American
naval officer), 250
Perry, Oliver Hazard (1785-1819, American
naval officer), 250
Pershing, John J. "Black Jack" (1860-1948,
American general), 277
Petain, Henri P. (1856-1951, marshal of
France), 278
Peter the Great (b. 1672, Russian emperor
and tsar 1682-1725), 180
Peter the Hermit (d. circa 1151, preacher of
the First Crusade), 35
Petrarch (1304-1374, Italian poet and
writer), 85
Phaer, Thomas (circa 1510-1560, English
physician), 154
Philip I (b. 1052, French king 1060-1108),
24-25
Philip II (b. 1527, Spanish king 1556-1598),
145, 148
Philip II Augustus (b. 1165, French king
1180-1223), 54, 56, 76
Philip IV the Fair (b. 1268, French king
1285-1314), 94, 95
Philip VI (b. 1293, French 1328-1350), 95
Philip Augustus. See Philip II
Phips, Sir William (1651-1695, American
colonial governor), 177
Photius (circa 820-circa 892, Greek
churchman and theologian), 29
Picard, Jean (1620-1682, French astrono-
mer), 164

Pitt, William "the Younger," (1759-1806,
Prime Minister of England 1783-1801,
1804-1806), 230
Pius IX (b. 1792, Pope 1846-1878), 244
Plato (circa 427-circa 347 B.C., Greek
philosopher), 16
Playfair, John (1748-1819, Scottish mathema-
tician), 219
Pocahontas (circa 1595-1617, daughter of
Powhatan), 175
Poe, Edgar Allan (1809-1849, American
author and critic), 223-224
Pogue, William (1930-, Skylab astronaut),
320
Polo, Marco (circa 1254-circa 1324, Venetian
traveler in China), 65
Pompadour, Jeanne Antoinette (1721-1764,
mistress of Louis XV of France), 205
Pope, Alexander (1688-1744, English poet),
163
Porphyry (233-circa 304, Greek scholar), 16
Porta, Baccio della (circa 1475-1517, Italian
painter), 118
Portinari, Beatrice (1266-1290, friend of
Dante), 86
Presley, Elvis (1935-1977, American rock
and roll singer), 266, 313
Priestley, Joseph (1733-1804 English
clergyman and chemist), 192-193
Primo de Rivera, Miguel (b. 1870, Spanish
general and dictator 1923-1930), 288-
289
Ptolemy, Claudius (2nd century astronomer),
13

Raikes, Robert (1735-1811, publisher of the
Gloucester Journal), 195
Raleigh, Sir Walter (circa 1552-1618, English
courtier, explorer, and author), 150
Rashi (1040-1105, Jewish Rabbi), 28
Reaumur, Rene Antoine (1683-1757, French
scientist), 193
Recalde, Inigo Lopez de (1491-1556, founder
of the Jesuits), 139
Reed, Walter (1851-1902, American army
surgeon), 268

Rembrandt van Rijn (1606-1669, Dutch painter), 166

Rhee, Syngman (875-1965, president Republic of Korea 1948-1960), 312

Richard I "the Lion-Hearted" (b. 1157, English king 1189-1199), 54-56

Richard III (b. 1452, English king 1483-1485), 125-126

Richard, Prince (1472-1483, duke of Gloucester), 125

Richthofen, Baron von (1892-1918, German aviator), 276

Rickenbacker, Edward "Eddie" (1890-1973, American aviator, 276

Ridgway, Matthew B. (1895-1993, American general), 313

Rivera, Miguel Primo de. See Primo de Rivera, Miguel

Robert of Sorbon (1201-1274, founder of the Sorbonne), 64

Robert "the Devil." See Robert I

Robert I (birth uncertain, duke of Normandy 1027-1035), 24

Robert II (circa 971, French king 996-1031), 25

Robert Guiscard (circa 1015-1085, Norman conqueror), 33

Rockne, Knute (1888-1931, American football coach), 263

Roentgen, Wilhelm Conrad. See Rontgen, Wilhelm Conrad

Rogers, Will (1879-1935, American humorist), 282

Romer, Ole (1644-1710, Danish astronomer), 168

Rommel, Erwin (1891-1944, German Field Marshal), 300

Romulus Augustulus (birth uncertain, last Roman emperor of the West 475-476), 21

Rontgen, (or Roentgen) Wilhelm Conrad (1845-1923, German physicist), 226

Roosa, Stuart (1933-,Skylab astronaut), 319

Roosevelt, Franklin (1882-1945, American president 1933-1945), 298, 303, 306

Roosevelt, Theodore (1858-1919, American president 1901-1909), 246, 311

Rudolph of Hapsburg (b. 1218, Holy Roman Emperor 1273-1291), 78

Rudolph II (b. 1552, Holy Roman Emperor 1576-1612), 156-157

Rufus, William (circa 1056, English king 1087-1100), 32, 38

Rumford, Count. See Thompson, Benjamin

Rumsey, James (1743-1792, American inventor), 215

Sabin, Albert (1906-1993 American physician), 268-269

Saladin (circa 1138-1193 Moslem warrior), 45, 53-54, 75

Salk, Jonas E. (1914-, American physician), 268

Sanctorius (1561-1636, Italian physiologist), 164

San Martin, Jose de (1778-1850, South American revolutionist), 251-252

Sarnoff, David (1891-1971, American radio and television pioneer, president of RCA), 265, 310

Savonarola, Girolamo (1452-1498, Italian religious reformer), 121

Sawyer, W. A. (1879-1951, American medical scientist), 268

Schiaparelli, Giovanni (1835-1910, Italian astronomer), 217

Schlieffen, Alfred (1833-1913, German field marshal), 274

Schmidt, Bernhard (1879-1935, Estonian telescope designer), 270

Schmitt, Harrison (1935-, Apollo 17 astronaut), 319

Schubert, Franz Peter (1797-1828, Austrian composer), 191

Schwarzschild, Karl (died in WWI, German astronomer), 270, 323

Scott, David (1932-, Apollo 15 astronaut), 319

Scott, Robert F. (1868-1912, British naval officer and arctic explorer), 264

Scott, Sir Walter (1771-1832, Scottish novelist and poet), 222

Segeralli, Gerard (d. 1300, founder of Order of the Apostles), 71

Seward, William Henry (1801-1872, American Secretary of State), 246-247

Seymour, Jane. *See* Jane Seymour

Shakespeare, William (1564-1616, English poet and dramatist), xii, 125, 152-153

Shapley, Harold (1885-1972, American astronomer), 270

Shelley, Mary Wollstonecraft (1797-1851, English author), 222

Shelley, Percy Bysshe (1792-1822, English poet), 221

Shepard, Alan B. Jr. (1923-, Apollo 14 astronaut), 318-319

Sherman, William Tecumseh (1820-1891 Union general in the American Civil War), 247-248

Shih Hauang (Chinese emperor 246-209 B.C.), 83

Sickingen, Franz von (1481-1523, German knight and supporter of the Reformation), 137

Sigebert of Gembloux (circa 1030-1112, Benedictine monk and writer), 33, 47

Simmons, Menno (circa 1496-1561, Dutch religious reformer), 138

Simpson, Sir James Young (1811-1870, Scottish physician), 225

Skelton, John (circa 1460-1529, English poet and clergyman), 151

Slater, Samuel (1768-1835, English-born industrialist in America), 198

Sloane, Hans (1660-1753, British Physician), 165

Smith, Adam (1723-1790, Scottish economist), 199

Smith, Eli (1801-1857, American missionary to Malta, Syria, Greece, and Armenia), 227

Smith, Joseph (1805-1844, founder of the Mormon Church), 228

Smith, Sarah Lanman (1802-1836, wife of missionary Eli Smith), 227-228

Snorri Sturluson (1179-1241, Islandic historian), 48

Sobrero, Ascanio (1812-1888, Italian chemist), 212

Sopwith, Thomas (1888-1989, English aviator and aircraft manufacturer), 275

Spaatz, Carl (1891-1974, American Air Force commander in World War II), 305

Spener, Philipp Jakob (1635-1705, founder of Pietism), 172

Spenser, Edmund (circa 1552-1599, English poet), 152

Spinoza, Baruch (or Benedict) (1632-1677, Dutch philosopher), 171

Spurgeon, Charles H. (1834-1892, English Baptist clergyman), 228

Stanley, Henry M. (1841-1904, British explorer in Africa and Journalist), 250-251

Starr, Ringo (1940-, member of the Beatles singing group), 341

Steinbeck, John (1902-1968, American author), 283-284

Stephen (b. circa 1097, English king 1135-1154), 55

Stephenson, George (1781-1848, English engineer), 215

Stigand (birth uncertain-1072, Archbishop of Canterbury), 23

Stimson, Henry Lewis (1867-1950, American lawyer and political leader), 305

Stokesley, John (circa 1475-1539, English ambassador to France), 144

Stoss, Viet (circa 1445-1533, German sculptor), 118

Stow, John (circa 1525-1605, English antiquary and historian), 152

Stradivari, Antonio (1644-1737, Italian violin maker of Cremona), 192

Strode, Ralph (1350-1400, Oxford professor), 87

Stuart, Henry (1545-1567, second husband of Mary Stuart), 147

Sturluson, Snorri. *See* Snorri Sturluson

Swain. *See* Sweyn

Sweyn (b. circa 960, king of Denmark 986-1014), 22, 37

Sylvester II (b. circa 940, Pope 999-1003), 26

Talbot, William Henry Fox (1800-1877,
English inventor of photographic
processes), 227
Tasman, A. J. (circa 1603-1659, Dutch
navigator), 254
Teniers, David the younger (1610-1690,
Flemish painter), 167
Tennyson, Alfred (1809-1892, English poet),
221, 345
Tertullian, Quintus (circa 150-circa 230,
Roman theologian), 17, 68
Tetzel, Johann (circa 1465-1519 German
friar), 136
Thackeray, William Makepeace (1811-1863,
English novelist), 221
Theodosius I (b. circa 346, Roman emperor
of the East,379-395 and of the West
392-395), 21
Theophano (Frankish regent, 983-991), 26
Theresa (or Teresa), Maria (b. 1717, Austrian
queen 1740-1780), 205, 207
Thomas á Becket, Saint (circa 1117-1170,
Archbishop of Canterbury), 52, 87
Thomas a Kempis. *See* Hamerken, Thomas
Thomas Aquinas, Saint (1225-1274, Italian
philosopher), 64, 67
Thompson, Benjamin (1753-1814, British-
American scientist), 193, 194
Togori, Iva (1916-, American-born Japanese
propagandist in World War II), 306
Tokyo Rose. *See* Togori, Iva
Tolstoy, Leo (1828-1910, Russian novelist
and philosopher), 223
Tombaugh, Clyde (1906-, American
astronomer), 270
Torquemada, Tomas de (1420-1498, Grand
Inquisitor of Castile and Aragon), 128
Torricelli, Evangelista (1608-1647, Italian
Scientist), 165
Toscanelli, Paolo dal Pozzo (1397-1482,
Italian cosmographer), 129
Toussaint L'Ouverture (1743-1803, Haitian
black patriot and martyr), 229
Trevithick, Richard (1771-1833, English
engineer and inventor), 215
Trotsky, Leon (1879-1940, Russian revolu-
tionist), 278, 289

Truman, Harry S. (1884-1972, American
president 1945-1953), 303, 311, 313
Tubman, Harriet (circa 1820-1913, American
abolitionist), 247
Twain, Mark (1835-1910, American humorist,
pen name of Samuel Langhorne
Clemens), 224
Tyndale, William (circa 1492-1536, English
religious reformer and martyr), 143

Uncas (circa 1588-circa 1683, Pequot chief),
175
Urban II (Pope 1088-1099), 34-35
Usher (or Ussher), Bishop James (1581-1656,
Irish prelate and scholar), 163

van Allen, James A. (1914-, American
physicist), 317
Van Dyck (or Vandyke), Sir Anthony (1599-
1641, Flemish painter), 167
van Gogh, Vincent (1853-1890, Dutch
painter), xii
Vasco da Gama. *See* Gama, Vasco da
Verne Jules (1828-1905, French novelist),
222, 317
Vernier, Pierre (1580-1637, French
mathematician), 164
Vesalius, Andreas (1514-1564, Flemish
anatomist), 154
Vespucci, Amerigo (1454-1512, Italian
merchant, astronomer, and explorer) ,
149
Victor Emmanuel II (1820-1878, last king of
Sardinia 1849-1861 and the first king
of Italy 1861-1878), 241
Victor Emmanuel III (1869-1947, Italian king
1900-1946), 243
Victoria (b. 1819, English queen 1837-1901),
245
Vladimir, Saint (d. 1015, Russian prince), 22,
30
Volstead, Joseph (1860-1947, American
legislator), 280
Volta, Alessandro (1745-1827 Italian
physicist), 188, 194

Voltaire, Francois (1694-1778 French philosopher and author), 189, 208

Von Braun, Wernher (1912-1977, German-American rocket scientist), 307-308

Waldseemuller, Martin (circa 1470-circa 1522, German geographer), 149

Walter de Merton (birth uncertain-died 1277, English bishop), 65

Walter the Penniless (d. 1096, led peasants in First Crusade), 35

Walton, Izaak (1593-1683, English author), 166

Warren, John Collins (1778-1856, American surgeon), 225

Washington, George (1732-1799, first American president), 202-203, 246

Webster, Daniel (1782-1852, American statesman, orator, and lawyer), 247

Webster, Noah (1758-1843, American lexicographer), 224

Weiss, Erich (1874-1926 American magician also known as Houdini), 231

Weitz, Paul (1932-, Skylab astronaut), 320

Wellesley, Sir Arthur (1769-1852, British soldier and statesman), 231

Wesley, Charles (1707-1788, founder, with brother John, of the Methodist Church), 195

Wesley, John (1703-1791, founder, with brother Charles, of the Methodist Church), 195

Wheatstone, Sir Charles (1802-1875, English physicist and inventor), 214

White, Edward H. II (1930-1967, Apollo astronaut), 318

Whittle, Frank (1907-, British inventor), 265

Wilkinson, John (1728-1808 English ironmaster), 188

William I the Conqueror (circa 1027, English king 1066-1087), 8, 19, 23-24

William I (b. 1797, king of Prussia 1861-1888,Emperor of Germany 1871-1888), 237

William I, Prince of Orange (1535-1584, Dutch Statesman), 170, 179

William III (b. 1650, English king 1689-1702), 177

William of Normandy. *See* William I the Conqueror

William of Orange. *See* William I, Prince of Orange, William III, King of England

Williams, Roger (circa 1603-1683, Puritan clergyman and founder of the colony of Rhode Island), 172

Wilson, Woodrow (1856-1924, American president 1913-1921), 217

Wise, John (1808-1879, American balloonist), 216

Wohler, Friedrich (1800-1882, German chemist), 225

Wolfe, James (1727-1759, British general), 201

Wolsey, Cardinal Thomas (circa 1471-1530, English prelate and statesman), 151

Worden, Alfred (1932-, Apollo 15 astronaut), 319

Wordsworth, William (1770-1850, English poet), 221

Wright, Orville (1871-1948, American airplane inventor), 264

Wright, Wilbur (1867-1912, American airplane inventor), 264

Wycliffe, John (circa 1328-1384, English religious reformer), 92

Xavier, Saint Francis (1506-1522, "Apostle of the Indies"), 139-140

Ximens, Francisco (1436-1517 Archbishop of Toledo), 128

Young, Brigham (1801-1877, American leader of the Church of Jesus Christ of Latter-Day Saints), 228

Young, Edward (1683-1765, English poet and dramatist), 163

Young, John (1930-, Apollo 16 astronaut), 319

Zelle, Margaretha Geertruida (1876-1917,
    German spy also known as Mata Hari),
    275
Zeppelin, Count Ferdinand von (1838-1917,
    German army officer, airship inventor,
    and builder), 217
Zevi, Sabbatai (1626-1676 self-proclaimed
    Jewish messiah), 173, 196
Zimmermann, Arthur (1864-1940, German
    ambassador to Mexico), 277
Zola, Emile (1840-1902, French novelist),
    222-223
Zwingli, Huldreich (1484-1531, Swiss
    religious leader of the Reformation),
    138

# Index by Subject

Abbess
    definition of, 66
    description of duties, 66
Abbey
    definition of, 30
    description of life in, 65-66
    Fountains Abbey, 120-121
Abbot
    definition of, 66
    duties of, 66
Aeronautics
    eighteenth century, 190
    jet engine, development of, 265
    nineteenth century, 216-217
    twentieth century, 264-265
Africa
    nineteenth century, 250-251
    twentieth century, 315-316
Alchemists, *See* also chemistry
    medieval, 63-64, 192
Aluminum
    new process for manufacturing in
    nineteenth century, 213
America, North
    after World War II, 310
    nineteenth century, 245-247
    "Seward's folly," 246
America, Latin, 251-252
American Civil War
    beginning of, 247
    important figures in, 247-248
    naval engagements during, 248
    Reconstruction after, 248
American Revolution
    Boston Tea Party, 202
    Continental Congress, 202
    Declaration of Independence, 202
    Lexington and Concord, 202
    Revolution, 201-203
Americans, Native, 176-177

Americas
    development of in sixteenth century,
    149-151
    development of in eighteenth century,
    200-201
    naming of, 149
Anabaptists, 137
Anti-Christ
    definition of, 50
    first, 50
    Ghibellines and, 50
    Guelphs and, 50
    origin of concept, 50
    seventeenth century, 171
    twelfth century and, 50 83
Anti-Semitism. *See* Jews
Apostles, Order of the, 71
Architecture
    Christian church
        cathedral windows, 92-93, 119-120
        dripping eaves, 71-72
        eleventh century, 31-32
        gargoyle, 72
        Gothic, 31-32
        parapet, 72
        Romanesque, 31
        thirteenth century, 71-72
        Winchester Cathedral, 31-32
    military
        barbicans, and 9
        castles and, 8
        drawbridges and, 8
        keeps (dungeons) and, 9
        motes and, 8
        portcullises and, 8
        towers and, 8, 9
Art
    attitudes toward by medieval man, 84
    Renaissance, 118-119
    seventeenth century Holland, 166-167

Astrology
astronomy and, 14-15
cautions about, 58
Astronomy
Almagest, influence on medieval, 13-14
black hole, 270, 323
Bubble Nebula, observations of in
sixteenth century, 156
comets and nineteenth century
discoveries, 218
comet of 1577, 156
Doppler Effect, 219-220, 259
Halley's Comet, 169
Hubble Space Telescope, 271
Jupiter, observations of in nineteenth
century, 218
Laws of Planetary Motion, 156
light, determination of speed of, 168
Lick Observatory, 218
Mars, studies of in nineteenth century,
217-218
medieval, 13-14
Milky Way Galaxy, determination of
size, 270
nebula, 14
nineteenth century, 217-219
observatories, 156, 270
Pluto, discovery of, 270
"Premium Mobile" and medieval
astronomy, 88
Radio, 270-271
religious interpretation of celestial
events, 14
seventeenth century, 164, 167-169
sixteenth century, 155-157
spectroscope, development of in
nineteenth century, 219
stars, determination of distances from
earth, 218-219
supernova of 1054, 14
telescope, 167, 188, 270
twentieth century, 269-271
universe, man's place in, 271
Atomic energy, 265
Audio devices
CD player, 266
eight-track tape player, 266

phonograph, 265
wire recorder, 265
Austria, 206-207

Baptists, 172
Barometer, 165
Battles, massacres, rebellions, revolts, sieges
Acre, siege of, 45
Austerlitz, battle of, 236
Bartholomew's Day Massacre, Saint, 142-143
Bosworth Field, battle of, 125
Crecy, battle of, 89
Friedland, battle of, 230
Hampton Roads, battle of, 248
Herrings, battle of, 124
Jacquerie, revolt of, 90
Jena, battle of, 230
Midway, battle of, 299
Nations, battle of, 232
Sadowa, battle of, 239
Saint Albans, battle of, 125
Saint Valentine's Day Massacre, 281
Svolder, battle of, 37
Towton Field, battle of, 125
Tyler, Watt, rebellion of, 90
Waterloo, battle of, 233
Benedictines
"Black Monks" and, 30
changes in during eleventh century, 30
origin of, 30
Berbers, 38
Black Death, See plague
"Black Monks", See Benedictines
Bordarii, 5
Buddhism, 72
Byzantine Empire
conquest of by Mohammed II, 21
early history of, 21-22
in eleventh century, 22

Cabala, 58
Canada, 253
Canon, 89

Castles
    customs and traditions in, 10
    entertainment in, 10
    quality of living and, 9
Cathedrals. *See also* Architecture, Christian
    church.
    and the people, 50
    definition of, 50
Charters
    Charter of Liberty, 55
    Magna Carta, 77
Chemistry
    discovery of oxygen, 193
    discovery of uranium, 188
    development of modern, 192-193
    petroleum, 188
Children, twentieth century, progress for,
    269
China, 248-249
Chivalry, *See* warfare, medieval
Christian Era, establishment of, 37
Christ, Order of, 91
Christianity
    acceptance of by Constantine I, 29
    drama and, 68-70
    early struggles of church fathers and, 29-
    30
    eleventh century, 29-30
    Jubilee Year, origin of, 68
    medieval views of hell, 88
    monasticism and, 67-68
    Ptlomeaic view of the universe and, 88
    seventeenth century, 171-173
    split in East and West church, 29-30
    twenty-first century, 323, 357-358
Cistercians
    origin of, 30-31
    "White Monks," and, 30-31
Clarendon, Constitutions of
    origin of, 52
Cluniac Revival
    origin of 31
    support of by Henry III, 26
Collar, Order of, 91
Communism,
    rise of in nineteenth century, 234-235
    rise of in twentieth century Russia,
    289-290

    twentieth century, 273
    compass, improvements in, 115
Computers, 265
Congregation of the Most Holy Redeemer,
    196
Constantinople, 128-129
Croft, 5
Crusades
    Albigensian Crusade, 70-71
    background of, 34
    Children's Crusade, 73-74
    Fifth Crusade, 74-75
    First Crusade, 34-36, 73
    Fourth Crusade, background of, 54
    Results of, 75-76
    Second Crusade, 52-53
    Sixth Crusade, 75
    Third Crusade, 53-54
Cuba
    America and the missile crisis, 314
    Spanish-American War and, 252-253

Dark Ages
    definition of, 4
    possible future, 357
Democracy, growth of during nineteenth
    century, , 234
Depression, Great
    background for, 281-282
    events during, 282-284
Divine Right of Kings, 140-141
Domesday Book, 5
Dominicans
    Albigensian Crusade and, 70-71
    duties of, 67
    origin of, 67
Drama
    English in sixteenth century, 152-153
    medieval church, 69-70
    medieval secular, 68-70
    Miracle Plays, 69
    Morality Plays, 69
    Mystery Plays, 69
    sixteenth century England, 151 153
Dunkards, 194-195
Dynamite, 213

Education
    Christian education in twentieth
    century, 266-267
    deductive reasoning, 155
    fifteenth century and, 116
    higher education in tenth century, 15
    higher education in twelfth century,
    46-47
    higher education in thirteenth century,
    64-65
    inductive reasoning, 155
    "Invisible College," 165
    medieval, 15-16, 46-47
    plague, effect on, 90-91
    Oxford Reformers, 119
    printing press, influence on, 117-118
    Quadrivium, 16
    reforms in sixteenth century, 155
    Royal Society, 165
    Saturn, discovery of 4 satellites of, 168
    scholasticism, 15-16
    scholasticism, definition of, 15-16
    scholasticism and the universities in
    the thirteenth century, 64
    schoolmen, 15
    Sic et non, 47
    seventeenth century, 166
    Sorbonne, founding of, 64-65
    Southwestern Baptist Theological
    Seminary, 266
    syllogism, 155
    twentieth century, 266
Eiffel Tower, 256
Electricity
    eighteenth century, 193-194
    nineteenth century, 214
    seventeenth century, 164
Energy
    nineteenth century, 213, 214
    twentieth century, 267
England
    Bores in South Africa and, in nineteenth
    century, 254-255
    Catholic Church and, in sixteenth
    century, 143-145
    early history of, 22-23
    eleventh century, 22-23

    fourteenth century, 122-123,
    France and England in thirteenth
    century, 77
    Hundred Years' War and, 122-126
    India and, during nineteenth century,
    255-256
    involvement in the New World, 118
    Norman conquest of, 23-24
    nineteenth century, 245
    origin of, 22-23
    Scotland and in sixteenth century, 146-
    148
    seventeenth century, 177
    sixteenth century, 143-148, 178-179
    Spain and in sixteenth century, 148
    thirteenth century, 76-77
    twelfth century, 55-56
Enlightenment, Age of, 188
Evolution. *See* geology
Explorers
    eighteenth century, 190-191
    New World, 129-130
    nineteenth century, 216
    thirteenth century overland, 65
    twentieth century, 264


Farming
    medieval, 7
    nineteenth century, 212
Fascism
    definition of, 323
Feud
    definition of, 4
Feudal Age
    definition of, 4
Feudal estates
    occupants of, 5
    classification of workers on, 6
Feudalism
    causes of in medieval Europe, 3
    decline of in fourteenth century, 89-91
    definition of, 3
    effect of on peasants, 2-4
    obligations of peasants under, 6
    obligations of feudal lord under, 6
Fief, 4

Flails, 7
France
    eighteenth century, 203-205
    eleventh century, 25
    fourteenth century, 123-125
    Hundred Years' War and, 122-125
    Indians and in New World, 176
    involvement in the New World, 118
    Mexico and in nineteenth century, 237
    nineteenth century, 229-233, 236-237
    origin of, 24-25
    Popes and in Fourteenth century, 94-95
    seventeenth century, 179-180
    sixteenth century, 142-143
    thirteenth century, 77-78
Franciscans
    origin of, 66
    duties of, 66-67
Freemen, 5
French Revolution
    attack on the Bastille, 204-205
    background for, 203-204

Geology
    catastrophism, theory of, 187
    Christian interpretation of, 220, 258
    evolution and, 219-220
    fossils, discovery of in nineteenth
    century, 219
    uniformism, doctrine of, 219-220
Germany
    origin of, 25-26
    eleventh century, 26-27
    Third Reich and, 285-288
    twelfth century, 56
    thirteenth century, 78
    twentieth century and, 285-288
Greece, independence from Turkey, 235
Guilds, See manufacturing
Gunpowder
    discovery of how it works, 165
    effect on feudalism, 89
    use of in Hundred Years' War, 96
Gunpowder Plot
    origin of, 177-178
    resolution of, 178

Huns, 89
Harrow , 7
Health, medieval, See medicine
Hide , 5
Holland, 150
Holy Roman Emperor
    origin of, 32
    in twelfth century, 56
    in thirteenth century, 78
    seventeenth century, 181-182
Homage, 4
Hospitalers, 36
Huguenots, 142
Humanism, See religion and philosophy

Index
    influence of, 140
    origin of, 140
India, 255-256
Indians, American, See Americans, Native
Industrial Revolution
    changes between government and
    industry because of, 198-199
    effect on the workers, 199-200
    in England, 197-198
    laissez-faire, 199
    outside of England, 1998
    sabots, 199
Inquisition
    Holy Office, 71
    origin of, 70-71
Investiture Controversy
    origin of, 32
    effect of in Germany in eleventh
    century, 33
Italy
    nineteenth century, 240-241, 242-243
    Pope and, 243-244
    twentieth century, 288

Japan
    nineteenth century, 249-250
    road to empire in twentieth century,
    291-292
    twentieth century, 291-292

Jerusalem, Kingdom of
changes in "ownership" of, 27
origin of in eleventh century, 35-36
Jesus, Society of
influence of, 139-140
origin of, 139
Jews
anti-Semitism, 49
medieval Cabalists and their concept of heaven, 88
eleventh century, 27
opportunities in Spain, 27
seventeenth century 173
victims of the First Crusade, 27

Knighthood. *See* warfare, medieval
Knights. *See* warfare, medieval)

Laser, 265
Liberty, Statue of, 256-257
Light bulb, 214
Literature
copyists, 47
in Renaissance England, 86-87
in Renaissance Italy 85-86
nineteenth century, 221-224
sixteenth century England, 151-153
twelfth century, 47-48
Vatican Library, founding of, 116
Lollards, 121

Magnetism, 164
Man, future of, 346-353
Manor , 7-8
Matter, atomic theory of, 213
Mattock, 7
Manufacturing
rise of the guilds because of, 62-63
rise of in medieval towns, 62-63
Medicine
acupuncture, medieval Chinese, 19
AIDS, 268
apothecary profession in sixteenth century, 154
barber-surgeons in fifteenth century, 117
barber-surgeons in sixteenth century, 153
blood circulation of, discovered, 165
body parts, artificial, 269
cancer, progress against, 269
children, interest in during sixteenth century, 154
copyists and medieval Christian, 17
doctors of the church and medieval Christian, 17
eighteenth century, 188,
fifteenth century, 116-118
Gregory of Tours and medieval Christian, 17
Hippocrates and influence on medieval Christian, 17
infection, progress in preventing, 224-225
medieval Arabian, 19
medieval attitudes about, 16-17
medieval Chinese, 19
medieval Christian, 17-18
microscope, compound, 154
microscope, improvements in 170
nineteenth century, 224-226
nursing, developments in during nineteenth century, 226
pain, progress in preventing, 224, 225-226
penicillin, discovery of, 268
polio, cure for, 268-269
prayer and medieval Christian, 17-18
public health issues in twentieth century, 267-268
Red Cross, 268
Royal College of Physicians of London, 153
secular European medieval medicine, 18-19
seventeenth century, 165, 169-170
sixteenth century, 153-154
surgeons in the fifteenth century, 117
syphilis, discovery of, 153
Tertullian and medieval Christian, 17
twentieth century, 267-269

World Health Organization, 268
X-Ray, discovery of, 226
yellow fever, progress against, 268
Meetings, religious
concordat, definition of, 51
Concordat of Worms, 51-52
Council, Fourth Lantern, 68
Nicaea, Council of, 29
Oxford, Council of, 121
Toulouse, Council of, 70-71
Mennonites, 138
Methodists, 195-196
Mexico, independence from Spain, 235-236
Millennium, end of first Christian, 1-2
Missionaries, 227-228
Monastery, 30
Monroe Doctrine, 260
Mormons, 228
Music
cantillation and, 20
cantor and, 20
clarinet, invention of, 165
eighteenth century, 191-192
Gregorian chants and, 20
Jewish use of music in medieval
period, 20
medieval religious, 19-20
plainsongs, definition of, 20
precentor, definition of, 20
Rock and Roll, 313-314
"Song of the Cid," 20
troubadours, definition of, 20


Nationalism, 234
New Zealand, 254
Nitroglycerin, 212
Northmen. See Vikings
North Atlantic Treaty Organization, 309


Oral tradition, 47


Peasants
in eleventh century, 1-2
in twelfth century, 43-44

Photography, 212, 227, 259
Pietism, 172-173
Plague
effect on feudalism, 89-90
bubonic, 90
description of, 90
pneumonic, 90
Plantagenets, 55
Portugal, 149-150
Presbyterianism
origin of, 138
seventeenth century, 172
Printing
fifteenth century, 117
italics, invention of, 118
Prohibition
background for, 280
problems during, 280-281
Saint Valentine's Day Massacre, 281
Volstead Act, 280
Protestant Revolt. See Reformation
Prussia
Hohenzollern Family and, 181-182
nineteenth century, 237-239
Puritans, 176


Quakers
beliefs of, 172
origin of, 172


Radio
development of in nineteenth century,
214
as propaganda device in World War II,
306
Radioactivity, 213
Reformation
Catholic church and, 139-140
indulgences and, 136
pre-Reformation events, 91-92, 121-122
sixteenth century, 136-138
Religion and philosophy
Cartesianism, 170-171
Christianity and Constantine, 29
eighteenth century, 189

equiprobabilism, 196
humanism, definition of, 119
missionary efforts in nineteenth century, 227
Mithra, 29
nineteenth century,, 227-228
pantheism, definition of, 47
persecutions in twentieth century, 273
Seraphic faith, 29
seventeenth century, 170-171
Sunday Schools, 195
Trinity, Doctrine of, acceptance of by
Constantine, 29
twentieth century, 271-273
Religious meetings, *See* meetings, religions
Renaissance
English literature in the Renaissance, 86-87
Italy as the source of, 84-85
limitations of, 88-89
literary revival in Italy, 85-86
origin of, 83-85
influence of on critical thinking and new
discoveries, 115-116
influence of printing press on, 117
results of, 158
Roads
ancient Roman, 37
medieval, 3
Rosicrucians, 173
Roses, Wars of the. *See* wars
Russia
Crimean War and, 244-245
seventeenth century, 180-181
twentieth century, 289-290

Safety lamp, development of for use in
mines in nineteenth century, 213
Salic law, 95
Sardinia, 241
Scales, 164
Scholasticism. *See* education, medieval
Science
eighteenth century, 192-194
nineteenth century, 212
sixteenth century, 155-157

Scotland
fifteenth century, 126-127
sixteenth century, 146-148
Serfs, 5
Sewing machine, 214
Skyscrapers, 266-267
Slaves
and feudalism, 5-6
and Christianity, 5-6
Social sciences, 194
Socialism, 273
Sound barrier, 212
Space age
background for, 316-317
deep space and planetary probes, 320-322
early artificial satellites and manned
space flight, 317-320
extraterrestrials, 353-356
Spain
England and in sixteenth century, 148
involvement in the New World, 150
Indians and the New World, 176
Portugal and in fifteenth century, 127-128
Submarine
American Civil War and, 248
first practical, 165
eighteenth century, 188-189
Superstitions
twelfth century, 45-46
twentieth century, 57-58
witchcraft, 88
Suzerain, 4
"Sweating sickness," 116

Television, 310-312
Templars
abolition of, 94-95
twelfth century, 45
origin of, 36
Teutonic Knights, 45
Thermometers
seventeenth century, 164
eighteenth century, 193

Towns
    formation of medieval, 44
    ancient Roman in medieval times, 44
    fairs and, 44
    in thirteenth century, 61-62
Transportation
    automobile, 215
    Automobile Club of France, 216
    canals, 215
    railroads, 215
    racing and automobiles, 215-216
    ships, 214
    steam power, 214-215
Treaties
    Ryswick, Treaty of, 177
    Troy, Treaty of, 123, 132
    Versailles, Treaty of, 279
Truce of God. *See* warfare, medieval
Turks, 128-129

Unitarianism, 173
United Nations
    examples of influence of, 308-309
    origin of, 308
Universal ether, 213
Universities. *See* education
Ursulines, 140

Vassal, 4
Vassalage
    definition of, 4
    and feudalism, 5
Vienna, Congress of, 234
Vikings,
    origin of, 28
    eleventh century, 28
Villeins
    definition of, 5
    full villeins, 5
    half villeins, 5

War. *See also* World War I, World War II
    American Civil War, 247-248
    Austrian Succession, war of, 200, 205

Cold War, 309
Crimean War, 244-145
Franco-Prussian (Franco-German) War,
    216, 239
French and Indian War, 176-177, 201
George's, King War, 200-201
Hundred Years' War, 95-96, 122-125
Jenkin's Ear, War of, 200
King William's War, 177
Korean War, 312-313
Peninsular War, 231
Queen Anne's War, 200
Roses, Wars of the, 125-126
Seven Weeks' War, 239
Seven Years' War, 201, 205-206
Spanish-American, 252-253
Spanish Civil War, 288-289
Spanish Succession, War of, 200
Vietnam War, 315
War of 1812, 250
Warfare, medieval
    chivalry, definition of, 12
    fighting as an occupation, 12
    in fourteenth century, 89
    in twelfth century, 45
    knight, process of becoming, 11
    knighthood and feudalism, 11
    movable towers used to attack castles,
        9
    origin of armed soldier on horse, 10-11
    Truce of God and, 12
    weaknesses of feudal warfare, 11-12
Warfare, modern, *See* War, Korean, Vietnam;
    World War I, World War II
"White Monks," *See* Cistercians
Witchcraft, *See* superstitions
Women
    church and, 66
    medieval society, 13
    twentieth century, gains for, 269
World
    after 1815, 233-235
    after World War I, 279-280
World War I
    American entrance into, 277-278
    airplane, role in , 275-276
    assassination of Ferdinand and Chotek,
        274

background for, 274
declarations of war, 274
Russia, changes in during, 278
ships on the sea, use of in, 276-277
spys, use of, 275
submarines, 277
surrender of Germany and its allies,
 279
tactics in field
Zimmermann Note, 277
World War II
 African invasion by the Allies, 300-301
 air war, 303-304
 American involvement in, 299-300
 American isolationism, 296
 atomic bomb, 304-306
 Austria, German invasion of, 292-293
 background and causes, 292
 Czechoslovakia, German invasion of,
 293-294
 England, German attack on, 297
 France, German invasion of, 295-296
 France, Allied invasion of, 301
 Germany and, 292-293, 293-294, 295-
 296, 297, 302-303
 Germany's, surrender of to Allies, 302-
 303
 Italy and, 294
 Italy, fall of to Allies, 301
 Japanese attack on Pearl Harbor, 298
 Japanese objectives in the war, 298-
 299
 Maginot Line, 296
 Midway, battle of, 299
 Norway, German invasion of, 295
 Poland, German invasion of, 295
 propaganda war, 306
 rockets and, 307-308
 Russia, German invasion of, 297
 "Second Front," 300